Norfolk 'n' G

NORFOLK 'N' GOOD
A Supporter's View of Norwich City's Best-Ever Season

Kevin Baldwin

Yellow Bird Publishing
London 1993

First published in 1993
by Yellow Bird Publishing
10 Cambridge Gardens, Muswell Hill,
London N10 2LL

Copyright © 1993 Kevin Baldwin
The author has asserted his moral rights

A CIP catalogue record for this book
is available from the British Library

ISBN 0 9522074 0 0

Printed and bound by
Ashford Colour Press, Gosport, Hants.

Acknowledgements

A raised hand of acknowledgement to: Bugle Songs Ltd for the extract from *Does Everyone Stare* by Stewart Copeland (© 1979 Magnetic Publishing Ltd. Used by permission); Plangent Visions Music Ltd for the extracts from two Specials songs – *Ghost Town* (Dammers) and *Friday Night, Saturday Morning* (Hall), both © 1981 Plangent Visions Music Ltd; and Faber and Faber Ltd for the extract from *High Windows* by Philip Larkin. A raised digit of contempt to BMG Music Publishing Ltd, who wouldn't let me quote one measly line from a Bee Gees song. A pat on the back for Roger Harris, who supplied the front cover photograph. A cowpat on the back for the *Daily Mirror* and Syndication International, who failed dismally to come up with the picture I originally wanted. A jocular punch on the shoulder of Neil Tunnicliffe, who edited the original manuscript. A kiss on the hand to Donna Head, who assisted with the production of said manuscript. And a prolonged bout of feet-kissing to Isabel Isaacson, without whose enormous help this book would not have appeared until around 1997.

To my family, friends and football team
I'd write you a sonnet but I don't know where to start.
I'm so used to laughing at the things in my heart.

The Police, *Does Everyone Stare*

I' the east my pleasure lies.

> William Shakespeare
> *Antony and Cleopatra*, II.iii.40

Introduction

Some reasons for writing this book were there from the beginning (obviously, or I wouldn't have started it); others materialised while it was in progress.

The primary motive, I have to admit, was self-justification. I've lost count of the number of times people have asked me why I spend so much of my life travelling around the country to watch football matches. I've never managed to offer a satisfactory explanation; I have always found that the more something means to me, the less able I am to articulate the reasons for my passion. This is my 'shit or bust' attempt to show what I get out of the game.

And whether you consider that I have shat or bust (which of the two options is supposed to be preferable, anyway?), it was worth making the attempt. In one of his more perceptive moments, Danny (Daz) Baker once said that the greatest shame connected with football is that so many people go through their lives without ever feeling what a supporter feels. If I can help just one person to appreciate how wonderful watching football can be as I pass along ... oh, you know.

It also seemed to be the right time to write a book about being a travelling supporter. On the one hand, the worst excesses of football hooliganism have been curbed. The chronicles of violence that are still to be found on the sports shelves of bookshops describe a phenomenon which, thankfully, has largely disappeared - though, in truth, they never bore any relation to my experience of attending matches. On the other hand, travelling fans are now being attacked from other quarters. It wouldn't be over-dramatic to suggest that our very existence is being threatened. The moves towards all-seater stadia have greatly reduced the number of places available to away fans at many grounds. Worse than this, there have been mutterings from some club chairmen that away fans may be excluded altogether to allow more home fans in. Even though the experiment of banning visiting supporters at Luton Town failed because there was less atmosphere there than on the moon.

On top of this, the increasing influence of television companies is causing more and more games to be scheduled for days and times which suit the casual armchair viewer but which are fiendishly awkward for the true supporters, who often have to take time off work to get there. We seem to have become an insignificant, neglected minority in the great scheme of things. With a new television deal funding a new Premier League, the 1992-93 season seemed to be the right time to examine the way in which the game's most loyal followers are being treated.

During the course of the season, two things happened which I had not foreseen. First, in mid-September, Nick Hornby's excellent book *Fever Pitch* was published. In this, he looks back over his life as an Arsenal supporter and analyses what it means to be a fan. My initial reaction to the appearance of this book was to go around kicking furniture for a week. Mum's dog cowered under the table whenever I came into the room. On reading Hornby's book, however, I realised that his experience of being a fan is somewhat different from mine. For example, he describes watching football as 'entertainment as pain', which doesn't square with my general experience of following Norwich (except at tense end-of-season matches). The attitude of Norwich supporters is, I would venture, far more light-hearted and humorous.

Of course, there is no reason why supporting Norwich should be anything like supporting Arsenal. The clubs are in very different parts of the country, for one thing. Life in London is far more grim and pressurised than in Norfolk, and the local temperaments differ accordingly. More important, Arsenal and Norwich fans have different expectations of their teams and use different criteria for judging success, largely because of the different histories of the clubs. Arsenal have won far more trophies and are a much 'bigger' club in terms of support and prestige - yet I rather think that this is a burden as much as a blessing. Norwich fans can consider that they have had a good season without winning anything, which I don't believe Arsenal fans could.

In *Norfolk 'n' Good*, I have also tried to show how football supporters simply live from one game to the next during the season; how moods change rapidly according to the team's fortunes; and how a rhythm and momentum is created by the succession of matches, with all sorts of coincidences, contrasts and repeated events along the way.

The second unexpected development during the year was the continued excellent form of the team. After the dismal end to the 1991-92 season, when we only just avoided relegation, I feared that this book might turn out to be a catalogue of dreadful defeats. I was praying at the outset that the players could at least string two or three decent results together at some stage to allow me a little joy and optimism - but, as it turned out, I needn't have worried. Indeed, by November, it occurred to me that this might well be the season that most deserved to be recorded for posterity. In the end, the team made history - and I will always be grateful to the players and staff for arranging to do this in the very season I was writing this book.

Not that *Norfolk 'n' Good* is intended to be the definitive or official account of the season. Far from it. What was it they used to say at the start of that old American TV programme? 'There are a million stories in the Naked City,' or something like that. There must be thousands of stories that could be told about Norwich City over the 1992-93 season, and mine is just one of them. Other fans will have different memories and opinions of particular games, and these are no less valid.

Equally, you may judge some of my remarks to be ill-informed, inconsistent, inconsiderate or incredibly biased. If this is the case, perhaps you should take them to be an authentic representation of the irreverence and impulsiveness of terrace opinion.

Hang on, my reasons are turning into excuses. Time I shut up and let you get on with the book.

I hope you enjoy my season. I did.

Saturday 15 August
Arsenal (away)

Hip hooray, it's New Year's Day!
 I've never understood why so much fuss is made about 1 January, when this merely marks the half-way point of the year. After all, isn't January named after the Roman god Janus, who had two faces so as to look forwards and backwards at the same time? Surely looking in two directions is something you do in the middle of an enterprise rather than at the start. (Except when crossing the road, of course, kids.)
 No, my year begins here. The football fixture list is my calendar. And my year doesn't have four seasons, but one. Well, perhaps two, if you count the close season. I don't recognise it as the cricket season, as some do. The way I see it, anyone who pays to watch a game that frequently fails to produce a result after five days is in greater need of supervision by men in white coats than the players.
 This is, of course, a time for hope. For optimism. For resolving that things will be much better this year than last. Though with our team, such optimism is not inspired by a rational assessment of our capabilities. Rather, it exists in spite of it. Just as the most fervent resolutions on 1 January are generally given up for Lent, it is a fair bet that our current hopes will be nestling among the fish heads and potato peelings in the dustbin by mid-October.
 Perhaps at this point I should announce (or should that be confess?) which team bears the burden of my affections. I feel I can do no better than quote from our customary song of introduction:

> Shall we tell 'em (Shall we tell 'em)
> Who we are? (Who we are?)
> Yellow and green (Yellow and green)
> World's best team. (World's best team.)

No, not Brazil. Norwich City. Of course, readers with a keen eye and a keen interest in football will have spotted that the phrase 'Yellow and green, world's best team' is not entirely accurate. After all, we don't always play in yellow and green. Perhaps an alternative version should be composed for those occasions when the change strip is worn. 'Purple and white, a load of old ...' - no, I can't think of an appropriate rhyme.

The omens for the new season are mixed, not to say contradictory. On the one hand, the pre-season friendlies have been going worryingly well. It is a scientifically-proven fact that our success once the official season starts is inversely proportional to our success in the kick-abouts. On the other hand, David Lacey in the *Guardian* has once again picked us as certainties for relegation, which as good as guarantees that we will finish in the top half of the table. His lack of knowledge of Norwich was amply demonstrated in this morning's paper, in which he remarked that we will be looking to Dean Coney to 'restore attacking momentum'. We'll need bloody good eyesight. He's been playing for Farnborough Town for the last eight months.

Perhaps I should sacrifice a Bernard Matthews Norfolk Turkey and examine the entrails.

The powers-that-aren't are claiming that this season represents the dawning of a new era for football. Apparently, we are witnessing a radical restructuring of the league that will change the face of the English game for ever. Really? Not from where I'm standing. Or, in line with the Taylor Report, sitting. What this major reorganisation actually boils down to is this.

What used to be called Division One is now the FA Premier League. There is a new Division One, but this is the old Division Two. Likewise, the old Division Three has become the new Division Two, while the new Division Three is the old Division Four. The GM Vauxhall Conference, which was known as the unofficial Division Five, is now the unofficial Division Four. There is no longer an official Division Four.

Apart from one or two minor matters such as the big clubs getting more money at the expense of the smaller ones, that's about it. Brilliant, eh? So much for the FA's Blueprint for Football. Misprint for Football, more like.

What makes these changes all the more annoying is the fact that it's taken me years to get some people I know to accept that Norwich are a First Division club. I've now got to try to impress upon them that we are a Premier League club and that, from now on, the term 'First Division club' is actually rather an insult.

As well as a confusing new league, we also have several confusing new rules to contend with, principally a new law to cut out passes back to the goalkeeper. The back-pass itself is not illegal, but the goalkeeper handling it is. I never thought I'd see the day when a keeper would be penalised for handball in his own area. He is, however, allowed to pick up the ball if it has been headed or chested to him. Unless, that is, the player heading it back is kneeling to do so or has flicked the ball up to himself, in which case the said player is booked for ungentlemanly conduct. Unless, that is, it is the second Saturday after Septuagesima, in which case ...oh, you get the idea.

The aim of this new law is apparently to cut down on time-wasting. No one seems to have considered how much time will be wasted in continually retrieving the ball from Row Z of the main stand after it has been inelegantly hoofed there by a panicking defender. Nor has any account been taken of the fact that a back-pass can often be a good piece of defensive play. Nor that this law is likely to encourage the long-ball 'chaos theory' brand of football (mentioning no names, Cambridge – oops, I did). Nor that more goalkeepers are likely to be injured in desperate challenges on the edge of the area.

'All right then,' I hear you say. 'Can you think of anything better?' Funny you should ask that. As it happens, I can. I would simply rule that the ball cannot be passed to the keeper unless a member of the opposition has touched it since the keeper last did. This would allow defenders to break up attacks with a neat back-pass, but still prevent the goalkeeper and defenders from knocking the ball backwards and forwards between themselves to waste time. No, it's no good, this is all far too sensible. They'd never adopt it.

It should be noted that the 'they' responsible for the new back-pass law are not our own sweet FA, much as it sounds like one of their ideas. In fact, it is the bright idea of FIFA, the world body. I have my own theory as to how they managed to come up with this gem. I'm sure they (and UEFA, the European body) are employing former European Community legislators. Think about it. It makes sense. Didn't the players' names on the backs of their shirts in the European Championship finals in Sweden remind you of EC foodstuffs labelling requirements? And don't the recent restrictions on the number of 'foreigners' allowed in European club competitions strike you as being reminiscent of moves to cut out artificial additives?

But back to Norwich, where there have been yet more pre-season changes. For a start, we have a new team manager. Our previous one, Dave Stringer, went because he felt he had reached his 'sell-by' date. Reached it? We'd been holding our noses on the terraces for months, saying, 'Poo, what's that? Something needs chucking out.' Canaries are, after all, traditionally renowned for their ability to detect noxious smells early.

Various names were put forward as possible replacements during the summer, the best-known being Bryan Robson, the Manchester United and former England captain dubbed Captain Marvel by Bobby Robson, presumably because his bones are white and crumbly. Fortunately, even I was able to spot that this piece of speculation was merely a PR stunt to try to make Norwich seem like an ambitious club, so I didn't even start trying to pretend that I've always liked him when, in fact, I never have. Not that I would expect him to like me. If he ever reads this, he certainly won't.

In the end, the job went to Mike Walker. I don't have a bad word to say about him. In fact, I don't have anything at all to say about him. I'm not sure he's even a household name in his own household. 'Who's your new manager again?' someone asked me at work a couple of weeks ago.

'Walker. Mike Walker,' I said. 'Just remember, he shares his name with a brand of crisps.'

I bumped into the same man a couple of days ago. 'How's your Mike Hedgehog getting on? Signed any new players yet?' Well, what can you expect of a Notts County supporter?

Actually, Mike Golden Wonder (damn, he's got me at it now) has signed a couple of players. He bought Mark Robins from Manchester United for £800,000 yesterday – just thirty seconds before the deadline to be eligible for today's game. And a month ago, he signed a much-travelled, highly-experienced professional in his 30s by the name of Gary. No, not that one. Gary Megson.

We also have a new club sponsor. It's a large financial institution based in Norwich. No, not that one. The Norwich and Peterborough Building Society. Do you get the impression that the club keeps getting it slightly wrong? It's like the time we had Rosario up front instead of Romario.

As is usual these days, the team strip has been changed yet again for the new season. Gone are the migraine-inducing diagonal stripes of the old Asics shirts. In their place we have yellow shirts covered with green and white flecks. Ironic, isn't it? We no longer have a Fleck in a Norwich shirt, but we have plenty on them. (More on the late, lamented laddie later, by the way.) Opinion is fairly evenly divided on the new kit. Some people think it's awful, others haven't actually seen it yet.

Norwich's local morning paper suggested that it was meant to represent the sandpaper on the floor of a canary's cage. I tend more towards a sabotage theory myself. My hunch is that an Ipswich-supporting motorcycle courier, entrusted with the job of taking what were originally rather tasteful patterns from the design studio to the factory, took the opportunity to smear Tipp-ex and snot all over them.

But the most plaintive and pertinent objection to date has come from a man who wrote to the Norwich evening paper. It's bad enough the chairman of the club making no secret of the fact that all the players are permanently in the shop window, he complained, but surely it's taking things a bit far to make them wear the curtains as well.

Perhaps we should think ourselves lucky that we don't play in black and white stripes like Newcastle United. The chairman would probably have changed them into barcodes.

While the new strip does not rank highly in the popularity stakes, however, it does come top in one respect. According to a table in today's *Daily Mirror* (so it must be true), it is the most expensive in the entire Premier League. Doesn't the club realise there's a recession? I can't see too many parents rushing out to buy new outfits for their offspring. Not because of meanness, but because of a lack of means.

I think I'll stick with my 1970s Norwich shirt. It's out-of-date enough to be up-to-date again.

I didn't wear it to today's game at Arsenal, though. I've always been a bit uncertain about going up the Arse since our match there three seasons ago. That was the occasion of what the newspapers always refer to as the 'infamous Highbury brawl'; an 'ugly mêlée' on the pitch after a second dubious, nay disgraceful, penalty award to Arsenal (biased? Me?) had given them a 4–3 win in injury time. No matter that the incident resembled nothing so much as a bunch of old biddies tussling over a pair of tights at a January sale; the media decided to make a Gazza out of a molehill, and both clubs were hauled up by the authorities. (Carry On joke, *circa* 1965.)

Arsenal received a £20,000 fine for being a fashionable, high-profile London club and getting involved. Norwich, unfashionable and provincial, were fined £50,000. Hmmm.

Despite this, I have to my own surprise found myself in sympathy with the Arsenal fans over the last year. The principal reason for this is the Arsenal Bond Scheme. In order to finance improvements to their ground, the clubs wants the supporters to cough up a huge amount of money just for the privilege of being able to buy season tickets in the future. Many fans who have followed the team for years understandably cannot afford this and now face the prospect of being unable to get into the ground, while those well-to-do types who only discovered football when Pavarotti started warbling over the top of it will be guaranteed seats for life.

Don't get me wrong. I'm all in favour of attracting new people to football. It is a wonderful game that everyone should enjoy and appreciate. But 'everyone' has to include those people who have been following the club – correction, who have *been* the club – all the time. We all know that money talks, but in this case it seems to be saying 'bugger off'.

I also warmed to the Highbury fans a little more after a flash of humour at our game there last season. A minute from the end of a dull 1–1 draw, the referee pulled a leg muscle. One of the linesmen took over for the final sixty seconds, but on jogging out to the centre of the pitch was greeted with a loud chorus of 'The referee's a wanker'. OK, so maybe you had to be there.

I set off for today's match just before 2pm. This did not require the use of a helicopter, Tardis or magical transportation. I actually live in North London, not Norwich, so going to Arsenal is one of the easiest journeys I have all season. Once inside the ground, I found that a large proportion of the home supporters were not real. No, I hadn't been smoking funny cigarettes. Some 8,000 fans had been painted on an enormous canvas at the other end of the ground. As part of the aforementioned redevelopment of the stadium, the North Bank had been demolished and this mural was supposed to prevent a loss of atmosphere. That was the official explanation, anyway. I'm not sure it wasn't to prevent the lumbering earth-movers on the construction site being mistaken for Arsenal's central defenders. From a distance, JCB could easily be confused with the JVC on their shirts.

Crowd noise was later piped through loudspeakers at that end. It wasn't very realistic, though. There were no cries of 'You're shit – aaarrgghhh!!!' as Bryan Gunn took his goal kicks. And they might have rigged up some mechanical arms to give gestures like Gareth Hunt's bean-shake in the coffee ads when a Norwich player missed from five yards out.

The pre-match entertainment was, for once, entertaining. The Red Devils parachute team, dressed in Arsenal kit, landed at the ground – but one missed the pitch completely and ended up on the sand and rubble behind the cardboard crowd. At the time, no one realised how prophetic this mistake would prove to be.

As is usual with the first game of the season, the match kicked off in sweltering heat. It's as if the weather always forgets it's time for football again and takes a couple of weeks to change accordingly. Nothing much happened on the field for the first half-hour, so we were left to amuse ourselves on the terraces. The Arsenal fans enquired as to the enjoyment to be derived from sexual congress with members of the ovine family (look it up if you can't guess) and whether we had parked our tractors outside. A ridiculous idea, of course. You can't park anywhere near Highbury on match days. The Norwich contingent in turn remarked on the uncanny resemblance of one Arsenal fan to the Freddie Boswell character in *Bread* and abused the chairman for selling Robert Fleck for a large amount of bread. (£2.1 million, to be precise.) A vendor moved through the crowd selling 'Premier League Peanuts'. These turned out to be just the same as last year's peanuts, except that they were 50 per cent more expensive.

Suddenly, Norwich discovered their form from the end of last season. A free kick, a free header, Arsenal 1 Norwich 0. A low cross, a low shot, Arsenal 2 Norwich 0.

The non-cardboard Arsenal fans kindly informed us that they were sure to win the league, whereas we were certainties for relegation. I could swear that was David Lacey in the middle of them. The painted variety at the other end of the ground remained strangely unmoved. Surely someone could have wobbled the canvas a bit to give an impression of jubilation?

Even at this early stage of the season, the man standing next to me felt the need to retire for a few moments of quiet contemplation. 'Fuck this, I'm going for a pasty,' he said.

Fifteen minutes into the second half, it still seemed that all we would be getting today was a tanning from both the sun and the opposition. Then Mark Robins was sent on as a substitute. It was generally agreed that we couldn't expect too much of him. He hadn't played in any of the pre-season friendlies and he had only had a couple of first-team games for United last year. Sure enough, the first time he got the ball, he miscontrolled it. His second touch was a wayward pass. His third touch – goooaaallll!!

Well, at least that'll make the last half-hour a bit more interesting, we thought with our usual unrestrained enthusiasm. Two minutes later, a long, high cross sailed over David Seaman in the Arsenal goal while he was practising his windmill impression, and David Phillips volleyed in the equaliser – despite the attentions of one defender who had grabbed his shirt for a closer look. The new Arsenal shirt, it has to be said, is even worse than the Norwich one. For some reason, there are now three V's on the sleeves, which makes it look as if all the players have been given the rank of sergeant. According to my dictionary, a gunner is only a private in the artillery.

Hey, we might be able to hang on for a point here, we conjectured, our optimism reaching new heights. But better was to come. A low drive from Ruel Fox made it 3–2. Finally, a beautiful, exquisite, delicate chip by Robins from thirty yards out (later described blasphemously as a 'hoof' by Charlotte Nicholl on Radio 5) clinched the match.

By now we really were going apeshit, our joy scarcely tempered by the worrying thought of what excruciating 'Canaries-Robins' jokes the tabloid headline writers would be coming up with. 'And now you're gonna believe us, we're gonna win the league,' sang a few over-excited souls. 'Staying up, staying up,' mumbled others, a touch more realistically. The only noise to come from the Arsenal supporters – who, as we remarked, were 'not singing any more' – was the clunk of 23,000 chins hitting the floor in unison. Even the fans on the mural started to leave early. There was no noise coming from the loudspeakers at that end, though canned laughter might have been appropriate.

It only remained for me to try to look miserable on the tube going home, so as not to draw attention to my being a Norwich follower. I just about managed this, thanks to the way my face naturally hangs, but as soon as I left my station, I was overcome by the irresistible urge to clench my fist discreetly every few yards and hiss, 'Yesss! Yesss!'

Having arrived back at the flat, changed my pants and put the kettle on (not in place of my pants, you understand), I settled down to compile the first league table of the season. Yesss! (Again accompanied by a clenched fist.) We're top! Europe here we come! I almost caught myself wishing for an earthquake or other act of God that would end the season now, while we're in front. Looking at the results down in Division One, though, I noticed that Wolves had won 2–0 away. Damn.

I spent the rest of the evening phoning around, telling people to watch *Match of the Day* ('I'll be asking questions afterwards'), and getting calls from friends who, while they are not all football fans themselves, know that if they ring when Norwich have won, I will be in a good mood. I hadn't spoken to some of them for some time.

God, I love football! I'd almost forgotten how much. A semblance of meaning has again been restored to my paltry existence. I had trouble getting to sleep that night, I was so excited. Even counting didn't help. 'Four-two, four-two, four-two, four-two ...'

Wednesday 19 August
Chelsea (home)

There was a film on TV on Monday afternoon called *The Arsenal Stadium Mystery*. Ha! Ha! Ha! I wonder how many Gunners fans turned on thinking it was a re-run of Saturday's game.

Not surprisingly, most of the national newspapers saw the match in that way, wondering how on earth the mighty Arsenal could throw away a two-goal lead rather than praising little Norwich for coming back. You get used to this kind of treatment as a Norwich supporter. We never win games; other teams lose them. We don't make chances; other teams make mistakes. We never have on-days; other teams have off-days. Or in the case of Liverpool, injury crises.

Did I say you get used to this? Actually you don't. Well I don't, anyway. It's bloody annoying.

Living in London was handy for Saturday's game, but midweek matches in Norwich are obviously more tricky to get to. Transport isn't a problem, as I am fortunate enough to own a car, but I have to sneak out of work early in order to drive back in time. Mum has always been more worried about this than me. 'You want to be careful,' she once warned me. 'You'll be getting the sack if they catch you.'

'Don't worry,' I said. 'They never notice I've gone. And, in any case, I'm too important for them to get rid of.'

'You can't be that important,' Mum replied, 'or they would notice you were missing.' I couldn't think of an answer to that. Now she had me worried.

Despite this – and despite the deliberately loud calls of 'See you then, Kev!' and 'Up the City!' from my ever-helpful colleagues in the office – I crept out of work at four in the afternoon and belted back up the M11. (At a constant 69½ miles per hour, honest, officer.) I made good time until I reached the outskirts of Norwich, where I was delayed by a diversion caused by a sewer under the main road doing a fair impression of the Arsenal defence on Saturday. As a result, I found that Mum and my brother had already left for the ground when I got back to the house.

Mum probably wouldn't strike you as being a typical football fan. After all, a little grey-haired woman of 68 isn't the image that usually springs to mind. Yet she isn't that unusual either, particularly at Norwich. According to a survey, Norwich and Ipswich have the highest proportion of female supporters in the country. It has been suggested that we also have the highest proportion of old women on the pitch, but that's another story.

It was from Mum that I inherited my love of football, as well as an easy-going nature, a generous spirit, and a big nose. Thanks, Mum.

Stephen is my big brother in more senses than one. He's 44, which is thirteen years older than me, but I suspect it's also his waist measurement, which would make it thirteen inches greater than mine. I'm not sure whether he's bigger in other dimensions, though. Emotional, intellectual dimensions, I meant.

I fended off the affectionate advances of the dog, grabbed the ham rolls Mum had left behind for me and trotted off to the ground. The evening was warm and sticky, and by the time I reached the top of Carrow Hill, I was too. Perhaps I shouldn't have put my scarf on until I reached the ground.

Yes, I did just say 'hill'. Norfolk, and in particular Norwich, is nothing like as flat, either physically or spiritually, as many people think. Noël Coward has a lot to answer for in this respect. Carrow Hill is very steep, which is fine when you're going down to the ground, but no fun on the way back. In this direction, it is known in our family as Jimmy Hill, as it is a long, painful drag that has to be endured after every game.

Descending the slope, I was met by those reassuringly familiar sights, sounds and smells which I had missed for months without always being aware of it. The floodlights glowed in the distance, drawing us closer like so many green- and yellow-speckled moths. The first strains of song wafted up through the trees, the words still indistinct – though this was perhaps not such a bad thing. The air was filled with the pungent smell of cheap pipe tobacco and spent matches. And, as I neared Carrow Road, of the hot dog and hamburger stall. Some things never change, I thought – especially not their cooking fat, judging by the reek of it. The stench catches you in the back of the throat like burning rubber. Paradoxically, this stall is just the place to visit if you are trying to lose weight. One whiff, and you don't feel hungry again for hours.

Inside the ground, much had changed.

There are four stands at Carrow Road: the Barclay Stand, named after Captain Evelyn Barclay, sometime vice-president of the club; the South Stand, named after Sir Arthur South, now honorary senior life vice-president; and the City and River End Stands, named after neither Dame Cecily City nor the Rt. Hon. Reginald Riverend. The Barclay used to be a large terrace where the most vociferous City supporters would stand. This was demolished at the end of last season, to be replaced by a two-tier all-seater stand with a row of executive boxes. The only boxes previously seen at that end were the ones little kids stood on. So far, only the lower tier is open, with the upper level due to be completed just before Christmas.

There also used to be a terrace on the lower level of the River End. This is where we have always stood, but this too has been filled with seats. In fact, it is no longer possible to stand in any stand at the ground. The reason for these changes is, of course, the report made by Lord Justice Taylor after the Hillsborough disaster in 1989. In this report, he recommended that the grounds of all leading football clubs should become all-seater to prevent a similar disaster from occurring.

14 Norfolk 'n' Good

The loss of over ninety lives at the Hillsborough semi-final was a terrible, terrible catastrophe. The horror of it was brought home to me all the more powerfully as I was standing on a jam-packed terrace at the other semi-final when the news broke. And yet ... and yet I can't help believing that the decision to scrap all terraces was an over-reaction. If an aeroplane crashes, an enquiry is set up to establish the cause of the disaster, and steps are taken as a result to make flights safer in future. If any individual still feels uneasy about travelling by air, he or she can choose not to do so. It is never suggested, however, that all aeroplanes should be banned. Similarly, it seems to me that enough measures can be taken (and, since Hillsborough, have been taken) to make standing at football matches safe without banning it altogether. Removing large fences, dividing terraces into smaller, more manageable sections, reducing the number of supporters in each section, installing more emergency exists, and improving the quality of the stewards, should work well enough.

Like many supporters, I positively prefer to stand. There are various practical reasons for this. It is easier to keep warm on a cold day and to move to somewhere dry on a wet day. It is much more comfortable than sitting on a plastic tea-tray with your knees digging into the back of the seat in front. It is easier to find a better view if you find yourself directly behind people taller than you – you know, the ones who invariably turn up at one minute to three when you think you have secured a perfect view. It would admittedly be easier to see in an all-seater ground were it not for the inevitable and irritating 'reverse domino' effect, whereby one person stands up, usually through great excitement, and everyone else has to stand up too. It is also quicker and safer to leave a terraced area in the event of an emergency. And the counter-argument that seated areas are inherently safer and ensure good behaviour is, sadly, fallacious.

But the main reason for my preference is one that is intangible, and thus all too easy to regard as insignificant: tradition. So many of my most treasured moments are of standing in a roaring, heaving crowd at Carrow Road. The FA Cup fifth round against Ipswich in 1983. The Milk Cup semi-final second leg in 1985 – by the purest coincidence, also against Ipswich. Swaying forward at moments of great excitement, my feet not touching the ground for five minutes after a Norwich goal. At one game a few seasons ago, I found myself squashed in the middle of an Under-18 girls team from Sweden who had come over for a youth tournament. My feet didn't touch the ground for a week.

The new safety measures I outlined above would necessarily make the crowd less tightly packed, and so less exciting, but the fact remains that I would prefer to be able to jump up and down on a terrace than have to sit and clap politely.

This issue has become very heated in Norwich over the last few months, with the decision of our beloved chairman Robert Chase to make Carrow Road all-seater a full two years before it needs to be. His argument is that the Government will not move from its present position and that we may as well comply with its directives now. Hmmm. Wasn't the Government equally insistent that it would press ahead with the football ID card scheme? And the poll tax, for that matter? And what about the Conservative doctrine of offering choice and letting the market decide, while we're on the subject?

More to the point, Mr Chase promised that we would have a piece of terracing this season. Now there's another fine example of a Tory U-turn. (He is a Conservative county councillor.) Even at a supporters' forum at the club in June, he conceded that he felt small areas of terracing should be retained and agreed to consider ways of achieving this. The next week, work began on installing seats on the River End terrace.

Not surprisingly, these broken promises have led to bitter resentment among the fans. 'I'll never sit at Carra Rud' T-shirts have been selling well, but it remains to be seen whether the wearers will actually stay away. My bet is that they turn up notwithstanding (geddit?). The chairman presumably thinks the same way – though, even if they do still come, he will derive no credit from it. Cynically playing on the loyalty of supporters is one of the lowest things a football club can do.

Once I had found Mum and Stephen, there was a lengthy discussion over who should sit where. The two of them were sitting together, and Mum had saved a seat between her and a weedy-looking man in an anorak (in this weather?). 'Here,' said Mum, 'I'll move over and you can sit in the middle if you want.'

'I'm not bothered,' I said. 'You can stay where you are.'

'She just wants to sit next to that bloke,' said Stephen. 'I think she fancies him.'

'I certainly don't,' she protested.

'Perhaps she just doesn't want to sit next to you,' I sneered at Stephen.

'Look, pack it in, you two,' sighed Mum. 'I'll stay where I am. I'll be a rose between two pricks.'

'Don't you mean thorns?' I corrected her.

'I know what I mean,' she said.

I couldn't see any of the usual faces around us. There were a couple of keen gardeners just behind having a conversation about how the pitch was made to look so green and lush. 'Probably because of all the crap that goes on it every two weeks,' someone interrupted. In front of us sat a quiet-looking chap in his 20s with his girlfriend.

Once the game started, however, the familiar chants rang out. 'Chase out! Chase out!'

'What are they shouting?' asked Mum. 'Chelsea?' It was the 'Rock Salmon' story all over again. When the Police released their single *Roxanne*, Mum thought for weeks that they were singing about fish. (Though, in a malodorous sort of way, I suppose they were.) 'No, Mum,' I said, 'they're on about the chairman again.'

Chase was being abused partly because the terraces had gone, as I have explained, but also because our star player Robert Fleck had been sold to our opponents Chelsea. Fleck was not playing in this game because of a 'gentlemen's agreement' between the clubs – though who the gentlemen concerned might be, I can't imagine. Last week Ken Bates, the Chelsea chairman, publicly admitted to having an affair – and what he has been doing to his mistress, Chase has done to our standing areas.

Given the performance of Fleck's replacement Robins on Saturday, such criticism may suggest a perverse determination to see a black cloud around a silver lining. Indeed, the chairman might have escaped censure were it not for an interview that appeared in the local paper on Monday. In this, he revealed that the club did have enough money to have kept Fleck, but that wage negotiations had not proceeded beyond a general discussion. More worryingly, he said that it is inevitable that we will sell Robins if he makes the grade. Not that 'sell' is a word he uses often. He generally uses the curious euphemism 'not stand in the way of'. This is similar to the way employees are sometimes 'let go' rather than being sacked. If we were to not stand in Robins's way for a large amount of money in three years' time, he would consider this to be a great success – '*however unpleasant this is for the supporters*' (Chase's words, my italics).

Success is thus seen in primarily financial terms. It is generally reckoned that, when a Norwich player scores, Chase can be heard chanting 'Going up, going up' – referring not to the team, but to the player's market value. His concern for money was all too evident in the newspaper interview when he praised our previous manager Dave Stringer for (first) the amount of revenue he had generated and (second) the average league position he had achieved during his time in charge. Much of this cash has been used to 'substantially increase the club's fixed asset base'. What this means in plain English is that the club has bought a car park. When Kevin Reeves was sold in 1980, the then new River End Stand was called the Reeves Stand by many. Are we to understand that people are now leaving their limos in the Dale Gordon Car Park?

There is nothing new in all this. The chairman has said many times before that we should accept that Norwich is a relatively small club and that players will always have to be sold or will want to move on. It is a reality we have to face. It doesn't get any easier to cope with this. He doesn't seem to realise that 'facing reality' has little or nothing to do with following a football team. For many, football is the last refuge of our dreams. We spend the rest of our lives lowering our sights, giving way to the relentless, restricting force of reality. When young, we may dream of delivering a great message to the world; we end up as postmen. We long to win a Nobel prize; later, we are dead chuffed to win third prize in the local pub quiz. We declare that we will only marry an outstandingly beautiful, intelligent partner with whom we are passionately in love; in the end, we settle for the best chance we are likely to get. Football is the only arena in which we can still harbour hopes of greatness. They may never be realised, but at least the possibility is there. When our rotund chairman just rolls over them again and again, though, what is left?

Even on the practical business level which Mr Chase urges us to consider, his pronouncements are short-sighted. Declaring that the best players will always leave the club is a self-fulfilling prophecy; saying it makes it happen. Even the ordinary players will think it's not worth staying with an unambitious club. And, judging by the way City's average attendances have fallen over the last three years, many supporters have already come to this conclusion. The chairman claims that this is due to the recession, but this has not stopped a general rise in attendances across the country.

I wonder what sort of crowds we will get this season. Not as low, probably, as they might have been if Fleck had gone before most fans had renewed their season tickets, though both player and club denied that the timing of the move was planned to take this into account.

There is, regrettably, one more distasteful facet of the Fleck transfer which has led many fans to call for the chairman's chair to be plugged in. Namely, the big fuss the Norwich board made when turning down Chelsea's initial offer of £2 million. This was presumably to make us, the gullible punters, believe that there was a new commitment to keep the best players at the club, that there was ambition after all. Even this feeble attempt at PR was blown by the admission that they could not stop Chelsea coming back with an improved bid if they wished.

This is not the only occasion on which our intelligence has been insulted by a transparent attempt to win us over. I have already mentioned the talk of appointing Bryan Robson as the new manager. Mr Chase referred to this episode himself in his interview, claiming that those who criticised it as a cheap publicity stunt (yep, sounds like me) were the same people who accuse the club of lacking ambition. Well, yes. He seems to have missed the point that precisely what we find so offensive is the club making grand noises in the newspapers when the reality of the situation is patently different.

But enough of our chairman. (For now, anyway.) There were plenty more people to shout at on the pitch. Andy Townsend for one was greeted with the special welcome traditionally reserved for former Norwich players. 'Judas!' yelled the quiet-looking bloke in front of us, to the evident consternation of his girlfriend. 'Judas! Fucking off for your forty pieces of silver!' Forty pieces? There's inflation for you.

'I think that's a bit unfair,' said the weedy figure next to me (no, not Mum – you obviously haven't met her). 'He gave us some good service when he was with us.' Quite right, I thought. He seemed an astute sort of judge.

After a quarter of an hour, our new hero Mark Robins made his acquaintance with the studs of one of the most famous, or infamous, characters in the English game:

> A wight ther was, yclept Vinny Jones.
> Y-wis, he was a stoute carl for the nones.
> He hadde heigh renoun in al the lande,

18 *Norfolk 'n' Good*

> Sin that he helde Gazzas spuddes in his hande.
> Ofte wolde he pleyen overmuchel harde
> And then receve the rede or yelow carde.
> Whan that oother men dide heren swich reportes,
> So biganne they to ploppen in there shortes.
> For they dide fere, as well they mote,
> That he wolde hem punchen up the throte.
>
> Geoffrey Chaucer, *The Harde Bastardes Tale*

Yes, I know Vinny is an easy target. But that's my favourite kind.

'He's a tough old boy,' said the *aficionado* beside me. 'I wish he was on our side.' Eh? Next thing, a Chelsea player hit a cross-field ball ('Ooh, look at that for a pass') straight into the dug-out, yards from its intended target. Then another boy in blue was caught around ten yards offside. 'If it weren't for the linesman, he'd have been through.' I scanned my neighbour's face for a trace of irony, but found ... oh, no, he was serious. Despite my first impression, I was sitting next to a fully paid-up member of the Pillocks Club. Worst of all, he was one of that particularly irritating species who can only see merit in the opposition.

When Chelsea scored, he was in his element. 'See that for a break? What a cross by Townsend, I've always rated him.' Except while he was at Norwich, I now began to suspect. 'Good header, too. That's the way to do it.' Thank you, Mr Punch. OK, so it was a good goal, but there was no need to go on about it.

If we'd still been on a terrace, I could have quietly slipped away from him. But this is yet another drawback of all-seater stadia; if you're next to a prat, it's impossible to escape. I couldn't now swap places with Mum as she had originally offered. To do so knowing full well what he was like would hardly have been fair. Yet I cannot deny that a certain measure of self-interest was involved. Mum does have a tendency to nod and agree with idiots, out of a misplaced sense of politeness or pity (or perhaps out of habit, having had to put up with me for so long), and this would have doubled the irritation for me.

Mr Anorak broadened the scope of his commentary in the second half, but it didn't get any less annoying. 'I like this new back-pass law,' he said. 'It makes the game a lot more exciting.' Well, if you find a lot of frantic wellying exciting, I suppose it does. It's like introducing the 'hit and run' rule into Test cricket to liven it up. Mind you, come to think of it ... He'll probably start suggesting changes to the offside rule next, I thought. 'They want to do something about that offside rule next,' he duly obliged. Good grief.

I began to wonder whether I was able to introduce thoughts into his pea-brain by some mysterious telepathic process. I tried to make him think his house was on fire and that he should return at once, but without success. Fortunately, the team came to my help and shut him up before he started extolling the virtues of national service, capital punishment and *Eldorado*. David Phillips, twenty-five yards, 1-1, Yesss! Mark Robins, a volleyed lob from the edge of the box, 2-1. Yeeaaahhooo!!

'I miss the scoreboard at the Barclay end,' said Mum. 'Without the little men running on and taking their hats off, I wasn't sure when to start jumping up and down.' Mothers.

Two games, two wins. And it seemed Mike Walker had come up with a new type of game-plan, apparently based on the old Muhammad Ali rope-a-dope technique. Do nothing for an hour, let the opposition score a goal or two – then surprise them late on.

We hardly noticed Jimmy Hill on the way home.

At 6:30 the next morning, having spent the night at Mum's, I stopped as arranged by the collapsed sewer on the main road to give a lift to another London-based Norwich fan – who, for reasons that will become clear, must remain nameless. 'Poo, what a stink!' I thought. Ten miles out of Norwich, I could still smell it. Bit persistent this, I frowned. Twenty miles, thirty miles on, it dawned on me that it wasn't the sewer at all. 'Sorry,' explained X. 'I overslept and didn't have time for a wash this morning.'

There still wasn't much news about Norwich in the papers. And what coverage we did get was somewhat overshadowed by Fergie's lack of coverage in her discussions with her financial adviser. Is there an Ipswich fan on the editorial staff at the *Daily Mirror*? 'Here, Norwich are still top of the league – let's run these snaps so no one will notice ...'

Saturday 22 August
Everton (home)

I began a fortnight off on Friday night, travelling straight after work to my favourite holiday location – yes, Norwich. I always spend a couple of weeks here around this time of year, the exact timing decided only when the season's fixtures are published in midsummer. Perhaps I would travel abroad if I lived in Norwich permanently; as things stand, with my job requiring me to live in London, the best I can do is spend all my available time in Norwich. Of course, I would be the first on the plane if Norwich ever went into Europe. I was going to trot out the old joke about this being unlikely unless the manager writes a song, but after the first two games, I'm beginning to wonder ... We did qualify for Europe by winning the Milk Cup in 1985. I saved up all my holiday in anticipation of glamorous trips to Reykjavik and Tirana, but then Heysel happened.

On Saturday morning, I visited the club shop to stock up on a few bits and pieces: a new mug ('You certainly need one of them,' said my sister, of whom much more later), a video of last season's highlight, and a couple of new team pictures. I tried to buy these a few weeks ago, but couldn't get near the place for the huge Jehovah's Witnesses convention that was on at the time. The ground was packed. Indeed, I wondered whether we might be able to recruit a few of them to boost attendances. They would also be useful in knocking on doors to preach the gospel and convert the unbelievers: 'Are you troubled and filled with despair at the moral emptiness of the long-ball game? Then come and rejoice with us at the purity and virtue of the short-passing creed.' Mind you, I suppose we'd lose their support as soon as we signed any new players, as they don't believe in introducing new blood into the system.

I needed a new Norwich mug for work after the last one got broken. I'd thought that no one else would want to touch it, but I hadn't reckoned with the possibility of sabotage. Is there a secret Ipswich fan in the building? OK, this is the third time I've suggested such a plot so far, which suggests that I am verging on paranoia, but I do have some grounds for suspicion here. A couple of weeks before the mug was smashed, the legend 'Pride of East Anglia' on the side was altered to read 'Pricks of East Anglia'. Just because you're paranoid, it doesn't mean they're not out to get you.

I couldn't find a compilation tape of Norwich's matches last season at the local video emporium in London. Perhaps I was making a mistake by looking in the sport section. After the way we finished the year (taking 1 point out of the last 18), it might have been on the comedy shelves. Or horror. It might have been next to the *Terminator* videos; after all, it terminated Dave Stringer's career as manager. I can see the blurb on the back now: 'It seems an average sort of year in the sleepy outpost of Canaryville. Everything appears normal ... until, that is, mysterious creaking noises suddenly begin to be heard. Previously solid structures start to crumble and fall. White spherical objects fly around out of control. Fit, healthy men are inexplicably paralysed, and even innocent bystanders are overcome by nausea. Only one person suspects the truth – that the city elders respected by all have been kidnapped and replaced by look-alikes ... The Brain-Dead Zombies from Planet Goof!'

It would have been less embarrassing to buy a mucky video. (I assume, never having bought a ... oh, never mind). Even in the club shop, I came in for some stick. 'What on earth do you want that for?' the man behind me in the queue asked. 'You might as well buy a blank tape. It'd be cheaper, an' all.' I tried to explain that I was only buying it out of a sense of duty and for the completeness of my collection, but my arguments sounded no more convincing then than they do now.

I didn't manage to get the team pictures, as they are apparently not ready yet. I hope this delay indicates that the club is taking more care over them than they did with last year's fiasco. The members of the squad were shown wearing different shirts and different boots. I wonder if our old sponsor Asics noticed how many players in the second row had Hi-Tec boots on. Come to think of it, is this the reason why Asics is now our old sponsor? The photographer's light could be seen glaring in the windows behind the team. Ian Crook looked as if he had a mouth full of sandwich when the shot was taken. And, worst of all, Mark Bowen, last season's captain, was put in the back row despite being very small, and you couldn't see his face at all.

I usually buy two pictures. One is for my wall at work. Some people put up pictures of their family – I put up one of the team. In fact, I have what amounts to a Norwich shrine in the corner of the office. It isn't only Muslims who pray to the East four times a day. The other is for the bedroom wall of my flat in London. I should point out that my flat is not entirely decorated in yellow and green, as you might have suspected. I do have some taste. Besides, I've been through that stage. Throughout my teenage years, my bedroom had three yellow walls, one green wall, a yellow bedspread and green curtains. My allegiance is demonstrated more subtly today. Apart from the team photo, there is just a Norwich City mirror and an inflatable bird in the window (no, missus, it's not what you're thinking). Oh, and a club towel in the bathroom. And a fixture list hanging up in the kitchen. OK, perhaps I'm not so subtle.

They sell some funny old stuff in the club shop. There are car mats featuring the club badge, babies' bibs (though, strangely enough, no potties with the Ipswich squad in the bottom) and even ladies' knickers (I wonder if Grimsby Town do these too). One cheering aspect, however, is something noticeable by its absence: there is nothing in the shop that bears the slogan 'I ♥ NCFC'. I hope we've finally seen the last of that particular symbol. It seemed new and fresh in 'I ♥ NY', but since then it has been used to praise anything and everything, e.g., 'I ♥ bonking' (I actually saw this on a hat in Scarborough once), 'I ♥ my dog' and, for all I know, 'I ♥ bonking my dog'. The only amusing variation I ever saw was a hand-written sign in the window of a vet's car: 'I ♠ my cat'.

The woman who served me didn't know who I was. There's no reason why she should, of course, but I know plenty about her as my brother briefly went out with her last year. She was certainly different from most of the women he's been out with. Usually, I have to be introduced to them before I can take a dislike to them, but in this case it wasn't necessary. She always gives me a sour look whenever she serves me, and I'm convinced there was a malicious glint in her eye two seasons ago when she told me that all the seats on the coach to Sunderland had been sold (the only match I missed that year).

Still, I don't suppose Stephen would like my choice of women. No one does. Even me, much. Thinking of which, Wolves won again in midweek (3-0). Gits.

I didn't tell the woman in the shop that we had a mutual acquaintance. Nor that the rest of our family have a nickname for her. Well, 'Iron T***' isn't exactly flattering, is it?

While I was buying these essentials, Mum was off throwing money around on such luxuries as food and drink. But in her defence, this is an essential part of her pre-match routine. Every Saturday, Mum calls in at the butcher's for a pound of mince, a small chicken, and a chat about football with the chief chopper. From what I can gather, it can hardly be called a conversation – each encounter consists of the butcher telling Mum how Norwich are going to get Paxoed in the afternoon, while she tries in vain to present a reasoned defence of our boys. Neither listens to the other, but then they don't need to, as they've heard it all before. I'm not sure the butcher knows anything about football anyway – it's just that he finds it fun to wind people up by the simple means of predicting the worst for Norwich. I wonder if he's related to David Lacey?

'The butcher reckons we'll lose 2-0 to Everton today,' said Mum as she served up dinner to Stephen and me.

'Did he know who we were playing or did you have to tell him?' asked Stephen.

'I told him,' she admitted.

'There, you see, he doesn't know sod all.'

Saturday dinner is itself a part of the ritual. Every time, Mum apologises profusely for having spoiled it – and every time, Stephen and I try without success to detect what she thinks she might have done wrong. Is this a ritual? Or merely a routine? That, I suppose, depends on whether you consider these events to be superstitiously observed or just regularly repeated. It isn't always easy to distinguish between the two.

For my part, I'm not normally a superstitious person. I'm not, honest. Cross my heart and hope to die. But where football is concerned, I have to admit to the odd habit. My faithful yellow and green scarf is washed when – and only when – City lose at home. 'Ugh, I should think it gets a bit smelly, doesn't it?' remarked a girl at work when I mentioned this.

'No, not really,' I replied sadly. Towards the end of last season, it was gleaming.

I generally wear yellow or green underpants to matches too. Mind you, they were white originally. Perhaps I should wash those more often.

On the way to the ground, Mum buys three packets of Polos for us. No more than two may be eaten during the pre-match warm-up, and no more than five during the first half, or there will be a great and terrible shaking of the earth, the jet-black skies will be riven by mighty thunderbolts, and we will lose to a dodgy penalty in the last minute.

Once inside the ground, we make a point of buying our Golden Goal lottery tickets from the same man every time. I don't know why – I've never come close to having the time of any goal scored. Failure to purchase said tickets would, however, mean ... I'd save 25p. Maybe I will give them a miss in future.

I'm by no means alone in having football superstitions, though. On the way to this game, I noticed a man telling his wife the road was clear to cross. 'I'm

Everton (h) 23

not crossing yet,' she told him. 'I didn't cross till the builder's yard on Wednesday night, and we won then.' Cuh! Pathetic or what?

We sat a few rows further back today in order to avoid that prat I had to put up with on Wednesday. This time, I actually spotted a few familiar faces. There was the Foghorn, who seems to be on a single-handed mission to prove that not all Norfolk people are quiet and reserved. And Silent Fingers, who seems equally determined to prove that most are. He never says a word, but settles for giving limp, languid V-signs whenever the opposition score. Still no sign of the BR boys (who, I suspect, sneak out of the depot up the road) or Mr I-remember-the-59-Cup-run-you-know Flatcap, though.

Another reunion was going on in front of me. 'Here, look who it is! I thought you said you were never coming back after last year.'

'Yeah, yeah, I know,' said a sheepish-looking man. 'But hey, I'm sure we've all said and done things we regret. I'm prepared to give this thing another try.'

Aaahhh. Touching, don't you think? Unfortunately for the man concerned, his mate didn't. 'Huh. Us winning our first two games wouldn't have anything to do with it, would it? Part-time supporter, part-time supporter . . .'

At around ten to three, the DJ put on *Atmosphere* by Russ Abbot. Perhaps he was being ironic, as there certainly wasn't any. The Everton fans weren't making much noise in their corner. I began to wonder whether their nickname was the Toffees because they chew them instead of singing.

Things didn't improve once the game got under way. After about a quarter of an hour, I heard some slapping a few rows behind me and thought someone might have started a fight to create a bit of interest. It turned out to be a couple of girls playing that game where one person tries to slap the other's hands before he/she takes them away. Honestly. It was as bad as that time a few years ago when I stood next to someone who spent a whole game trying to solve a Rubik's cube. And failed.

Someone remarked that the ref looked like Alexei Sayle – which he didn't, especially – and we were treated to a few shouts of 'Ullo John, gotta new motor?' whenever he came near. This only drew confused looks from people sitting too far away to have heard the initial remark and who thus failed to grasp what little relevance there was.

Even I resorted to flicking idly through the match programme while the game was going on. I found a piece entitled 'Who do you believe?' which turned out to be about the article in the *Daily Mirror* on the price of replica kit that I mentioned before. According to the club, the *Mirror* had it all wrong. There was even a new table to prove that the City kit is one of the cheapest around. Fine. Except that this new table in the programme showed the price of children's kit, whereas the *Mirror* one seemed to be dealing with adult strips. I still don't know who to believe – but the fact remains that the price increases are too great at a time like this. So there.

'One good thing about this new back-pass rule', said a voice at half-time, which I was disappointed to discover belonged to my brother. 'At least it's making Everton play ninety minutes instead of the usual sixty.' True, on their previous visits (and in the 1989 FA Cup semi-final), they had spent much of the time knocking the ball back to Neville Southall from the half-way line, but as Mum pointed out before I could reply, this new rule had led to the players sending more balls over fences than an average hacker on a golf course.

In the second half, certain sections of the Norwich crowd began singing songs about Peter Beardsley's film-star looks. Trouble was, the film star they had in mind was Charles Laughton in *The Hunchback of Notre Dame*. While this was undoubtedly unkind, there did seem to be some cunning thinking behind it. After all, it did provoke Beardsley into scoring a goal – 'I had a hunch he'd do that,' said the man in front of me – which, if the previous two games were anything to go by, would now be the cue for a stirring comeback.

Sure enough, the equaliser soon came. (No, not Edward Woodward.) Robins swung over a first-time cross, and Ruel Fox, only 5ft 7in, somehow outjumped the six-footers in the Everton defence to score. It looked as though he must have taken something to enhance his performance on the field, such as a stepladder, but apparently he hadn't.

The winner, however, did not materialise on this occasion. Robins curled a shot past the far post in the last minute, but no one was too disappointed with a draw. Except possibly Mum's butcher.

Wolves also drew today. They did score in the last minute. Jammy sods.

Wednesday 26 August
Manchester City (away)

I didn't fancy driving all the way from Norwich to Manchester and back at night, so I decided to travel on the coach organised by the club. This group of travelling supporters is officially called Club Canary, but in certain quarters it is known as Club Cabbage. This reputation is to a large extent self-created; the Cabbage Crew are forever singing a song which goes, as all the worst nightclub singers say, just a little bit like this:

> I can't read
> And I can't write,
> But that don't really matter.
> 'Cause I'm a Norwich City fan

And I can drive a tractor.
(Ooh arr, ooh arr,
Ooh to be a farmer.)

It is with great regret that I have to report that this assessment of their intellectual (in)capacity is not far from the truth in several cases. The preponderance of *Suns* and *Stars* on the coaches hardly suggests a strong interest in the written word, after all.

In their defence, it should be said that they are Norwich's most loyal and vociferous fans. They never cause trouble (though I am aware that this may change at my expense if anyone ever reads the above paragraphs to them), and consequently Norwich fans have an excellent reputation throughout the country. Parents need have no fears about letting their kids go on these trips. In fact, I'd recommend all parents in the Norwich area to send their offspring on at least one trip whether they like football or not, if only so that they can see for themselves what can become of you if you don't do your homework. (Er – just kidding ...)

Mum was keen to come on the trip too – but even if she were not interested in football, it would be necessary to take her, given the high statistical probability of sitting next to someone a bit strange otherwise. 'I know what you mean,' she once said. 'I always end up sitting next to someone strange.'

Getting a double seat on the coach can be difficult, as people seem to turn up so far in advance, you'd think they were queueing for a January sale. The coach tickets informed us that we'd be setting off at 12:45pm and advised us to be in our seats by 12:30. 'We ought to get there at about quarter past,' reckoned Mum, though as the morning progressed, this estimate was revised earlier and earlier so that we actually arrived at the ground at five to twelve. Even at that time, there were only three double seats free, so it was just as well we did.

As soon as we boarded the coach – me with my flimsy carrier bag containing just a book, a Walkman and a couple of tapes, Mum with a holdall crammed with enough food to sustain us for a couple of months as long as we restricted ourselves to three meals a day – I could smell something was up. Every so often, a hideous odour assaulted our nostrils, making us flinch as if it were smelling salts (though it was nothing like as pleasant as that). What was it? More to the point, where was it coming from? Every time I tried to identify the nature and source of the stink, it disappeared like a name on a page that leaps out to grab your attention and then vanishes when you try to find it again. Checking the soles of our shoes and the little sweet-wrapper holders on the backs of the seats in front revealed nothing.

Once the driver closed the door so that we could set off, Mum and I named that stench in one. It smelt as though someone had been marinading fully-clothed in a bath full of mouldy cabbage for a week. The coach's nickname seemed more appropriate than ever.

It still wasn't easy to tell who had doused himself in *eau de chou*, however. It wasn't like judging the direction of the wind, where you can lick your finger and stick it in the air. In the end, we settled on a man of around 50 sitting a couple of seats in front of us, a verdict based solely on his rather shabby appearance. True, this was flimsy evidence on which to judge him, but we had nothing else to go on.

I tried sticking my nose in the curtain by the window, as even the odour of stale cigarette smoke was preferable to the cabbage, but this made reading rather difficult. It was made downright impossible by the assault on our ears. At the front of the coach, the driver had put on a tape of an unfunny, and not surprisingly unknown, Irish stand-up comic 'by popular request' (which presumably meant just him). At the rear, a radio/cassette offered the alternative 'entertainment' of Dexy's Midnight Runners, who appeared to be style gurus as well as musical heroes to several of our number. My knowledge of physics is a bit ropy these days, but it seemed to me that the sound waves from the two sources were meeting just above my head and fighting out a particularly messy battle, with me caught in the crossfire.

Still, at least I was soon given some justification for my previously arbitrary nomination of the scruffy article in front as Cabbage Man when he stood up to close one of the skylights above the central aisle. 'He must be in a draught,' commented Mum.

'Not at all,' I said. 'He's just trying to keep his smell in.'

'Are you sure it's him? You could always stand next to him when we stop for a cup of tea and find out.'

'You must be joking. The effect's probably toxic at close quarters.'

When we did stop, after an hour and a half, it came as little relief.

Such establishments as the Little Chef and Happy Eater have a policy of not welcoming coachloads of football supporters, presumably because they believe we would shatter their refined ambience and would be unworthy of their equally refined cuisine. But surely there must be a more salubrious eatery between Norwich and Manchester than the place we called at. An appropriate name for it would have been the Unhappy Eater. They should have a logo showing a sick-looking face with two fingers pointing down the throat. Even as we pulled into the parking area, shielding our retinas from the hand-scrawled dayglo lime and orange signs plastered all over the building, I could feel my skin taking on the complexion of a lard-coated Lego brick.

The moment we stopped, there was a tremendous stampede to get off. I hoped that this might indicate a pressing need to use the toilets, as the thought that anyone might actually be keen to taste the wares here was frankly too horrible to contemplate. Mum and I stepped off after the rush to stretch our legs and take a much-needed breath of fresh air, but no sooner had we done so than the rain began to fall, forcing us against our will into the café. Sheltering just inside the door was not an option, as the entrances to the toilets were there and to loiter outside for a half-hour or so would have made us appear incontinent or indecent or both. So it was that we were both drawn inexorably to what might be termed the inner sphinctum.

Here we had two choices. We could opt for the baked beans and formica of the main café area and risk further optical damage from the indoor explosion of fluorescent notices, the only relief from which came when one of the enormous waitresses obscured them in passing. Some were so large, you couldn't help wondering whether they had any food left to sell, in much the same way that one always suspects that make-up demonstrators in department stores have used their entire stock in getting ready for work in the morning. It only occurred to me later that it might be management policy to hire lardy ladies to show that some people are prepared to eat there.

Alternatively, there was a small bar area which at least looked quieter and had a more sober brown decor (if a bar may legitimately be described as sober). On entering, however, we found this to be equally nightmarish in its own way. The interior appeared to have been designed by someone who had developed their aesthetic sensibilities by studying the Argos catalogue. Horse-brasses hung everywhere (I couldn't tell whether they were genuine or genuine-imitation, but who cares?), along with patterned plates, olde-fashioned clocks offering a wide and varied range of times, and pictures which would have been considered tacky even by the art buyer at Boots. Elvis lurked insidiously in the background. Not in person, you understand – unless one of the staff was called Elvis, which seemed highly likely – but on tape. Yes, it was from the Vegas years. How did you guess?

Mum and I had the usual disagreement over who should pay for the coffees. I said I should, as I was earning. She said she wanted to, to prove that she wasn't a 'helpless OAP'. For once, we stopped short of arm-wrestling to settle the matter – just as well, as she generally wins – and decided to go Dutch. Unfortunately, another argument began as soon as we tasted the coffee. 'You have mine.' 'No, no, you have mine.' 'No, I insist ... '

Our hopes that conditions on the coach would be better on reboarding, or that we might feel more able to withstand them, proved short-lived. The stop had only served to make things worse.

Cabbage Man had evidently been for a stroll in the rain, and the moisture had begun to activate other noxious odours that had been hiding in the fibres of his jacket for some time. I'm not keen on farmyard impressions at the best of times, but a version in Odorama?

The boys in the seats across the aisle had bought new batteries for their computer game, which sounded like Kraftwerk rehearsing on a bad day. Some people believe that these games exert a pernicious influence on our young people, rendering them less capable of relating to people around them. I did note, however, that on occasion they can actively stimulate conversation. 'Why is it I can never get past this level?' asked one lad, seeking some advice or at least a little encouragement. 'Cause you're a twat, hur hur hur,' explained the other. Hmm. Perhaps some people are right.

The whole coach seemed more animated after the break. Someone a few seats back was entertaining the troops with a few impromptu witticisms, e.g., 'Why are Cambridge United fuckin' shit?' 'Cause they're crap!' Thank you, Peter Ustinov.

Now I might just have been able to put up with all this. I had, after all, been afforded some relief through changing seats with Mum so that she was digging me in the right side with her elbow rather than the left. But then it happened: the man in the seat directly behind me began to commit the most anti-social act possible in an enclosed space. No, not smoking. Eating cheese and onion crisps.

The two offences are similar, it is true, in that the secondary effects are the most repugnant, while the people enjoying their vice are at the most risk of suffering long-term harm to their health. In the case of cheese and onion crisps, this is because I have resolved that the next time an eater breathes over me, I will shove the crisps somewhere that will make them look like Bovril ones when they re-emerge.

You must understand that I am by nature a liberal-minded, easy-going sort of person. Little stirs me, and I can forgive much. There are just two occasions when I turn into a rabid fascist.

One is when people whisper in the cinema or theatre – or, heaven forbid, start fellating one of those revolting Plonkers hot dogs with gulping, slurping noises. The other is when anyone eats cheese and onion crisps within a hundred yards of me. Or two hundred, if I'm downwind. I have no rational explanation for this. I love cheese with all its tastes and textures (with the exception of those continental varieties which have the consistency of congealed phlegm). I enjoy the tang of onions, whether raw in salads, pickled in vinegar or cooked in meals. But put the two together and – ugh! The combination just doesn't work. It's like Butch Cassidy and the Milky Bar Kid. Or Abbot and Costello (Russ and Elvis). Or Little and Large (Sid and Eddie). And to think they put them in yellow and green packets.

Certain shallow, chauvinistic types (with whom I in no way associate myself, obviously) judge the physical allure of a woman by weighing up whether or not they would kick her out of bed for farting. Surely a more stringent test would be to consider whether she would be expelled for eating cheese and onion crisps. Frankly, even Tara Fitzgerald wouldn't last five seconds in my bed if she did. Sorry, Tara, but that's the way things are.

I decided to escape from all this in the only way possible: by sleeping. The continual rhythmic rocking of the coach made this easier to do than might have been anticipated, and it wasn't long before I began to drift off to ... before I began to drift ... before I began ... before I ... before ...

'Sweep!'

Huh?

'Sweep, 20p a go. For the scorer of the first goal,' said a man brandishing a small plastic bag containing several small, folded-up pieces of paper.

'OK,' I said, 'we'll have one each.' Mum's ticket had the Norwich substitutes on it. How I laughed! I got the goalkeeper. 'Oh do shut up, Mum, I'm trying to sleep ... '

I must have nodded off again for some time after that because, the next thing I knew, we were travelling along the M62. Or rather we weren't. We were slowly crawling up an incline in the wrong gear, which was making the whole coach vibrate at precisely the natural frequency of the human vertebrae. Why do all coach drivers seem to do this at least once on every journey? Do they win a prize if they manage to shake someone's dentures out? Add to this the selection of songs from *Grease* that were being belted out by the massed choir of the back seat, and it was astonishing that I'd been able to sleep for so long.

The weather by now was filthy. Great swirling billows of spray chased every vehicle along the opposite carriageway. The line of hills was smudged by low cloud and rain and was waiting in vain to be redrawn. At last the weather has realised it's the football season, I thought. Or was it just because we were approaching Manchester? I know it's a cliché to say that it always rains there. But clichés become clichés because they're often founded on truth. And the truth is that it has rained every time I have ever been to Manchester.

The reason we were chugging along so slowly was an accident some way ahead that was causing a long tailback. As ever, I seized the chance to worry. Would we get to the ground in time? Would they delay the kick-off until we arrived? Would there be any hot pies left? I looked at a rather mournful-looking sheep out of the left-hand window for a sign, but it turned away from me in apparent despair. Nice arse, though.

Then the driver uttered that terrifying phrase, 'Don't worry, everyone, I know a short cut.' This had the ring of famous last words – and I knew I had reason to be concerned when I caught sight of the map he was using. It was a hand-sketched one on a sheet of A4 paper, which showed the route he had originally intended to follow and none other. In other words, once you deviated from that route, you were floating around in blank space.

We duly turned off at the next junction and immediately climbed a long, steep hill – half-way up which I looked back down at the motorway and saw that it was completely clear a short distance past the point at which we had left it. Great. After that, things went downhill as quickly as I had feared.

Now I'm sure Oldham, Ashton and Stockport are towns of considerable life and character (you see how you get to develop a keen understanding of the use of the patronising remark when you come from Norfolk), but this was not the time for a guided tour, let alone an unguided one. The Madness version of the old Labi Siffre song *It Must Be Love* came on the radio, and the coach chorused: 'We must be lost, lost, lost ... '

To cut a long detour short, we finally arrived at Maine Road around twenty-five minutes before kick-off. We wasted no time in going into the ground, apart from Mum insisting on going round twice when we were frisked by the stewards. We bought a couple of meat and potato pies, which were excellent (Kev's

Gourmand Rating – $8/10$), and found our seats, which were not. Like many other grounds in the First Div ... – sorry, the Premier League (I still can't get used to calling it that) – Manchester City's is being redeveloped, and the huge stand which used to contain the away fans has now been flattened. Thus we found ourselves in seats which provided a first-class view if you happen to have a particular interest in the brands of footwear chosen by the players, but a crap view of any action.

Not that there would be much action we wanted to see, we suspected. I should explain.

Manchester City is our number one, supreme, uncontested, all-time bogey team. The last time we won at Maine Road was in 1964. To put that into some sort of context, the Beatles topped the charts with *A Hard Day's Night*, the United States were starting to build up their military presence in Vietnam, and I was beginning and ending my life of crime. I stole a packet of flower seeds from Key Markets while in my pushchair – but before the DPP gets on the phone, Mum took them back the next day.

Over the years, I have come to the conclusion that if a World XI – including, say, Ronald Koeman, Roberto Baggio, Jean-Pierre Papin and Mark Robins – turned out at Maine Road in the Norwich kit against eleven traffic cones painted light blue, the cones would still sneak a 1-0 win.

So why travel all this way if I think they're going to lose? Well, all sequences have to end sometime, and I want to be there when it finally happens. I realise that this is much more likely to happen if I stay away, in the same way that a goal is almost certain to be scored in a match on TV if you've nipped out for a pee, but this is a sacrifice I am not prepared to make.

The first half went pretty well ... as expected. We were under pressure virtually the whole time – but just as we thought we would reach the interval on level terms, the other City scored. So much for the sweep.

I got the impression that the Manchester fans almost felt sorry for us. They made none of the usual chants of 'One-nil, one-nil' or 'You're not singing any more'. It was as if they were bored with seeing this bunch in yellow and green turn up every year just to get beaten again. Reading the match programme later, I found an item expressing sympathy for the Norwich fans at having to make such a long journey in midweek. 'If they'd known about the cabbage on the coach, they might have let us in for nothing,' said Mum.

About the only noise from the home fans was made by some woman with a bell. She's been ringing it for years, but I still haven't worked out what the point is. It can't be to lead the chanting, as the only shout that would really go with it is 'Unclean! Unclean!' Still, if it keeps her happy ...

Here, I wonder if she calls it Colin. (Younger readers should ask their parents who he was.)

Ten minutes into the second half, the unexpected happened. We equalised. I should really have seen it coming, for the goal was scored by Gary Megson, whom we signed from Manchester City during the close season. This brings me to ...

Kevin's Alternative Laws of Football (No. 1 in an occasional series)

'Any player facing a team whom he has just left will play well, the quality and impact of his performance being in inverse proportion to the opinion held of him by his former club's supporters. Outfield players are guaranteed to score or at the very least make a goal, while a goalkeeper is sure to keep a clean sheet.'

This phenomenon is well recognised in Italy, where they have an expression which translates roughly as 'the immutable law of the ex'. I know this because Brian Glanville, formerly with the *Sunday Times* and now with the *People*, mentions it in every article he writes. OK, maybe not every one, but it seems to be there whenever I read one of his articles.

This is a phenomenon of its own, which also deserves its own phrase. *Toujours vu*, perhaps. Other examples would include Kenny Ball and his Jazzmen, who always played *Hello Dolly* whenever I saw them on TV, though they must have known another couple of tunes at least. And the only episode of *Whatever Happened to the Likely Lads?* that I ever saw was the one where they try to avoid hearing the England score all day. Yet I've seen this one three or four times.

As the second half wore on, Norwich took more and more control of the game, and I began to wonder whether the 'law of the ex' might just be strong enough to break the jinx. Ten minutes from the end, however, it was as if a director had run on to the pitch waving a sheaf of paper and shouting, 'Stick to the script, boys, stick to the script.' Both sides – and one linesman – obliged, and the final score was 3-1 to the wrong City.

When you lose an away game, the worst part is always the journey home. Considering how awful the trip to the match had been, I was now fearing the worst. I wasn't wrong to do so. The coach driver was clearly determined that there would be no repeat of the dithering and uncertainty we had experienced earlier. He made straight for the M56 and headed directly, confidently and swiftly towards ... North Wales? When this was pointed out to him ('Oh, are we lost again? I think we're lost again, oh-oh-oh' – apologies to Phil Collins), he grew most aggrieved that anyone should question his competence or sense of direction. We passed three junctions before he was finally persuaded to turn off, go round a roundabout and head back the way we had come. Even on the roundabout, the whole coach had to yell, 'No! No!' to prevent him from leaving at the wrong exit and taking us to Wigan. Which I'm sure is a town of considerable ... oh, you know.

The upshot of all this was that we had been on the road for fifty minutes before we reached the point at which we should have been after fifteen. Just as well Mum did bring all that food.

Cabbage Man, who must have eaten heartily himself, had apparently started farting. It was as if he was trying to demonstrate his versatility; having filled the coach earlier with the odour of compost made from decomposing vegetable matter, he was now providing a pungent example of excreted manure. I wonder if Patrick Süskind came up with the idea for *Perfume* on a football coach.

Mum was becoming increasingly indiscreet in her scorn for the driver. 'Are we at John O'Groats yet?' she asked in a loud voice as we passed Leeds. In the Country Kitchen at Ferrybridge Services, she said she hoped the driver hadn't gone to use the toilet, as he'd never find his way out again. The conversation on the other side of an adjacent partition suddenly died out and, on leaving the cafeteria, we saw the driver sitting there glaring at us.

Almost as soon as we boarded the coach again, the draw for the second round of the Coca-Cola Cup was announced on the radio. Carlisle. Bloody Carlisle. How am I going to get up there for a midweek match? We couldn't have been given a longer journey. That just about rounded off the day.

Just about, but not quite. Approaching Norwich two and a half hours later, I was woken up (which came as all the more of a surprise as I hadn't realised I was asleep) by the same man who had organised the sweep earlier. 'Wakey, wakey, folks,' he announced, sounding like a cross between Billy Cotton and a sub-editor on the *Sun*. 'Collection for the driver!' Mum gave 10p, presumably out of embarrassment at the incident in the cafeteria, but this was more than he deserved. I gave nothing, which was also more than he deserved.

We finally arrived back at Carrow Road just before 3am, half an hour later than we were supposed to. When we got home, we fought off the soppy dog, whose joy at seeing us showed that she couldn't have heard the score on the radio we had left on for her, and went straight to bed.

I had a weird dream that night. Tara Fitzgerald was in my bed in the middle of Maine Road, inviting me to share her Scampi Fries, but every time I approached, I was pulled away by a man wearing a traffic cone on his head and shouting, 'Wakey wakey!' Work that one out, Sigmund.

Saturday 29 August
Crystal Palace (away)

After the Manchester City excursion, which had proved to be a manky trip in every respect, Mum and I decided we would travel to Crystal Palace by car rather than coach. That way, we could have a nice quiet journey free from all irritations except each other, which we were quite used to coping with. We wouldn't be able to avoid other people at Selhurst Park as we would if we were playing Wimbledon there, but we shouldn't be any more disturbed than we already were.

As it happens, I did get a call on Thursday evening from a Palace fan I used to be close friends with (we'll call him Graham, for the simple reason that it's his name), asking if I wanted to sit next to him. I was able to decline politely by informing him that we had already bought tickets, but even if this had not been the case and if we had not been filled with this Garbo-like need to be alone, I would still have turned down his offer. I have, you see, sat next to him at Palace-Norwich games a couple of times before.

Watching with Graham can't be all that bad if I was prepared to go along with him a second time, you might think. Well, yes, it can. The fact is that I tend to make most of my mistakes twice. Once bitten, twice mauled, if you like. After the first occasion, I convince myself over a period of time that things couldn't have been that bad really, that I must have been in a particularly intolerant mood that day, and that everyone deserves a second chance – only to find that the experience is worse the second time around, the misery compounded by the knowledge that I have been stupid enough to ask for a second helping.

It's always hard to contain yourself when surrounded by opposing fans. Your hands get sore and crease-marked from being sat on, and you are more than likely to induce a hernia by trying to suppress shouts for your own team. (A problem exacerbated by the fact that Norwich have won at Palace for the last two seasons.) Palace fans are generally good-natured, it must be said; the atmosphere is nothing like as threatening as that described by Jasper Carrott in his wonderful routine about watching Birmingham City at Manchester United in the late 1970s, or as it was when, for some reason I have long since forgotten, I had a seat in the middle of the Leicester fans at a Cup-tie at Filbert Street. But it only takes one idiot to start trouble, so it's best to keep stumm.

The man who always sits in front of Graham is an idiot. Not in the hooligan sense of the word, fortunately, but in the eight-draws-short-of-a-jackpot intellectual sense. He really got on my nerves last season. Whenever Palace attacked, he stood up, raised an imaginary bugle to his lips, and sounded a cavalry charge. Who wants some pillock going 'Da-doot, da-doot!' in front of you every twenty minutes? OK, every ten minutes. Then there were the frequent comings and goings while the match was in progress. First he went to get a pie. Having squelched his way through that, he disappeared again and returned with a packet of crisps. Then he went for a cup of tea. Then he went for a Kit-Kat. The only sane explanation for this behaviour that I could come up with was that he had a thing about the woman in the refreshment kiosk. 'Where's he going now?' asked a voice as he inched his way along the fully-occupied row of seats for the fifth time. 'To buy a Teach Yourself Football book, with any luck,' I said.

He certainly didn't understand anything about the game. The only comments he made were cheap insults of a disgracefully ruralist nature. 'Come on,

Palace, stick it up the carrot-crunchers,' he shouted. Ah well, I thought, at least he hasn't resorted to those tired old jibes about us being sheepshaggers. 'Sheepshaggers!' he bawled. 'Baaa! Baaa!'

Regrettably, Graham was making the same sort of remarks. 'Where are your horses and carts parked? Can you buy yellow and green smocks at the club shop? It's good of you to have washed off the woad before coming down.' With all the fuss last year about whether the Palace chairman Ron Noades is a racist or not, you'd think their fans would refrain from making such jokes about ethnic minorities like us.

You may be starting to see why Graham isn't such a close friend these days. There is another reason, but I'll come to that shortly.

The drive down to London for this match was a routine affair. I make the journey up and down the A11 and M11 so often during the course of a season that the route no longer has anything remarkable about it, if indeed it ever had. Nothing worth relating occurred on the way to Selhurst Park (or on the way back, for that matter), which may not be wonderfully enthralling as far as this chronicle is concerned, but it was just what I wanted in order to maintain my composure. I did have a slight feeling of queasiness as we approached London – partly because the whole point of my holiday was to get away from the craphole and here I was returning to it, but mainly because I had a bad feeling about the game to come.

I always have a presentiment of the outcome of a match. This often has some basis in rational thought – in this case, the facts were: a) we had lost our last game; b) Fox and Robins had been injured on Wednesday night and would miss this game; and c) having won at Palace for the last two years, we surely couldn't do it again. Funny, that. If we're on a bad streak, as at Manchester City, I think it will never end. Yet if we have been winning, I think it can't last. Are all fans this pessimistic, or is it just me?

But as you could probably tell from the direction in which point c) above was heading, my sense of foreboding sprang mainly from an inexplicable, irrational gut feeling. This feeling is by no means always accurate. For example, I was utterly convinced before last season's FA Cup semi-final against Sunderland that we would win, and look what happened there. (Possibly because the players were equally sure that they would sail through.) In fact, I'm wrong so often that I don't know why I pay as much attention to these feelings as I do.

We arrived at Selhurst Park in good time, as I had not taken a detour via Oldham, and were able to park quite close. As on Wednesday, our first move when inside the ground was to buy a couple of pies, but these scored only $\frac{4}{10}$ on my Gourmand Scale. The insides were filled with a warm, runny, brown liquid with the odd slightly more solid lump floating around in it. In fact, they looked just like ... ah, I think you're ahead of me on this one.

'Where are your friends?' asked Mum. Where indeed, I mused, thinking that she was initiating a general discussion on my lack of inter-personal skills. What she was actually referring to was the Norwich City London Area Supporters' Club, or Capital Canaries for short. We ought to be known as the Disciples. After all, we are devoted followers, we spread the gospel, and there are twelve of us. Our official membership stands at around four hundred, but I've never met more than a dozen, despite being on the committee. But getting back to Mum's question, I knew exactly where they would all be until ten to three. In the pub. They're always in the pub. Perhaps the reason I have met so few of them is that I don't drink.

That's right, I don't drink. I realise that this makes me rather unusual, not to say abnormal since, for many football fans, the glass and the game are inextricably linked. There are superficial, practical reasons for this. Some people say they need a stiff drink before they can watch their team play. Some suggest that if you drink so much that you start seeing double, you get twice the number of players (and balls) for your money. But there are more profound links between the two; alcohol is what you might call (though only if you were a pretentious git, which I'm sure you're not) an integral element in the total recreational experience.

Take, for example, the following song:

> Norwich boys, we are here,
> Shag your women and drink your beer.

Drink is seen to be an essential component in the ethos and lifestyle of the football supporter (who is automatically, and chauvinistically, assumed to be male). The idea that there may be those who choose not to booze is not given consideration for a moment. An alternative, much healthier version might run:

> Norwich persons, shun all abuses,
> Forge a meaningful relationship over
>   a couple of orange juices.

For all its sensitivity, though, it has to be admitted that this lacks some of the impact of the original.

Finding somewhere to drink before a match is not always as straightforward as you might think. Even today, with the much-improved behaviour of supporters in general, plenty of pubs still put up 'No football supporters' signs on match days. Mind you, how can they tell? Perhaps the landlord wonders aloud who won the FA Cup in 1958, for example. Anyone who fails to stop him- or herself from blurting out, 'Bolton Wanderers, 2-0 against Manchester United' is then sent flying out on to the pavement.

When the capital contingent rolled in five minutes before kick-off, I was relieved that they failed to spot me. They are decent enough sorts, but I didn't want to suffer the effects of passive drunkenness from their alcohol fumes. As the game progressed, however, I reverted to being relieved that I wasn't sitting next to Graham. I knew exactly what he'd be saying – namely, that Palace were by far the superior team and that Norwich were so lucky, they ought to be sponsored by Hartley's.

I know full well that there is no such thing as objectivity. It's one of those many words that describe something that doesn't actually exist. Such as 'God'. Or 'girlfriend'. And I accept that all football fans are biased to a greater or greater extent. But Graham has steered his partisanship into totally unchartered waters. He calls for handball when the opposition takes a throw-in. He screams for a penalty if a Palace player stumbles when getting off the team bus. When they were thrashed 9-0 at Liverpool three seasons ago, all Graham could say about it was that two of the goals looked offside and that Palace had had their chances too.

Such bias becomes very wearing after a while. And the problem with any extreme views is that they always provoke equally strong counter-opinions. The further one child is from the centre of a see-saw, the further away the child on the other end has to be. What this means is that, when talking to Graham, I find my own attitude becoming more and more fanatical until I end up annoying myself far more than he did in the first place.

In this game, it was true that our goalkeeper Bryan Gunn made three or four outstanding saves in the first half. But then that's his job. One header from a Palace forward grazed the bar. But this means that he was off-target. And yes, one shot was blocked right on the line between Mark Bowen's boot and a post before the ball squirted out like an orange-pip. But as all supporters who regularly go to away games know, the home side will always have chances and near-misses. What really matters is how the away team copes with them, whether they can absorb the pressure and survive the odd hairy moment and then show the confidence to hit back.

It became clear that Norwich had such resilience when we took the hitherto unprecedented step of scoring the first goal. Graham would doubtless have said that this was a complete fluke and that the Norwich players must all be wearing lucky horseshoes around their necks. David Phillips's cross to Lee Power was admittedly a mishit shot. But to call the goal lucky would be to ignore Power's lightning reactions in converting the chance, and the lovely passing build-up in which he had been instrumental and which had made the Palace defenders look as though they were wearing horseshoes on their feet.

Ten minutes later, Palace equalised. This was a gem of a goal, created by subtly teasing and stretching the Norwich defence and then striking like a panther once the inevitable weakness had been exposed. Well, that's how Graham would have described it. In fact, it was just a long throw that Phillips failed to clear and McGoldrick prodded in.

The second half similarly lent itself to diametrically-opposed interpretations. Delete as applicable:

Palace were all over us like a rash/had a reasonable amount of possession but lacked penetration. They should have had a hatful of goals/might possibly have scored if the City defence and goalkeeper had gone for a cup of tea. Norwich kept scrambling the ball away in a blind panic/covered well and passed the ball out of defence. In the end, City sneaked an undeserved winner/put together a classic counter-attack which ended with a beautiful mid-air scissor-kick volley at the far post by David Phillips.

You might have expected an august publication such as the *Observer* to provide an impartial account of the game. Scouring its pages on Sunday morning, however, I found ... nothing. Rien. Nichts. Sod all. I realise we can't expect a full match report every week, but you'd think a team who have just gone third in the league, even at this early stage, would merit at least a mention in the round-up. I'm surprised they remembered to include us in the classified results.

I mentioned earlier that the national newspapers rarely give Norwich any credit for our victories. Some have already been downright snide. Last Monday, the Guardian remarked on the fact that Mark Robins had scored two goals in his first game, one in his second and none in his third. This surely meant, the paper concluded, that he would score an own goal in the fourth. Oh, ha ha ha. Excuse me while I darn my sides.

I realise that I make jokes at the team's expense now and then, but this is a quite different matter. There are always insults flying around within a family or a circle of friends, but these are generally playful signs of affection. The bottom line, to borrow a revolting business phrase, is that the parties involved love each other. But when an outsider comes along and starts slinging 'light-hearted' abuse around, the effect is at best presumptuous and at worst bloody offensive.

Would it be offensive of me to say what a marvellously entertaining team Wolves must be to have drawn 0-0 at Oxford? It would? I won't, then.

Monday 31 August
Nottingham Forest (home)

This match was originally scheduled to take place on Wednesday evening, but was brought forward at the request of the satellite television company BSkyB. Since securing the sole rights to offer live coverage of the Premier League, BSkyB has had a considerable effect on the game. The company is the first to acknowledge this, and has been proclaiming loudly in its TV and poster advertisements that 'it's a whole new ball game'.

What, however, is the average supporter to make of the changes in the availability of live televised football, the presentation of the game, and the rescheduling of matches? After much deliberation, in the course of which I endeavoured as far as possible to put to one side any mistrust of innovation *per se*, as well as any preconceptions I may have had regarding the nature of satellite broadcasting, I came to the conclusion that the supporters' response to BSkyB should be threefold:

1) Fuck off.
2) Fuck off even further.
3) Fuck off so far over the horizon that you will never ever be seen again thank you very much good riddance.

The 'new ball game' is the shameless exploitation of, and disregard for, football fans. For whose benefit was BSkyB acting when it won the TV contract? Was it the company's overriding intention to offer superior presentation and put a large amount of money into the game to help provide better conditions in the grounds? It would doubtless claim so. But it is clear that the real aim was to force football followers all over the country to stick designer dustbin lids on their houses and take out subscriptions to the sports channel. The mentality is akin to that of the kidnapper who snatches a hostage and then demands a ransom. It would have been more honest (or more openly dishonest, anyway) to run ads with letters cut out of newspapers arranged to form the message: 'If you want to see your loved ones again, you'd better cough up.'

As it is, the Sky commercial currently on air is offensive in its insensitive portrayal of footballers living in grand houses and driving flashy cars. Emphasising that many players are rolling in it while asking the public to fork out more money is tantamount to rubbing our noses in it. How appropriate that the music backing the commercial (*Alive And Kicking*) should be by Simple Minds. The Football League should have responded by advertising its matches with *Don't You Forget About Me*.

Of course, the FA and the Premier League chairmen are as much to blame as BSkyB for this hijacking of our game. They awarded the live TV rights in extremely shady circumstances. It appears that the FA led ITV, who previously held the rights, to believe that it would almost certainly continue to cover the top league matches. In the days before the final decision was to be made, however, ITV began to suspect that the BSkyB bid would be accepted. Accordingly, ITV raised its bid to a far higher level than the FA and chairmen had anticipated. Before BSkyB tendered its offer, though, it was given details of the new ITV bid by both Rick Parry of the FA and Alan Sugar, chairman of Tottenham Hotspur plc and (you can draw your own conclusions from this) head of Amstrad, suppliers of satellite TV equipment. BSkyB duly raised its offer still higher and was awarded the contract.

ITV protested vehemently about this, and even offered to go still higher than the BSkyB bid, but to no avail. The latter kept the contract and the value of Mr Sugar's shares in Amstrad reportedly rose by several million pounds on the day it was awarded. The whole business stinks even more than the coach to the Manchester City game did. If the FA is to charge anyone this season with bringing the game into disrepute, it should start with itself. No newspaper articles by players or managers could possibly damage the game and its image more than the Premier League has by behaving so shabbily.

The FA professes to be concerned with the game's image, of course. One of the considerations in awarding the TV rights to the Rupert Murdoch-owned Sky was that the publications (I hesitate to use the word 'newspapers') in his News International organisation could be relied upon to promote a positive image of the league. However, it is already clear that all they really want to promote is the sale of satellite equipment and subscriptions. Even worse, we are being treated to articles in all our match programmes by Rick P. (or should that be P. Rick?) of the FA which are nothing more than thinly-veiled advertisements for BSkyB. They've sold their souls. They've sold our souls. And they're talking through their arseholes.

A favourite argument of the satellite station is that it is only fair that people watching live football matches at home should pay for the privilege, since those actually attending them have had to. I trust that Northampton Town fans will forgive me if I use the word 'cobblers' at this point. First, any television company is seriously deluded if it believes that TV coverage of any event – but especially football – comes anywhere near the experience of actually being present. TV can only ever be a very poor substitute, and it is wrong to expect viewers to pay extra money (monthly subscriptions this season, with the lawless ogre of 'pay-as-you-view' due to lurch over the horizon next year) to watch this.

Second, many people have to settle for watching matches on television because they can no longer afford to attend them. Are they now to be priced out of enjoying top-class football by these secondary means as well?

Third, what of the old and the young? People who do not feel strong enough to go to matches and who cannot afford a satellite subscription may never see their team play live again. And how are young children who have just started to take an interest in a Premier League side ever to see their favourites if their parents are unable or unwilling to pay? Saturday-night highlights are likely to be way past their bedtime.

Finally, why should people have to pay if other commercial television companies are quite prepared to pay on their behalf? Pay-as-you-view TV is not inevitable, no matter how often we are told it is. It will only come if greed is allowed to win the day.

Since I attend virtually every Norwich match, you might suppose that the question of who televises live football should not really bother me. Indeed, I have to admit that altruistic objections alone could probably not have provoked such anger towards BSkyB. What infuriates and disgusts me most, for the simple reason that it directly affects me and people like me, is the fact that BSkyB can ask for matches to be played at inconvenient times on inconvenient days, and the FA will willingly accede. Travelling supporters are treated as irrelevant. No matter that fans will often have to take time off work on a Monday to get to an away match in the evening and then won't get home until the early hours of Tuesday morning. As long as the viewers at home are comfortable, that's all that matters.

True, there have always been midweek matches requiring great efforts to attend. This game against Forest was originally scheduled, as I mentioned earlier, for Wednesday evening. But many of this season's Monday-night matches were originally supposed to be played on a Saturday afternoon, which is both the traditional and a more convenient time for watching football. Furthermore, many teams playing on a Monday are likely to find themselves playing again on Wednesday in a cup match. This is far too much for both the side and its supporters. And yes, I am aware that ITV has moved matches in the past – but not on such a regular basis throughout the season.

I suspect that some club chairmen were quite aware that travelling supporters would find the new arrangements inconvenient, and approved of them because they in turn find travelling supporters inconvenient. Most Premier League grounds are having their capacities reduced as they become all-seater, and there are probably clubs which would like to reduce the number of away fans to nought eventually, thereby allowing them to fill the place with their own.

Travelling support is an integral part of British football, however. For many, myself included, the journeys around the country are an integral part of our lives. And the drawbacks of barring away fans altogether were all too evident in the morgue-like atmosphere at Kenilworth Road when Luton Town experimented with this policy a few years ago. (I managed to get in to witness this for myself.)

I cannot see the BSkyB venture succeeding in the long term. Many fans will refuse to pay the ransom on principle. Others will be satisfied with the other football shown on television (the BBC is showing Premier League highlights on '*Match of the Day*', regional ITV stations are offering live coverage of local Football League matches, while Channel 4 is to broadcast live games from Serie A of the Italian league). And many who might otherwise be persuaded to invest in a satellite dish will be unable to afford it given the current recession.

The failure of the BSkyB enterprise would doubtless have serious repercussions for the Premier League clubs and their followers. One can envisage admission prices having to be raised yet again to cover large financial commitments made by clubs in the belief that they were to receive equally large sums of money from the TV company. I also appreciate that it is churlish to wish misfortune on any company, especially in the present economic climate. Despite all this, however, I shall take great pleasure in waving goodbye in the manner of Silent Fingers if and when BSkyB's football coverage disappears with a swoosh down the pan.

There didn't seem to be many people around as Mum, Stephen and I made our way to the ground this evening. Was this because they were going to watch the game on TV? Or had the majority of the crowd gone to Carrow Road early to see the pre-match 'entertainment' provided by Sky? The word used at every opportunity by the local media to describe this was 'razzmatazz'. My dictionary is unhelpful on this point, but I suspect that this term must derive from an American euphemism for the public display of the male genitalia. (Bollocks, to you.)

Once again, the Red Devils parachuted in before the match. Do they ever pay to get in like the rest of us? Then there was a display by a troupe of inanely beaming dancing girls who released bunches of balloons into the air and kicked plastic footballs into the crowd. 'Puffery and balls' just about summed it up. They were accompanied by fireworks and 'the one and only Mr Bart Simpson'. What the hell has a juvenile American cartoon character got to do with football? The whole spectacle was like a bizarre, drug-induced nightmare, with its visual cacophony of bright colours and flashes and the incongruity of its elements which had been thrown together without logic, meaning or relevance.

True, it made a greater impact than some previous attempts by the club to entertain the crowd before a match. Or during a match, on some occasions. Around ten years ago, we were regularly treated to dance routines by the 'Canary Girls'. Frankly, being treated at the dentist's was less painful. They were a collection of six pale, anorexic-looking 13-year-olds who would be shoved out on to the pitch in skimpy skirts and vests on the coldest February days. The goose-pimpled group would then perform what could most kindly be called free-form jazz dancing, as their uncoordinated movements bore little relation to one another's and none at all to the music, which was generally a crackly copy of *Work That Body* by Diana Ross.

If their efforts were amateurish crap, the dancing of the Sky girls this evening was professional crap. Yet it seemed, it pains me to report, that most of the crowd enjoyed it. I could imagine the pillock I sat next to at the Chelsea game lapping it all up. But what did Mum think she was doing, signifying her approval by tapping her feet? 'You're an old stick-in-the-mud,' she replied when challenged. 'You don't like anything different.'

'I do,' I said, 'only this is different in the way that you say, "It's, er, different" when someone asks what you think of their ghastly new hat.' It is true, however, that I am a traditionalist where football is concerned. My preferred timetable of pre-match entertainment would read:

    7.00   Floodlights turned on
    7.40   Teams come out
    7.45   Game starts

Evening games have an atmosphere of their own without having to be jazzed up. And even on dull Saturday afternoons, prancing around on the pitch beforehand makes the time pass more slowly rather than more quickly. It makes me even more impatient for the game to start, and I generally find myself muttering, 'Get off so we can get on with it'. The game is our *raison de venir*, not to mention *raison d'être;* nothing else is important. After all, is anyone likely to walk home thinking, 'Oh well, we lost 3–0 today, but the brass band was good'? Or: 'We may be in the bottom three, but at least I've just enjoyed a total recreational package'? Of course not. Such frivolous foreplay is as irrelevant and irritating as the interminable series of ads that has to be endured before any main feature at the cinema these days. ('Rank Screen Advertising' is a pretty accurate description.) At least you can occasionally remember a commercial afterwards, though, which is more than can be said for the dancing girls of Dregs & Co.

Half-time has been extended to a rather excessive fifteen minutes in all Premier League matches this season, but this was made to seem longer still by our mid-match entertainment. This was provided by a pop group called KWS, who a year from now will, I suspect, be just another curious combination of letters knocked off the great Scrabble board of history, along with BOAC, ATV, SDP and the DDR. To date, they have had two hits, both reinterpretations of classic compositions by great icons in the history of popular music: *Rock Your Baby* by George McCrae and *Please Don't Go* by KC and the Sunshine Band. 'No, *please* go,' I thought, as they proceeded to make the originals sound good, though not in the way they had intended.

It seems that KW ... (er, what was the name again?) were chosen because they come from Nottingham, home of this evening's opponents. This much was understandable. After all, what successful chart acts has Norfolk produced over the years? The Singing Postman, Cathy Dennis and, so legend has it, the bloke who played the drums on the Fiddler's Dram hit *Day Trip to Bangor*. Marvellous. Are you listening, Liverpool?

The heavyweight boxer Lennox Lewis was also introduced to the crowd at half-time. I don't know why. He was interviewed briefly, but we couldn't hear a word he said. Now if they'd arranged a pro-am bout against our chairman, that might have been interesting.

After the match, there was another fireworks display. This would have been extremely irritating if we had lost, since it would have looked as if they were celebrating the fact. Fortunately, the players provided their own fireworks on the pitch, putting on a performance that cannot have failed to impress both of Sky's viewers.

Mum seemed preoccupied with another matter, however – namely, the presence of the Forest manager Brian Clough. 'I hate him,' she repeated, as if it were a mantra. In truth, she doesn't really hate him in the generally understood sense of the word. Such a mixture of rage and loathing is reserved for child abusers, female Prime Ministers of Britain, and Bill Tidy's cartoons on *Countdown*. Her attitude to Clough is only slightly on the aversion side of indifference. The reason it is expressed with the word 'hate' is down to the semantics of the football crowd, whereby every action and sentiment is magnified and exaggerated in its description. Players are caught a mile offside, linesmen are blind, poor back-passes are catastrophic, and even the lowliest team enjoying an undeserved 1–0 lead is likely to be acclaimed by some as 'by far the greatest team the world has ever seen'. But, of course, this is all part of the fun.

Quite why Mum dislikes Clough in the first place is unclear. I know that she respects his managerial achievements in terms of the trophies he has won and the manner in which he makes his teams play. What she seems to resent is the fact that he is fully aware of his stature and acts accordingly. She never liked Cassius Clay/Muhammad Ali in his Louisville Lip period for the same reason. Even false humility would be better than none in Mum's book.

Mum viewed every event in the match in relation to Brian Clough. When Ian Crook's free kick flew into the top corner in the second minute, she said, 'Hooray! I hate Clough'. When Forest equalised through Nigel Clough, she moaned, 'Huh. I hate Clough.' I'm pretty sure she was referring to the father and not the son. We even had the odd *non sequitur*: 'Would you like a Polo, Mum?' – 'Ta. I don't like that Clough, though.'

Such petty concerns were finally forgotten when Power and Phillips scored late goals, and it was realised that we had regained our place (or, as the tabloids predictably put it, given our nickname, our 'lofty perch') at the head of the division. 'Say we are top of the league, say we are top of the league,' came the chant to the tune of *Oops Upside Your Head*. 'Safe by Christmas, safe by Christmas,' sang a small group near me.

My natural pessimism inclines me more towards the latter outlook at the moment. Of course, I'd love to see Norwich stay at the top, but that will be so difficult to do. I'd be happy just to see them on Saturday, but even that won't be possible.

Saturday 5 September
Southampton (home)

When the invitation to my friend Martin's wedding arrived back in June, I didn't realise at first what it was. Martin, you see, is a doctor in Birmingham (Doc Martin – ha!), so I had to take the letter down to the chemist's to be deciphered before I knew what he was on about.

This task accomplished, I quickly realised that the timing of his big match left me with a dilemma. Should I miss Norwich's big match on the same day? At the time, the fixtures for the season hadn't been published, so I didn't know how big a match this would be. All the same, I couldn't help but find his lack of consideration quite appalling.

What on earth possesses people to get married during the football season? Don't they realise that that is precisely what the close season is for? A few years ago, in the days before she knew better, my sister Karen committed this heinous error. She chose to get hitched on the last Saturday of the league season, when Norwich needed to win at Arsenal to finish fifth, which would be our highest-ever final position. To be fair to her, she had tried to take into account the feelings of the football-loving contingent in the family (i.e. everyone else). Her original preference had been for the following Saturday, but on discovering that this was FA Cup final day, she had thought it best to change the date. Whether this was purely out of consideration for us, or because she feared the attendance for her own 'all-important showpiece occasion' would be adversely affected, is unclear to this day. The trouble was, she brought the date of the wedding forward a week instead of putting it back, not realising that she was making matters worse. We weren't in the Cup final that year – OK, we never have been – so no one would have been too bothered about missing it. The Arsenal game, on the other hand, looked like being a cracker.

In the event, virtually the whole congregation (the only exceptions being the bride and groom) spent virtually the whole afternoon huddled around radios. The reception didn't get underway until we heard that Arsenal had missed a penalty in injury time to leave us 2–1 winners.

Karen was furious. I tried to point out that things could have been worse. After all, Norwich might have lost, which would have had an effect on the general mood like a wet blanket on the bed first thing in the morning. (I'm assuming that's unpleasant – I wouldn't know ...) As it was, we had lost one guest because of the football results. It was a cousin who supported Manchester City, who were relegated to Division Two that afternoon. 'Kevin and his Mum will understand,' he said as he went home early in some distress.

Karen was also lucky that we weren't all cheesed off at having missed what had indeed proved to be an excellent game. She didn't thank me for presenting this line of argument at the time, but she understood a few years later ...

'What time of year would you get married, then?' Mum once asked me. That was easy.

'Late July or early August, so we could spend our honeymoon in Scandinavia watching Norwich thrash Norwegian Third Division teams on the annual pre-season tour.'

You may be surprised that Mum needed to ask this, knowing football and me as well as she does. She didn't need to, of course. It was just another way of bringing up the perennial subject of my marriage or, more precisely, of the increasingly remote possibility of this ever occurring. 'I'd like to see you happily settled down before I go,' she always says.

'Go? Go where? What have you got planned? Are you off on holiday somewhere without telling me?'

'Oh, you know what I mean.'

Southampton (h)   45

Who could I marry, though? Assuming, of course, that anyone would be prepared to have me, which many would regard as too improbable a hypothesis to warrant serious consideration. Another football supporter? This seems unlikely. If there were an eligible Norwich fan around, I would surely have met her by now. And the prospect of setting up home with the follower of another team appears fraught with difficulties. Take the Wolverine. (Please, just take her away.) No, a mixed marriage just isn't on.

Perhaps my best bet would be to find a woman who knows nothing about football but wouldn't mind me going, and whom I might eventually be able to convert to the cause. This, however, is a longer shot than the one Jason Cundy scored with for Spurs at Ipswich last week. (It flew in from fifty yards. I wasn't at the game, obviously, but I still enjoyed it.)

But back to Doc Martin. Should I go to his wedding or not? I managed to delay giving a reply until the fixtures came out, when I saw that we were due to play Southampton at home. This was not as big a match as a clash with Manchester United, Liverpool or Ipswich would have been. Moreover, I saw four games against Southampton last season, none of which was very pretty – especially the FA Cup sixth-round replay in which they had two players sent off. Some Saints.

On the other hand, I hadn't missed a home league game for four and a half years, which wasn't bad going considering I'd been living in Birmingham and London all that time.

Back on the first hand again, I wanted to stay on Martin's good side. Apart from anything else, he would often let me kip on his sofa overnight on the way to or from matches in the north. (Mercenary? Me?)

Yet returning once more to the other hand, the prospect of having to wear a suit for the day was almost as traumatic as the thought of missing a game. One of the very few good things about the office where I work is that we can wear casual clothes. In fact, I would have to buy a new suit, as Old Faithful had been around since 1982 and now made me look like Norman Wisdom. Despite the fact that it was rarely worn, it had also developed such a shine on the seat of the trousers that people would check their hair in it. Unless, of course, they were just having a good stare at my arse, which doesn't bear thinking about. Them staring, I mean, not my arse. Oh, I don't know, though.

The matter was finally resolved when Martin rang and threatened extreme physical violence if I didn't turn up. Always a persuasive argument, that. Had I known back in the summer that Norwich would be top of the league come the day of the wedding, I might have risked his wrath. But having no balls, crystal or otherwise, I agreed to be there.

The wedding was to take place at a church in the wilds of darkest Shropshire. 'Hmm', said Mum, 'does that mean you'll be going anywhere near Wolverhampton on the way?'

'No I won't', I snapped back, my general bad mood at the now looming prospect of being elsewhere during a Norwich home game exacerbated further by the anticipation of what Mum would ask next. As sure as night follows day and Day follows Mervyn, the dreaded question came along.

'Have you heard anything from that girl in Wolverhampton lately?'

'What, the Wolverine? No, I think I've finally heard the last of her,' I said. 'She hasn't rung me for a while now.' I neglected to mention that I'd rung her three times in the last month, only to find her either busy or out.

'Why do you keep calling her the Wolverine?' I started to explain to her for the umpteenth time that as well as being an appropriate name for a female Wolves supporter, it serves as an abbreviation of 'Wolverhampton bitch queen' – but her question turned out to be a rhetorical one and she carried on talking. 'You were so keen on her at one time. I did wonder if we might hear wedding bells for you at last.'

'Good grief, Mum, I only have to mention a girl's name and you're off buying a new hat.'

'No, I'm not. But I would like to see you settled before … '

At that point, I decided it was time to go myself.

I didn't bother tying white ribbons on to the car for fear of looking like a Leeds supporter on tour. I did wonder about letting my yellow and green tie flutter out of the window instead, but even I realised that this would look stupid.

Or rather, wet. As I neared the tiny church, which was an achievement in itself as it wasn't near anywhere or anything, the rain began to bucket down. Well, what can you expect if you get married during the football season? I almost knocked over the photographer who was trying to snap the arriving guests in my haste to get inside the church. It was the first time I'd ever run to a church; what the beckoning of Heaven could never achieve, the opening of the heavens found easy. A piece of piss, in fact.

The congregation didn't exactly look like an all-ticket crowd. The turn-out was more like that for a reserve match, which in a sense I suppose this was. Mind you, I was a bit early; the kick-off wasn't until three o'clock. I settled down to read the programme and listen to the music.

The musical selection was not dissimilar to that of the DJ at Carrow Road. That is to say, most of the songs played were several years old. Slim Whitman's *Happy Anniversary* and *A Glass Of Champagne* by Sailor both seemed to be played at every home game from the mid-1970s to the early 1980s. And even today, you can still hear the occasional rendition of *Kinky Boots*.

After a while, it occurred to me that the organist was probably not responsible for the choice. Left to his own devices, he would presumably have opted for a classical piece of appropriate grandeur. Instead, we were treated to what were apparently extracts from Martin's sadly limited record collection. Procul Harum's *Whiter Shade Of Pale* was followed by Andy Williams's *I Can't Help Falling In Love With You*. Then came Ian – sorry, Jennifer – Rush's *The Power of Love*. I seem to recall Martin having a few Meatloaf tapes. Wonder why we didn't hear *Two Out Of Three Ain't Bad*? Still, at least we didn't get Color Me Badd's *I Wanna Sex You Up*.

Southampton (h)

As the moment neared when the three teams were to appear (Norwich, Southampton and the bride's entourage), I felt myself tensing up. This was partly a climax of the day's build-up; I had been listening to all the pre-match football talk on Radio 5 in the car, and the music I have just mentioned had got me in the mood. It was partly because I can feel intuitively when a Norwich match is about to start; should I ever suffer the misfortune of being held hostage in a darkened room (though the only circumstances I can envisage for this would involve the kidnappers threatening to release me if the ransom were not paid), I would be able to keep some track of time by sensing when it was three o'clock on a Saturday afternoon. And it was partly because I was debating whether I should go ahead and use the tiny radio concealed in my pocket during the service.

In the end, I wimped out – not for any moral reasons, but because I could easily imagine myself blurting out my reactions to the radio at inopportune moments during the ceremony.

'If any persons here know of any reason why this couple should not be joined in holy matrimony, let them speak now or forever hold their peace.' – 'You're shit, aaagghhh!!'

'Do you, Catherine Margaret ... ' – 'Easy! Easy!'

'You may now kiss the bride.' – 'Go on, get stuck in there, my son!'

I settled for trying to imagine what was happening at Carrow Road. Southampton break – Hurlock hoofs a long ball forward to Le Tissier – he beats one man – he beats two – he cuts inside and shoots – Gunn tips the ball away. Norwich press again – Power is tripped – Crook steps up to take the free kick – the ball curls into the top corner – yeesss!! Doubtless this was all completely wrong, but I couldn't help myself. Physically I was in a cold, damp, half-empty church in the middle of nowhere, but mentally I was in the warm, dry, quarter-empty ground at Norwich. Even when I did pay attention to what was going on around me, I found that my reactions were those of a fan on the terraces.

The ceremony was interrupted several times by the arrival of latecomers who had clearly had as much trouble as me in finding the place. The more discreetly they attempted to creep into the church, the more attention they attracted. ('We can see you sneaking in, we can see you sneaking in.') One old granny knocked over a metal flowerpot and stand, which hit the stone floor with an almighty crash. ('She fell over, she fell over.') Hopefully, this was not an Almighty omen. Then two or three brats started howling ('Little boys, little boys, little boys ... ') and, of course, they couldn't be taken outside because of the rain. Perhaps churches, like most football grounds now, should have separate family enclosures. 'If this doesn't put them off having kids, nothing will,' the woman next to me whispered.

The vicar ('Who's the wanker in the black?') carried on regardless. 'We will now sing ... ' ('Get your books out for the lads') ' ... hymn number one ... ' ('One-nil, one-nil, one-nil, one-nil') ' ... twenty-seven.' ('One-twenty-seven, the hymn is one-twenty-seven, one-twenty-seeeeven, the hymn is one-twenty-seven.')

I had decided beforehand that I would mime to the hymns in classic *Top of the Pops* fashion, as: a) I can't sing to save my life; and b) this would hopefully reduce the chances of the church roof being cleft in twain by a thunderbolt as a deep voice boomed, 'Hypocrite!' In the event, though, the whole congregation seemed to have the same idea ('Can you hear the bride's lot sing? No-o, no-o. Can you hear the bride's lot sing? I can't hear a ... thing at all. Wo-oh, wo-oh-oh. Sssshh. Aaagghhh!!'), so I ended up having to give it a go anyway.

The vicar tried to introduce some life and spontaneity to the proceedings by initiating a round of applause after declaring the couple man and wife ('Clap, clap, clap-clap-clap, clap-clap-clap-clap, they're hitched'), but the dearly beloved who had gathered there today remained as vibrant as a wet flannel.

Once the names of the bride and groom had gone into the vicar's book and he had urged them to follow the teachings of the Lord ('He taught, he led, he rose up from the dead, Jesus Christ, Jesus Christ ...'), I went off ('Off! Off!') to the car, thereby avoiding the photographer (again!) and the bride's bouquet, which Mum had specifically ordered me to catch. According to the radio, the Norwich score was still 0–0, so my earlier attempts at visualising the game had indeed been pathetic rather than telepathic.

I drove in advance of everyone else to the charming country club where the reception was to be held. Well, I'm sure it will be charming once it's completed. At the moment, it looks more like the sight, or site, that the North Bank mural is intended to cover up at Arsenal. I was, however, the last to go inside, as I remained in the car for another forty-five minutes listening to the football scores coming through. Finally, at around 4:55, I heard the news that Norwich had won with a goal from Mark Robins a couple of minutes before the end. I got some very strange looks through the windows as I did my happy dance in the pouring rain in the car park.

Slightly moist, through excitement as much as the weather, I went into the club to celebrate the happy event. Oh, and the wedding. Unfortunately, all my attempts to socialise proved to be in vain. The trouble was that, with both Martin and his bride being doctors, almost everyone there was in the medical profession. If you have ever been confronted by a group of medics, you will know that, when together, they use impenetrable medical terms even when discussing everyday matters, e.g., 'Care to implant some Twiglets into your duodenum via your oesophagus?' or 'Sorry! A temporary dysfunction of my equilibrium caused by an OD of amontillado sherry.'

I once lived in a house with a couple of dentists who used to ruin every song on *Top of the Pops* by loudly discussing the bridgework and crowning that the various performers had had done. Mind you, I suppose people who don't follow football find the discussions of groups of supporters equally strange. After all, everyone sees the world in terms of their own interests and concerns. When Nigel Kennedy plays Vivaldi's *Four Seasons*, I do not appreciate the sensitivity with which he plays each movement. I am thinking, 'Bloody Aston Villa fan.'

Similarly, when Roy Hattersley sprays anything on *Question Time*, I am not considering the persuasiveness or validity of his arguments. All I have in mind is that he supports Sheffield Wednesday.

Having given up on holding an intelligible, let alone intelligent, conversation with the other guests, I sought out a phone to get a match report from Mum. 'It wasn't much of a game,' she said. 'You didn't miss anything apart from the goal. Oh, and one moment when Gunn knocked the ball to one side of David Speedie and ran round the other side to pass it.' Even if it was a dull encounter, I would have expected Mum to make it sound more exciting, if only to rub in the fact that I hadn't been there. 'Well, I would have done,' she said when I put this to her, 'but the game's on *Match of the Day* tonight, so you'll see it for yourself anyway.'

Or would I? Could I get away from the wedding and back down to London in time?

I soon made up my mind when we sat down to dinner. The main course was roast beef and potatoes, but it was piping cold. (9/10 in Kev's Gourmand Guide.) I asked for some orange juice, but was given squash that was watered down so much, it was really only coloured water. Or was it ... ? No, it doesn't bear thinking about. On top of all this, the meal took place in a marquee, which was being battered so intensely by the wind and rain that no one could hear themselves think. (As if you can normally.) I could make out very little of the after-dinner speeches, but I did hear perfectly when the bride's father wished his daughter and Martin 'all the happiness in the world as they begin their married life together in London'. London? So I wouldn't be able to use his place in Birmingham as a free B&B any more? I needn't have bothered keeping on his good side after all.

As the Sunday tabloid reporters always say, I made my excuses and left. 'Thanks for being here,' said Martin. But I hadn't really, of course.

'That's OK,' I said, 'give me a ring when you get back from your honeymoon.' ('Score in a minute, he's gonna score in a minute ... ')

I had a rather worrying journey back to London. I was so tired, I had to do all sorts of things to make sure I stayed awake, such as blasting cold air out of the vents into my face and singing along with the Smiths for all I was worth (all qualms about my voice having been shelved for the time being). Looking back, I know I should have stopped for a doze at a service station, but seeing Norwich on TV was my only concern. (Well, apart from being worried about getting bludgeoned to death in my sleep by a mad axe murderer – I've watched too many *Crimewatch* programmes, I think.) I made it back to the flat with five minutes to spare, but I needn't have rushed after all. Mum's assessment of the game proved to be spot-on, judging by the highlights. Or rather highlight, as they didn't show Gunn's piece of skill.

Despite this oversight, I must remark on how pleased I am that *Match of the Day* is back on Saturday nights, not least because I feel I ought to say something positive after having given the Sky coverage such a slagging earlier. True, the presenters (Desmond Lynam with Gary Lineker and Alan Hansen) are just a bit too staid and polite – especially coming after the liveliness and irreverence of *Six-0-Six*, Danny Baker's football phone-in programme on Radio 5. But then they don't try to be matey and popular in the excruciating manner of Elton Welsby or Jimmy Greaves on ITV. When I bemoaned the fact that ITV had lost the live TV rights for the Premier League, it wasn't because I was sorry to see the end of their coverage; it was simply because the Sky deal is so distasteful.

There is also a strong element of – here comes that word again – tradition with *Match of the Day*. It was a reassuringly constant presence in my life until the BBC lost the TV rights for the Football League four years ago. Seeing it return now is like renewing acquaintance with a friend you grew up with, but who went to work abroad for a few years. Of course, there was the odd FA Cup match during this period, like an occasional letter or phone call, but it is only now that you realise how much you have missed it.

Last, and most important, I prefer the highlights shown by *Match of the Day* to full, unedited coverage of matches. I didn't always feel this way. I used to object strongly to the way edited highlights distort a game. Which they do, as the aforementioned omission of Gunn's bravado demonstrates. It often seemed that deliberate attempts had been made to turn one-sided matches into evenly-balanced ones by showing alternate clips of each team attacking. I welcomed the introduction of full, live coverage on a regular basis, thinking that this would present a better sense of the ebb and flow of a game, showing more accurately the way it builds to a climax or throws up a sudden surprise in the middle of a drab period.

Over the last few years, however, I have changed my mind completely on this and now feel that full coverage does football a much greater disservice than extracts do. For one thing, a match has to be absolutely outstanding to come across at all on television, and football cannot often reach these heights. Even if a game is very good, it loses a great deal in transmission.

But the main point is this. When people turn on to watch a game in full, they imagine that they are going to get the full experience. As soon as you start to think about this, you realise that this cannot be true. After all, you get a restricted view of the play, even with endless action replays and silly camera angles (e.g., inside the net), and precious little of the atmosphere of the crowd. Yet many people do not think about this. They blithely imagine that watching on TV will be, as near as makes no difference, as good as being at the match. And the TV companies are naturally loath to dissuade them of this impression. Consequently, if a match comes across as only averagely entertaining, the viewer will assume that it would have been boring to be there. My sister was put off football for years because she found live televised football on a Sunday afternoon dull and, believing that she had seen everything there was to the game, she refused to come along and watch a match for herself. (There was a little more to her resistance than this, but I'll come to that later.)

With highlights, on the other hand, everyone knows that they are only seeing bits and pieces, and can make allowances accordingly. Extracts may give a distorted picture of the game, but they arguably come closer to conveying the mood and definitely offer more sustained excitement. I believe they are far more likely to encourage people to attend matches. In fact, they may usefully be compared to film trailers which pick out the best moments of a movie to entice you along to the cinema. Live coverage, conversely, is the TV version of the movie; you are led to believe that you are seeing the whole thing, but with the smaller screen and the sanitised language, the original product has actually been butchered.

The clips from the Norwich-Southampton game wouldn't, it must be admitted, attract anyone new to Carrow Road. Still, they cheered me up as I realised I hadn't missed a classic. For once it was a case of 'Never mind the quality, feel the 3 points'.

Mike Walker made the point that it is the sign of a successful team to win when not playing well. This is true, but unfortunately most of the media took the view that Norwich would not remain at the top of the league for long precisely because we had not played well. Similarly, Mark Robins was criticised in some quarters for his overall contribution, although he had popped up to score the winner. Yet his critics were probably the same people who always marvel at the likes of Ian Rush or Clive Allen who can 'do nothing for eighty-nine minutes and then nick it'. It seems we can't win, even when we do.

Talking of winning, it was announced today that Mike Walker has been named Premier League Manager of the Month for August. Quite right, too. He has turned out to be Mike Golden Wonder so far. I just hope this award isn't a bad omen. The last time he won a monthly award, as Colchester's manager a few years ago, he got the sack soon after.

Saturday 12 September
Chelsea (away)

With the Canaries still flying high (oh no – have I really just written that?), you might expect me to be floating around in a constant state of euphoria at the moment. Not so.

The awful reality of having to return to work in London this week negated all that completely. The Norwich joke about the M11 being the best thing to come out of London is not wrong. Living there feels like being crushed under an enormous rock – and you know what slugs and bugs you find under rocks when you roll them back. So why don't I haul my khyber back up the frog-and-toad to Norfolk, you ask? Believe me, I'm working on it.

Moreover, my regret at missing the win over Southampton has, improbably and irrationally, grown steadily greater since last weekend. In fact, 'regret' is no longer the most accurate word for it. 'Guilt' comes closer.

It is also far too early in the season, and I have followed Norwich for far too long, to start going around annoying people with a cheesy grin and mock-serious enquiries as to where their teams are in the league. I am well aware that in the (hopefully non-occurring) event of our slide down the table, I would be subjected to the same treatment, only ten times more malicious. I'm likely to get this even though I have tried to be restrained and considerate, but it's worth a try.

Still, at least I had this game at Chelsea to look forward to, which wouldn't involve too much travelling. Though why we should be playing them in the league again after only three and a half weeks is a mystery. The only explanation I can come up with is that the FA's computer has gone haywire. Have Zenith Data Systems hacked into it to get their own back for their cup being dropped this season? Or has Alan Sugar flogged the FA a computer from the reject pile?

I only discovered on Friday evening that Mum and Stephen were coming down for the game. 'Typical,' I sneered on the phone. 'A few good results, and all the part-timers crawl out of the woodwork.'

'Cheeky little bugger,' she retorted. 'You're not too grown-up to have your backside stung, you know.' The worrying thing is, I'm probably not.

I was pleased to hear they were coming, even if it was the match they wanted to see rather than me. Mum only ever visits me when Norwich are playing nearby – though I daresay she says exactly the same about me. Don't get me wrong, we are very close. It's just that we allow Norwich fixtures to dictate when we see each other.

By half past one on the Saturday afternoon, I was wondering whether I would see Mum and Stephen at all. They were supposed to arrive at the flat at around midday, and they still hadn't turned up. I was starting to get rather worried for them – after all, if they left it much later, they'd miss the start of the game. Note that I said 'they' rather than 'we'. I was in the middle of scribbling a note for the front door to tell them I'd gone on ahead when they finally appeared. It seems they'd been stuck in a huge jam caused by an accident. Not wishing to get stuck in any more traffic on the way through Central London, we decided to drive to the nearest Underground station and travel by tube. This proved to be an excellent plan – indeed, it's a pity the City team didn't follow it.

We only discovered after the game that the team coach didn't arrive at Stamford Bridge until five to three. The players, having changed on the coach when it was held up by roadworks in Battersea, apparently got off, ran through the tunnel at the ground (pausing only briefly to enlist the help of a policeman to tighten their studs) and on to the pitch. Next time, boys, pop round to my place for lunch, and I'll sort out the One-Day Travelcards.

You might wonder whether Stamford Bridge is really a suitable place for your mother to visit. Chelsea seem to have cleaned up their act somewhat in the last couple of years. The T-shirts on sale outside the ground are not as vicious and belligerent as they were. I once saw one that said 'I hate Leeds and Leeds and Leeds and Leeds and ... (etc., etc.)' – I wonder what the designer of that particular creation was trying to say. And the club is trying to foster a less crude atmosphere inside the ground, albeit by bizarre methods. In the programme for this match, the Chelsea chairman Ken Bates challenged those who use bad language to 'pack it up or bugger off'. Too fucking right, Ken. You tell the cunts.

However, I regret to say that Chelsea still have a small, obnoxious and disproportionately publicised group of followers whose acts of hooliganism have caused untold suffering all over the country. I refer, of course, to the likes of Major, Mellor and Coe. Their highly-organised gang is one of those particularly vicious ones who leave chilling calling-cards with their victims after giving them a kicking. Well, what else do you think those poll tax demands were?

One of the ringleaders, David Mellor, made an appearance at this match and received a rapturous reception from the followers of the Blues. This was a show of support after a week in which he had been featured on the front page of most of the tabloids as a result of his affair with an actress. According to the allegations, he used to make love to her while wearing the Chelsea kit (minus the shorts, obviously). I would have thought that most of the fans would regard this as sacrilegious, but they seemed more impressed by the thought that anyone in a Chelsea shirt could score five times in one night.

The reaction from the Norwich end was, predictably, rather different. Thatcher's phrase 'the oxygen of publicity' did not properly describe the effect of Mellor's prominence in the papers; 'laughing gas' would be nearer the mark in this case. The Minister of Fun was now merely a figure of fun, as the hoots of derision from around me testified. The old Peter Shilton taunt of 'Does your missus know you're here?' was revived by a few. And the nearest anyone came to an expression of sympathy was when someone behind me remarked that it made a change for an arts minister to put something into the acting profession.

Most of our attention, however, was focused on Robert Fleck – particularly as the Norwich team had not yet appeared on the pitch.

When Flecky joined Norwich from Glasgow Rangers in 1987, both he and the club were in a bad way. We were at the bottom of what was then the First Division. Uncle Ken Brown had been sacked as manager amid bitter protests. Flecky had separated from his wife and (so the rumours had it) was drinking too much. Ironically, the Norwich shirts bore the words 'Foster's Lager' on them at the time. The joke in the city was that, in Flecky's case, it wasn't the sponsor's name but a list of contents.

Yet the relationship took off straight away. His goals (and those of Kevin Drinkell) kept us up that season, and in subsequent years he scored some of the most spectacular ones we have ever seen. The late winner in the televised 3–2 victory over Millwall which caused the jubilant destruction of countless living-rooms around Norfolk one Sunday afternoon; the one-two and low drive after a wonderful passing move in a televised 2–0 win over Manchester United (have you spotted the pattern yet? It was generally reckoned that the way to get the best out of Flecky was to tell him the TV cameras, or the Scottish coach Andy Roxburgh, or preferably both, were present); and a cracking volley from twenty-five yards when we won 3–0 at Stamford Bridge last season.

He became the most popular player at Norwich for years, probably since Martin Peters. In fact, he was more popular than Peters, for whereas the latter was simply revered, Flecky was loved. He didn't just score goals and make beautifully subtle passes; he had cheek, he played to the crowd, he was the sort of character the modern game isn't supposed to have these days. He was by no means perfect; he could be niggly, petulant and, on occasions, violent. And there were the tiffs with the crowd, when he called us fickle and announced that he would be prepared to walk to Leeds to join them. (They promptly announced that they didn't want him.)

But we forgave (and even secretly admired) his bouts of obnoxiousness and excused him his threats to leave. By the end of last season, he was as popular as ever, as proved by the deafening roar that acclaimed him when he came out for the FA Cup semi-final at Hillsborough, having been sidelined since the previous round with two broken ribs. It was fitting that Flecky should have scored the goal (in a dreadful 1–1 draw against Wimbledon) that ensured our safety from relegation in our penultimate game last May.

When his move to Chelsea finally went through a month ago, it was as if he had died. Suddenly, he was referred to in the past tense. 'He was a good player.' 'He used to have a great shot.' In fact, while I was on holiday at Mum's a couple of weeks ago, we all found ourselves reminiscing about him as if we were at a memorial service for the recently departed. We all remembered him in different ways.

Karen, my sister, recalled how he used to go shopping with his girlfriend (a local girl with whom he has settled down) in Sainsbury's on a Thursday if Norwich had won the previous evening. 'He'd be strutting up and down the aisles in his shell suit,' she said. 'Funny, though, you never saw him in there if City had lost.'

Mum will probably never forget the time Flecky hit her in the face. Not personally or intentionally, you understand. It happened during a pre-match warm-up when our late hero thumped a shot off-target into the crowd. I didn't realise what had happened at first, as I was standing a little way away. I glanced round to see where the ball had gone and saw her standing there – though only just standing, as she was clearly dazed – with her glasses broken and blood pouring from her nose. 'Why didn't you duck?' I asked.

'I wanted to, but I couldn't,' she replied. 'I was mesmerised by this white circle getting larger and larger, and then everything went dark.'

There is a postscript to this story. A few weeks later, Karen's husband saw Flecky in the city. OK, so it was in a pub. 'Here, I want a word with you,' my brother-in-law said. 'You hit the wife's mother in the face with the ball the other week.'

'Sorry,' came the reply. 'I didn't mean to.'

'That's not why I'm complaining. You didn't kick it hard enough.'

Stephen picked out the incomprehensible post-match interviews that Rab C. Fleck used to give:

> 'A goal? A bliddy goal, is it? Well I'll tell yi this, boy, I will tell yi this. See me, by the way? Stoatin' aroona box like a Govan guy waitin' on a Giro, know? See the ball hit me on the napper? I kinna brung it doon, gied the big numpty in defence the old hipsway an' left his arse in the keech. Then di yi see the flyness of me? A wee dunt o' the toecap and the tube in front o' thae sticks cudnae keep it oot. Pure bliddy magic, so it was!'

All right, so he never actually said that. But he should have done.

I will remember Rab above all for his little flicks and dummies. Like the idiosyncrasies of a lover, they could be enchanting or infuriating depending on the circumstances and on one's attitude towards him at the time. And depending on whether or not they came off, of course.

It seemed very strange to see him now wearing blue as he began his afterlife at Chelsea. And yet I am well aware that, by Christmas, I will no longer be able to imagine him in yellow and green. This has been the case with every player who has ever left Norwich. Dave Watson lifted the Milk Cup when we won it in 1985, but I cannot see him in anything other than Everton blue today. Similarly, Steve Bruce scored the goal against Ipswich that took us to the final, but I can only picture him in Man. Utd red. In fact, when I look at photos from the period, they both seem strangely out of place.

It is impossible to forget that they once played for us, of course. The choruses of 'Norwich reject' ensure that. But as soon as a player joins another club, his loyalty necessarily changes, and ours does too. Indeed, it disappears, and everything the player ever did for us is conveniently overlooked until the day he stops playing, when his case may come up for reconsideration.

Only three former players have managed in recent years to receive a warm welcome back to Carrow Road: Chris Woods and Kevin Drinkell, possibly because both originally moved away to a Scottish club (Rangers), and Andy Linighan who, it is widely believed in Norwich, was sold against his will and has had a miserable time since he joined Arsenal.

Fleck (who has now lost the affectionate 'y' at the end of his name when Norwich fans mention him – a sign that his popularity has already diminished) has attempted to join this select group by praising the City supporters and claiming that the Norwich result will be the first he looks for on a Saturday. Hmm. I don't think these efforts will do him much good. Getting into the Non-Abused Ex-Canaries Group is like getting on to *Desert Island Discs*; you have to be invited, and actively canvassing for selection is severely frowned upon.

As well as remarking on Fleck's presence in a Chelsea shirt, we couldn't fail to notice the absence of another.

> For in the squadde ther was no mencioun
> Of Vinny – nat fro som suspencioun,
> But sin that he hadde left for Wimbledonne,
> Wher that his wrecched dedes hadde first bigonne.
> His steye at Chelsea was, for al the bred,
> As shorte as the haer upon his head.

> Geoffrey Chaucer, *The Harde Bastardes Tale*

The turn-out from Norwich was pretty good, inspite of the taunts from the Shed end of 'Is that all you take away?' It was especially impressive given that Stamford Bridge is one of the grounds that City fans do not often visit in large numbers. (Villa Park is another. What do you mean, so is Carrow Road?) This is because the weather is usually cold and windy when we play at Chelsea, which is particularly unpleasant as we are forced to stand on an exposed open terrace.

Mum, Stephen and I didn't mind the wind too much today, though, as it provided us with considerable amusement. Just in front of us stood a man in his 40s with the most spectacular Bobby Charlton haircut I have seen in years. After all, even Bobby Charlton doesn't have a Bobby Charlton these days. With every gust, a two-foot long mass of matted grey hair (he was evidently of the opinion that washing it would cause the tragic loss of further strands) shot up off his bald pate and extended horizontally just above his left ear. It looked like a dead rat nailed to the top of a Belisha beacon. Time and again he swept his hair back into place. Time and again Roland Rat made a dash for it. Who was he trying to kid? Did he really think he could persuade us that he wasn't bald? Still, this was what I would call pre-match entertainment. It was far better than any fireworks or dancing girls.

Our mood was less jolly once the game started. After five minutes, Fleck waltzed around our defence (who looked as though they'd only just got out of bed, never mind the coach) and set up Mick Harford for the first goal, thereby wrecking immediately what slim chance he had of remaining popular with us. It gave me no satisfaction at all to see that my First Law of Football (see above) had been proved yet again. Chants were directed at Fleck for the rest of the half, the most wilfully stupid being 'What a waste of money', ignoring as it did his contribution over the last five years as well as the first five minutes today. True to form, he responded by ostentatiously kissing his blue shirt just in front of us, and in so doing kissed us all goodbye.

Worse was to come. Chelsea went 2–0 up with a goal from Andy Townsend, another former Canary.

By half-time, Mum and Stephen were beginning to regret coming down for the game. As the seasoned traveller who had trod this path before (at Arsenal on the opening day), I tried to reassure these day-trippers that we could easily come back again. We'd created a few good chances and, judging from the impassioned orders being yelled from the bench, the management team had a definite plan in mind to shore up the defence against the runs of Chelsea's midfielders. (Poo!) Yet, deep down, I didn't really believe we could come back. The fact that we had managed it at Arsenal paradoxically reduced our chances of doing it again. (The old 'lightning never strikes twice' theory.) But I had reckoned without help from an unexpected quarter.

Unexpected, but not unlikely. Dave Beasant, the Chelsea goalkeeper, had come in for much criticism earlier in the season. Five minutes from the end of a home game against Oldham, with Chelsea 1–0 up, he had rushed out of his area and kicked the ball straight to a grateful opponent, who duly equalised. Then last week, with the scores level at Anfield, he dived over a low cross in injury time to allow Liverpool to take all the points.

Normally this would be a bad sign according to:

Kevin's Alternative Laws of Football (No.2)

> *'Any player making an horrendous mistake the week before playing your team will play an absolute blinder when you see him.'*

. . . but this proved to be the exception to the rule. If anything, last week's error had merely been a rehearsal for today's spectacular finale.

The first mistake came after only two minutes of the second half, when a long ball from Crook was weakly toe-poked towards the goal by Mark Robins. The Norwich contingent groaned as we regretted the missed chance – but suddenly Beasant was sitting on his backside and the ball, having glanced off his elbow, was nestling in the back of the net. The Chelsea and Norwich fans went equally wild, but for different reasons. The fact that no defender had moved to cover Robins was overlooked; the glaringly obvious culprit was Beasant.

The City crowd were quite merciless, as is only right and proper. It is the job of all supporters not just to support their own team, but to undermine the confidence of the opposition, confidence being the only difference between most teams in the division. Attempts to do this are generally misguided, often taking the form of direct abuse. This just serves to encourage the target to redouble his efforts on the pitch (e.g., Fleck in the first half). Mocking laughter is a much more powerful, though much less employed, weapon. Thus we had choruses of 'We love you, Beasant, we do', 'Beasant for England', 'There's only one Dave Teflon' plus, of course, exaggerated applause when he gathered the simplest balls.

Sarcasm may be the lowest form of wit, but it is arguably the most effective. It induced more and more mistakes from Beasant. He was nowhere to be seen when Robins tapped in the equaliser from five yards out. But in the words of the song, he saved the best for last. (In the words of another song, 'you're no good, you're no good, you're no good, baby you're no good'.)

Ten minutes from time, David Phillips produced a shot from the edge of the box which, as a caller to Radio 5 later put it, was about as hard as that of a mascot in a pre-match warm-up. As before, we all groaned at the miskick – but as Beasant dived to collect the ball, it seemed to dematerialise in *Star Trek* fashion, passed invisibly through him, and reappeared in the back of the net.

Our joy was unconfined, but the roar that greeted the goal came mainly from the home supporters. If they had not been confined to the stands by a cordon of police and stewards, they would have strung Beasant up from the crossbar there and then. The contrast between this reaction and the welcome given to David Mellor only occurred to me later – I was too busy jumping up and down at the time. Both had brought public humiliation and disgrace upon themselves by screwing around in a Chelsea shirt. (Allegedly, allegedly – lawyers, please note.) Yet while the gap-toothed one had been forgiven, the gap-handed one was in danger of seeing two more balls slip out of his grasp.

Why the different responses? It wasn't easy to tell at first. It's not as if Mellor is all that popular. As I overheard one Chelsea fan say at the tube station after the match, 'He's a prat, but at least he's a Chelsea prat.' Yet the second half of this remark is illuminating. It shows that the fans' overriding loyalty is to their club and their fellow supporters, rather than to any individual players. Players come and go (imminently, in the case of Beasant), but fans are fans for life.

Then there is the different hierarchy of values that football supporters have. Consider the circumstances and implications of the two Davids' actions. David Mellor had knowingly entered into an affair, the revelation of which must have had a terrible effect on his wife and family and which had embarrassed the Government. Dave Beasant had tried his best not to make mistakes, and had merely given away 3 points in the league. But to the Chelsea supporters, these 'mere' 3 points were of far greater importance than someone's domestic unhappiness and the destabilisation of the Government. Furthermore, Beasant had brought embarrassment and shame on them all, whereas Mellor had only done so on himself.

At the end of the match, one or two Norwich players commiserated with Beasant. But were they really sorry for him? I doubt it. We certainly weren't on the terraces. It was time to dust off some favourite jokes and given them another airing. 'He'll go in the dressing-room now, put his head in his hands – and drop it.' 'If he throws himself under a bus, it'll only go under his body.' Ah, it was good to hear them again. I did feel a twinge of sympathy when the Chelsea manager publicly sacked him later in the evening. But only a twinge.

For the record, though, it should be pointed out that the whole Chelsea team was awful in the second half. John Major apparently wants to see a classless society. Well, he's certainly picked the right team to follow, as there was very little class evident here. His allegiance is also consistent with his environmental aims. If they keep playing like this, we'll have a CFC-free Premier League by the end of the season.

On returning to the flat, I found a message waiting for me on my answerphone. 'Kevin, what on earth have you got on this machine now?' Actually, it's *The Canaries* by the 1971–72 Second Division Championship squad. 'And how much did you pay their goalie today? I'm just ringing to let you know I'm off to Portugal for two weeks. I'll ring you when I get back. Bye!'

'Who was that?' asked Mum.

'Who do you think?'

'Well, she obviously thinks something of you if she keeps ringing you up.'

I accidentally failed to mention that I'd rung her during the week, but found her busy again. 'No she doesn't. Why do you think I call her the Wolverine?'

'Surely even wolverines are capable of love and affection,' said Mum, clearly thinking she'd got me there.

'Possibly,' I conceded, 'but only to their own kind.'

If she and her boyfriend get the Portuguese Plops while they're away, they'll get as much sympathy from me as Dave Beasant did.

Saturday 19 September
Sheffield Wednesday (home)

My sister Karen came to the game today.

A prosaic statement on the face of it, but in fact this represents one of the most satisfying achievements of my life. Getting Karen interested in football was a drawn-out, arduous struggle of the first magnitude. If I may tell the story here, it is in the hope that it will encourage others who have been trying without success to persuade someone to come to a match to persevere, no matter how many times they have been told no for the last time.

For years, Karen was the white sheep of the family (as she saw it). She wasn't interested in football at all – indeed, she openly disparaged the game and all who watch it. 'What's the point of 22 men running around a field chasing a bit of leather? It's stupid. And you're even more stupid, paying good money to watch them do it.'

No, she was more interested in other things. If I tell you that she had three children by the time she was 22, you can guess what her chief hobby was. If I may give Oscar Wilde a severe buggering, to have one child by this age may be judged imprudent, to have two is reckless, but to have three smacks of out-and-out rampant shagging. On the other hand, the style mags reckon that kids are the ultimate fashion accessories of the '90s so, on those grounds, she's the trendiest person I know.

As her husband Chris has no interest in the game, she declared their house a football-free zone. No conversations on the subject were allowed. 'And don't you go buying the kids green and yellow scarves or bibs or anything else,' she warned me. 'I won't have them in the house. I don't want you leading them into bad ways.'

I kept on at her to come along anyway. The simple reason for this was that I like football and I wanted her to like it too. But there was also the notion that, with football being such an important part of my life (and Mum's and Stephen's), Karen couldn't fully understand us until she attended a match. Even if she didn't enjoy it, she would see why we did. She would see us acting differently to any way she had known before. She would no longer be an outsider.

I tried every argument, every approach conceivable to persuade her. I tried to convey the excitement of the game; she said it didn't look that exciting on TV. I told her that it was completely different when you were actually there; she said she'd seen games in the local park, but they weren't at all interesting. Mum attempted to describe the atmosphere of a large crowd. 'It's so moving when there are thousands of people there, all singing those wonderful football songs. "You'll Never Walk Alone". "On the ball, City". "Who's the wanker in the black?".' Even I sprayed my mouthful of tea over the carpet when she said this, and I'm used to her.

This season, incidentally, referees in the Premier League are wearing not black, but green. This has completely ruined the third of the classic songs Mum mentioned. Does the FA have no sense of tradition? 'Who's the wanker in the green?' just doesn't sound right. There is an added drawback for Norwich supporters, in that half the team would turn round if we sang it. Referees in the lower divisions were supposed to wear purple this year, but thankfully this hasn't happened. 'Who's the wanker in the purple?' doesn't even scan. It would have to be 'Who's the purple-wearing prat?' or 'Who's the moron in the mauve?' No, no, no.

But let's get back on to Karen, as her husband might say. I tried to impress upon her the importance of the football club to Norwich. It is the most visible expression of the city's identity. Think of London, and you think of Big Ben, Buckingham Palace, Oxford Street. Think of Birmingham, and you think of the Bull Ring, Jasper Carrott and the NEC. Think of Norwich, and you think of the football team – unless you have a particular interest in insurance. Football gives Norwich most of its mentions in the national media. It provides a rare chance to see famous national figures on our doorstep. And what other event in Norwich regularly attracts fifteen to twenty thousand people to one place? 'So many people can't be wrong,' I said to Karen.

'Eat shit – fifty billion flies can't be wrong,' she replied. I walked into that one, I suppose.

I tried a completely different tack, proceeding in a roundabout manner before getting to the point. I cited all the things I had recommended to her that she had subsequently enjoyed, such as Victoria Wood, Tamla Motown, *The Purple Rose of Cairo*, Thai food, Brambles card shop in Norwich, *Death of a Salesman* – but when I suggested that she should trust my judgement again and come to Carrow Road, she declared that this was a completely different matter. She just kept picking off my approaches like a sniper, so I decided to turn the argument around to make her defend her position.

'What about all the violence?' she protested. 'I don't want to get beaten up.' I pointed out that the only people who would beat her up were Mum, Stephen and me if she didn't come along.

'I'll get tired standing all that time.' (This, you understand, was in those halcyon days of yore when standing was possible at Norwich.) I offered to buy her a seat, but she said she wouldn't want to sit away from us.

Eventually, I abandoned reasoning and persuasion; I tried pleading, bribery, moral blackmail (I bought her tickets, but they all went to waste), coercion (but my physical threats have never worked since she found out how ticklish I am). Nothing worked. In all, I spent over ten years trying everything bar chloroform to get her inside a football ground, but always there was this impasse. I couldn't see any way around it, especially as the battle was not really about football any more. Honour was now at stake. Karen had said no so often and for so long that to give in now would mean a tremendous loss of face. I despaired.

Gradually, however, and despite her best efforts, Karen began to show the tiniest signs of interest. She knew where Norwich were in the league, who we were playing in any given week, and the names of most of the players. She was like one of those people who always claim that they are not influenced by advertisements, but who can tell you what all of them are for.

Mum told me not to seize on these signs. If I charged in now like a hurricane, I would extinguish this spark rather than kindle it. It was very difficult keeping quiet – harder than being among a group of opposing supporters when your team scores – but I managed it. And Mum proved to be right – but then that's her job.

What ignited the spark was the 1990 World Cup tournament in Italy. After the first week, I found out from Chris (for she obviously wasn't going to admit this to me herself) that she'd got hooked and had watched all the games. Her interest had nothing to do with Pavarotti or the fact that football was now seen by many as a key element in a hip, designer lifestyle. She actually appreciated the game for itself, enjoying the naive but ebullient Cameroonians, admiring the efficiency and organisation of the Germans, swooning over Baggio's solo goal for Italy against Czechoslovakia. England's semi-final against West Germany was the clincher. When Gazza burst into tears over the yellow card that would have ruled him out of the final even if England had won, his tears were like paraffin on the flame of Karen's interest.

If the English domestic season had started the next week, she would have been first in the queue at Carrow Road. But over the next month and a half, the memories – not of the games themselves, but of how she'd felt when watching them – faded somewhat, and the suggestion that she should come along was rebuffed again.

It was in the following spring that she finally succumbed. Again, Gazza was responsible. He may be a bit of a git, but I have a lot to be grateful to him for. He'd been out of the game for a few matches after a hernia operation, and the papers were full of speculation as to whether he would be back for the FA Cup semi-final against Arsenal at Wembley. If he was going to make it, he would need a run-out in the game at Norwich on the preceding Wednesday. Karen said she wanted to see him and would go if he played. Did she think he wouldn't be fit? Suddenly, I found myself scouring the papers for the latest news, hoping for the first and probably last time that the opposition's star player would make the game. At the last minute, it was confirmed that he would play. If Karen had been bluffing, her bluff had been called – though I got the impression as she took her place on the terrace with us that she was pleased and excited to be there.

I was so happy she was there – not because it meant that I had won ... though, of course, I had – but because we were finally together as a family unit at the place I love most. At last she would get to see why football is such a big part of our lives.

Or would she ... ?

Kevin's Alternative Laws of Football (No.3)

> *'The more a supporter extols the game of football in general or his/her team in particular, the greater the likelihood that the game or team will be dreadful when any person, acting upon this recommendation, sees the game/team for him/herself.'*

This law holds true for television programmes too. Haven't you ever noticed that, when you recommend a TV series to someone, the next episode is always crap? No matter how much you protest, 'Well it's usually good, honest,' you know that irreparable damage has been done to the credibility of your opinions. Fortunately, this game with Spurs proved to be an exception to the rule. It was an entertaining, competitive match, Gazza impressed for the hour he was on the pitch, a couple of good goals were scored in the first half, and Norwich got a spectacular winner through Ian Crook five minutes from the end.

Before the start of the game, Karen had implored us all not to shout, fearing that we would be making a spectacle of ourselves – and, more to the point, that we would be embarrassing to her. Like a 'Wet Paint' sign, however, her request merely served to encourage the behaviour she had sought to prevent. 'Come on, you yellows!' we all bellowed as the team took the pitch. 'You're so fat, it's unbelievable!' we roared whenever Gazza touched the ball. 'He's gonna cry in a minute!' we yelled on the few occasions he lost it. Karen was so astonished at seeing her mother behave like this that she completely forgot to stick up for her lachrymose lover-boy. Gradually, she became more and more caught up by the game herself. She forgot Gazza and was won over to the Norwich cause. At first, she just clapped politely when she noticed everyone else applauding. Then she became confident enough to follow her own judgement and applaud by herself. By half-time, there had even been one or two suppressed whimpers as she began to shout, then stopped herself.

In the second half, it dawned on her that she could shout, scream and groan as much as she liked, and no one would mind at all. I knew she was a natural when Norwich did their usual act of stringing together fifteen or sixteen passes around the Spurs area without entering it, before a misdirected ball rolled out gently for a Spurs throw. 'Stop mucking about, Norwich, that's rubbish!' she yelled.

'See, I told you you'd soon get the hang of this,' I said.

She leapt around as much as the rest of us when the winner went in but, as we left the ground, she became very sheepish about this. She realised – far too late, of course, to conceal the fact convincingly – that her enjoyment and her conversion had been total. She had been wrong to resist for so long. And I had been right! Everything I had told her about going to a football match had been true. Yet despite the incontrovertible evidence of the previous ninety minutes, she was determined not to admit this in public to her smug, smart-arse, I-told-you-so-ing brother. 'Well?' I asked.

'Well what?'
'You know very well what.'
'No I don't.'
'The game. Did we enjoy it?'
'I don't know. Did you?'
'You know I'm talking about you. Did you enjoy the game?'

'It was OK.'

'Just OK? But ... '

Mum intervened at this point to spare Karen from squirming and to stop me from being even more unbearable than usual. 'Just leave her be for now,' she whispered to me. 'She'll admit it in her own time.' In fact, this happened the very next day, when she confessed to Mum that she'd loved it and wanted to go again.

Since then, she's become a member in her own right and been to as many games as her having such a large tribe will permit. She came to the FA Cup semi-final at Hillsborough last season, which she found almost overwhelming. She even went so far as to say that, even if she had known in advance that Norwich were going to play so poorly and lose, she still wouldn't have missed it for anything. Had we reached the final, she would apparently have gone in for the full face-painting and hair-dyeing treatment. Frankly, I'm not sure the world is ready for this yet, so perhaps our failure was a blessing in disguise.

She certainly wouldn't arrange her wedding on a football Saturday now. (Not that she's planning another one.) However, I did worry at the time of last season's semi-final that I might have created a monster that was getting out of control. Her interest in football was growing so intense that I feared it may wreak untold damage on her home life.

I didn't spot the danger when she produced a bowl of fruit one day and asked me to explain the offside law to her. I was too stunned. I'd have thought there was more chance of me buying a season ticket for Ipswich than of her bringing this up. I didn't miss the opportunity, though. 'At the moment when the Cox's Pippin plays the grape forward to Granny Smith, there have to be at least two satsumas between her and the bunch of bananas ... '

Nor did I worry unduly when I noticed she'd started reading the papers from back to front and knew the numbers of the football pages on both Ceefax and Oracle. I was alerted, however, on the way to last year's home game with Arsenal. 'I hope we win tonight,' said Karen.

'Well, obviously,' I replied.

'After all, we haven't beaten Arsenal at home in the league since Boxing Day 1984.' What? Had she swallowed the *Rothmans Football Yearbook*?

Then it turned out that her two eldest children, aged only 5 and 3, were able to give a complete rendition of 'On the ball, City', and even the youngest could shout 'Ummonnalelloes'. (Toddler-speak for 'Come on, you yellows'.) I'm not too happy about her indoctrinating her kids at such an early age. I wanted to do that myself.

She had hinted that she would like me to buy Norwich shirts for all three daughters, but she changed her mind when she saw the new designs and the new prices.

For the time being, though, football has again slipped a place or two in her Premier League of priorities. The reason for this is that she is now pregnant for the fourth time. She obviously hasn't given up her other pastime. Yet I still have a nagging suspicion that football may have had something to do with her present condition. The baby is due in January. Even someone with an arthritic grip on arithmetic (i.e., me) can work out that he/she/it must have been conceived in April, when there was all the excitement over the semi-final. He sees a gap, he gets his head to it, he's scored!

Moreover, it is not inconceivable that Karen is carrying out a single-handed campaign to boost Norwich attendances in the future. It's just as well she is. The chances of me fulfilling my quota seem remote, to say the least.

Whatever her motivation, we hadn't expected to see Karen at Carrow Road while she is expecting. After our start to the season, though, she couldn't keep away. 'Are you sure you'll be all right?' asked Mum.

'Well, the doctor did say I should avoid too much excitement,' she replied. 'But when I asked if it was OK to watch Norwich, she said that would be fine.'

For the first half of today's game, this medical opinion seemed pretty sound. One shot on target in 44 minutes was hardly likely to provoke anything untoward. On the other hand, the game certainly wasn't uninteresting. At least, I didn't think so. But did Karen?

This was the type of game which indicates, probably better than any other, how much a spectator really understands football. Anyone can enjoy a 4–4 draw with a couple of sendings-off and a missed penalty in injury time. And there are dire goalless games which everyone can see have no redeeming features at all. But there are games which have no goals and which are superficially uneventful (the opening games of World Cup tournaments usually fall into this category) that still offer much for people with a knowledge of the game to appreciate.

In this case, it was intriguing to watch Norwich and Wednesday weighing each other up like cagey boxers. Norwich in particular were knocking the ball around in neat triangles, probing one side, then switching the play to the other flank to seek an opening there. Sometimes the ball would be played forward for Newman to hold up with his back to the Wednesday goal, on other occasions diagonal through-balls would be laid on for Phillips or Goss to run on to. But all the time, the running off the ball to create space was excellent.

This, more than anything else, is what creates a good team and largely explains our current run of success. Again, this is not something that the casual observer realises at first. I remember our sports master at junior school telling us that what you did without the ball was far more important than what you did with it. I couldn't fathom this at first. Surely you had to have the ball to show you were a good player. After all, the television would pick out outstanding goals, saves or even passes, but I couldn't recall them ever highlighting people just running around. It took me ages to see (well, I was only 10) that it is the movement of the players off the ball which gives the man with the ball the opportunity to play a brilliant pass, or which creates the space to receive the ball and put in a brilliant shot.

I sometimes wonder whether even the so-called experts on the game really appreciate this. TV commentators and newspaper reporters rarely refer to the quality of the movement off the ball. Occasionally, they will describe a team as 'hard-running', but this is generally a euphemism for 'industrious, but unskilful'. Instead, they talk in vague terms about whether teams 'gel together' or not, implying that this is an unfathomable mystery which is purely down to chance. What actually 'gels' a team together is the enthusiasm, wit and understanding with which the players run for each other.

The failure to grasp this is largely responsible for the incomprehension expressed by the media at Norwich's current position in the league. If we do slip (and I am beginning to think we might not), the 'experts' will doubtless claim that this is because our players are mediocre and have been 'found out'. Wrong. If it happens, it will be because the standard of movement has dropped (as it did at the end of last season, when the players were as static as Subbuteo men) or because other teams have started to match us.

Even the current England manager does not seem to know what makes a team click. Since he got the job, Graham Taylor has picked over fifty players for the national team, apparently in the hope that he will stumble on a successful formula by accident. I realise that Bobby Robson had a measure of success using this method, but it's hardly likely to work again. None of Taylor's players seems to have any idea what the others are doing, or are intending to do, and so the movement is lousy. But more on this later.

Karen, I was pleased to see, was totally absorbed in the game. She actually commented on the movement of the team. Though I should say that this was not an entirely spontaneous observation, as I had told her what to look out for in previous Norwich matches. She also demonstrated her sound, if curiously expressed, knowledge of the offside law when the large contingent of Sheffield fans continually hurled abuse at the linesman covering the Norwich attacks. 'If Phillips was level with the satsuma when the grape was played, he's OK ... '

Norwich finally broke the deadlock with an excellent Newman header from an excellent Robins cross after 44 minutes and 44 seconds. Yes, the exact time is important, and not just because of the neat duplication of digits. Remember those Golden Goal lottery tickets that I mentioned a few games ago? They were my brother's second thought as the ball flew in. The first being 'Yeeesss!!'

'My goal time is around now!' he said, delving enthusiastically into his pocket. He produced his ticket, opened it up and read ... 44 minutes 43 seconds. Now you do get a fiver for being within five seconds of the first goal, as Mum tried to point out, but Stephen was in no mood to look on the bright side. He was preoccupied with what he had almost won.

'A hundred quid. One bloody second away from a hundred quid! Bollocks. Bollocks! A fiver isn't even half of what it cost me to get in today.'

It was a fatal mistake to let Karen see that this had got to him, for she would walk off with the gold medal if winding people up were an Olympic sport. Even on the podium, she'd probably be saying, 'Silver and bronze aren't bad, you know. It's nice to have something to remind you ... that you didn't win.' During the summer, she'd said to me, 'Why didn't you take me to the football earlier? You should have told me that it's much better being there than watching it on telly.' Of course, I realised that she was deliberately trying to wind me up, but I found that I was getting wound up anyway – and this served to wind me up even more.

She was like a dog with a bone during half-time. (An unfortunate analogy, I admit, but the only one that springs to mind.) 'Ninety-five quid,' she said. 'Think what you could have done with that. Ten albums. Fifty pints of beer. Forty gallons of petrol. Golden Goal tickets for the next fifteen years.'

'Oh, shut up,' said Stephen.

She did. For about a minute. 'You know, they might have made a mistake with the timing. What if the timekeeper's finger slipped and he was a second late? Do you think they stop the watch when the ball crosses the line or when it hits the back of the net? Suppose it was a digital stopwatch? If it said 44 minutes 43.5 seconds, they probably rounded it up. I'd ask if I were you.'

'Look ... '

'And while you're at it, I'd tell them to change their prize system. It's not fair. Two people will have been four seconds further away from the correct time than you, but they'll still get the same money.'

'If you weren't pregnant, I'd ... '

'Of course, it might be a Maxwell-type scam. Perhaps they programme the times of all the unsold tickets into a computer before the game and pick one out when someone scores.'

Karen let the matter drop for another ten minutes to make Stephen think she'd exhausted her theme. Then she applied the *coup de grâce*. 'Here's a good one, Stephen. What's the difference between this [she clicked her fingers] and this [another click]?'

'I don't know.'

'Ninety-five quid! Ha!'

He was spared any further irritations she might have had up her sleeve by the excellence of the second half, which demanded our full attention. There were no further goals, but Norwich created a string of good chances. Karen gave a great shriek as each was missed, and the one she emitted when Newman somehow managed to thump the ball over from three yards out had Mum seriously worried. 'Steady on,' she said. 'We don't want to see your baby for another four months.'

'You can see it now if you want,' Karen said, and produced a Polaroid of a scan she'd had at the hospital two days before. That's what she said it was, anyway. It looked like a shot of the surface of the moon to me.

Despite her condition, she tackled Jimmy Hill with no trouble after the game.

If the team stays this high in the league for much longer, we're all going to have to invest in oxygen masks. We're not used to being 4 points clear. Still,

Mum's butcher seems unimpressed by the current run. 'He reckoned we'd lose 2–0 today,' Mum said. He's consistent, I'll say that for him.

The following morning saw the start of my Sunday football season. I play for the Norwich Supporters' team in Division Four of the West Fulham League. This doesn't sound too bad until you discover that there is no Division Five.

You may be surprised to hear that such a team exists. After all, I did mention before that I'd only met around a dozen Norwich followers in London. The explanation is simple: most of the players don't follow Norwich. The player-manager and a couple more support Liverpool, while others follow Arsenal, Manchester United, Oxford and Leyton Orient. All, however, are friends, or friends of friends (or friends of … oh, you know) of City fans. Even so, I can't really understand why they are prepared to play for us. I certainly couldn't turn out every week wearing the shirt of another club.

You may also be wondering why I haven't mentioned any training sessions before now. Again, there is a simple reason. You guessed it. Because the players live all over the South-East, from Milton Keynes to Basingstoke to Tonbridge, it's hard enough getting everyone together for the matches, let alone training. No one lives anywhere near Fulham. I suspect that whoever started the team years ago lived in the area and simply entered it in his local league.

I did try to do some training when I was in Norwich for a fortnight, but this proved abortive. I took a ball down to a nearby playing field to practise, but made the mistake of wearing green shorts and yellow socks. As I dribbled round a football pitch for the third time, I became aware that I was being watched intently by a group of four or five kids aged around 10. Eventually, they came over.

'Hey mister, do you play for Norwich?'

Should I be flattered that they thought I was of Premier League standard, or was their question more an indictment of the City team? 'No,' I replied.

'What team do you play for, then?' they continued, undeterred.

Explaining about the Norwich Supporters' team would be too confusing, so I settled for, 'Oh, you wouldn't know.'

'Are you on the telly?' asked one.

I might be on *Crimestoppers* soon, I thought, for beating up a gang of annoying kids. I finally managed to persuade them that I was not famous, and they trooped off in disappointment. Yet no sooner had they disappeared than another group came up from the bottom end of the field, clearly thinking that the first group had discovered a celeb. I then had to go through the whole rigmarole again. Perhaps it would have been easier to say I did play for Norwich and to charge each kid a quid for my autograph.

Or maybe I should have said my name was Robert Chase and told them all to piss off, the idea being that they would go home and tell their parents, who would then write angry letters to the local press complaining that the Norwich chairman had been rude to their children. Why is it you never think of these schemes at the time?

I gave up on training after that, and decided that adopting a high-energy diet of pasta and bananas the day before the first game would do just as well. After five minutes, it seemed to be working. I crossed from the left, and one of the few genuine Norwich supporters in the team headed in. Here we go, here we go, here we go (repeat as necessary). Division Three here we come! Unfortunately, my banana turned out not to be big enough. We were 5–1 down by half time and eventually lost 8–3. Damn.

Tuesday 22 September
Carlisle United (away)
COCA-COLA CUP SECOND ROUND, FIRST LEG

Ever since the draw for this round of the cup was made (while Mum and I were travelling back from Manchester City on the Club Cabbage coach, you will recall), I had been wrestling with the question of whether to travel up for the away leg or not.

The first matter to determine was whether it was actually possible for me to get to Carlisle and back in the middle of the week. Capital Canaries weren't running an official trip, so I would have to make my own arrangements. I checked the mileage chart in my road atlas, but when I looked at the intersection of the Carlisle column and the London row, I found a blue Biroed asterisk. At the foot of the page, there was another asterisk with the comment: 'Forget it, Kevin, it's far too far.' Funny, I could have sworn it was Mum's writing.

Even without roadworks or jams, it would clearly take at least five hours to drive up, and the same to get back. I'd be shattered for days. That option was out.

On checking the rail timetable, I discovered that there was a train that left Euston at 2:25pm and arrived in Carlisle at six. Perfect! Now, could I get back? There was a train leaving Carlisle at 1:30 in the morning and getting into London at 6:30, but I didn't fancy hanging around on Carlisle Station in the cold for four hours. 'Is there a sleeper you could catch?' suggested Mum helpfully – if she had been writing in my atlas, she was obviously feeling guilty about it. It turned out there was. Hooray! It would cost £72. Damn.

Having established that I could go to the game, albeit at a price, I then had to decide whether I should or not. Unfortunately, I found this all but impossible. Even tossing a coin didn't help. This usually works because you realise what you want the outcome to be when the coin is in mid-air. The trouble was, I was observing my reactions so intently, I wasn't reacting naturally any more. In the end, I resorted to drawing up a list of pros and cons. Such an exercise is necessarily quantitative rather than qualitative; that is, the number of points on each side counts whereas their relative importance is ignored. Still, it was the best I could come up with.

Reasons for going to game
1) I always enjoy watching Norwich play. Well, nearly always. Well, enough to warrant putting this in the 'pro' rather than the 'con' list.
2) The boys are playing particularly well at the moment.
3) I'm a bag of nerves if I'm not at a Norwich game. I pace up and down like an expectant father outside a delivery room, flicking dementedly between Ceefax, Oracle and the various radio stations for the latest news. It's actually far less stressful just to go to the game.
4) Having missed one game this season, I don't want to miss any more.
5) What else am I to spend my money on? The Wolverine? Chance would be a fine thing.
6) I've never been on a sleeper, and it might be an adventure.
7) If I'm trying to chronicle a season, I should go to all the games I can.
8) If I don't go to support the team, who will? There aren't that many of us.
9) If the supporters don't make an effort, how can we expect the team to?

Reasons for not going
1) The price! £72 is a lot of money to wave goodbye to (though not as much as £95, eh, Stephen?), especially for a relatively unimportant match like this.
2) We will get no credit if we win (Carlisle being in the Third, formerly Fourth, Division), and will be a target for scorn if we lose.
3) Defeat would make the journey home horrendous.
4) Whatever the score, it will not be decisive, as there will still be the second leg to come in a fortnight's time.
5) I've been to Carlisle before ('85–'86 season), so it's not as if I'd be visiting a new ground.
6) Since I've missed one game already, why should I worry about missing another?
7) They'd be sure to spot my absence at work this time.
8) Do I really only want to go so that I can point to the sacrifice of time and money and tell myself and everyone else what a loyal supporter I am?
9) Several people have told me that the word 'sleeper' is in fact a misnomer.
10) I could always make up the entry for this book and say I'd gone when I hadn't.

Well, let's take a look at the final score. Pros 9 Cons 10. So that was decided. Close as the tally was, I wasn't going. Definitely. Positively. Irrevocably.

At work on Monday morning, I was accosted by an Arsenal fan. (Four-two, four-two ...) 'Are you going up to Carlisle tomorrow night, then?' he asked. 'No,' I said. 'For one thing, it'd cost £72, for another ... ' 'Part-time supporter, part-time supporter,' he chanted. 'As soon as things get a bit difficult and require a bit of effort, you can't be bothered.' He only goes to about three matches a year himself, but that didn't matter. I went to Euston Station at lunchtime to book my tickets.

Sneaking out of work with my overnight bag at lunchtime the following day, I bumped into my boss in reception. 'Er ... where are you going?' he asked.

'I've just got to go and see some important people,' I replied. 'I'll be back early.' I didn't tell him I meant early the next morning.

I wasn't sure what to expect when I boarded the train. I hadn't been on one since around the time they started running those black and white Intercity ads on TV. You know, the ones where the music sounds as if it's been recorded by an old bloke dosed up on Valium and then played at the wrong speed. The image of train travel presented in these commercials always seemed to me to bear as much relation to reality as an Anfield penalty decision.

Things did seem to have improved, though. The carriage was clean and warm, without the slightest whiff of cabbage. The hot chocolate from the buffet car was drinkable. I even had a group of four seats and a table to myself because three people had not taken up their reservations. I might even have taken the advice of the song in the TV ad to loosen my tie and take off my shoes, were it not for the fact that I wasn't wearing a tie and that it might seriously distress the others in the carriage if I removed my trainers.

As we approached Carlisle, I was further heartened to see lots of fields with sheep in them. At least our sexual behaviour wouldn't be questioned here. As it turned out, the Carlisle fans seemed to be proud of their love of lamb. At half-time, a toy sheep was tossed around at the other end of the ground for a full ten minutes.

The train pulled in at six on the dot. I waited at the station for a few minutes to see if any other Norwich fans had caught the same train, but it seemed they hadn't. I had half-expected to see an old chap called Charlie who travels to all the City games from Preston, but he'd obviously found another way of getting to Carlisle.

The town centre was virtually deserted. You would never have thought there was to be a cup match against the Premier League leaders that night. In fact, I started to worry that I might have come up on the wrong day, and even glanced at my paper to check I was right. Eventually, I spotted a couple of boys and their father wearing blue and white scarves and followed them to the ground.

Brunton Park stands about a mile out of town and is surrounded by what seems to be a moat of mud, which serves to reinforce the feeling that you are visiting a real football outpost. It therefore struck me as particularly ironic when a group of home fans pointed out someone in a Norwich shirt (no, not me) and treated him to a chorus of 'Who the fucking hell are you?' Norwich supporters come to expect this welcome at large Premier League grounds, but this was a bit rich.

Still, at least the match prices were somewhat removed from what I am used to paying on my travels. The sign above the turnstiles said £5, so I not unreasonably presented a fiver to the operator. 'Oy!' he grunted. 'Six quid.'
'Sorry?'
'Another quid. It's six quid to get in.'
'Well, it does say five pounds outside.'
'It's six quid, right? Bloody Premier Leaguers, trying to get in cheap.' I gave him the other pound and bit my tongue. I hadn't come all this way to be chucked out for calling him a wanker.

The match programme reminded me of a TV programme – the *Beverly Hillbillies*. After all, it was largely black and white, the headings of each page were in the same jokey '60s typeface used for the credits of the show, and the content was a mixture of the quaint, the unfamiliar and the unintentionally hilarious. There were adverts for multinational conglomerates such as Monkhouse's Brown Eggs (available at the covered market), Stewarts the Saddlers (repairers of equestrian requisites – and try saying that three times quickly), and Trotter's Waste Services (Del Boy must be branching out). A column entitled 'Brewster's Brunton Beat' reminisced about Carlisle's League Cup run in 1969–70. 'United had just sold Hughie McIlmoyle to Middlesbrough, remember.' Er – no, actually. There was also an appeal to fans to become members or agents of the club's Digit. Don't ask me what that is.

The amusement was provided by the chairman and the physio. The former is Michael Knighton, who will forever be remembered by Manchester United fans for running on to the Old Trafford pitch juggling a ball a few seasons ago when it appeared that he was about to buy the club. He doesn't seem to have quite the same skill with words. The attendance for the previous home game (against York City) was described as 'FAN-tastic!' (his capitals). Hur! Hur! Geddit? The lads 'gave their usual 200%+ effort'. And there was a rather strange use of pronouns in the sentence: 'Let's hope we can clip the wings of these marvellous flying canaries with some scintillatingly stylish soccer we know you can produce.' Mind you, even this does not compare with the interview Rob Newman gave on *Match of the Day* last Saturday, in which he appeared to be going for the all-comers cliché record. In the space of just twenty seconds, he informed us that 'the game lasts for ninety minutes', 'it only takes a second to score a goal', and 'the lads showed tremendous character to battle back and get our just rewards'. At the end of the day, Brian, the boy done crap.

On the next page, the physio revealed some of the secrets of his medical bag. Apparently, it always contains sissors. I'd have thought scissors would be more useful. And there is always a spare pair of shorts. Why? Is it because his mother was one of those who always said to wear clean underpants in case of an accident? I can just see him now. 'Your leg looks broken, son. It's the hospital for you. But we can't let the doctor see you in those mucky shorts. Whatever would he think? Stop yelling and put these nice clean ones on ... '

I was disturbed from reading the programme by a bit of fuss to my left. A small group of close-cropped Carlisle youths had infiltrated the Norwich section, but had been spotted by a steward and were being led away to rejoin the home fans. As they passed in front of us, I understood for the first time what the United Digit was. Later on, an appeal was made over the loudspeakers for people to stop throwing coins.

Neither of these incidents was particularly serious (unless you happened to get hit by a coin, I suppose), but they did confirm a general phenomenon I have noticed; namely, that it tends to be more dangerous to go to smaller clubs than larger ones. With the exception of a couple of skirmishes at Aston Villa in 1990 when a late equaliser ruled out any chance they had of winning the Championship that season, the only trouble I have seen at Norwich games in recent years has been at Wigan, Port Vale and Exeter.

I'm sure it isn't always this bad at these grounds. My theory is that the local hooligans have this notion that every big club (which, from their point of view, Norwich are) has a large following of trouble-makers. This has not been the case with most clubs for some time now – and never has been with Norwich – but the idiots still come out of the woodwork to take on the big boys off the field as well as on it.

The vast majority of the Carlisle crowd were, it must be stressed, perfectly behaved, yet passionate. And the word 'vast' is not entirely inappropriate, given that 10,300 people were packed into the ground by the kick-off – almost double their previous highest gate of the season, and only a couple of thousand short of Liverpool's attendance the same evening. The turn-out from Norwich was also encouraging: our contingent numbered considerably more than the odd 300, despite the length of the trip.

Two things became apparent after five minutes of the match. First, the Carlisle players were giving it everything. This wasn't going to be easy. Second, and this is going to sound like an excuse worthy of British Rail, the grass seemed rather longer than we were used to. And it was very wet. I hesitate to suggest that the pitch had been deliberately prepared to render our close-passing style impossible, but that was the net result. The match became a wellying contest, with which Carlisle were clearly happier.

The Norwich defence was under pressure for most of the half, and eventually conceded a goal from a penalty. It looked on the TV later as though the penalty had been won by a dive, but since the referee had missed an obvious handball by John Polston after five minutes, we couldn't really complain. The Carlisle fans must have been wondering what all the fuss about Norwich was. To be honest, I was starting to wonder too. We didn't win our first corner until the stroke of half-time.

O me of little faith! Mark Robins scored only twelve seconds after the restart, and ten minutes later Jerry Goss made it 2–1 with a shot that squirmed under the keeper's body. Sound familiar?

'Are you Beasant in disguise?' came the cry. 'Two Dave Beasants, there's [*sic*] only two Dave Beasants ... ' On this occasion, though, the Beasant-fingers in question was too far away, and our numbers were just too small, for us to undermine his confidence seriously. Attention turned instead to the linesman just in front of us who, it was generally thought, kept failing to spot Carlisle players in offside positions. As far as I could see, he was right every time. If only Karen were here with her bowl of fruit to give those around me a quick explanation. But they continued to jeer him anyway, starting with the usual comments about needing new glasses and moving on for some reason to laughing at his boots. 'Woolworths boots! Woolworths boots!' they shouted. The linesman didn't seem to hear – but suddenly the ball was crossed to a Carlisle player who looked four yards offside to me, and he didn't raise his flag. Two all. If this was the linesman's petty idea of revenge ... it was very effective.

Still, 2–2 was a fair result, and everyone seemed happy enough as we all filed out of the ground. I quickly blended in with the home fans and made my way back into town. At the railway station, everything went as smoothly as it had on the train earlier. The buffet was, surprisingly, still open – and when it closed, I was able to board the sleeper. Perfect!

What can I tell you about the cabin? Very little, really, as there was very little of it. There wasn't enough room to swing a penis. Not that I planned to do so, but I didn't fancy getting a wet smack in the ear if the man booked into the other berth did. 'If he doesn't turn up before quarter to twelve, I'll put him in another cabin so he won't disturb you,' said the steward.

Midnight arrived, and I realised I would have the cabin all to myself. Yesss! As well as not having to take turns with the other man in holding our stomachs in to allow each other enough room to get dressed in the morning, I was now free to go to the toilet in the sink instead of traipsing down to the other end of the carriage. Mind you, it took a while to force the turds down the plughole. I definitely shouldn't have had that sweetcorn the evening before. (I'm only kidding about this, of course. I didn't really have sweetcorn.)

Everything had worked out as I had hoped. I duly set my alarm for the morning and went to sleep. I was woken briefly when the train started to move at half past two (it felt as if someone was jumping enthusiastically up and down on my bed and, of course, I'm not used to that), but I soon nodded off again.

Looking back, I should have realised that things were going too smoothly. Even when I woke up at ten to seven, I suspected nothing. The train wasn't moving, but I took this to mean that we had arrived at Euston Station ahead of time. I got up, dum de dum de dum, washed, doo doo de doo, got dressed, tum te tum. Only then did I raise the blind over the window. Bollocks. Nuneaton.

The steward explained that torrential rain during the night had flooded tunnels, closed stations and caused signal equipment to break down. The train wouldn't be going any further. 'But I have to be in London by nine because of a testicular replacement,' I said.

'You're having an operation?'

'If I'm not in work by nine, I'll need one.'

In the end, a coach was laid on for us. And BR did try to make amends by offering free crisps and coffee on the way. But by the time we'd taken a huge detour via the M40 (the M1 was blocked, apparently), we didn't get to Euston until twenty past eleven. Fourteen hours to get back from a match. We'd better win the second leg now.

I walked into work twenty minutes later, as prepared as I could be for my bollocking. Or de-bollocking. But where was my lord and bast ... er, master? 'Ill. He won't be in today,' said his secretary. Thank you, God! And sorry about that small matter of not believing in you.

I got myself a cup of tea and settled down to read the paper. Wolves lost at Notts County in the cup. Ha! I hope the Wolverine's getting the British papers in Portugal. I don't care if she did send me a postcard.

Saturday 26 September
Coventry City (away)

Many people seem to think of Coventry as a dull, dreary place. After all, it is not pleasant to be 'sent to Coventry', so the assumption is that the city cannot be congenial. I would like to set the record straight once and for all. Such assumptions are totally with foundation. In fact, Coventry is the saddest, most depressing place I know.

And yes, I do know it. I have spent enervating evenings in dingy pubs in Spon End. I have zig-zagged my way down streets to avoid people fighting and pissing in doorways at nine o'clock at night. I have been gobbed on for no reason by ugly-looking youths in the uglier-looking precinct. I have been shat on by birds in the bleak bus station as they return to the cak-covered Lanchester Poly buildings across the street. (I believe this establishment has undergone a transformation recently, though. It is now the cak-covered Coventry University.) Life in Coventry seems to take place in black and white. And grey, of course. It is entirely appropriate that the city's symbol should be a ponderous grey elephant.

You want more evidence? Hard luck, you're going to get it anyway.

Take the Coventry Carol. Is this a happy celebration of the birth of Christ? Tidings of comfort and joy, 'tis the season to be jolly, and all that? Hardly. It is a mournful dirge that focuses instead on the possibility of the baby Jesus being brutally slaughtered:

> Herod the king, in his raging,
> Charged he hath this day
> His men of might, in his own sight,
> All young children to slay.
> That woe is me, poor child, for thee!
> And ever mourn and say . . .

What an uplifting little number that is.

More recent musical compositions from Coventry have scarcely been more cheerful. Which town were the Specials singing about in *Ghost Town*?

> This town is coming like a ghost town.
> Why must the youth fight against themselves?
> Government leaving the youth on the shelf . . .
> . . . No job to be found in this country.
> Can't go on no more, the people getting angry.

On the other side of the twelve-inch version of this was a song which, for me, encapsulates perfectly the experience of being in Coventry at night — *Friday Night Saturday Morning*:

> I'll eat it [a pie from the chip shop] in the taxi queue
> Standing in someone else's spew.
> Wish I had lipstick on my shirt
> Instead of piss stains in my shoes.

In the mid-1980s, there was a band called King who tried to present a jollier image by painting their Doc Martens different colours. They didn't last, though. The lead singer is now a daytime presenter on MTV. What a sad job that is.

Who else comes from Coventry? The poet Philip Larkin was born and brought up there, which may explain a lot:

> Man hands on misery to man,
> It deepens like a coastal shelf.
> Get out as early as you can,
> And don't have any kids yourself.

This be the Verse

The only famous Coventry women I can think of are Lady Godiva and the Page Three model Debee Ashby, both of whom became well-known for getting their kit off. The circumstances were different, it is true, but both cases are sad in their own way.

Finally, of course, we come to Coventry City Football Club, where it always seems to be dull and devoid of atmosphere. When the weather isn't grey, it's pouring with rain. I once travelled the 160-odd miles there from Norwich with Mum and Stephen, only to find that the game had been called off because of a waterlogged pitch. Not fun. The club's nickname is the Sky Blues. Terminal Blues would be nearer the mark.

The main reason for finding the place so depressing is, however, the fact that Coventry, like Manchester City, are another of our bogey sides. What is it about teams that wear light blue? I've never seen us win at Highfield Road, a couple of dreadful 0-0 draws being the best results we've managed there lately. We didn't even get a result the time I went along to support Norwich at a Coventry-Luton game. Perhaps I should explain.

At the end of the 1984-85 season, Coventry needed to win their last three league matches to stay in Division One and send us down instead. They won the first at Stoke (though only after Stoke missed a penalty in the last ten minutes), and then played Luton in midweek. This match took place so long after the season was supposed to have finished that Luton had to come back from their club holiday to play it. Even so, they were by far the better team – yet they missed a stack of chances, and Coventry won with a miskicked shot six minutes from time. They went on to win a Sunday-morning game against an under-strength and uninterested Everton side, and we were relegated.

It is probably this jinx that makes me see the whole city as a miserable place. If we always won there, I'd probably think Coventry was marvellous. Hmm, I wonder if anyone thinks Norwich is a craphole because their team always loses at Carrow Road. I can't think of any who do, though.

I should make it clear that, when I criticise Coventry, I do so in full awareness of my own status as a sad person. For years I refused to admit that there is an inherent pathos in those who follow their teams home and away, but recently I have come to admit that this is true. The most fanatical followers often have severe problems relating to the outside world, and more particularly to the opposite sex.

Football grounds have frequently been described as recruitment centres for extremist groups such as the National Front. I have never seen any evidence of this myself, but it occurs to me that organisations such as Dateline might profitably hand out their leaflets on the terraces to attract new members. The die-hards would be prime fodder. Many of them (OK, OK - of us) started travelling everywhere to watch football precisely because of a lack of social success. Being a committed supporter has many comforting compensations. You become part of a group. You feel that you belong somewhere. No personal interaction is required with the object of your affections (apart from the odd shout at long range). And while you may be let down now and then, you are never rejected.

This is all very well, but the trouble is that football can assume such importance in a person's life that it renders social interaction even more difficult, even impossible, as time goes on. What was originally a refuge becomes a prison. True, it is an open prison. But, after a time, you become institutionalised and incapable of dealing with the outside world.

There are two particularly horrendous examples of my obsession with football wrecking my chances of personal happiness. Even now, I cringe when I look back at them. And what makes it worse is that both incidents involved the same girl.

In February 1985, a witty, pretty law student called Judith rang me out of the blue to invite me to a party in Cambridge. I was bowled over. I didn't get asked to parties very often, and certainly not by anyone like Judith. No other girl could compete with her. But, of course, it wasn't other girls she was competing with. The date of the party was the same as that of the Milk Cup semi-final first leg at Ipswich. Tickets were like gold dust in Norwich – and I had one. Having no car (and less money) at the time, I couldn't go to both, so I had to make a choice between the two. Which did I go to? You guessed it.

My reasoning was that I would always follow Norwich, whereas the chances of spending the rest of my life with Judith were remote at best. This game could be a great moment in the club's history that would stay with me forever, but I probably wouldn't remember her name in a few years' time. OK, so I do still remember it. And we lost the game 1-0. But we did go on to win the second leg and the final, so I can't have too many regrets about my choice.

Judith wasn't pleased with me at all. In fact, it took a year of fawning and apologising to get back into her good books, but in February 1986 she finally agreed to let me visit her. This was arranged for a Saturday when Norwich were playing at Barnsley, but I felt I had to make some sort of sacrifice to prove my affection for her.

It was a wonderful afternoon. (Even though we only drew 2-2, thanks to a disputed late goal by some Barnsley youngster called David Hirst.) We walked, we talked, we laughed. We were on exactly the same wavelength, whereas all I had ever encountered previously was whistling and complaints of interference. Our souls touched, entwined, and would have had a bucket of cold water thrown over them if they had been visible to the general public. We ate at an Italian restaurant in the market square and, as we walked back to her flat, she asked me softly, looking at me with those piercing yet beautiful blue eyes, 'Kevin, do you really have to go and watch Norwich play every week?'

Now what would you take this question to mean? What would the *Annie Hall*-type subtitle be saying there? Right. And did I see this at the time? Did I Hurlocks. What I thought she was saying was: 'Discuss, with particular reference to Norwich City Football Club, the sporting, psychological and sociological reasons for following football. Candidates should give examples and show all working. The time allowed for this exercise is three hours.'

There was no stopping me. I was like a racehorse that unseats its rider, veers off to jump the siderails of the course, and then disappears across the fields into the distance. 'Football matches are always the same, yet always different. They can be ugly and depressing, beautiful and uplifting – you can never tell in advance. Some players are graceful and skilful, some are disgracefully dirty, some are both. There's the overall contest and the individual battles within it. And it's about being with your family, being part of the crowd, part of the city you were born in and wish you still lived in. I love the good humour of the terraces, even the bad humour of the terraces. Being able to shout your head off. Or trying to shout and finding out you're so tense that nothing comes out ...'

And so I went on. It was the most complete synthesis of reasons for loving football that I'd ever come up with. And it was the most completely wrong time to do it.

You don't have to tell me how stupid I was. God knows, I know now. I just wasn't able to read the game or make the right pass when I was there in the middle of the action. Come to that, I'm still not. Football and love are very similar in that respect. It's much easier to be an expert when you're watching from the sidelines. Or after the event.

Not surprisingly, I never saw Judith again. No, tell a lie, I did bump into her on the tube about a year ago. After a few minutes of squinting quizzically at each other over our newspapers, we spoke for a couple of stops before she had to get off. She was still beautiful, had got a First, had been called to the Bar, and was now based in Lincoln's Inn. She was also married. Damn, damn, damn.

The Wolverine should be back from her holiday today. Unless she has to spend six months in quarantine, of course.

While it wasn't football that made me a sad person, you could say it has kept me one. But I am not as pathetic as I was, according to:

Kevin's Alternative Laws of Football (No. 4)

> *'The point at which a supporter who attends all of his/her team's games passes from being admirably keen to being a sad old git may be determined by the following criterion. When he/she is older than any member of the first-team squad, the said supporter may officially be deemed sad.'*

I failed this test last season, but the arrival of Gary Megson has granted me a temporary reprieve. Let's hope they offer him an extended contract.

I also console myself with the knowledge that I am not as sorry a character as some. For, as with all things, there are degrees of sadness. Here are ten (by no means mutually exclusive) groups of fans who are even more pitiful than me.

1) People who wave at the TV cameras whenever the ball comes near them.
2) People who hold up 'Hello Mum' signs. This wasn't funny the first time it was done, for goodness sake. Regrettably, this appears to be an international affliction. During the 1992 European Championships, I noticed a

large banner at a France match which read: 'Maman, on est là.' Maman, on est demeuré, more like.
3) People who keep videos of themselves at matches. The only time I have been guilty of this was after an FA Cup match at Exeter a couple of years ago. The ground was so small that everyone there got their Warhol-predicted fifteen minutes of fame that day. And being positioned right behind one of the goals meant that I was on screen longer than some of the players. The BBC had to keep powdering my head, though, as the reflection of the floodlights on my dome kept dazzling the cameraman. I would like to state, however, that I did record over the tape after a fortnight.
4) People who start the Mexican wave. Get a life.
5) People who keep count of the consecutive number of a team's games that they've attended. Who cares? You can't reduce loyalty to a number. Trying to quantify it merely renders it meaningless.
6) People who send requests to the club DJ every week. (Not counting the DJs themselves, who probably have to write to themselves every week out of necessity.)
7) People who listen to their radios during a game. If you're so interested in the other match being broadcast, why don't you go to that one instead?
8) Adults who do the junior crossword in the match programme. (Or, even worse, adults who can't manage it.)
9) People who run fantasy football teams. These are the same losers who used to play dice cricket at school with made-up teams such as a World XI v Dinner Ladies.
10) People who buy two programmes – one to read and one to keep flat and unopened forever. You can tell these types fairly easily at matches, as they get hysterical if anyone comes within five yards of them, for fear that they may crease their pristine collection copy.

You will notice that I have not included in this list those people who wear stupid costumes on the pitch, such as the eagle at Crystal Palace and that strange-looking creature in the Chelsea kit. No, not David Mellor – a mangy-looking lion. On the subject of Mellor, incidentally, he resigned from the Cabinet this week. It seems that the laughing gas has turned into poison gas.

This omission is because these are rotten jobs, on a par with putting broken biscuits at either end of packets of Rich Tea, drilling tiny holes in the side of ballpoint pens, or being a daytime presenter on MTV – jobs that people do out of desperation. They deserve our sympathy rather than our scorn. And at least their anonymity is preserved under their costumes, unlike the pillocks who wave at the TV cameras to draw attention to themselves.

Having established that the city of Coventry is dismal and that a large number of football supporters are dysfunctional, what of today's game? Was it a cheering experience or not? Well, if I tell you that, before the match, we were treated to a display of baton-twirling that was slightly less exciting than a routine by the Canary Girls; that they were outperformed by the seated Norwich fans, who were so troubled by wasps that they looked like the St Vitus Formation Ballroom Team; and that the meat pie I had was as dry as a teabag and only marginally bigger ($^3/_{10}$) – you would come to the wrong conclusion. It was actually a very bright and enjoyable day. That's the thing about football – it surprises you so often, it's surprising that you can still be surprised.

This was actually a 'top-of-the-table' clash, for Coventry were second in the league before the match. William Hill (and, for all I know, David Lacey) would have given you good odds on this being a first-versus-second match at the start of the season. It seemed that everyone had turned out for the occasion. There was a decent crowd for once (16,000), the TV cameras were present, and even the sun made an appearance. This fixture usually feels like it is just making up the numbers on the coupon, but this time it had the atmosphere of a Match of the Day.

Everyone was in a good mood, perhaps because the two sets of fans sensed a common cause in being 'unglamorous' clubs at the top of the league. The banter was cheery, 'We are top of the league' being met with 'We'll be top at ten to five', and 'On the ball, City' being countered by the Coventry version of the Eton Boating Song which, for once, didn't seem totally incongruous in this setting. Even when the home supporters pointed out one rather, er, rotund Norwich fan with 'You're so fat, it's unbelievable' and 'Go on a diet, you ought to go on a diet', he waved back with a broad grin on his face.

The 17-year-old girl sitting next to me with her father got particularly excited as the game got underway. Her commentary during the build-up to Ian Crook's goal after thirteen minutes went something like, 'Go on, yes, yes, yes, go on, there, that's it, yes, yes, get it in, hit it, yeeeessss, oh yeeeessss! Yeeeaaahhhooooo!!!' Now where had I heard a girl say that before? It sounded vaguely familiar, but it must have been a long time ago. And why did I suddenly have an irrational longing for a cigarette?

Incidentally, you may be wondering why I was sitting at the match when I made such a fuss earlier about wanting to carry on standing at Norwich. I do sometimes have a seat at away matches if the away terrace offers a poor view or is open to the elements. Both factors applied here – though the terrace still isn't as bad as at Southampton.

The game offered an entertaining contrast in styles. Norwich showed better technique and put together better passing moves, while Coventry were faster and seemed more determined. It was easy to see why Coventry had made such a good start to the season: up front they had three very good players, and Robert Rosario.

No, that's a bit unfair on Big Bob. I often used to stick up for him when the crowd gave him stick at Norwich. He is strong, hard-working, and more skilful on the ground than he is generally given credit for. His only flaw is that he doesn't score enough goals, which is admittedly a bit of a problem for a striker. He scored the ITV Goal of the Season against Southampton three years ago –

but the joke in Norwich was that it was his only goal of the season. I once heard a rumour that someone was selling 'I've seen Rosario score' badges, but I never saw any myself.

The three good Coventry forwards were: John Williams, a summer signing from Swansea who won the Rumbelows Sprint Challenge last season and who used to be a postman (are the two facts linked in some way? Was he wearing a Walkman and listening to the sound of a rabid Alsatian barking when he competed?); Kevin Gallacher, who is one of the few Kevins in the Premier League and who really ought to be providing me with more headlines to stick on the wall at work ('Kevin's hat-trick wins it', 'Hero Kev', that sort of thing); and Peter Ndlovu (pronounced 'that kid from Zimbabwe').

It was Ndlovu who scored the equaliser five minutes before half-time, taking the ball past three defenders and leaving Gunn on his backside with a brilliant change of feet before chipping it in. Even some Norwich supporters clapped ... though I didn't. I was tempted to, through appreciation and sportsmanship (it was that sort of day), but somehow I found I couldn't. It was as if my hands were programmed not to respond to such signals from the brain. I may now be mature enough to recognise skilful play by the opposition, but I don't believe I will ever be able to applaud it. Is this further confirmation of my sadness? Perhaps. But stuff it, I don't like seeing other sides score against us.

The second half was good, if not spectacular. The crowd was only roused when Sutton grabbed Gallacher as he ran towards the Norwich goal. There were calls for him to be sent off, but Sutton escaped with a yellow card by angrily accusing Gallacher of taking a dive. This was an underhand piece of cunning which cannot be condoned by any fair-minded individual. Well done, Chris.

Press opinion on the match was divided. Some discerning journalists enjoyed it and were able to identify the reasons why both teams are doing so well. Other thickheads (including some of the broadsheet reporters) sounded as if they had written most of their reports before the match, rambling on about how mediocre the Premier League must be for two teams like this to be at the top. Or maybe they just watched the highlights on TV, which didn't look so good. So much for my praise of *Match of the Day* earlier. Much of the action, such as Robins's late chance to win the game, was left out.

I wonder how they edit the games. Perhaps they use the same method as the priest in *Cinema Paradiso* (my joint favourite film – along with *Gregory's Girl*, of course – which just happened to be on Channel 4 at the same time as the match). The priest views all the films at the cinema before the public sees them and rings a little bell whenever there is a scene he finds offensive. The projectionist then takes it out. I suspect that Jimmy Hill (the chinny one, rather than the steep incline on this occasion) must have been holding his ding-a-ling in the editing suite tonight, as he has strong connections with Coventry.

Here, I've just thought. If this theory is correct, is there a large pile of film and videotape at the BBC showing great Norwich moves through the years that we've never been allowed to see?

Our Sunday-morning game was uneventful in the sense that nothing officially happened. We were due to play the mighty Hammersmith Academicals at 10:30, but our manager Brian (elected principally because he has the best name for the job – for example, in such phrases as 'I'll give it 110 per cent at the end of the game of two halves, Brian') broke down on the way to the ground and he had all the kit. By the time the RAC had rescued him, the referee had called the game off and gone home.

We played a friendly instead. We won 4-2, and I scored my first goal for two years. 'It doesn't count,' said the others. 'It's only a friendly.'

'Sod off,' I wittily replied. 'I write the newsletter reports, and this is going in.' The goal was only a toe-poke from a yard out (and at the second attempt). I didn't even see the ball go in. I was flattened by a defender as I hit it, and only realised I'd scored when I heard him mutter 'Shit' under his breath. I was going to run to the corner flag and do a Roger Milla wiggle, but by the time I had picked myself up, the moment had passed. I just trudged back to the halfway line.

By the time I rang Mum in the afternoon, though, the goal had mutated into a screaming volley into the top corner from the edge of the area.

'Rubbish,' she said, 'I bet it was a toe-poke from a yard out.'

How do Mums know?

Saturday 3 October
Blackburn Rovers (away)

For reasons that will soon become clear (if you do not already know the score of this game), I am inclined to write 'Bollocks' for this entry and leave the next few pages blank. But as this would make me look an even worse loser than I actually am, I'd better carry on.

I received one of Mum's Red Cross parcels of Norwich newspapers during the week. The local rags are always strongly biased towards City, but I'm strongly in favour of this, as they help to counteract the sneering of the national press. Among the features ('Why City are bloody great', 'Mike Walker tipped for knighthood', etc.), there were two articles of particular interest.

One drew parallels between Norwich's start this year and the beginning of the 1988-89 season (our best-ever, when we finished fourth in the league). Then, as now, we won seven, drew two and lost one of our first ten games. Now, as then, our goal difference is plus seven. Mark Robins is currently our top scorer with seven goals (six league, one cup). In 1988, Robert Fleck had hit six in the league and one in the Littlewoods Cup at this point. In 1988, our tenth league game was a 1-1 draw refereed by Alf Buksh. This year ... yes, you got it.

I'm never sure what to make of patterns like this. Are they just coincidences? Or are there too many similarities for this to be the case? What, for example, are we to make of all the parallels between the assassinated US Presidents Lincoln and Kennedy? Lincoln became President in 1860; Kennedy in 1960. Lincoln had a secretary called Kennedy; Kennedy had one called Lincoln. Both men were shot in the head on a Friday by a Southerner in his 20s (if we overlook Oliver Stone's arguments in *JFK* for the moment). Lincoln was killed in a theatre by a man who ran off to a warehouse; Kennedy was (supposedly) killed by a shot fired from a warehouse by a man who hid in a theatre. Both men were succeeded by a President Johnson, who was born in a year ending 08.

On balance, I tend towards the coincidence view. After all, if you look hard enough, you can often find similarities between separate situations. In 1988, Norwich won the eleventh league game 2-0 away from home. This time, we were away from home, but ... no, no, all in good time.

The other article of note in the papers announced that our away fixture at Oldham scheduled for Saturday 7 November has been moved to the evening of Monday 9 for live BSkyB transmission. Did I say 'fixture'? The word is becoming less appropriate by the week as the TV companies shift more and more matches around to suit themselves.

Yet there is a redeeming aspect to the switch. The club has decided to use the money it will receive from Sky for the game to subsidise a plane trip for the supporters. The price will be the same as on Club Cabbage, around £13. Has this been arranged because the coach driver on the Manchester City trip got so horribly lost? (Though he did inadvertently find Oldham.) Does the club feel that an airline pilot might do a better job in getting us there? He couldn't do any worse.

I suspect that this is actually a scheme devised by our beloved chairman to try to get into the supporters' good books. Honestly. If he thinks he can win us over by laying on cheap air travel to matches ... well, it's a start, I suppose. Robert Chase, Robert Chase, Robert Chase . . .

According to the paper, booking priority for the trip will be given to supporters who travelled on the coach to last season's game at Oldham. As it happens, Mum and I did; it fell in the fortnight I spent in Norwich last September. I'm not sure how we can prove this, but I rang Mum at once and told her to apply for tickets. If we get them, I'll take another week off in Norwich so we can fly up to the match.

But back to Blackburn. I'd been looking forward to this game all week. For one thing, it was a ground I hadn't visited before. For another, it would be my first long Saturday trip of the season.

There is always a special sense of occasion about an all-day excursion to watch a game. This is partly because of the sheer amount of time involved. But there is more to it than that for me.

Even at 31, I feel that I am still trying to make up for time I lost in my youth. Between the ages of 12 and 18, I had to go to school on Saturday mornings. I never learned a thing on a Saturday (what do you mean, obviously not on any other day either?) and always had the feeling I was missing out on things. Saturday-morning television, for example. I still feel I ought to watch it now to catch up on all those programmes I missed. When I stop to think more clearly about this, however, I remember that the main Saturday programme of the time was *Multi-Coloured Swap Shop*. Seeing Noel Edmonds on TV now, I realise I wasn't missing out on much at all.

Of course, I was also unable to travel to away matches while I was at school. I couldn't have afforded to go even if I had been free, but my memory generally overlooks such minor details. Today, a long away trip still feels like a treat.

There were other reasons for eagerly anticipating the Blackburn game. As at Coventry last week, it would be between the top two teams in the table. And it would be a chance to compare a team put together relatively cheaply by Premier League standards (i.e., us) with one assembled for millions of pounds (them).

Blackburn's money has been provided by Jack Walker, a lifelong Rovers fan who sold his steel business for a fortune and now wants to buy his club success. It is curious how much this is resented by the supporters of other clubs – even, I understand, by some Blackburn fans. It is seen as unfair, cheating even, and there was much glee around the country last season when it appeared that Blackburn would miss out on promotion. Yet if you asked any true football supporters what they would do if they suddenly had over £300 million at their disposal, they would undoubtedly want to put a large amount into their club. Walker is a genuine fan who simply wants to see Rovers succeed and cannot be criticised for that. Let's see what spare cash I've got at the moment. Hmm, a tenner. I suppose we could make a bid for Rosario.

The first indication I had that the day would not be all bunting and frolics came in the morning when another batch of newspapers from Mum arrived. They were torn, soaking wet, and bore a Post Office sticker which read: 'Your mail's all shitty. What a pity. Tough titty.' That was the gist of it, anyway. I laid the papers out all over the floor of the flat before they turned into papier-mâché and hoped I would be able to read them properly on my return in the evening. I did notice one item as I put the sheets down: Paul Blades has been sold to Wolves for around £350,000 – half what we paid for him a couple of years ago. Oh well, it'll save me having to buy the Wolverine a Christmas present. I'll tell her he must be a gift at that price.

After the soggy mail, the day went steadily downhill. In fact, I feel it is only fair to warn you that what follows is a tale of unmitigated misery. If you are of a depressive nature, or can't stand people who are, you are strongly advised to skip to the next section. If, on the other hand, you derive a sadistic pleasure from the suffering of others, or are an Ipswich fan who loves to see Norwich supporters squirming in abject wretchedness, you'll love this.

I set off from London at around quarter to ten, thinking I would have plenty of time to stop for lunch on the way and still be early enough to find a handy place to park. No such luck.

To say that it poured with rain would be like saying Robert Maxwell was a bit of a rascal. I wondered whether I should make for some high ground and start building an ark. But what animals would I take with me? Two cheetahs, perhaps (Maradona and Klinsmann). Two from the rabbit family (Paul Ince and Les Sealey). Two donkeys (no, I'm not going to say it. It would be a cheap shot to mention the Arsenal centre-backs – oops). There definitely wouldn't be any wolves or wolverines.

I got stuck in jam after jam up the M1 and M6. On top of the creeping fear that I might not arrive in time for the game, I was almost driven nuts by the incessant to-and-fro, to-and-fro of the windscreen wipers for hour after hour. I was only saved by the calming influence of two tapes I bought the day before – *Happy in Hell* by the Christians and *Us* by the Archangel Gabriel. I mean St Peter. I mean Peter Gabriel.

When I finally reached Blackburn, just after half past two, I made the mistake of getting too close to the ground before trying to park. I turned round and drove away again in search of a space – and the next thing I knew, I was in some village two miles south of Blackburn with the time now 2:46. I don't remember the name of the village, but 'Blind Panic' would have been appropriate. More by luck than judgement, I managed to find my way back to the right part of town, parked around half a mile from Ewood Park and ran all the way there (splashing my jeans in the deepest, dirtiest puddles, of course). The strains of *The Final Countdown* by Europe blaring out from the loudspeakers in the ground told me that kick-off was imminent. I passed through the turnstile with about thirty seconds to spare.

I was agitated, irritated, irrigated, exhausted, starving for a pie and dying for a pee. However, I decided not to do anything about the latter problems until half-time in case I missed any goals. I wish I had missed them. We were 4-1 down by then.

We were destroyed (see, it's that over-dramatic football terminology again) by Alan Shearer. On two occasions, he gave Ian Butterworth a huge start in a chase for a long ball, beat him and crossed for Roy Wegerle to score. On the first, Wegerle had so much time that he fell over and got up again before sticking the ball in the net. He could have gone and bought me a pie if he'd wanted – we still wouldn't have stopped him.

Just before half-time, Shearer ran fifty yards and scored with a brilliant chip over Butterworth and Gunn. It should be pointed out that Butterworth was making his return from injury. After this, though, he may need psychiatric treatment to restore his confidence and self-esteem.

Since the game, I have been wondering whether I have ever seen a more outstanding individual performance than Shearer's that day. I don't believe I have. On that form, he looked worth more than the £3 million-plus that Blackburn paid for him. On the other hand, I saw him play for Southampton four times last season – or rather, I didn't see him play at all. What has brought on this inspired form? More to the point, will it disappear as suddenly as it materialised? Perhaps we'll know when we play Rovers again at the end of February.

Also, was it really necessary for Shearer to elbow Culverhouse in the face for no apparent reason? He received a yellow card for it – the only blot on his afternoon – but some referees would have made it a red one.

I have mentioned three of Blackburn's first-half goals. The other one was the most painful from the Norwich supporters' point of view. We just knew it was coming, and its inevitability made it all the more depressing.

If you were to play a word-association game in Norwich and mentioned the word 'Sherwood', the most common response would not be 'forest', but 'rubbish'. Not that Tim Sherwood is an untalented player; he has almost as much ability as he thinks he has. However, the crowd at Carrow Road always considered him lazy and unbothered when he was with Norwich, and frequently told him so. A hate-hate relationship soon developed. Sherwood took to gesturing at his critics during matches (though not individually – it would have taken too long), and the abuse intensified. Any hopes he had of winning the crowd over (and I'm not sure he was concerned whether he did or not) vanished when he went AWOL with John Polston before a pre-season friendly last year. Polston was suitably contrite afterwards and was quickly forgiven; Sherwood was reviled even more, the general opinion on the terraces being that evil Tim had led innocent John astray.

But what earned Sherwood the soubriquet 'Rubbish' was his £50 fine in court last year for dumping a load of garbage in a picturesque village just outside Norwich. It isn't clear why he did it, nor how he thought he could possibly get away with it. After all, the Norwich players are the best-known people in the area. So it was that several villagers nudged each other on the day in question and said 'Ooh look, there's Tim Sherwood,' followed by, 'Here, what's he up to?' followed by, 'Git!' Well, something like that. Letters addressed to Dim – er, Tim – were found in the rubbish and proved him to be the culprit. Suggestions that he should be converted to sweeper were not taken up, and he was sold to Blackburn.

If ever a player was guaranteed to score against his former club, it was Sherwood. He hadn't scored for Rovers before this match, but it was clear to all Norwich fans that he was saving his first goal for us. Sure enough, after 27 minutes, he turned up unmarked in the box and looped a header over Gunn. And wouldn't you know it, he made sure that he scored at the end where we were all standing. He leapt into the air, beaming all over his face, and waved at us. The Norwich supporters waved back, but not using all their fingers.

Half-time offered little relief, except to my bladder. The meat and potato pie was a flabby effort ($^3/_{10}$), and we were assaulted by a deafening medley of Abba songs. Though surprisingly not *Money Money Money*, which I'd have thought they'd have played as a tribute to their benefactor. What's with this current Abba revival, by the way? It all seems to have been started by that Australian group, Bjorn Again. What ghastly '70s combo will be the next to return in mutant form? Phoney M? The New New Seekers? Stepbrotherhood of Man?

Nor did the break offer any respite from the thrashing. Newman's goal in the first half had offered the faintest glimmer of hope, but there was to be no glorious second-half recovery this time. Five, six, seven – I could see the video of this being sold in Early Learning Centres with the title 'Learn to count with the Blackburn Boys'. It could have been 8-1, but Wegerle somehow chipped over a completely open goal from ten yards out.

'Say we're not top of the league, say we're not top of the league.'

How did we react to seeing our team taken apart like this? The only parallel I can offer is the sequence of stages one goes through when a loved one dies. The first was sheer disbelief, the phase when the mind simply cannot take in the enormity of the loss. Even the Blackburn supporters seemed incredulous. They cheered every goal, but didn't jeer at us as much as you might have expected.

Then came cheerfulness. Apparently, it is very common for people to be good-humoured, even euphoric, when they are bereaved. (No, not when the will is read.) It is as if their defence mechanism over-compensates for their grief. Accordingly, the 2,000 or so City fans, easily our best away following of the season so far, sang louder and longer the further behind we fell. At 6-1 down, there was a huge chorus of 'Now you're gonna believe us, we're gonna win the league'. The home fans were totally nonplussed by this. At 7-1, 'On the ball, City' rang out again and again. This actually helped the team to keep playing, and a few useful chances were made at the end.

I bumped into some other members of Capital Canaries on the way out of the ground. 'You had to be there, didn't you?' said one, as if we'd just been to the Live Aid concert. 'I've never seen us let in seven before,' said another, 'I'm glad I came.'

'?!' I thought.

Of course, moods are never pure and simple. Other feelings are constantly weaving in and out. Pride and defiance were certainly part of the Norwich contingent's reaction. We don't expect the team to lie down in defeat, so why should we? It also has to be said that there was a large degree of self-aggrandisement. Some fans used their continued vocal support to prove (to themselves as much as to others) that they were loyal and committed. After all, who but a true fan would keep singing when the team was 7-1 down? This masturbatory element might not have been spotted but for the chorus of 'Loyal supporters' which gave it away.

I was still in a reasonably good mood when I got back to the car. I had been heartened by the overheard comments of Blackburn fans who had praised the way we had continued trying to play attractive football to the end. Looking back, I can see these remarks for the patronising drivel they were. Oh, it's very easy to be generous when you've just won 7-1. They wouldn't have been as gracious if we'd won, I bet.

I glanced at the tapes on the front seat of the car. *Us – Happy in Hell*. I suppose we were in a way.

Then the next stage of grief began. This is when the good mood wears off, and you are dragged down inexorably into despair. It is similar to the experience of a wild animal when it is shot with a tranquilliser dart. It senses that something has happened when it feels an initial twinge, but it keeps on running as normal. Then, as the sedative works its way around the animal's system, it becomes aware that its legs are not functioning properly. It tries to resist the inevitable, but finally falls to the ground in a crumpled heap.

With a death, this stage (the 'sinking-in') can take weeks, even months, to happen. In the case of this defeat, several factors combined to precipitate it. First, there was the news that Ipswich had beaten the champions Leeds 4-2. As Tommy Steele never sang:

> I never felt more like singin' the blues
> When Ipswich win and Norwich lose.

Then there was our match report on Radio 5. I didn't catch the reporter's name (I wish I had), but he was convinced that Norwich would now plummet down the table. This thought honestly had not occurred to me before. We had merely lost a game and dropped to second in the league. In his mind, however, Norwich were dead, an ex-team, they had ceased to be, and it was time to send out invitations to a party on the grave.

I cannot recall which analogies he used to describe our anticipated decline. I heard and read several over the next few days, including: a sinking stone; a sinking ship; a bursting bubble; leaves falling in autumn; the stick of a spectacular, but now spent, firework rocket; a marathon runner falling behind after leading for the first lap in the stadium; the effect of gravity; and the king whose nakedness was pointed out by a young, fresh-faced boy. At any rate, I'm sure he used one or two from this selection.

I thought this was disgraceful reporting. How could he possibly know how the team would react? This result could well be a one-off. In fact, the freakish scoreline might well help the players to write the game off as an untypical aberration. However, this reporter's dismissal of our prospects was as nothing compared to the scorn poured on us by Danny Baker on his programme *Six-0-Six*. When I heard that this was to be the last time he would host the show, I was very disappointed. This, I thought, was yet another item to add to the list of things I have liked which have disappeared too quickly: Heinz Ideal Sauce, the *Sunday Correspondent*, Cluster bars and Opal Mints, to name but a few.

Then he started. First, he suggested that *Match of the Day* should show all the Blackburn goals, run a pop video while the tape was rewound, then show them again with comedy music underneath. This should be followed by vox-pops with Norwich supporters coming out of the ground, during which we would be asked questions like: 'How far did you come to see this?', 'How much has it cost you?' and 'How did you feel when the seventh went in?'.

Some Norwich fans rang in and tried to point out that we had played well going forward, but were simply laughed at. One cited the example of Sheffield Wednesday, who lost 6-1 and 7-1 last season, yet still finished third in the league, but he was given equally short shrift. Another recalled that Norwich beat Millwall (Baker's team) 6-1 a few seasons ago, but was told that the difference between six and seven is not a goal but a gulf. It was clear that Baker simply wanted to rub our noses in it.

I grew increasingly angry. After all, you aren't subjected to this sort of treatment when attempting to cope with a death. You don't get people gathering outside the house singing, 'Hello, hello, Granny is dead, Granny is dead.'

What's that you say? I can't take a joke? Yes I can, but this wasn't a joke. What did Danny Baker know about our game? Sod all. By the time 7:30 came, when he finished the show for the last time, I was shouting, 'Piss off and don't come back!' at the radio. I have also stopped listening to his breakfast programme on Radio 5 until such time as Norwich stick seven past Millwall.

My depression continued to intensify as I drove back to London. Now and then I would twitch with impotent rage against the cruel fate that had decreed our downfall. 'Why us? Why me? Why now? There are others who deserve it more.' Nature itself seemed to be laughing at us, as the evening was now clear and dry.

Like a widower gazing sadly and enviously at couples going about their normal business, I thought of all the people out there whose teams had got a result, yet who took it for granted. How many were moaning about drawing 0-0? They should be grateful, I thought. Nil-nil, that's a point. That's something to be appreciated, treasured even. What I wouldn't have given for a dull 0-0 draw.

I was utterly disconsolate by the time I reached the flat and phoned Mum. The call was like one between two members of a support group trying to comfort each other after a disaster. Mum told me to think about all the good times we have had up to now this season. 'That's all gone now,' I said. 'In the past. This overshadows all that.'

Indeed, our run of wins already seemed a very long time ago. The magnitude of our defeat weighed heavily on my mind – so heavily that I couldn't budge it. Seven-one. Seven-sodding-one. I thoughht seven was supposed to be a lucky number. Still, I suppose it is for Blackburn supporters. Seven-pissing-one. So much for the pattern suggested in the local paper. And I bet even Mum's butcher didn't predict this. Seven-bastard-one. For some reason, I even imagined Fred Astaire singing about the score in *Cheek to Cheek*:

> Seven, they scored seven,
> And I'm so astonished I can hardly speak.
> 'Cause poor Norwich do no longer top the league.
> They'll be falling further down it week by week.

What corner of the cortex did that spring from? Did it suggest that I was now worried that we might slide down the table, which I hadn't been before? If the players were entertaining such doubts, I hoped Mike Walker would be able to knock them out of their heads before the next game.

I don't know why I watched *Match of the Day*. To see exactly what went wrong? To see if they had taken up Danny Baker's suggestions? Force of habit? Latent masochistic tendencies? To prove I am a 'loyal supporter'? Or was it just that there was nothing else on?

This Saturday's 'Film on Four' was *La vie est un long fleuve tranquil*. Rubbish. La vie est plutôt une tranchée de merde. The day had been a total disaster. The only positive aspect of it was that it would be a year before I returned to Blackburn.

I avoided the newspapers on the Sunday morning, but I couldn't escape the horror of the result that easily. The Norwich Supporters' team played a side in blue and white and ... go on, have a guess at the score. Yes, that's right. No, Alan Shearer wasn't playing for the opposition – but at least we had the excuse that our goalkeeper (a last-minute, press-ganged volunteer) hurt his leg after twenty minutes and couldn't move. The other team scored their seventh goal with a quarter of an hour to go and could have had more, but they eased off, thinking it hilarious that Norwich had lost 7-1 again. Oh, ha ha ha.

Then there was work on Monday. As I had anticipated earlier, my consideration in not crowing about our start to the season counted for precisely nothing. There was a can of 7-Up on my desk when I arrived in the morning. I tried a few pre-emptive visits on colleagues who I thought would be particularly derisive – 'Come on, then, let's get the wisecracks out of the way' – but people from other floors who hardly know me (or anything about football, in many cases) kept turning up at the door of my office to say, 'Seven-one, eh? Cuh!' Even the girl on reception shook her head and drew a sharp intake of breath as I passed – and she's a temp who only started last week.

This carried on for the rest of the day. Ever more elaborate wind-ups were devised. Some started out in the guise of sympathy in order to make the final

barb sharper: 'Never mind, Kev. How about if we buy you an orange juice at the pub after work?'
'OK, thanks.'
'We'll be going down by around seven, but then you're used to that, aren't you?'
Uproarious laughter. Sods.

Wednesday 7 October
Carlisle United (home)
COCA-COLA CUP SECOND ROUND, SECOND LEG

The Coca-Cola Cup is the new name for the old Football League Cup. (Technically, Norwich – like all Premier League clubs – are no longer members of the Football League, but no one seems to have noticed this.) The previous sponsors were Rumbelows, who suddenly terminated their rental agreement before the start of the season. Are we to infer from this that the public has not exactly been flocking into their shops to buy satellite equipment? We can only hope so.

I thought they might have taken the time to explain to the fans why they no longer wanted to sponsor the cup. Perhaps an advertisement based on their slogan ('We don't play any more, Mrs Moore ... ')? Still, they did at least introduce one or two novel touches to the competition during their two years. They gave every Man of the Match a new TV set (though I can't imagine there are any professional footballers who don't already own one or ten) and – a praiseworthy move, this – chose their Employee of the Year rather than some decrepit dignitary or tatty royal to present the trophy.

I wonder what Coca-Cola will do. Will the winners have to drink Coke instead of champagne out of the trophy? And will the trophy itself be made out of aluminium so that it can be recycled and turned into a new one every year? So far they have resisted the temptation to call this competition the 'real thing'. Quite right, too. Although this cup has been around for over thirty years, the FA Cup is still more highly regarded. It hasn't helped that the League Cup has had so many different sponsors in recent years. Before Coca-Cola and Rumbelows, Littlewoods and the Milk Marketing Board put their names to it. Will we ever see the Butter Cup or the Playtex Bra Cup?

It occurs to me that Pepsi should have tried to take over the sponsorship instead of Coke. For one thing, they could have got Michael Jackson to present the trophy. He would be an appropriate choice given that his appearance has changed as many times as the cup. And for another, it would make the chants on the terraces scan. Try this one: 'We're gonna win the Coca-Cola Cup this year.' Doesn't sound right, does it? How about 'When Ian goes up to lift the Coca-Cola Cup, we'll be there'? Nah.

I wonder how active a role the various sponsors play in their competitions. Do Barclays, for example, write snotty letters to clubs whose goal difference has gone into the red? Probably not. After all, if they did run the league the way they run their banks, all matches would finish at 4:30pm (12:30 on Saturdays), grounds would only have one turnstile open at the busiest times, and the referee's pen would be attached to his shirt by a metal chain.

I do believe, however, that when Fine Fare sponsored the Scottish League, the prize for the champions was a sixty-second trolley dash. But now that B&Q are in charge, things are different. The winners still don't get a trophy, but are given a rather nice self-assembly, teak-effect cabinet which will come in handy if the team ever wins any others.

I was almost awarded something for attending this game against Carlisle, but it wasn't a medal or a trophy. My problems began at around four in the afternoon. This is when I usually leave work to get back to evening games in Norwich, but this time I was called into a meeting. I gabbled away like the racing commentator Peter O'Sullevan to try to get it over with as quickly as possible ('Idon'tthinkweneeddecideonthisjustyetlet'sleaveitaweekandreview-itthencanIgonowplease?'), but I still didn't get out until twenty to five. However, I had taken the precaution of leaving my jacket on reception so that I was able to saunter casually down the glass-surrounded staircase in the centre of the building before grabbing it and making good (or, as it turned out, bad) my escape.

The journey back to Norwich was more frustrating than usual. Earthmovers, bulldozers, abnormal loads – you name them, I followed them. It was as if there was a 'vehicles-with-flashing-orange-lights-on' convention in Norfolk that night. I spent the whole journey yelling, 'Come on, you bastards, move it!' Still, it was good practice for the match, I suppose. What little breath I had left after this was used on running non-stop from Mum's house to the ground. Still, it was good practice for Sunday morning's match, I suppose.

I missed the first thirty seconds. I hate it when that happens. I was so out of breath, I didn't really take in any of the first ten minutes, but it was the lost half-minute that concerned me. Mum, Stephen and Karen eventually convinced me that nothing important had happened before my arrival. 'Apart from that streaker who ran on during the warm-up,' said Karen.

'What?'

'Oh, she wasn't much to look at', she went on. 'That punch-up in the crowd was far more entertaining.'

Wha ... ? Hang on a minute. 'Oh, very funny,' I sneered.

Karen grinned. 'Nearly got you.'

I decided to change the subject. 'Did any of you get me a Golden Goal ticket? Our usual man had gone by the time I got here.'

'We didn't get any either,' said Mum. 'I don't think they're selling them tonight. Probably because they're not expecting many here.'

'They could have sold a few,' Karen piped up. 'And they could have relaxed the prize arrangements to make up for the numbers. I mean, they could have decided to give a hundred quid to anyone a second out from the time of the first goal.'

After a moment, Stephen realised what (or whom) she was getting at. 'Here we go again.'

I laughed loudly, mainly in relief that Karen had found another target for her wind-ups. Not for long, though. 'I hear you had a postcard,' she smirked.

'Did I?' I glared at Mum, who must have told her, but she was engrossed in the match (or pretending to be).

'Come on, you know the one I mean. From your girlfriend.'

'How many times? The Wolverine is not my girlfriend.'

'Ah, but I bet you wish she was.'

'No, I don't. She's bloody awful.'

'There, that proves it. You make such a fuss about not liking her, it's obvious you do.'

'What sort of logic is that? I moan about Ipswich. Are you suggesting I secretly love them too?'

'Well, now you mention it …'

'Oh, shut up,' I reasoned cleverly.

'Anyway,' Karen continued regardless, 'I came across "wolverine" in the dictionary the other day when I was looking something up.'

'And what word was that, then? "Wool"? How did you think it was spelt, W-U-L?'

Karen refused to be deflected. 'A wolverine isn't a female wolf like you reckon it is.'

'What is it then, smart-arse?'

'A vicious weasel.'

'Thank you, m'lud. I rest my case.'

You will gather from all this nattering that the game was less than exciting. There was little atmosphere – indeed, the crowd was smaller than at the away leg in Carlisle. 'Well, it was a big game for them up there,' Stephen pointed out. 'I remember when we were always the underdogs and got all excited about playing someone from a higher division. It still feels a bit strange to be one of the big clubs now.'

'Yes,' agreed Mum. 'I remember the '59 Cup run when we were in the Third Division … ' Yawn, yawn, yawn, the rest of us went, patting our lips. 'Sod you, then,' said Mum.

The Carlisle players were putting up less of a fight than in the first leg, possibly because they had lost their manager since then. 'Lost'? What am I saying? It's not as if he wandered off from his mum by the fish counter in Tesco's. Michael Knighton sacked him.

The Norwich team and crowd were similarly subdued, partly through complacency, but mainly because of the absence of our goalkeeper Bryan Gunn. He missed this game because of the worsening condition of one of his daughters, who has had leukaemia for some time. Our thoughts were with him and, as they couldn't be in two places at once, were not really on the match. For the record, we missed a stack of chances, but in the second half Chris Sutton scored with two identical headers from two identical Culverhouse crosses. Sutton then missed a penalty in the last few minutes. Maybe he should have headed that as well.

Considering we'd won, Jimmy Hill was particularly tiresome afterwards.

We'd been indoors around ten minutes when the phone rang. My half of the ensuing conversation went something like: 'Hello? Hello. Yes, 2-0. You? Oh. Never mind. Look, can I ring you back? No, not tonight. Whenever. OK, bye'. The others managed to rein in their curiosity for a good thirty seconds. I reluctantly admitted that it had been the Wolverine.

'Ringing you up, you see,' nodded Karen. 'You're in there.'

'I thought you were very rude,' said Mum. 'I'm not surprised you don't get anywhere with her.'

'I wasn't rude. And even if I was, it was nothing she doesn't deserve.'

'How did she know you'd be here, anyway?' asked Stephen. That was easy. As a football fan herself, she would know that all she needed to do to ascertain my whereabouts was to look at the fixture list.

I could never have been a spy. Or a supergrass (not that I've ever had any inside information I could reveal). I could never do a Reggie Perrin and disappear into thin air (but don't think I haven't considered this on occasions). I would be ridiculously easy to track down, assuming in the latter case that anyone would want to. Any pursuer would merely have to wait by the appropriate turnstile at a Norwich game for me to turn up.

The interrogation continued. 'What did she want?' asked Mum.

'A smack in the teeth for a start. I don't know, I didn't talk to her long enough to find out. All she said was that Wolves lost in the cup tonight.'

'See,' said Karen. 'She was ringing to cheer you up. And did she ring you after the Blackburn game?'

'Well, no.'

'There you are, she's showing you some consideration as well.' I found it hard to argue with Karen. But then I always do.

'Are you going to ring her back?' Mum pressed.

'Some time. Perhaps.' Perhaps! I wasn't fooling anyone, least of all myself.

After the highlights on TV, we all waited expectantly for the third-round draw. Anyone at home would do – failing which, anywhere in the London area so that the game would be easy for me to get to. What we got was ... Blackburn away. And verily, there was much wailing and gnashing of teeth. So much for thinking I wouldn't be returning there for a while. If Butterworth is to mark Shearer again, they'd better give him a motorbike and a shotgun first.

But worse was to come the next morning. On arriving at work, I was tipped off by my colleagues that the plop had really hit the propeller after I'd left early the previous afternoon. 'The boss went spare,' said one. 'We told him you'd gone to an important function you'd had arranged for some time, but he looked at your poster on the wall, put two and two together and for once made four.'

Typical. No one notices when I travel to Carlisle, but all hell breaks loose when I go to the home leg. 'So what's he going to do about it?'

'He said if you do this again, you'll be watching Norwich full-time.' That was the wrong way to phrase it, of course. Watching Norwich full-time sounds an attractive proposition to me. All the same, I prepared myself for a big confrontation. I knew there could be no easy resolution of the situation; we were dealing with completely different views of life. To my superior (and I use the term solely with regard to our relative positions in the company hierarchy), work is the 'real world', the most important thing in life. Pastimes such as football are marginal trivia, to be indulged only in rare free moments. To me, football is what matters, and the job is significant only in that it takes up eight hours of each weekday (six and a half on certain Wednesdays).

On the other hand, I do have rent to pay and food to buy. And given the current state of the job market, the chances of finding new employment if I am sacked are minimal. Forced to make a choice between the job and football, I would have to go for ... football.

As things turned out, the confrontation never took place. My boss had cooled down overnight and alluded to my absence only once (and that obliquely). All the same, I've booked the afternoon of the Blackburn game as official holiday.

Saturday 10 October
No Match

At five minutes to three on a Saturday afternoon in October, I would expect to be standing on a terrace somewhere listening to *We Are The Champions* and a list of team changes coming over a muffled loudspeaker system. I would not expect to be pushing a trolley round a supermarket listening to *The Girl From Ipanema* and a list of price changes.

We had no game this weekend as there is an England match next Wednesday. No Premier League matches take place the Saturday before an important international, to give the squad time to prepare and to reduce the risk of late injuries.

I felt very strange all afternoon. I wondered about going up the road to see Barnet play, but whenever I have been to a game where I am not bothered who wins, I have been bored to tears. The only match on today which might have been able to involve me was Southend v Wolves, but I wasn't interested enough to drive out to Essex to see it. Besides, the Wolverine didn't go today. OK, OK, so I rang and asked her. Just don't tell the family.

Every time the fixtures are disrupted, or the suggestion is made that the number of clubs in the Premier League should be reduced, the fans are posed the same question: do we want a successful national team or not? After all, it is stressed, such measures are essential to give England the best possible chance at international level. To me, though, club football is far more important. The infrequency of England matches serves to make them less, not more, special. Can I be the only football fan who doesn't give a toss what the national team does? Personal experience suggests that I may well be, but here are my reasons anyway.

For a start, I am not patriotic in the conventional sense of the word. I find it impossible to identify with the country as a whole. Not that I would call myself anything as right-on and trendy as a European or World Citizen, either. I consider myself to be a Norwich man – or, at a push, a Norfolk man – rather than an Englishman.

I love the place I come from. I am even proud of our insularity and pleased that there is no motorway in the county to make it easy for hordes of other people to visit Norwich. I stop short of wanting independence for Norfolk, with border patrols stationed on all the main roads, though it might be an idea to require Ipswich supporters to obtain visas before entering the county. I am aware that such an outlook may be seen as unhealthy parochialism, and that my attitude to outsiders (or 'furriners') could appear dangerously close to racism. I am not sure I can offer adequate defences to such suggestions, but I can at least try to explain myself.

My parochial views may be compared to fish and chips covered in batter, or a fried breakfast: they may not be healthy, but that doesn't stop me enjoying them. My wish to keep Norwich free from large influxes of outsiders is more difficult to defend. Arguments such as 'they would change the tone of the place' and 'they'd be all right if they fitted in with our ways' sound frighteningly fascist. All I can do is stress that my attitude has nothing whatsoever to do with the colour of a person's skin. If I do ever prejudge anyone on colour grounds, it is only on the colour of their football shirt. Rather, it is based on a dislike of the attitudes of certain groups of people, e.g., the arrogance and patronising manner of many Londoners. In the mid-1980s, I was very worried about the threatened 'yuppie invasion' of Norwich. Fortunately, this never materialised, not least because the yuppies suddenly dematerialised.

I feel no affinity with London (yes, I know, so why am I living here?), nor for that matter with Birmingham, Manchester, Liverpool, Leeds or Newcastle. They are like other countries, in some cases with their own language. Being lumped together under the banner of 'England' makes no difference to me at all.

This brings me to my second reason for not being bothered about the national team. It is made up of players I spend most Saturdays cursing because they play for teams trying to beat Norwich. How can I suddenly switch my sympathies? Am I really supposed to admire and support Stuart Pearce, David Batty and Alan Shearer in the England team when, for the rest of the year, I am praying that their form will go down the toilet? Even if I could manage this, the team changes so often that I would find it impossible to form any sort of attachment to it.

If there were any Norwich players in the England team (and I realise we are straying into hypothetical territory here), it still wouldn't make much difference to my overall view. I would want our boys to do well for themselves, but I wouldn't suddenly become a great fan of the team. When Phillips, Bowen and, occasionally, Goss play for Wales, I hope they have good games, but I can hardly be called a Wales supporter there's lovely boyo bach.

Third, I feel I have nothing in common with the large group of supporters who follow the England team around. Yes, I know generalisations are odious. Yes, I know the tabloids exaggerate the slightest suggestion of trouble when England play abroad. Yes, I know how glib it sounds to trot out Samuel Johnson's remark that 'patriotism is the last refuge of a scoundrel'. But I've seen and heard the scoundrels getting tanked up in Central London before going to see 'Engerland, Engerland' at 'Wemberley, Wemberley' to play the Wogs, Frogs, Krauts or Brussels Sprouts. Suddenly, any worries I may have had about the implications of my wishing to preserve the character of Norwich and Norfolk are exposed as over-intellectual, self-indulgent soul-searching. If you want to see real racists (not that everyone wants to), an England match is the place to go.

Reason number four: the joyless way in which the England team almost always plays. I generally prefer watching other countries. The only time England have played really well in recent years was in the 1990 World Cup semi-final against West Germany.

It is often argued that there are not enough outstanding individual players in England. I am not sure that this is relevant. We do not have any big names at Norwich (we've sold them all), but we still play attractive football. We play as a team. It may sound strange if I say that watching Norwich every week spoils you for watching the national team, but it happens to be true.

'But what have Norwich won recently?' you ask. Nothing since the Milk Cup in 1985 and the Second Division Championship in 1986, it is true. But I am not sure this is relevant either. As the old saying has it, whether you win or lose is less important than how you play the game. This is an unfashionable idea these days (how often are we told by managers and chairmen that football is all about getting results?), and I must admit that it has taken me some time to agree with it. But winning, while it is important, while it is the aim of every team, is not everything. If it were, the Wimbledon FA Cup win in 1988 would be seen as one of the greatest stories of all time: the romantic rise of a tiny club from the Southern League to such heights in such a short time would fill every fan with admiration. However, the fact that the club achieved its success through thuggery, intimidation and the ugliest football imaginable means that it is still reviled rather than revered.

I would derive no satisfaction from seeing Norwich win a trophy in that way. Honestly. I've given this a lot of thought. If we are to win anything, it has to be achieved in the right way, otherwise it would be a hollow triumph. For, ultimately, winning trophies doesn't matter. The style, the emotions, the memories of particular moments are what count.

Think of the 1974 World Cup finals. You remember the wonderful Holland team, and especially their outstanding performance against a Brazil side in an unfamiliar dark blue kit – but can you recall anything about the West German side that beat them in the final?

Think of the 1986 finals in Mexico. The Brazil-France match was one of the greatest in World Cup history, yet neither side reached the final.

Think of Italia '90. You remember Platt's late goal against Belgium, and Lineker's goal and Gascoigne's tears in the semi-final against West Germany. What do you recall of the final, other than a general feeling of sickness at the ugliness on show? In the end, it doesn't matter that England didn't reach the final; the moments that moved the country and the quality of the semi-final performance are far more valuable than the results in the record books.

If only an England manager would realise that trying to grind out dull wins and draws in the short term with a cobbled-together team is less important than building a stable, attractive team. The twin demons of public expectation and media pressure admittedly make his job very difficult, as they demand that the national team should always win. England need a manager who does not mind losing a few games – and can ignore the inevitable criticism – but who has a clear view of the sort of team he wants to build and will stick to that, confident that the results will come in time. A manager who sees European Championship and World Cup final tournaments as football showpieces, where national teams should endeavour to present the game at its most exciting and beautiful, not as the football equivalents of dental appointments to be approached with fear and foreboding.

This is easy for me to say, of course, As it is of little consequence to me whether England win or lose, I can afford to adopt a more relaxed attitude. Paradoxically, however, this insouciance probably makes me just the sort of fan the England manager needs.

Does such a clear-sighted, high-principled manager exist? If he does, he is not called Graham Taylor. (We are on to reason number five now, by the way.) I have never been a lover of the way his teams played, but when he took the England job in 1990, I did think that he might be the manager the country had been waiting for. He seemed then to have definite ideas for the future and – most encouragingly – said that his aim was to prepare for the 1994 World Cup, the implication being that the 1992 European Championships were merely a stepping-stone on the way.

Things have not quite turned out this way. After two years in which he has picked so many players that members of our Sunday-morning team are becoming hopeful of a call-up, Taylor is still no nearer to blending a team with any shape or understanding, let alone flair. The European Championships turned into an event of huge import, the players were so tense that they turned in performances of dreadful mediocrity, and Taylor turned into Bobby Robson.

The excuses he came out with after England had been knocked out were astonishing. The Swedes, he said, were bigger and stronger because of their national love of outdoor pursuits. Really, Graham? So why is it that these Scandinavian supermen never do much in the track and field events at the Olympics? He also claimed that the Swedes had triumphed by playing a long-ball game. So what about the succession of short, first-time passes that led to Brolin's goal that won the game? The fact is that Sweden varied their approach play in just the right way.

It seems to me that Graham Taylor has missed his true vocation. He should have been a PR officer for British Rail. In fact, it's probably only a matter of time before he starts borrowing their excuses. 'Ladies and Gentlemen, we apologise for the adverse result. This was due to leaves on the pitch.' 'We regret that it was the wrong type of grass, which our players are not designed to cope with.'

Saturday 17 October
Queen's Park Rangers (home)

While Mum paid her usual Saturday-morning visit to the butcher's (his predictable prediction for the game: Norwich 0 QPR 2), I went to get my hair cut. That's hair in the singular rather than the plural these days. Karen reckons I should ask for off-cuts instead of a haircut.

In the chair, I discovered a new explanation for our heavy defeat at Blackburn a fortnight ago. It turns out that it was the first time the 'boy' of the salon (he's about 22 now, but he's been called this ever since he started) had been to see Norwich play away. He has already been told not to travel again, but I ordered him not to go to Blackburn for the cup match under any circumstances. Strangely enough, he didn't seem that keen to go anyway.

The conversation turned inevitably to the QPR game, and the question of whether Bryan Gunn would return in goal or not. Sadly, his daughter died last weekend – but although he was offered as much time off as he wanted, he returned to training during the week. Officially, it still hadn't been decided whether he would play, but all of us in the hairdresser's felt that he would.

Looking back, drawing a parallel between my reaction to defeat at Blackburn and the stages of coping with bereavement seems crass to say the least. What we suffered that day is nothing compared to what Gunn and his family must be going through at the moment. Yet while I sympathise with them, I cannot say that their loss has affected me deeply, much as I would like to be able to. I often refer to the team, not entirely in jest, as my surrogate family. I have their pictures hanging up at home and at work, where you might expect to see portraits of my relatives. But an event such as this reminds me that there is actually a huge gulf between myself and the individual players; a gulf which I have been careful to maintain over the years.

I am sure that I would be disappointed if I were to meet the players in person. Distance lends people a certain aura. Think of the stars who rarely, if ever, give television interviews, such as Marlon Brando, Michael Jackson or the late Greta Garbo. Their talent marks them out as exceptional people, but their remoteness gives them a mystique. What we do not know about them, we make up for with hazy fantasy. (Weren't they a pop group?)

Familiarity, on the other hand, does breed contempt. And if the 'player profiles' in the match programmes are anything to go by (favourite drink: lager; favourite band: Simply Red; favourite place: Ibiza; favourite film: *Terminator 2*), most professional footballers would have no difficulty inspiring this in me. The closest I have come to talking to a Norwich player was when the father of Dave Bennett came round to Mum's a few years ago in his capacity as area manager of an insurance company. I only spoke to him for five minutes, but I never had as much respect for his son after that.

Now I think of it, I did find myself standing behind Mark Bowen and his wife in a cinema queue earlier this year. They were going to see *Cape Fear* – though I'd have thought he'd have had enough tension and excitement the night before in the FA Cup sixth-round replay against Southampton, which we won 2–1 in extra time. I kept myself to myself, but a couple of lads came up to him and said, 'Er – well done last night.'

'Thanks,' replied Bowen. Both parties looked at each other for a moment, then the lads realised that their conversation was exhausted and wandered off again.

All I want to know about the players is what they are like on the pitch. There, they are quick and intelligent; elsewhere, they could not possibly live up to that. They have their idiosyncrasies when they play – Gunn, for example, almost heads the crossbar before the start of every half, and teases the crowd during the game, cupping a hand to his ear as if he cannot hear the shouts of 'Bryan, Bryan, give us a wave' – and, for me, that is enough.

Occasionally, the gap between the crowd and the players can cause unfortunate misunderstandings. A few months ago, Gunn shaved his head and we all laughed at him. I was especially keen to mock, as my own receding hairline means that I have few opportunities to shout 'Baldy!' at anyone else. It now turns out that his daughter was undergoing chemotherapy at the time, which made her hair fall out. He shaved his head to show her that this was nothing to be ashamed of. Sorry, Bryan.

In the end, Gunn decided to play against QPR, and received a standing ovation from the whole crowd as he ran on to the pitch. The atmosphere was by no means solemn, however. In fact, it was very jovial. It was as if everyone had resolved that we should carry on as normal in the same way as Gunn.

The first big laugh came when an advertisement for the *Sunday Express* was played over the loudspeakers, promising in-depth articles on Graham Taylor's England stars. Stars? Ha! After they missed a heap of chances against Norway in midweek and only drew 1–1 at home? At least Taylor didn't make the usual lame excuses afterwards. I wondered if he might borrow an idea from the Olympic weightlifting tournament during the summer and suggest that, while England and Norway were level on goals, England should win by virtue of a lower body weight. Mind you, with Gazza back in the team, that probably isn't the case.

Then the group of blokes sitting behind us started commenting on the name 'Classic FM' that is now emblazoned across the front of the QPR shirts. 'What does that stand for?' asked one. 'Fanny Merchants?'

Other suggestions were put forward, including 'Football Machine', 'Fit Men', 'Fat Men' and 'Flagrant Masturbators'. Once this seam had been exhausted, we were treated to a string of classical music puns. 'Here, I suppose they'll play with two full-Bachs.' 'And the goalkeeper will Handel the ball.' 'And the centre-backs will be Chopin us down outside the box.'

Groan. This did set me thinking about the subject of sponsorship again, however. I'm not sure what companies hope to gain by sticking their names on footballers' chests. Do they think they can influence the purchasing decisions of the public by doing this? Actually, I am influenced – though not in the way that is intended. I won't be listening to Classic FM, but even if I did, I would not be using Sharp or JVC equipment. I don't drink, but if I did, I wouldn't touch Labatt's, McEwan's, Carlsberg or Holsten. I am not writing this on a Commodore, NEC, Brother or Tulip computer, and I will not be taking photostats of it on a Mita copier. If I redecorate my flat, I will not be using Draper Tools or Arnold Laver timber. If I buy sportswear, it will not be made by Admiral, and I certainly won't be driving to JD Sports in a Peugeot fitted with Goodyear tyres. And if I put fertiliser on the garden, I will not be using ICI or Fisons varieties.

I wouldn't be entirely surprised if firms started to sponsor individual players and make them change their names. Well, it happened to horses in showjumping a few years back – I half-expected Princess Anne's children to be called Sanyo Hi-Fi and Mitsubishi Music Centre. At Norwich, we would have Lee National Power, Ruel 20th-Century Fox, David Philips CD Player and Ian I-can't-believe-it's-not-Butterworth. And looking at the QPR team, Alan McDonald could become Ronald McDonald and play alongside Dennis Bailey's Irish Cream.

During the first half, the conversation behind moved from names on shirts to names in seats. At the Barclay end, two-thirds of the upper-tier seats have now been installed, with the green and yellow ones arranged to spell 'ARIES'. Are we now to be seated according to our astrological signs? Is this the first New Age football club in the country?

'Shouldn't that green one at the bottom of the S be yellow?' someone asked.
'Yeah. And what about that one at the top of the R?'
'Isn't that where the away supporters are going to sit when it's all finished?'
'I think so.'
'The seats ought to spell something other than "CANARIES", then.'
'Like what?'
'Like "TWATS SIT HERE". I mean, if they're sitting in the seats, they won't be able to see what they spell.' They then went on to discuss the feasibility of assembling a crack squad of seat-fitters and breaking into Portman Road one night to rearrange the seats to spell 'IPSHIT TOWN'.

At half-time (score: 0–0) the usual presentation was made on the pitch to a long-serving (or was it 'long-suffering'?) supporter. This time, it was to a 90-year-old man who has apparently been following Norwich for seventy years.
'Poor old bugger,' muttered one of the wags behind us. 'He's seen some hard times.'
'What, war, rationing, rickets?'
'No, Division Three football for years on end, then that rubbish in the late '60s.'
'How do we know he's really supported Norwich all this time?' someone asked. 'Anyone getting on a bit could say that.'
'Yeah, he might just have looked up the names of some of the old players for all we know.'
'Here, if he's 90 and he says he's been watching City for seventy years, that means he was 20 before he came along.'
'Bloody Johnny-come-lately. Boo! Boo!' Norwich have only been in the league for seventy-one years, but they obviously didn't know this.
'You know,' Stephen whispered to Mum, 'you'd probably qualify for a tankard if you wrote in.'
'Bloody cheek,' she replied, thumping him. Child-beating and football violence in one. I don't know.

One of the group who had been sitting behind us returned from the refreshment bar with a cup of tea and a big grin. 'I've just seen Malcolm downstairs,' he said. 'He's freezing.' It was the first really cold day of the season.
'Why?' asked another. 'Hasn't he got a coat?'

'Well, yes. But he hasn't got it on. His missus bought him a loud pink one for his birthday and expected him to wear it today. He was too embarrassed to come here in it, so he's left it at the pub near the bus stop and he's going to pick it up again on the way home.' They all laughed and resolved to lie in wait for Malcolm outside the pub later on so that they could poke fun at his pretty pink number.

The fun continued in the second half, with a 10-year-old boy blurting out, 'You fucking wanker!' just when everyone else had fallen quiet. From the look on his father's face, he would have more than his tea waiting for him when he got home.

After 52 minutes, Chris Sutton was hauled down in the penalty area. This time, Mark Bowen took the spot kick and duly scored. 'Oh shit,' moaned Stephen.

'What is it?' I asked. He waved a Golden Goal ticket under my nose. 'Nine seconds out,' he said. 'Why couldn't they have taken that penalty a bit quicker?'

'Karen will love this,' I laughed.

'Oh, do you have to tell her?'

' 'Fraid so.'

After 64 minutes, Sutton darted in from the blind side and planted a powerful header into the net from the edge of the box. 'Looks like Rangers' defending is about as harmonious as Stockhausen,' I wittily remarked. Well, not that wittily. OK, so no one got it at all.

Stephen wasn't nine seconds out this time. His other ticket was six away. He just sat there silently shaking his head. 'You'll have to try to buy your tickets a few seconds later than usual,' suggested Mum, but he didn't seem to hear.

QPR scored a late goal, but Gunn made some important saves and earned another standing ovation and more praise all round. Top of the league again! So much for the predictions of doom on Radio 5 a couple of weeks ago. Danny Baker can eat . . . well, it begins with 'sh', ends with 't', and isn't sherbet.

The next morning, Carrow Road was open for aromatherapy and reflexology classes as part of National Healing Week. Perhaps we are turning into a New Age club! The 3 points against QPR were all the healing I needed, though. I'm even able to look forward to the cup match at Blackburn now; we can quickly atone for our nightmare a couple of weeks ago and be all the stronger for it.

In any case, I had to be back in London on Sunday morning to lead the Norwich Supporters' team in the absence of our manager. My team talk wasn't exactly up to the standard of Henry V – it was more like, 'Er, do your best, boys' – but with ten minutes left, we were 3–2 up and the opposition were down to ten men. Faced with the unnerving prospect of actually winning a game, we gave away an own goal and a penalty to return to comfortably familiar territory. Ah well. I'd much rather watch a successful team and play for an unsuccessful one than the other way round.

Sunday 25 October
Liverpool (away)

The phone rang at seven on Thursday morning. 'Huh?' I grunted. Civility is out of the question for the first hour after I get up, let alone half an hour before I am supposed to.

'We are flying, we are flying ... ,' warbled Mum, as melodiously as a knife scraping on a plate. She'd just received the letter that said we'd both been allotted seats on the plane to Oldham in a couple of weeks. She was very excited, as she hasn't flown before – though she did quieten down a bit when I pointed out that we wouldn't qualify for duty-frees.

I had another call at around eleven on Friday morning. I'm able to remember the times with some accuracy, as I don't get that many calls – cue violins ...

'Wanker!' yelled a voice. Who was that? It could have been any one of a hundred people.

'Wankerwankerwankerwankaarrgghhh!!'

'No, I'm sorry, you'll have to give me a clue.'

'Liverpool, Liverpool, Liverpool ... '

'Hello, Gary.' Gary, you will gather, is a Liverpool fan. Well, he says he is. In fact, he's never seen them play and has never been further north than the NEC in Birmingham. And even then, one of his lungs collapsed, presumably because he was unused to the air. You don't get much of it in Central London.

Claiming to support a team from another city just because it happens to be successful is a sign of insecurity in my book. It shows a desperate need to be associated with winners and an inability to cope with the opprobrium (as they perceive it) of mediocrity. For my part, I think I'd get bored if Norwich won every week. On second thoughts, perhaps I wouldn't.

'Did you by any chance support Leeds in the early '70s?' I once asked Gary.

'Yeah,' he replied, astonished. 'How did you know?'

'Oh, just an intelligent guess.'

I would imagine that the genuine fans of Leeds and Liverpool resent the intrusions of such 'pseudo-supporters'. As well as being annoyed at these outsiders coming along to appropriate a share of the glory, to enjoy the thick without ever having experienced the thin, the real supporters probably feel less comfortable about proclaiming their own allegiance for fear that others will think that they have only just jumped on to the bandwagon themselves. At least this is an irritation I am unlikely to experience as a Norwich supporter. Or is it?

It has also been my experience that those people who do not actually go to matches are the quickest to jeer the followers of other teams. When we lost 7–1 to Blackburn the other week, those in the office who regularly watch their teams play made only mild comments about it, while the can of 7-up and the loud calls of 'Seven-one, seven-one' came from individuals who have not been near a football ground for years. The armchair followers do not seem to look any deeper into football than the results; only the real fans understand how much more there is to the game and how much feeling is invested in it by those who travel every week to watch their team.

This match with Liverpool was originally supposed to take place on Saturday. However, they had a European Cup-Winners' Cup match in Moscow last Thursday, so they asked Norwich to allow them more time to recover by switching the fixture to Sunday. Norwich agreed – but if it had been left to me, I'd have made them play when they were knackered. I still haven't forgotten that it was Liverpool fans who robbed us of the chance to play in Europe in 1985. Did I say earlier that I was generous of spirit? I guess I lied.

I was disappointed at having to miss the Sunday-morning match. Still, with most members of the Norwich Supporters' team not being Norwich supporters, the side wasn't affected too much. In fact, I was the only one to drop out to make the trip to Anfield. Did no one else consider that getting a result at Liverpool was more important than getting one against East Barnes Reserves?

Getting a result at Liverpool does not just mean securing a win or a draw. It means getting away with the car still in one piece. This is not an idle slur on the character of Liverpudlians. Last year, the door of my car was kicked in and 'FUK OFF' (*sic*) written on the bonnet. Why? It's not as though I had any provocative stickers in the window saying things like 'Canaries do it from a great height'. And the car's red, for goodness sake. Scouse wit? Half-wits, more like.

I realise I am not doing myself any favours by saying this – I can see myself becoming the target of a Scouse *fatwa* if I am not careful – but I have never understood why Liverpool is so often described as being a warm, funny city. This strikes me as being an unsubstantiated urban myth to rank alongside the tarantula in the yucca plant or the Kentucky Fried Rat. In my experience, Liverpool is probably the coldest, most vicious place I have ever been.

I tried to get there early so that I could leave the car in the large car park near the ground. I arrived at 1:20, but it was full already. What time do you have to go to get in? Or had all these other people forgotten to put their clocks back the night before? I parked a few streets away – but no sooner had I applied the handbrake than there was a tap on the window.

'Can I mind your car, mate?' This is by no means exclusive to Liverpool, but it sums the place up for me. These boys may seem to be cheeky, enterprising scamps to some, but what they are actually doing is running a protection racket at a frighteningly early age.

'I'll do a good job, mate.'

'I bet you will, too,' I thought, and handed over two quid. Pausing only to visit the Shankly Gates and the Hillsborough Memorial, I went inside the ground for a drink so that I could take a couple of aspirins. I had a splitting headache, brought on (as on the trip to Blackburn) by the incessant motion of the windscreen-wipers on the journey up. I couldn't face a meat pie.

There seemed to be a different type of crowd from Norwich today. Several families had decided to have a special Sunday excursion to see the game, and tweeds, waxed jackets and smart coats were much in evidence. Goodness knows what they made of the hostile reception inside Anfield when the game got underway.

We were 1–0 up within a couple of minutes. I couldn't see exactly what happened, as I was sitting behind the goal at the other end with the crossbar obscuring my view as soon as the ball went beyond the half-way line. If I wanted to see where the ball was, I had to squat so that it looked as if the players were running around without heads (which some of them were, in a sense); if I sat up to see which player was which, the position of the bar meant I had to play 'Spot the Ball', using my skill and judgement to guess where it was. I spent the whole match bobbing up and down like a condom on the North Sea.

'One-nil, one-nil,' sang the Norwich fans, as you do.

'Fuck off, fuck off,' came the reply from the Kop. How witty.

They used to have a sense of humour, apparently. I remember hearing about a mounted policeman who helped a colleague on to the back of his horse and was given a rendition of *Two Little Boys*. And on another occasion, Gary Sprake of Leeds threw the ball into his own net, and the Kop sang *Careless Hands*. But you can tell from these songs that both incidents happened some years ago. The Kop rarely sang today. They whistled loudly when the Norwich team was announced, gave a chorus of 'You'll Never Walk Alone' before the kick-off and 'We hate Mancs' in the second half, and that was that.

At most games, the away fans make more noise than the home ones, despite the numerical imbalance. This is probably because travelling supporters are thinking about nothing but the game from the moment they get up in the morning, whereas home fans often have other things to do before the game, such as the shopping, and aren't as psyched-up. Away sections also bring the noisiest, most dedicated fans together, thereby intensifying their passion further. Having said all this, I still find it disappointing when a group of supporters as famous as the Kop remain so quiet.

Still, they did chant the name of the scorer after every Liverpool goal. This must be because there is no electronic scoreboard at Anfield. The members of the Kop have clearly taken it upon themselves to confirm the identity of the scorer for anyone who couldn't see.

They'd scored two after half an hour, but this hadn't improved the mood of the home supporters. In fact, it had made them even more unpleasant. Those on the other side of the gangway just a few feet from us had been transformed from a fairly normal-looking assembly into a pack of snarling, sneering, jeering, gesturing monsters with horribly contorted features. I'm not exaggerating. The new two-tier stand to our left that had looked so impressive before the game now looked awful, since it contained twice as many home fans as the old one. If Anfield is this hostile when we are there, whatever is it like when Manchester United are the visitors? It doesn't bear thinking about.

As I've said, I've never found Liverpool friendly in the past, but things have never been this bad. What's brought this about? My guess is that it's because the team has gone downhill in the last couple of years. (And it has, despite winning the FA Cup last season.) When Championship wins were as regular as a man on a prunes and All-Bran diet, there was a certain arrogance about the place. This was understandable. The level of success achieved and sustained by the team could not help but induce a feeling of superiority in the supporters. And this was just about tolerable, since the team was just about the only positive expression of the city's identity at the time. The arrogance also reflected the self-belief of the team on the pitch, a characteristic which is essential for success in football (and life in general) as it improves your own performance and puts others in awe of you.

Since the team has deteriorated, however, the inflated balloon of the supporters' arrogance has developed a slow leak, and now pure bile is seeping out. Perhaps it is wounded pride. Or a refusal to accept what is happening. Or the fact that, with decay and unemployment still rife on Merseyside, there is little else to hold on to. Perhaps it was just lying beneath the surface all the time, waiting to emerge. Whatever the case, it isn't pleasant to witness.

The appointment of Graeme Souness as their manager hasn't helped either. Just as the fans' attitude in the past mirrored that of the team, they now appear to have adopted some of the less appealing characteristics of Souness. He was guilty of some appalling acts as a player – and even at the match in Moscow on Thursday, he was abusing the officials in a disgracefully undisciplined manner.

While the home fans were screaming and gesticulating at us, the stewards and police just looked on, grinning. What would they have done if we'd behaved in this way, I wonder? And, talking of the police in Liverpool, are there any young ones? All those at the game seemed to be carrying walking sticks.

A minute before the end of the first half, a penalty was awarded at the Kop end. This won't sound surprising to anyone who's been to Anfield – until I tell you that it was awarded to us. We then witnessed a blatant display of gamesmanship. Liverpool players surrounded the referee to protest. Someone threw a toilet roll on to the pitch, and Grobbelaar decided to do his duty as a good citizen and tidied it up. All this time, the home fans were making a deafening noise. (Though this was fair enough.)

You can always tell when a player is going to miss a penalty and, sure enough, Mark Bowen stepped up and sent the ball soaring over the bar. He said afterwards that he thought Grobbelaar might have seen where he put last week's penalty on TV, and he wanted to put it somewhere different. Well, he certainly managed that.

At half-time, I realised that my headache hadn't got any better. Indeed, it was now blinding. They say that nothing works faster than Anadin. Next time

I'll try nothing. As well as the scoreline and the annoying position of the crossbar, the people around me had exacerbated it. In front were two girls who kept going on about which men in the crowd they fancied (though, with their looks and personality, the chances of their feelings being reciprocated were minimal); behind were two men who clearly didn't know the rules about offside, or when a goalkeeper can pick the ball up, or that deliberately kicking the ball away after a stoppage automatically earns a booking this season. Pillocks! (I was not at my most tolerant at this match, you will gather.)

Not that the referee was any more clued-up than the men behind. Before this match, Norwich had been second in the Fair Play League. And no one could accuse us of being a dirty side. (OK, so Southampton did earlier in the season, but that's like being called ugly by a frog.) Yet the referee showed the yellow card to four of our players. No wonder he lives in Bookham.

Five minutes into the second half, Liverpool went 3–1 up. Once again, the fans on the other side of the gangway bayed at us and regrettably provoked some Norwich supporters into renditions of 'You'll never get a job' and 'In your Liverpool slums'. These were neither funny nor original, it is true, but they were just about understandable in this atmosphere.

As the half progressed, attention turned to Bruce Grobbelaar in the goal in front of us. In midweek he had produced another of his famous eccentric goalkeeping displays, giving away a soft goal and getting sent off, so the Norwich following attempted to prompt more mistakes in the manner that had proved so successful at Chelsea. 'Moscow, Moscow' came the shout, followed by 'You're even worse than Beasant'. When these had no effect, a note of desperation crept in: 'Brucie, Brucie, give us a goal'. Grobbelaar responded with a quite astonishing save from a Phillips header. I was in mid-air yelling 'Goal!' when he sprang to his left and somehow scooped the ball round the post.

Liverpool rounded off the game by demonstrating how to take a penalty at the Kop end and left us with a negative goal difference despite still being second in the table. My headache was worse than ever, and I now had the worry that the car might be on four piles of bricks when I returned to it. Fortunately, it was OK, though the small extortioner was still hanging around. 'What was the score?' he asked.

'Two–two,' I replied. The little shit.

The journey back to London was horrendous. I'd been warned that the M6 and M1 were busy on a Sunday evening, but they were far worse than I'd expected. It took me over five hours to get back to London and, at the point where the two motorways meet, it took an hour to travel ten miles.

Football supporters probably know more about the state of Britain's roads and transport systems then anyone else. After all, we travel to all parts of the country at all sorts of times in the course of a season. It would help matters considerably if the Secretary of State responsible followed a team around. On second thoughts, John MacGregor is MP for South Norfolk. Do we really want him travelling around with us?

It is very rare for me to travel to a match without experiencing jams, roadworks or hold-ups of some sort. You might say that, as a motorist, I am part of the problem myself – and you would have a point. But what is the alternative? Public transport is hugely expensive (e.g., my trip to Carlisle) and generally very inconvenient. This should be the way forward, for environmental reasons as well as to improve efficiency, and more investment is desperately needed. However, if British Rail is to be privatised, as now seems likely, the danger is that fares will rise higher and higher and services will be sacrificed on the altar of profit.

If you were thinking that there is another option available to me, namely not travelling to all the away matches, I would respectfully suggest that you put this book down at once, as you have obviously missed the point.

On Monday morning, my picture appeared in the *Daily Mirror*. 'Where?' asked the others at work.

'Look, there,' I said. 'At the extreme right of that photo with the crossbar in front of my face.'

'How can you tell it's you?' someone wondered.

'Believe me, I know. That's the view I had of the match.'

'You're really proud of this picture, aren't you?'

'Well, I ... '

'You sad git.'

The small gathering dispersed, with one person muttering something about Damien in *The Omen*. Not having seen the film, I had to ask him to explain. Apparently, there is a part in the film where strange shadows mysteriously appear on a photograph of a priest, and these presage the manner of his death. 'If that photo in the *Mirror* is anything to go by, Kev, you're going to get finished off by a crossbar falling on your face.' Gulp.

I rang Brian, our Sunday football manager, to see how the team had done in my absence. 'We lost 1–0,' he said. Never mind, I thought, at least that means I'll get back in the side next week. 'We played really well, though,' Brian continued. 'So you'll be starting as sub next week, if that's OK.'

Tits on toast.

At least Brian was fairly sympathetic about the result at Anfield, considering that he is a genuine Liverpool supporter from up north. Unlike Gary, who is neither genuine nor sympathetic. He rang before my second cup of tea of the day (i.e., very early). 'Four-one, four-one, four-one, four-one. Wanker–wankerwankerwankaarrgghhh!!'

He has a very short memory, but then that's consistent with being a part-time supporter, I suppose. Last season, we beat Liverpool 3–0 at home, but I didn't ring him up to rub it in. In fact, he rang me a few days after the game to ask why I hadn't. 'I'm not that type,' I explained. 'Besides, I didn't need to.'

'How do you mean?'

'I knew very well what you'd think of the result. And I knew you'd know what I was thinking. And I knew you'd be expecting me to ring. If anything, not ringing you has kept it on your mind all the more, otherwise you wouldn't be ringing me now.'

'You calculating bastard,' he said, once he'd worked it out.

It occurs to me that all three of the games we have lost so far this season have been in the North-West. I'm now starting to worry about Wednesday's trip to Blackburn again. I don't think I could face another defeat up there so soon.

Wednesday 28 October
Blackburn Rovers (away)
COCA-COLA CUP, THIRD ROUND

Bollocks.

What? You really want to know what happened? Are you sure it's not just because you feel cheated at finding a few blank pages when you've spent good money on this book? I thought they were a rather eloquent appraisal of the match and of my reaction to it, but if you insist . . .

For a start, it absolutely pissed down. Again. And the away turnstiles weren't opened until 7pm, even though the kick-off was at 7:45, so most of us were sodding wet by the time we got inside. (Or do I mean sodden? No, I don't think so.) All the home supporters' turnstiles were open long before, though. Curious, that. The Norwich turn-out was depressingly low, though this owed less to the result here at the start of the month than to the fact that Blackburn had only allowed us a few tickets.

When I found my seat, I discovered that I had a dirty great steel pillar blocking my view of the goal to the left. Whereas at Liverpool I had had to bounce up and down to see, here I was going to have to rock backwards and forwards like Val Doonican on speed. It's a pity this pillar wasn't part of the steel that Jack Walker sold off. Mind you, the roof would have fallen down if he had.

Talking of Jack Walker, they did play *Money Money Money* over the loudspeakers this time. In fact, they played a whole selection of Abba songs again. Never mind Kenny Dalglish this month, Jack. How about slipping the club DJ a few quid so he can go and buy some more records?

As well as the steel pillar, there was a man to my left who hhhad hhhorrendous hhhalitosis and who was annoyingly chatty. 'Hhhave you come far tonight?' 'Hhhow did hhhe miss that?' 'Hhhe was unlucky there, wasn't hhhe?' You'd think a close friend would have told him about his problem by now. Then again, if he does have any friends, I don't suppose they get that close.

He was right about one thing, though. We were unlucky. Goss hit the post from thirty yards with the keeper well beaten, and Newman had a header cleared off the goal-line. In between, bloody Shearer bloody scored another bloody goal against us. And I bloody missed it, as he took the free kick just outside the area before either Gunn or I was ready. I was actually looking the other way at the time.

Smoking was not allowed in our stand, and every time a Norwich supporter lit up (which happened quite frequently, as several had arrived late and missed the reminders that it was forbidden), the stewards fussed around like ARP wardens during the war. 'Oi, you, put that bleedin' light out!' Someone lit a cigarette just as the free kick was awarded and, as I glanced round to see the stewards clucking officiously at the culprit, there was a great roar at the other end of the ground. The free kick was dodgy in the first place ...

Kevin's Alternative Laws of Football (No.5)

> *'The more dubious the award of a corner or free kick just outside the area, the greater the likelihood that a goal will result from it.'*

We conceded another soft goal after an hour. Time, we all thought, to bring

Mark Robins on. After all, when you're 2–0 down in a cup match, you don't leave your leading goalscorer on the bench, do you? Apparently, you do – until the 85th minute, anyway. This reluctance to make substitutions was worryingly reminiscent of last season, as was the performance of the team in general. There was plenty of pretty passing, but no sting up front. For the first time this season, we failed to score.

Curiously, Mike Walker declared after the game that he was quite happy with the way things had gone. Why? Did he not realise that this round of the cup is not over two legs? Or was there a deliberate plan to get knocked out early so that the team can concentrate on the league? Perhaps he was simply displaying an ability to look on the bright side (de-dum, de-dum-de-dum-de-dum) which I do not possess. I can think of few positive aspects to the evening. One was the undampened spirit of the damp Norwich following before the game. The home fans looked bewildered as our contingent pointed at them chanting 'One-seven, one-seven, one-seven, one-seven' and 'We're only gonna lose six-one tonight'.

The fact that we didn't lose 7–1 again was a good point, I suppose. And Sherwood didn't score, though I feared that all the taunts directed at him would provoke him into doing so. The abuse of Mr Rubbish actually started at Anfield on Sunday, where he had been spotted in the crowd. Here, he was greeted by a couple of hundred people shouting 'Sherwood's a self-abuser' and 'We've all shagged your missus' whenever he came near. When the chant 'If you all hate Sherwood, clap your hands' went up, he joined in the applause, which I thought displayed a remarkable capacity for self-criticism, especially for a professional footballer. On the other hand, he may have been taking the piss.

There were a few amusing misprints in the match programme. According to one feature, Tottenham are now in the 'post-Lineker, post-Gazza ear'. However, they have tried to strengthen the team by buying 'Neil Ruccock' from Southampton for a mere '3750,000'. What a bargain. I'm surprised the article didn't go on to mention that Blackbum's next visitors play at Shite Fart Lane.

The only other good thing about the evening was that this really was the last time I would have to visit Blackburn for a year. Oh no, I shouldn't have said that again. What's the betting we get them in the FA Cup now?

Saturday 31 October
Middlesbrough (home)

Thursday saw the first Capital Canaries committee meeting of the season. I was present as the representative of the Sunday football team. There were eight of us in total – which is more than the turn-out for the London branch at the Liverpool and Blackburn games. At Liverpool, there were five including me. At Blackburn, one including me. 'I didn't see any of you at Carlisle either,' I said.

'Did you go?' someone asked.

'Of course.'

'I haven't been able to watch Norwich as much this season because of work commitments,' protested one.

'I haven't done much work this season because of Norwich commitments,' I retorted.

The various secretaries – travel, balls and tossers (pool and darts) – gave their reports. We discussed the club's forthcoming sports quiz, a prestigious annual event that takes place in a leading London phone box. I won last year, but I won't be able to defend my title as I will be in Norwich on the night in question. I handed the winner's shield back. That will leave a gap at the bottom of my wardrobe where it has sat for the last twelve months in a Tesco carrier bag.

Finally, we came to my report. 'So far we have a 100 per cent record in the league this season,' I began.

'Oh, jolly good!' exclaimed the chairman.

'Not exactly,' I said. 'We've lost every game. But then we always have a poor run before Christmas.'

'This one seems to have started last Christmas,' someone commented.

'Have you managed to get a photo of the team for the newsletter yet?' another committee member asked. 'We've been asking you for months now.'

'I know,' I replied. 'But it's hard enough getting eleven players out every week, let alone having anyone spare to hold the camera.'

During 'Any Other Business', the chairman read a letter from two club members who have decided to resign because they consider the newsletter to be too negative and critical. We duly had a good moan about them for a quarter of an hour. We have also lost another member, though this is because he died of old age. Apparently, he has left a sum of money to Capital Canaries, though we don't know how much yet. In the absence of solid fact, we began to speculate wildly. Could he be another Jack Walker? Could we buy Alan Shearer for the Sunday team? Could we afford a purpose-built stadium? 'Probably not,' said the treasurer, handing out lottery tickets for us to sell to raise some funds. I'll sell some to Stephen, then buy the next ones myself. They're bound to be winners.

On Friday evening, I gave a lift back to Norfolk to Jon, another Norwich supporter who lives about a mile away from me in London. I haven't seen much of him lately, as he's been abroad. In the middle of the season! He's been on a tour of Eastern Europe and saw games in most of the countries of the old Eastern Bloc – though he missed Norwich playing a friendly in Romania on their free weekend. He didn't know they were there!

Our conversation turned to the poor level of support from the London-based fans this year. I remarked that I had been the only one to make the trek to Carlisle from the South, but Jon quickly corrected me. It turns out that there is a teacher in Reading who goes to all the games and who went to even greater lengths than me to get to Carlisle. At the end of the school day, he drove to Heathrow and caught a plane to Newcastle. There, he hired a car and drove to Carlisle. After the match, he left the car at Carlisle railway station and caught the same sleeper as me back to London. Or rather, to Nuneaton. I was horrendously late for work that day. What on earth did he do?

Jon then recounted the story of how he had once travelled by air to get to a match when he was supposed to be at his cousin's wedding. It happened four years ago, when City were playing away at Middlesbrough. Jon went round to his cousin's house in Kensington on the Saturday morning, dressed in his best suit. He said he would see him in the afternoon – and dashed off to Heathrow and caught a flight to Teesside Airport. He jumped into a taxi and stood among the home supporters at Ayresome Park so that he wouldn't be kept in the ground by the police at the end. After seeing Norwich win 3–2, he dashed back to the airport, caught another plane, and eventually arrived back at the wedding reception before the food was served. Only his parents knew what he'd done. No one else noticed.

'It must have cost you a fortune,' I said.

'Yes,' he admitted, 'but it's the sort of thing you have to do once just for the story.' I should have done that during the doctor's wedding.

At the Middlesbrough match this weekend, I bumped into two other Capital Canaries committee members. Would they have come to this game anyway, or had I pricked their consciences? There wasn't much happening on the pitch to persuade them to make the effort more often. The omens were bad from the start. For the first time this season, we kicked off towards the River End. Statistics show that Norwich do much better when playing towards the River End in the second half. Besides which, as a River End regular, I prefer to see any exciting late winners scored in front of me.

As at Blackburn, City put together some neat moves and fancy approach work, but never actually got into the box. (Sounds like my sex life.) The crowd was very quiet, presumably concerned at seeing the return to last season's form. The speed and directness of the performances at the start of the season had disappeared, and the closest we came to a goal was when the Boro keeper Pears had to head a back-pass over his own bar. I suppose this was entertaining in a way, though only if you find the Keystone Kops amusing.

The only noise came from a party of schoolchildren singing 'You're worse than Maradona' to a Middlesbrough player. This may sound self-evident, but they were actually referring to a handball incident. The boy who had sworn loudly at the last home game was being kept quiet, if not kept away. A case of being obscene and not heard?

'Shall I start the singing?' asked Mum.

'Things aren't that desperate yet,' I said, But, twenty minutes into the second half, they were. A cross into our box was met by Wilkinson and he headed the ball past Gunn, who was busy writing a letter to the 'Missing Persons' section of the Salvation Army to see if they could find our central defenders. For the first time this season, the crowd started to pick on the team. (Still, it's late October, so it's not bad going.) As usual, one player was singled out. The choice was not entirely arbitrary; some degree of consensus was involved. The attempts to get the abuse going were like trying to start a motorbike that hadn't been used for a while.

'That Newman's too bloody slow for this level.' Rud-dud-dud-dud-dud.

'Is Crook ever going to make a tackle today?' Rud-dud-dud-dud.

'You're ruddy useless, Goss.' Rud-dud-dud-dud-rrm-rrrmmmm-RRRRMMMMM!!

Yes, Jerry Goss was the unlucky winner of today's unpopularity poll. There were soon all sorts of variations being produced on the general theme of incompetence. 'My granny's faster than you, Goss.' 'You should never have left Bros.' 'These Golden Goal tickets ought to be for the time of your first tackle, Goss.' 'Yeah, except the tickets saying "No tackle" would win every week.' There was also a suggestion that Goss should be used as an extra man to push the still-injured Megson around the pitch in a wheelchair, rather like a batsman's runner in cricket.

This abuse can't help. I mean, I wouldn't like it if people kept shouting 'Wanker' at me when I'm at work. Come to think of it, I don't ... The truth was that Goss was not playing that badly, and he's had a good season so far. Still, the amount of criticism did mean that the crowd was generating some noise at last.

Ten minutes from the end, Norwich were finally building up some momentum in the search for an equaliser. Walker brought on two subs (a bit late again, I thought, but never mind). Four minutes from time, Crook crossed, Beckford leapt higher than Zebedee to knock the ball down, and Daryl Sutch thumped it in from eight yards. As the papers cornily put it, everyone screamed to laud Sutch. Bet he hasn't heard that one before.

All things considered, a point was OK from this game. And it had ended excitingly. And Wolves lost 2–0 at home to Derby. (Paul Blades, Paul Blades, what a difference you have made ...)

The next morning, the Norwich Supporters' team won their first game of the season. Six-one! And we only had ten men (so I wasn't a substitute after all). I didn't know what to say to our opponents at the end, as we don't find ourselves in this position very often. 'Thanks for the game' sounded patronising, while 'Well played' sounded sarcastic. In the end, I settled for a simple 'Cheers'.

My colleagues at work weren't stuck for words when I told them about our win on Monday morning. 'The other side must have been crap.' 'Who were you playing, the blind school?' What a disgraceful suggestion. For the record, they were partially sighted.

Monday 9 November
Oldham Athletic (away)

Ah, the romance of the cup! No one gave the minnows from Capital Canaries a chance before they took on the mighty West Barnes Reserves from Division Three in the first round of the Margaret Gray Cup. Yet after 120 minutes of pulsating, end-to-end action, the score was still 1–1. To be honest, it wasn't so pulsating by the end. In the second half of extra time, the teams were like two bloated heavyweight boxers lolling over each other in the final round. I wouldn't have minded the effort so much if I'd seen a bit more of the ball during the game. I kept making runs down the right, covered by the opposition's left-sided midfielder, then had to run back and cover him. This happened countless times without either of us being picked out by our team-mates, so in the end we called a truce and decided to have a rest together on the half-way line.

We now have to have a replay at West Barnes's all-seater stadium (there's a park bench next to their pitch, they said). Still, at least we're in the hat for the next round, and it's the first time we've got that far in the three years I've played for the team.

'Are you arranging a plane for the replay?' asked Stephen when I told him about our glorious draw. I knew what he was referring to. On Monday evening, the eagerly-anticipated (by Mum, at least) plane trip to Oldham was to happen at last.

Norwich Airport was one of the few places in the city I'd never been before – though I still haven't got round to visiting the Sainsbury Art Centre at the UEA to see such masterpieces as 'Lean Cuisine sur l'herbe' or 'Adoration of the marrowfat peas.' Still, Mum and I soon checked in and were minding our own business in the queue waiting to pass into the departure lounge when a young woman came up and tapped Mum on the shoulder. At first, we both thought that she was an airport official who was about to tell Mum that she had dropped her purse or something, but suddenly she produced a big, black, bulbous microphone and announced that she was from BBC Radio Norfolk. I didn't quite catch her name. Gormley? Gormless? Something like that, anyway.

She proceeded to ask Mum the usual inane questions. It seems to me that local reporters, whether they work for TV, radio or rag, have only three questions which they use whether they are interviewing a granny at her 100th birthday party or someone who has just lost all their relatives in a plane – er, car – crash: 'How do you feel?'; 'Has this come as a surprise?'; 'Are you looking forward to the future?' Mum dealt with these searching questions quite well, though she gaped incredulously when she was asked, 'How will you feel if they lose tonight?'

'You should have said, "Pissed off, how do you think?"' I told Mum later. But it's not so easy to think of apt replies at the time, as I was about to discover.

I had been standing there smirking at Mum – but then the reporter turned towards me. 'Excuse me, sir ... ,' she began. I was about to say, 'I'm sorry, I'd rather you didn't' – but it was too late. She had her finger on the 'record' button, and I had a fuzzy black ice-cream cone wedged up my left nostril. 'Are you excited about the flight?' she asked.

'Er, not really,' I said. 'I've been busy doing other things all day, and I haven't had a chance to think about it till now.' This was the truth, but Kate Adie couldn't accept it at all. It was just too dull and matter-of-fact. I suppose this is because local journalists spend their lives trying to turn the mundane into something dramatic, e.g., a bit of dog plop on the pavement is reported as seriously as arms limitation talks.

'What? You're flying on a plane to a football match and you're not excited?'

Irritated, I acted more sullen than I actually was. 'Well, I guess that's the sort of miserable bloke I am.' At this, she wandered off to pester someone else.

I cursed for the next hour. Why hadn't I known what to say to her? Why didn't I tell her that this flight was a PR exercise by the chairman and turn on her for giving him the publicity he was after? This interviewing lark isn't as simple as it looks. I shouldn't have been so scornful of Rob Newman on *Match of the Day* the other week.

'Never mind,' said Mum. 'They probably won't use it.'

It took some time to get through the scans and searches. There was a big notice warning us not to take compressed-air devices or offensive weapons on board, so Mum handed over her CS gas canisters and flick-knife. Explosives were banned too. 'I suppose that means we can't go and bomb Ipswich on the way,' said a woman of similar age behind us.

There were more media people on board the plane. A television camera crew kept walking up and down the central aisle. 'Who are they?' asked Mum.

'I don't care as long as they're not from the *Krypton Factor* filming contestants landing the plane,' I replied. As it turned out, they were from Sky. Boo!

Some fans had brought pocket cameras to record the occasion. Some even had leather flying hats and white silk scarves. As the plane took off, there was a loud rendition of the *Dambusters* theme. I thought everyone would be singing 'Going up, going up', but no one did. Though I am ashamed to report that one or two sang 'Always look on the runway for ice', an adaptation of 'Always look on the bright side of life' devised by Liverpool fans to taunt Manchester United supporters about the Munich air crash. Why is there always an element of sickness in every crowd? Is it because there is an element of it in every individual?

On the whole, the plane was much better than the Club Cabbage coach. There was no sign of Cabbage Man. No one ate cheese and onion crisps. We didn't stop at the Unhappy Eater. Instead, we were each given a small plastic tray with an only slightly less plastic roll on it. The man sitting next to me had some trouble getting his knife and fork out of their plastic packet. 'You need a GCSE in engineering to get this open,' he moaned.

Everyone adjusted to this new mode of transport easily enough, though one person asked if we could have a skylight open to let some air in. And Chairman Chase didn't go around being smarmy and ingratiating, which was a relief – though he may have been told not to move in case his shifting weight destabilised the plane.

The only real irritation was the peculiar tone of voice used by the stewardesses. To convey it accurately, you would need musical notation to show how the pitch rose and fell without regard to the sense of the words – though the words themselves were used in a strange way. Do they talk like this at home as well? 'Good evening, darling. Please be advised that I am amorous towards you and wish to demonstrate my passion with due expeditiousness here, here and here. Loved ones are respectfully requested to unfasten their belts and kindly reminded to extinguish all smoking materials until landing. Thank you.'

There was no in-flight movie, but the trip was over so quickly that we would scarcely have had time to watch an episode of *The Magic Roundabout*. We touched down safely at Manchester Airport and stepped out into pouring rain. How unusual.

Coaches had been laid on to take us to Oldham. The driver of ours had a virtually impenetrable Lancashire accent, and we had to try to identify the odd word and reconstruct the rest of the sentence from that, rather like cloning. He remarked (I think) on the plane trip and the presence of the TV cameras at the match. 'Bit of a do, in't it? Anyone'd think tha were a proper team. No, lad, only joking. Tha'll beat Oldham, they're bloody rubbish.'

So whom did he support? Not Manchester City, from what he said when we passed their ground. 'Maine Road? That's where tha goes when tha's tired of watching football.'

Manchester United? 'Tha's bloody joking. I score more than they do. No, I'm a Rochdale man, though I don't get to see them much as I'm usually working on Saturdays.'

'Taking supporters around the country?' I asked.

'Aye. And it's OK, unless I have to take the Goon Squad from United anywhere.' He told us about the coachload of United fans whom he took to Glasgow for a friendly with Celtic before the season started. They travelled up early, all got tanked up, and many were so sloshed that they missed the game altogether. Then he told us how the coach had been stoned after United's game at West Ham at the end of last season.

'You don't get that at Norwich,' said Mum. 'Have you ever been there?' 'Only once,' he replied. 'I took a party from the Women's Guild there. Mind you, in some ways I'd rather have the Goon Squad on board.'

With all the fuss about the flight, I had almost forgotten that this was another Sky TV game, even though this was the reason for playing on a Monday night. I was soon reminded when we arrived at the ground. We had to put up with the same deafening music as at our home game with Forest, and there was the same meretricious display by Bart Simpson and the dancing girls. The only amusing part was when the fireworks were set off and the wind blew the smoke straight into the main stand, leaving the home supporters coughing and spitting into their hankies. For some reason, Oldham always play *Mouldy Old Dough* by Lieutenant Pigeon before their games. I don't know why, but on this occasion it served as an appropriate comment on the Sky entertainment.

The match programme was scarcely more entertaining. There was a feature on the new Rochdale Road Stand in which we were sitting, complete with a list of 'interesting facts'. Apparently, 5,500m^3 of poured concrete was used in its construction. And 369 gallons of paint. Well, that's handy to know. The next time I'm at a dinner party or a similar social function, and it falls to me to pick up the conversation by saying something interesting, I'll inform the others that the Rochdale Road Stand contains 4,000m^2 of cladding. That'll be bound to get me invited again.

I was pleased to see Darren Beckford starting a match for the first time this season. He was bought for a club record fee (£925,000) at the start of last season and presented as the shit-hot striker we'd needed for so long. So far, however, this assessment has proved to be only 50 per cent accurate. Actually, that's not entirely fair. He did score a hat-trick against Everton last season. And it was just unfortunate that he never really hit it off with Fleck on the pitch. They went together like chalk and cheese – or should that be cheese and onion? Mind you, Beckford did insist on making runs into silly positions, e.g., in the box waiting for a cross. Did no one tell him that we don't do anything as vulgar as crossing the ball early?

I hoped that he would be able to strike up a good relationship with Mark Robins. After fourteen minutes, the signs looked good. Beckford back-heeled the ball into the path of Ian Culverhouse, who crossed for the unmarked Robins to head home. Robins hadn't scored in the last seven games – so where better to start again than in his home town in front of his father, a high-ranking police officer who was here on crowd control duty?

For the first time in a while, the Norwich fans sang 'Say we are top of the league'. This was a little presumptuous at this stage of the match, it is true, but everyone was keen to give the chant another airing after our treatment on *Grandstand* and *Match of the Day* on Saturday. We weren't mentioned at all. 'Arsenal go top,' Des Lynam had said, 'Villa are up to second, Blackburn are down to third ... ' – I waited for him to point out that we were fourth but poised to go top if we won our game in hand at Oldham – ' ... and at the bottom of the table ... '

This is by no means the first time this sort of thing has happened. Once, *Grandstand* used to show only the top few clubs in their round-up of the divisions at the end of the programme. If Norwich were seventh, they would show the top six. If we were sixth, they would show the top five. This was all the more annoying as we didn't use to get that high very often. 'It's always been the same,' Mum said on Saturday. 'During the '59 Cup run [yawn], there was a man at the BBC who always put us down. Sam Leitch, that was him.'

'If we do win the league, they'll have to give us some credit,' said Stephen. I'm not sure they would. They would just use the fact to argue that the league was mediocre this year and move on swiftly to the cricket season. And would the TV companies be scrambling for the rights to show 'Norwich in Europe'? I doubt it.

After twenty minutes, Oldham equalised with a goal from Graeme Sharp. His finish lived up to his name. 'Say you're not top of the league,' sang the Oldham fans.

'Say you're not top of the league,' responded the Norwich fans, which rather confused the home supporters.

There was an even better response a couple of minutes later. Fox broke away down the right (the whole Oldham crowd and team appealed for offside, but I'm sure he wasn't – Ruel's an honest lad and would certainly have stopped if he was) and squared the ball for Robins to side-foot it into an empty net. But just before the interval, Oldham equalised again. Ian Marshall ran on to a flick and lobbed the ball over the advancing Gunn before they collided and fell to the ground like two sacks of spuds.

At half-time, Sky's entertainment plumbed new depths. I have never been that interested in sumo wrestling, but I am aware that the solemn, traditional ritual is as important to the Japanese as the outcome. Every detail of the ceremony must be scrupulously observed. Even the mound of mud on which the bouts take place is sacred. In Sky's hands, however, the sport was turned into a tawdry travesty.

Two sumo dummies, each around twenty feet high (like *It's a Knockout* figures, but less classy), ran into each other for ten minutes while some berk in a black T-shirt and red braces exhorted the crowd to yell 'Sumo!' The 'contest' was choreographed like an ordinary wrestling bout and planned so that the dummies ended up in positions from a sex manual. They would have no place in a genuine sumo contest, but if they did, the falls would probably be given names such as 'sukifuki', 'dikiliki', 'upachutni' and 'analingi'.

How would we feel if one of our revered sports, surrounded by sacred ritual, were to be debased to give cheap thrills to an uncomprehending public? We may find out at the 1994 World Cup finals in the United States.

Norwich were under pressure for most of the second half, but Oldham didn't create any clear openings. Beckford had a shot saved at point-blank range, but when Fox lobbed just wide with five minutes to go, we thought our chance of victory had gone. Mike Walker seemed to have settled for a point, sending on

Sutton to use up some more time. Thirty seconds into injury time, however, Robins collected the ball on the edge of the Oldham area and, despite having three defenders around him, shuffled to his left and hit it across the goal and in off the far post. Verily, it was easier for a camel to pass through the eye of a rich man than to thread the ball into the net, but somehow he managed it.

What a finish! A last-minute winner is always exciting, since it comes just when you have given up hope of victory, it gives the opposition no time to come back and, most important, it gives you a delicious feeling of having got away with theft, even if you deserved to win in any case (as we did here). But when it means that the scorer has got his hat-trick and has sent the team to the top of the league ... ohhh!! The fireworks exploded, *Land Of Hope And Glory* blared out (rather too jingoistic for my taste, but forgivable for once), and all was well with the world.

'I bet you're glad you don't have to drive all the way back to London now,' said Mum as we boarded the coach.

'I wouldn't have minded after seeing that,' I said. 'Besides, there's something quite romantic about driving through the night because you wanted to see your loved ones.'

This rare expression of sentimentality on my part (attributable directly to the win) seemed to put Mum in a reflective mood. 'People a hundred years ago could never have imagined travelling on motorways or in planes,' she mused on the way back to the airport.

'Yes,' I said, 'it must have made it bloody difficult to get to away games.'

At the airport, our flight was delayed by three-quarters of an hour as we had to wait for the team. In the circumstances, we didn't mind – though if we'd suffered another Blackburn, I suppose we might have insisted that the plane take off at the appointed time. While we waited, we rang Stephen, who had watched the game on TV at a pub in Norwich. Apparently, there was mayhem when the winner went in, with beer and glasses flying all over the place. Yet somehow the goal escaped the attention of some imbecile on Radio Broadland who announced the final score as 2–2. Whoever it was should be put on to hospital radio – at the listening end.

The players received an enormous ovation when they arrived, and the party continued on the plane. Once again, the old *Dambusters* theme was sung on take-off – or should that be the Oldham-busters theme? Oh, please yourselves. The captain offered his congratulations over the tannoy and mentioned that we would be flying south towards Birmingham before hanging a left to Norwich. 'Let's hope they empty the toilets over Wolverhampton,' I muttered.

Half an hour later, with *To Dream The Impossible Dream* now playing over the speakers, we touched down. The players waited by the door and let all the supporters get off first. I didn't speak to them, for reasons I have already explained, though Mum thanked them for making our trip worthwhile. 'Goodnight, my darling,' said Mike Walker. Mum bored everyone she knows with this over the next few days.

The news with which she woke me the next morning met with no more enthusiasm. 'Guess who's just been on Radio Norfolk, then?' she asked.
'You?'
'No. You.'
'Oh, no. They didn't use the bit when I said what a miserable bloke I was, though, did they?' Mum grinned and nodded. 'Oh, shit in a swimming pool. Did they say anything about what I'd said?'
'Well, the presenter did say he hoped you cheered up a bit on the way home.'
At least they didn't mention my name, so no one should know it was me. And, in any case, half of Radio Norfolk's audience is senile, and the other half is Mum.

Saturday 14 November
No Match (again)

Another free Saturday so that Graham Taylor can get his squad together and work on tactics for Wednesday night and excuses for Thursday morning. For one reason and another, Norwich have played on only two of the last six Saturday afternoons. What is the world – well, football – well, same thing, really – coming to?

Still, it does give me an opportunity to look back over what I've written so far to see whether my views on anything have changed. Surprisingly, given the general fluidity of football supporters' opinions, they haven't much. I still think the new back-pass law is spoiling the game. I still think the Sky TV deal is obnoxious, as is their method of 'packaging' the game. The new Premier League is, as I suspected, no different from the old First Division. And I remain as suspicious of our chairman as ever, despite the cheap flight to Oldham.

In the edition of *On the Ball* which came out this week (this magazine being 'the official publication of Norwich City Football Club'), he claimed that the new Premier League 'has served to increase interest in the game amongst both loyal supporters and newcomers'. No, it hasn't. My interest could hardly have been increased. The satellite TV coverage 'has not only won over its critics, but caught the imagination of football fans everywhere'. NO, IT HASN'T! To cap it all, he suggested that the new back-pass rule 'improves the excitement in every game'. Mike Walker got it right in his column on the following page when he said that the law 'has robbed the game of a little more skill'.

I am a little ashamed of my pessimism at the start of the season. I had my reasons at the time, primarily the dismal way in which we finished last season. And my general approach to life has become, through experience, 'Prepare for the worst, and what follows can only exceed your expectations'. I now accept that this attitude was not altogether helpful to the team and that I have been proved wonderfully wrong.

I also have to admit that I've rather grown to like the new shirts now. However, I suspect that this is because we have played so well in them rather than because my aesthetic opinion has changed.

Looking back, I see that I was very patronising about Carlisle United's match programme. Sorry, Carlisle. I also looked down my nose at the size of Exeter City's ground. Sorry, Exeter. And I was very scathing about Liverpool.

I suppose it is time I explained who the Wolverine is. If for no other reason, any Wolves fans reading this deserve to know why I keep laughing every time they have a bad result. The following history of my relationship with her (or lack of it) is admittedly selective, partly to prevent it from dragging on too long, partly because I'm sure my memory has erased many of the more painful moments. And the Wolverine's point of view would doubtless be very different from mine. In my defence, I would point out that: a) all history is necessarily selective; and b) you should have learned to allow for my natural bias by now.

It all began in August 1988, when I was living in Birmingham. I was invited along to a pop quiz at a local pub (the Scarlet Pimpernel in Harborne, should anyone want to commemorate the event with a wall plaque) by an accountant friend of mine. I'm not sure why she wanted me to be on her team. It might have been because I'd given her the impression that I had a memory that retained trivial facts when I once told her that the only member of ZZ Top not to have a beard is called Frank Beard. Or it might have been because I had mentioned that all the records played at Carrow Road were old, so my knowledge of pop history was good. Anyway, I agreed to go along.

The pub was full of young accountants. It would have been easier to hold the quiz in their firm's offices, but perhaps it was felt that each team's score could be kept more accurately in a different environment, as the participants would be less ready to massage the figures to make them look good. Everyone looked casual and scruffy. It seems to me that most junior accountants try to react against the dull, boring image of their profession. It is only when they approach 30, and promotion is in the offing, that they succumb to the sensible slacks and Marks and Spencer cardigans. However, one girl stood out in the crowd – and she turned out to be on our team.

She was wearing a shapeless, full-length dress in a tastelessly loud shade of blue. Her hair was a mess. She was fairly ordinary-looking. She hardly answered a question all evening. I was utterly captivated.

I don't know why I thought she was so wonderful then. There was no rational explanation for being so attracted. (Though how many people choose their football team after logical, reasoned thought?) There was just an indefinable spark. I was strangely drawn, and I don't mean like a Ralph Steadman cartoon.

After the quiz (which we won!), I asked some of her colleagues about her in a casual way, so as not to arouse any suspicion about my motives. This is precisely what I did, of course. They all tried to warn me off – but this had precisely the opposite effect too.

'She's always moaning,' said one. 'There's always something wrong.' Great, I thought, she's just like me!

'She's not that sociable,' said another. 'She doesn't come out much.' That's like me as well!

'She's only really interested in one thing,' someone else remarked. What? What? 'Football.' Yeeessss!! My ideal woman! OK, it turned out that she supported Wolves, but that wasn't too far away from football.

The fact that she wasn't universally popular made me all the keener. I saw her as an undiscovered gem, or a dull-looking painting whose qualities would not be appreciated by the casual observer until it had been cleaned and restored. There was another parallel between us here in that I often think of myself in this way. I could see her hidden worth. Could she see mine?

I also thought that I might stand a chance with her if no one else was interested. It is often said that unavailability makes people seem more desirable. This may be true for some, but not me. Realism and experience have made me more inclined towards women who I think may be as, er, desperate as me.

At this early stage, I had no idea just how deep my affection for her was. I only realised this when she passed two tests by which I am generally able to gauge how strongly I feel about someone. First, I found myself thinking about her when I went back to Norwich for the weekend. There have been several girls I've thought I liked, but as soon as I've returned home for a match, I have become completely oblivious of their existence. I have only remembered about them on my return to Birmingham or London, and then realised how unimportant they were to me. It was different with the Wolverine. Even in the middle of a Norwich match, I wondered about her and hoped that Wolves were winning so that she would be happy. That seems a long time ago now.

Second, I couldn't picture her face. I have no trouble visualising the features of people I care nothing for. But with loved ones, I can't manage it at all. I couldn't put together a photofit picture of them. It is as if I see through their exterior and into their essence, their soul if you like. I can picture the Norwich players, incidentally, but this is presumably because they are figures rather than people I know personally.

Mum and Karen always complain if I don't notice their new shoes or hairdo. But these things aren't important, really – I see only them when they come into a room, not such superficial details. In fact, you might say (I often have) that they should be flattered when I don't notice any difference; it shows how much I think of them as people. The trouble is, of course, it looks as though I am taking them for granted. It might be more legitimate to argue that I have imprisoned them in my own fixed conceptions of them, that I can only see them in a certain way. This is possibly true, but it does not deny what I feel about them.

Anyway, as I said, I soon realised that I couldn't picture the Wolverine's face and took this as a sign that I must think an awful lot of her. So I rang and asked her if she'd like to come to the pictures. She didn't come, but on reflection it was just as well. I thought *Midnight Express* was a jolly film about a train, like *Silver Streak*. How wrong can you be?

Undeterred, I rang her again. And again. In those early calls, I talked too much to avoid any embarrassing silences on the phone and, of course, became embarrassing in the process. Then I tried to plan, almost script my calls in advance so that I could be suitably witty and amusing. This didn't work either. As soon as the conversation deviated from the prepared outline, I was thrown. I should have realised that life never follows an American football-type game-plan. It is much more like our football. You can work on one or two set-pieces and have a general aim in mind, but you have to improvise in the short term.

Despite this, we soon got on wonderfully well. The conversations became longer and longer, and I became less and less popular with the other members of the house I lived in, as I was always on the phone. The only problem was that I still had trouble getting her to come out. Weekends were difficult anyway, as we were usually watching football at different ends of the country, but I had no more success in midweek. Was it down to me? Or was she simply unsociable as her colleagues at work had told me? For once, I chose to believe the latter and pressed on. Nothing worthwhile is easy, I told myself. No pain, no gain, and all that. Revealing the glory of a shabby painting is a painstaking job. I never actually offered to miss any Norwich games to go and watch Wolves with her, but I would have done if she'd asked.

When I did see her, it was always as part of a group. And she was nothing like the bright, warm, funny person that I talked to on the phone. The way she acted towards me, Electrolux should have named a freezer after her. I understand that, when a suspected criminal is being interrogated, one policeman will be nice and another nasty in order to unnerve him. I was all the more disconcerted by the Wolverine, as these two personae were inhabiting the same body. More evidence of this dichotomy: she has Guns 'n' Roses and Debbie Gibson albums next to each other in her record rack.

I continued to pursue her with the relentlessness, charm and success rate of book club mailers until Christmas of that year, when things came to a head. I knew it was time to do something drastic to try to win her over. Apart from the fact that I had been prostrating myself – or prostituting myself – before her for months without success and was getting tired and desperate, I had found a new job in London and knew that I would be moving down to start in January. I was in the Last Chance Saloon, it was a minute before noon, and I had only one bullet in my gun.

I had to buy her a present that would knock her out. Expensive perfume? Lingerie? A trip to Paris? No, none of these would impress her or show her how I felt. In the end, I hit on the perfect gift: I bought an orange football (the nearest I could find to gold) and arranged for the whole Wolves first-team squad to sign it. I tried to deliver it in person one evening, but she was out. (Where?) The train back to Birmingham was late, and I didn't get home until half past midnight. I tried again on the Saturday morning, breaking my train journey to Liverpool, but she'd gone shopping. I left the present by her door and carried on to Anfield. We won 1–0 there that day, and I took this as an omen, a sign that anything was possible.

What happened? Nothing. She never said anything about it. I know that she got it, as one of her work-mates told me that she was overcome by curiosity (or the fear that it might start ticking) and opened it a few days before Christmas. Apparently, she was touched (ha!), but she didn't admit this to me. I got the message and moved to London, resigned to the fact that my efforts had been in vain. 'See you,' I said to her, thinking that I never would again.

Yet somehow I couldn't let go. I kept ringing her and hated myself for doing so. A new set of flat-mates hated me for doing so. Once in a while, she'd call me and I'd be encouraged again, reading things into the conversation as I tried to detect interest on her part, then realising how foolish I was to do this, then going ahead and doing it again anyway. It might have been different if I'd found another woman to fancy and fail with in London. After all, I don't subscribe to the thoery that there is only one ideal partner for any person in the world. There are any number of potentially good matches out there.

This is one respect in which love and football differ. You generally love the same club for life, whereas you may have several partners over the years. It's not so hard to see why. A football club may disappoint you and let you down, but they will never turn you away (barring any acts of hooliganism). And they appreciate a football when you give them one.

The simple fact was that I met no one else who was in the same league, let alone division, as her. Furthermore, the possibility of anyone matching up to her decreased as time went on. She acquired the aura of distance that I talked about in connection with the Norwich players. Other women couldn't compete with her, as they were up against an image which maybe didn't have much basis in reality – though whenever we spoke on the phone, she always lived up to it.

It also has to be said that I was not exactly beating admirers off with a big stick. In the surveys that purport to show what 'gals' fancy about 'guys', the two most desirable attributes are generally a sense of humour and a small bum. I thought I must have a sense of humour, as 'gals' often laugh in my company. I now suspect that they are just laughing at the size of my bum.

I did manage to see the Wolverine once around that time. One Saturday when, for some reason, Norwich weren't playing, I went with her to see Wolves play Bolton. Wolves got a result (1–0, Bull). I didn't. Once again, she was so frosty, I feared I might lose some of my extremities. Not that I would miss them.

This wholly unsatisfactory situation carried on until around August 1989, when she said that she was now going out with someone. They had even been on holiday together, though this blow was softened by the news that they had had to cut it short because he had food poisoning. What was so great about him, I wondered. He was a robotic welder by profession, she said. Hmm. That sounded rather risky, having to do all those jerky movements while holding a blow-torch. Perhaps she was attracted by the danger.

I finally accepted defeat. It was never going to happen. I resolved not to call her again, as it would be too painful and embarrassing. I summoned up what remained of my dignity and self-respect and managed to keep to this resolution, though I was sorely tempted at times. I even picked up the phone receiver once or twice, but managed to put it down again.

She rang a couple of times to talk about her boyfriend. Was she cruelly rubbing it in? Or did she just see me as a good friend she could talk to? I gave her the benefit of the doubt and chose the latter explanation, though believing the former would have made it easier not to phone her – but no, I didn't anyway.

After September, there was no communication between us. There were no Christmas cards, no footballs, no Valentines. It got to the stage where I rarely thought about her, which showed that I had broken the attachment.

Then, the following April, a card and letter turned up from her. 'I bet you thought you'd never hear from me again,' she wrote. How true. She sounded very friendly. What did this mean? That she'd chucked the body-popping blow-torch? That she had belatedly realised what a sterling chap I am? I debated whether or not to get in touch. I had invested so much emotion in my previous attempts to woo her, I wasn't sure that I was prepared to go through it all again.

Once again, it was in Norwich that I realised what I felt for her. I saw someone walking towards the football ground who looked like her. It wasn't her, of course, but the way my heart leapt on seeing the cover version told me how much I thought of the original. Like the fan who returned to the Everton game earlier this season, I went back on all I'd vowed and decided to write back.

She rang back virtually straight away, and I discovered ... the boyfriend was still in tow. Nothing had changed at all. At this point, I became very bitter towards her and towards Wolves. I felt that she was deliberately toying with me. Why get in touch with me again? Even if she weren't doing it for malicious pleasure, she knew how I had felt about her and should have realised the effect her note would have.

This was when I began referring to her as the Wolverine. I understand that derogatory epithets – in fact, any nicknames – are limiting in that they present a narrow and over-simplified view of a person. I moan enough when Norwich followers are called turkeys or dumplings. But in the Wolverine's case, I couldn't give a toss. I was so confused and hurt by the whole business, it was comforting to refer to her by this term of abuse. She deserved it.

Now that contact had been re-established, though, I found I couldn't break it again. Over the next few months, the mixture of unrequited love and self-disgust became more and more painful. I use the word 'love' only now, as up to this point I had not been sure that it was not mere infatuation. But to last so long and to survive such a break indicated that it had to be something more.

I thought I'd found a way to end it when she complained how much weight she'd put on. She'd been to a function with her former colleagues (she had left during the break), and some had asked whether she was pregnant. I conceived the notion that if I went to see her, and if she was as repulsive as she made out, it might shatter my illusions and put me off once and for all. I know I said earlier that appearances are unimportant – and, ultimately, I believe they are – but I resorted to this ill-considered scheme out of desperation. I wasn't thinking consistently.

When I arrived at her house (after a drab 0–0 draw at Derby), she was wearing jeans that were indeed far too tight around her bum, and there was a 'Nora Batty' effect around her calves. She had a drab navy jumper on, and her hair was crimped, which I have always hated. She looked wonderful. Oh shit. I was back to square one. Again, I was treated with indifference. I wondered whether I was visiting the same person I talked to on the phone. I really can't stress enough how well we get on via BT. The conversations are funny, flowing, and last for ages.

Why did I put up with this treatment? You may well ask. What friends I have did. They urged me to ask her exactly where I stood. I said I would, but always knew I wouldn't. I just couldn't face the ultimate rejection. I know that when football teams are crippled with fear and are desperately trying not to lose, they invariably do, in a dour, joyless struggle. Even so, I couldn't force myself to seize the initiative and go for broke.

I have always been reluctant to express myself outside football grounds. It's easy to vent your feelings at a match, as the objects of your praise, abuse or advice are so far away, they can't pick you out as the person shouting at them. Doing it face to face with one person is a different matter. You're on your own, you can't hide, you have to argue and defend your point of view.

It's much simpler to direct my anger and frustration at Wolverhampton Wanderers – though it wasn't me who started the fire there last season. The Wolverine did accuse me of this.

I have let the situation drag on ever since. The phone calls are still long, she still has her boyfriend, and I have found the drawbridge up and portcullis down whenever I have called in to see her. She was supposed to visit me last year. I cleaned the flat (a major personal commitment), had a bath (ditto) – and she didn't turn up. It took her two weeks to ring and claim that she had lost my address.

I think I know my position now. I'm sitting on the sub's bench, waiting to see if the first-choice striker is dropped or asks for a transfer. I've been running up and down the touchline, I've done all my stretches – on occasions I thought I was about to be called into action and prepared to take my tracksuit bottoms off, but it never happened. Yet I still harbour hopes of coming on to score a last-minute winner.

My hopes have increased in the last six months. She has rung me more often than I've rung her. And as often as not, she's in the bath when she rings. (Friends have told me that this is significant.) There is also a strange buzzing noise in the background, though she claims that this is because the batteries in her cordless phone are fading. It couldn't possibly be what you're thinking. Could it? No, surely not.

And that's more or less the story of the Wolverine and me. Boy meets girl, boy doesn't get girl, boy leaves girl, boy meets girl again, boy still doesn't get girl. Pathetic, isn't it? I really ought to settle it one way or the other. But Wolves will probably have to bear the brunt of my dissatisfaction for a while yet.

This weekend they were 2–0 up at Notts County, but let in two late goals and dropped 2 points. Ha! Ha!

Our Sunday team had a game against Newcastle Supporters at Wormwood Scrubs. No, not inside the prison – though I have heard that, when we play there, persistent offenders are put in the cells overlooking the pitch. Our unbeaten run was stretched to a magnificent three when we sneaked a 2–2 draw with a highly dubious penalty in the last minute. Still, all gifts gratefully received.

Except for the kit, that is. It's my turn to wash it this week. It would be, when the pitch is so muddy that, by the end of the match, everyone looks like turds in boots (though, in a sense, we always do).

Mum asked how long it would take to iron everything. I told her I wasn't going to bother, as: a) the creases drop out by themselves; and b) the first time I ever washed the kit I ironed it, and the next week I had to put up with comments like 'Mmm, Kev, this shirt has never felt so soft' and 'Yes, it's got that spring freshness!' Never again.

Saturday 21 November
Sheffield United (home)

After spending most of last weekend writing about the Wolverine, I did some thinking. Yes, I know, it makes a change. I decided that I really should make more of an effort to find a suitable woman in London, so on Wednesday I went to lunch with someone from the office. She is still only GM Vauxhall Conference standard compared to you-know-who, but that's far better than most down here.

To be honest, we had sort of agreed to 'do lunch' some time ago, though she had had to 'put it on a pencil' for a while before she felt able to 'action it', as she's been 'eyeballs-out' with the company being 'under-resourced people-wise'. You will gather that these phrases are hers, not mine, and go some way towards explaining why she is unlikely ever to achieve full league status.

Inevitably, the subject of our conversation turned to football. I hadn't consciously led it there; somehow it is always drawn in that direction as if attached by elastic. This is possibly because the first analogies to spring to mind when discussing any subject are football ones. Though I'm not sure whether this is because football is a good analogy for life or vice versa. In this case, we were talking about the company Christmas party next month. This year, the theme is hedonism. We are all supposed to dress in a way that suggests our ultimate pleasure. I said I was thinking of turning up in full Norwich kit, with a life-size model of the Premier League Championship trophy and a box of Kleenex.

'What, for your tears of joy?' she asked.

'Er, something like that,' I said.

'Are Norwich in the Premier League anyway?' she went on.

'Of course we are,' I spluttered, and all over the table-cloth too.

'Oh. Have they just been promoted?'

Barely concealing my irritation, I explained that Norwich have been in the top division for all but three of the last twenty seasons. 'And we're top of the league at the moment.'

'Really? You won't win it though, will you?'

'How do you know?' I snapped. 'We might. I think we will.' It was the first time I'd said this aloud, and I was more than a little surprised to catch myself doing it. I was only saying it now because I had been provoked by my companion's scornful comments, but I have been starting to wonder lately whether we might actually be able to do it. The result at Oldham felt as if it marked a crucial point in the season. Had we lost, we would have remained fourth and possibly started to fade; as it was, we had played well and returned to the top again.

'Well, I don't really know much about football,' she said. I thought she might be trying to atone for her earlier remarks and gave her the benefit of the doubt. And I did say before that a girlfriend wouldn't necessarily have to follow football. But then she really put her foot in it. 'I can't see the point of it. It's silly. Twenty-two grown men kicking a piece of leather around a field.'

Yes, this was exactly the same description of football that my sister had given in the years before her enlightenment. Not that there is anything extraordinary about this. Most people who disparage football come out with it. It is ridiculous, though. Anything of value can be reduced to a banal description if you wish. A Jackson Pollock painting can be called a load of splodges of paint on a canvas. Henry Moore's sculptures could be dismissed as being merely odd-shaped chunks of stone. OK, bad examples.

This was looking like a lost cause. Well, not irrevocably lost, perhaps. The example of Karen's conversion shows that. But look how long that took. Still, I decided to make a token effort while waiting for our coffee. 'Have you ever actually been to a football match?'

'No, and I don't want to.' Very open-minded, I thought. I tried making a similar speech to the one I had inflicted on my lawyer friend in Cambridge all those years ago but, though the timing was more appropriate, the outcome was just the same. I tried to explain how I become a better person in a crowd; more passionate, more expressive, more animated.

'Like Goofy, you mean?'

She couldn't grasp the importance of football at all. She finally killed off the subject by asking what I would do if Norwich City went out of business tomorrow. This was such a stupid question, it was worthy of a local radio reporter – though if her aim was to render me speechless, it was brilliant. I began several sentences in reply, but didn't get past the second or third syllable with any of them. The very idea was just too catastrophic to contemplate, let alone talk about coherently. I believe I eventually mumbled something about a length of rope and a stout beam, but that was it.

Fortunately, of course, there is little chance of the club going bust tomorrow or in the foreseeable future. You can say what you like about Chairman Chase – as indeed I have – but his constant concern for the financial side of the club has put us on a sound footing.

On Thursday, feeling guilty at having had such a large lunch the day before, but also because I was encouraged by the Sunday team's recent improvement in form, I took the radical step of doing some exercises in the office at lunchtime. I looked to see if the coast was clear, shut the door and started to change into a T-shirt and jogging pants. My jeans were around my ankles when a temp who'd only begun that morning burst in, screamed and ran out again. I don't think she saw anything ('Well, she wouldn't, would she?' the others said later), but I am now being called 'Paddy Pantsdown' in the office. I wondered about explaining how nicknames distort and over-simplify the truth, but decided this would be fruitless. I've settled for giving up this midweek training idea instead.

It was good to have a game to go to on a Saturday afternoon for a change. However, it has just been decreed that yet another match is to be switched. Our game at Sheffield Wednesday in early January will now be played on a Sunday afternoon for Sky's benefit. The club is considering whether to organise another plane trip, following the success of the one to Oldham. I suggested to Karen that, if we could get tickets again, she might like to travel with Mum this time and I would drive up from London to meet them. 'Aren't you forgetting someone?' she asked. I couldn't think who she meant. 'Someone who's coming to stay around that time?' The penny didn't drop until she started tapping the bulge in her belly. I had completely forgotten ab[out her being preg]nant. This bears out what I was saying earlier about not notic[ing] the appearance of people close to me, though it should be rememb[ered]. Karen has been in an almost continuous state of gravidity since she was 18; it [is] such a normal condition for her that I tend to forget when the babies are due.

'Couldn't you try to have it before the game?' I asked. 'Not too early, though – I don't want to have to rush out and buy another Christmas present at the last minute.' For some reason, this suggestion didn't go down too well. Must be her hormones going haywire and preventing her from spotting tongues firmly planted in cheeks. I tried to make amends by showing a fraternal/avuncular interest and asking how the pregnancy was progressing. It turns out that he/she keeps kicking hell out of Karen. 'I think it's going to be a striker,' she said. 'It'll probably leap out of the womb arms aloft, kiss the midwife and shout "One-nil!"' Ugh!

I asked if she'd thought of any names yet. In her pre-football days, she'd been very keen on the name Chelsea for a girl, and it had taken a lot of persuasion to make her change her mind. I hoped I wouldn't have to do the same thing again. 'We haven't decided yet', she replied. I suggested that, if it is a boy, he could be given the names of the first-team squad. Karen was unconvinced, though she did say she might consider Mark Robin or David Philip.

Mum, Stephen and I (Karen didn't feel too well) were rather later than usual in arriving at the ground for this match. The rain was pouring down, and we thought we would leave it until the last moment to go along to see if it eased off at all. It didn't. According to Bobby Charlton's daughter Suzanne (whose name I cannot mention without imagining what she would look like with a bald head and a few strands of hair swept over it – there, I've just done it again), this downpour was caused by a cold front sweeping across the country towards the east coast. Rubbish. It was caused by Michael Peck of Kendal, who refereed our soggy cup match at Blackburn recently and who had now brought the rain with him for this one. I think he should be obliged to inform the Met Office of his movements at all times, especially on bank holidays, so that we all know where to avoid.

We weren't too late to buy our Golden Goal tickets at Carrow Road, 'Perhaps you'll have a winner now that we've come at a different time,' Mum suggested to Stephen. His expression suggested that he didn't think this was very likely. Unfortunately, we were too late to secure our usual seats. We ended up having to sit right at the end of the stand, where the wind and rain were swirling around so that it was like being in a washing machine. On the cold cycle. We were all drenched before the game even started. Perhaps this was one game where I wouldn't be so animated. (If the stand were still a terrace, it is worth noting, it would have been possible to find a place out of the rain.)

I was further depressed when I was accosted by a woman who sits on the Capital Canaries committee. 'Wasn't that you I heard on the radio the other day?' she asked. I tried to protest my innocence, but to no avail. 'I'm sure it was you, saying what a miserable person you are.' And I thought no one would recognise me. Damn.

As in the Middlesbrough match, Norwich played towards the River End in the first half. On this occasion, however, it didn't seem such a bad sign, as we would at least be playing with the tide in the second half. Flippers rather than boots were the order of the day.

Despite the conditions, it turned out to be a cracking match. United started strongly, playing in a manner that gave the lie to the notion that all teams managed by Dave Bassett always play in an unsophisticated, hit-and-hope style. As the first half wore on, Norwich came more into the game, with Ruel Fox and Daryl Sutch flying down the wings. I use the word 'flying' deliberately in Fox's case – not because of 'flying foxes', but because the match programme revealed his middle name to be Adrian, which makes his initials R.A.F. These are the most amusing initials of any Norwich player since Viv Busby. He became the target of much laughter in the 1970s when it was discovered that his middle name is Dennis.

Somehow, the score was still 0-0 at half-time. Both teams left to great applause. Even the old boy sitting next to me in a Barbour patted the back of his hand in appreciation. Nice of him to put himself out, I thought.

During the break, a prize draw was held on the pitch, though it wasn't clear for some time what the prize was, as the announcer was quite unintelligible. I suspect that the loudspeakers at Carrow Road were bought second-hand from a British Rail station. Either that, or the announcer was. He sounded like a record being played backwards, though even the most fanatical Bible-basher would have been hard pressed to detect a message, demonic or otherwise. Fortunately, a man in front of us kindly explained that this was a draw for free air tickets to ... 'Sheffield Wednesday?' Mum interrupted excitedly.

'No,' the man replied, 'Amsterdam.' Mum seemed unimpressed. Apparently, the draw tickets had been handed out before the game, but being late, we'd missed out. When the winning number was chosen, the announcer asked the holder of this ticket to stand up and wave it. As one, ten thousand people rose and waved their tickets like the delegates at a Neville Chamberlain fan club convention. 'Oh, come on, play fair,' pleaded the announcer.

'What a shambles,' muttered Mum. 'I think I'd rather have the dancing girls out there again.'

'Would you go out there in a skimpy skirt in this weather?' asked the man in front.

'She'll do most things for a cup of tea and a pasty,' I said, and was rewarded with an elbow in the ribs.

The weather actually deteriorated still further during the interval, and we were now so wet that the oft-quoted statistic about the human body being 65 per cent water felt like a gross underestimate. Mum asked if her little boys wanted to go home and get out of the nasty rain. 'We'll just give it another 45 minutes and then go,' said Stephen.

Some people at the extreme end of the stand had belatedly decided to get up and put up their umbrellas. They weren't obscuring anyone's view, but a steward still came along and tried to get them to sit down. He didn't have any success, as his approach was as ineffectual as that of Sergeant Wilson in *Dad's Army*. 'I say, you chaps, would you mind awfully not standing up?' Those holding the brollies explained that they were trying not to catch pneumonia. At least, I assume that's what 'For cough' meant.

Amazingly, the quality of play remained wonderfully high in the second half. After sixty minutes, we finally took the lead, with Beckford's low, hard cross hitting a defender and just crossing the line before being hacked away. Beckford still tried to claim the goal. Soon after, United's veteran striker Alan Cork equalised with no Norwich defender within five yards of him. The idea that he may have outpaced our players even with his Zimmer frame is very worrying. Perhaps we should assume that the defence was simply showing him the deference due to persons of advanced years.

Stephen looked particularly miserable. Surely the Golden Goal curse hadn't struck again? It had. This time his ticket was five seconds too late. Mum and I would normally have wet ourselves at this point but, given the weather, it hardly seemed worth it.

Ten minutes from time, however, the buffeting wind felt like a gentle, fragrant zephyr and the hammering rain like droplets of blessed water sprinkled from an aspergill as City scored the winner. And what a winner. Phillips played a perfect forty-yard pass from the centre circle into the path of Fox, whose first-time cross was volleyed in at the near post from ten yards out by Robins as he ran in. According to Mike Walker, Beckford tried to claim this goal too.

Yeeesss! And Arsenal had lost 3-0 at Leeds, so we were now 4 points clear at the top of the league. Weather-beaten but victorious, we returned home eagerly looking forward to a hot cup of tea and warm reviews.

All we got was the tea. Once again, the national media were utterly uninterested in us. The match reporter on Ceefax clearly hadn't been to the game, describing Robins's winner as being a header at the far post instead of a shot at the near post. The ITN sports round-up led with the story of Arsenal's defeat, followed by Manchester United's game, followed by Manchester City's game, and only then made a slight and slighting reference to Norwich 'snatching' (i.e., seizing wrongfully) a late winner. *Match of the Day* devoted just over a minute to the highlights of the game, concluding: 'Waiting for Norwich to fade is becoming a time-consuming business.' Which was tantamount to saying: 'Why don't these bloody yokels get out of the way and let the proper teams through?'

I can just about accept the girl from work with whom I had lunch writing off our chances; as she admitted, she knows nothing about football. I can understand Norwich supporters being reluctant to get carried away too soon; after all, I am only just starting to believe myself. But for national television to sneer at us when we are well clear with a quarter of the season gone is frankly disgraceful.

At least the national papers are slowly beginning to take some notice. True, the *Mail on Sunday* had no report on our game, and the one in the *Observer* began: 'Turkey may have been on the end of a roasting last week [England won 4-0], but the Norfolk variety still rule the roost in the Premier League.' But the *Sunday Times* gave us a glowing report, and even the *Guardian* commented that 'one should not assume that Norwich are simply there for the plucking.'

I am also pleased to see that no newspaper has yet made the appalling geographical error of describing Norwich as a Fenland town. This happens most seasons, and it isn't just the tabloid reporters who get it wrong. I distinctly remember a *Times* journalist reporting that, after a stirring midweek cup victory, 'the cheers from Carrow Road rang out around the surrounding Fens'. Mind you, I suppose it is possible that he actually said 'fans' to the copytaker on the other end of the phone, but his posh accent was misunderstood.

I wondered whether our Sunday-morning match would be on this week after we had had so much rain, but the groundsman didn't seem concerned with the mass of slippery yet clinging mud or Olympic-size pools of water on the pitch. I got the impression that, even if a bomb were to land on the pitch, he would dismiss the resulting crater as a divot and tell us to get on with it.

The game wasn't bad in the circumstances, and we held on for another 2-2 draw thanks to another late penalty. This was a particularly good result as only ten players turned up – and we were reduced to nine for fifteen minutes of the second half when one of our centre-backs remembered he had to ring for a motor insurance quote and went to look for a phone box.

I got back to the flat just in time to catch the start of the Wolves-Charlton game on TV. I settled down to watch it but, on waking two hours later, I discovered that Wolves had won 2-1. Just as well I missed it, I suppose.

Saturday 28 November
Aston Villa (away)

a) I spent four and a half crazy years in Birmingham. Friday nights at the bar in the Midland Hotel (I haven't always been teetotal), late-night film shows at the Midland Arts Centre, sweaty gigs at the Hummingbird club, that blues party in Hockley two days before the Handsworth riots. And, of course, meeting the Wolverine.

b) I was crazy to spend four and a half years in Birmingham. The concrete misery of the city centre, the bleak job-free zones dotted around it, the legions of prostitutes in Balsall Heath, the stench of bad chips, samosas and sick on the late-night buses, the difficulty of getting back to Norwich without a car. And, of course, meeting the Wolverine.

Which of the two versions above is closer to the truth? You may as well decide, because I'm blowed if I can.

Travelling back to Birmingham this weekend, I was more concerned with the match than with my memories of my time there. It would only be a flying visit after all, and I wouldn't be going anywhere near where I used to live. Villa Park is in the north of Birmingham, very close to the M6. It used to be easy to pick out the ground from there when it had large floodlight pylons with the lights in the shape of A and V, but these have now been taken down. I hoped we could dart in, pick up the 3 points, and make off before anyone noticed.

On arriving at the ground, I wondered if I might make off with more than that. Inside was a Ladbrokes betting kiosk, with boards showing the prices for the scorer of the first goal and the score at full-time.

Apart from doing the pools every week, I'm not really a betting man. I'll stick a fiver on a horse in the National, but that's about it. I daren't put money on Norwich winning a trophy, as this would be the kiss of death – as proved in 1987 when I had a rush of blood to the head and put £20 on us to win the FA Cup. We lost 1-0 at Wigan in the next round.

So why was I tempted to have a bet here? I still don't know exactly. I had accumulated a lot of change in my pockets that I wanted to get rid of, and the odds on offer looked rather attractive. I decided to risk a pound – then, at the last moment as I waited in the queue, two pounds – on Norwich winning 3-2 at odds of 50-1. At least this would keep me in with a chance for some time, I thought. If you go for 1-0 and the wrong team scores in the first minute, that's it. You've lost. Besides which, we have been scoring and conceding a lot of goals this season.

I didn't consider betting against Norwich for a moment. I know some City fans who do this in the belief that, if we lose, the winnings offer some sort of consolation. I can't come to terms with this at all. When Norwich lose, no amount of money – with the possible exception of a multi-million-pound pools win at the end of a season when we are in mid-table – can make up for it. I would feel guilty and ashamed at having profited from our defeat. The only justification I can see for betting against Norwich is if you are trying to divert your bad luck in the bookie's on to the opposition.

Having bought a steak and kidney pie ($^7/_{10}$ – not bad at all), I settled down to watch Aston Villa thrash Norwich 9-2. In a ladies' five-a-side match in one corner of the pitch, you understand. What really caught my eye, however, was how few police officers there were in evidence. Instead, there seemed to be more stewards and crowd control officers with walkie-talkies scurrying around than usual. More and more clubs are trying to replace police officers with stewards for financial reasons, but this is an especially welcome development at Villa Park. On previous visits, I have found the members of the West Midlands force to be so surly and unpleasant, I'd swear they were trying to get talent-spotted by the Serious Crimes Squad. The worst occasion was a couple of years ago, when we drew 3-3 in a game at the end of the season. As we jumped around to celebrate City's opening goal, a pointy-headed posse charged in among us for the rest of the first half (a good thirty minutes) so that I couldn't see a thing. One Norwich fan then spotted a friend of his a few yards away on the terrace and called and waved to attract his attention. This was interpreted as being a provocative gesture – and when the fan tried to explain himself, the police decided that he must have been giving a signal to start a riot and gave him a stern warning. When Villa equalised, thousands of home fans began gesticulating at the massive Holte End. Our innocent subversive rashly pointed this out and suggested that the attention of the constabulary should be directed towards them instead. He was immediately surrounded by several thick-necked upholders of the law, one of whom put his nose so close to the fan's that I suspected he must be of Innuit stock. He threatened him at length about what could happen to him if he persisted with his insolence, such as being detained at the local nick until the early hours of Sunday morning, when he would be released – presumably for lack of evidence, though this has not always been a concern in the past.

What is it about the police in the Midlands? If Sting had been born in Birmingham rather than Newcastle, I doubt whether he'd have been so keen to name his group after the local force. If he had, some of his compositions might have turned out very differently. 'Falsified Message In A Bottle'. 'The Cell's Too Big Without You'. 'Every Breath You Take May Be Used In Evidence Against You'. 'De Did Did Did De Didn't Didn't ... Ooof, Ow, Ouch, OK, I did'.

This match had been built up all week as the biggest test yet of Norwich's credibility as title contenders. Villa were on an unbeaten run of thirteen matches and being tipped by more and more people as potential champions. As the loudspeakers blared out *We Will Rock You* and 29,000 voices roared the teams on to the pitch, I wondered whether the occasion might make City too tense and nervous to be able to perform.

It soon became clear that they felt enormously confident. They were even laughing and smiling. When Gunn needed two attempts to turn a shot over the bar, when Culverhouse knocked the ball just a yard wide of his own goal, when the strikers missed good chances, no one shouted angrily or apportioned blame. They actually joked about it.

The confidence of the team spread to the supporters and was boosted when David Phillips scored after a wonderful, sweeping move involving Crook, Sutch, Fox and Robins. Fox and Beckford then missed one-on-ones with Spink in the

Aston Villa (a) 141

Villa goal, and a deflected Phillips shot dipped just over. Eventually, after a succession of corners, Beckford prodded home the second from close range. 'We don't need a cheque book, we don't need a cheque book, la la la la', sang the Norwich end, followed by a quick burst of 'Cheque book 0 Norwich 2, Hallelujah'.

Villa weren't in the game at all. The only player to catch the eye on their side was a young defender called Ehiogu, and that was because he was playing so badly, he'd struggle to get in our Sunday side. Even if we only had ten players turn up. Apparently, he is a regular in the England Under-21 side. I may be guilty of bias here, but how on earth is he keeping Chris Sutton out?

The referee, Alf Buksh, felt sorry for Villa. At least, I assume that was why he played over three minutes of injury time at the end of a half in which there had been no injuries, time-wasting or other long stoppages. He seemed determined to play on until Villa scored, no matter how long it took. Sure enough, they got a goal back when a long-range shot from Houghton squeezed under Gunn's diving body like a rabbit scurrying away from a falling oak tree. Or Scots pine.

Poo.

At half-time, the man who had been sitting next to me wandered off and a different one took his place. While I was still fuming at Villa's late goal, my new neighbour was simply relieved that he was still in one piece. He had come to the game with a Villa fan and stood with him at the Holte End. When Norwich had dared to score not once, but twice, he realised from the looks and comments around him that he ought to move for his own safety. The police, who had not been responsible for the looks and comments on this occasion, had brought him down to our end.

He had come all the way from Spain to see the game. 'I've been living out there for two years,' he said, 'but with the boys doing so well, I had to come back and watch them.' From Spain? And I thought I'd done well to get to Carlisle. Mind you, if he was such a big fan, how could he possibly consider moving abroad in the first place?

'The last time I came here, we drew 3-3,' he went on.

'I know the game you mean,' I replied – then, at precisely the same moment, we both added, 'Rosario scored!' The rarity of such an event made it memorable – even more so than the actions of the police that day.

Twenty-two seconds into the second half, the score was 2-2. The home crowd roared again, and for a minute we wondered whether the game was about to slip away from us. But only for a minute. Then Daryl Sutch drove the ball home to put us 3-2 up.

Three-two? Hang on, that was the score I'd put my money on! I didn't allow myself to get too excited, though. After all, there were still over forty minutes left to play.

With ten minutes left, however, my hopes (and greed) refused to be restrained any longer. A hundred pounds might soon be mine! Pity I hadn't put on a fiver – I'd have stood to pick up £250. Or a tenner, to win £500. Or a hundred, to ... no, it was ridiculous to think like this. I told myself I should be grateful I'd changed the bet from one pound to two.

With the clock showing 89 minutes, I was presented with a dreadful moral dilemma. Mark Robins had broken through and was bearing down on the Villa goal. What did I want him to do? Should he score and make the game safe, or miss for the sake of my bet? A third option would have been to take the ball to the corner flag and stand on it to waste some time, but this only occurred to me afterwards.

I am being utterly honest when I say that I really wanted Robins to score – but I have to admit that, when he squared the ball to Sutch and his shot was charged down for a corner, I clenched my fist and hissed 'Yesss!' This might, I guess, have attracted inquisitive looks from the Norwich fans around me had I not already told them about my prospective winnings.

A nerve-racking three minutes later, the final whistle signalled that 3 points and a hundred quid had been secured. Yeeaahhooo!! Our visitor from Spain thumped me on the back so enthusiastically that I began to wonder if I was being mugged without realising it.

My first coherent thought was to find a phone and tell Stephen about my good fortune. Yet when I did so later, he sounded less than delighted for me. Perhaps I shouldn't have kept saying what a shame it was that he has been so unlucky with his Golden Goal tickets this season. Karen was scarcely more congratulatory. 'Why don't the people who really deserve it ever win? Like me?' And Mum seemed worried that I might take up gambling more seriously after this. She needn't be. I know I should quit while I'm ahead.

My second thought was of all the Villa fans I had known and who had given me stick when I lived in Birmingham. I knew that they knew that I would be at the game and going mad about the result. I was the only Norwich fan whom any of them had ever met, which I usually find to be the case as there aren't that many of us around the country. In all the time I travelled to Norwich matches from Birmingham, I never met a fellow Canary on the train.

My third thought was of the Wolverine, whom I had arranged to visit after the match. Did I not mention that I rang her last weekend? It must have slipped my mind. They say that good things come in threes; after the victories against Villa and Ladbrokes, would I now receive a warm welcome from her?

Unusually, I did. Whenever she had greeted me with the enquiry 'How are you?' in the past, she had managed to make it sound defensive and hostile, but this time she seemed almost affectionate. Even Wolves' win over Grimsby in the afternoon couldn't entirely account for this. Something was different today.

We nattered away, with me annoying her by telling her about my successful bet and her annoying me by telling me about a football rule change of which I had been quite unaware. In the Barclays League, teams on the same number of points are ranked according to the number of goals they have scored rather than on goal difference. After the initial shock of being told something I didn't know about football by the Wolverine, I thought again what a wonderful woman she was.

After about an hour, I was just telling her that I had considered buying her a Wolves shirt for Christmas, but that all the ones I had seen in the shops had dirty black marks on them (and she was unnecessarily pointing out that they are supposed to look like that) when the living-room door opened and the boyfriend walked in. So that was why she had been acting in such a friendly way. She had felt more confident and assured because her loved one had been upstairs all the time.

Quite why she loved him was not immediately apparent. Come to that, it didn't become apparent either. It couldn't be for his looks. He's into cricket but, judging by his waistline, he would be best employed as a sightscreen. He's also into playing Nintendo computer games. In fact, that's what he'd been doing upstairs all afternoon, even ignoring the phone when it rang in the middle of a game. He'd only come down to watch *Noel's House Party* (having set the video for *Gladiators* on the other side) before going out to have a skinful with his mates. 'Got any money?' he asked her. He had a slab of cake for his tea. 'She don't feed me properly, you know,' he muttered three times in twenty minutes. Probably because she can't find a trough big enough, I thought.

Even with my low opinion of myself, I couldn't believe that the Wolverine preferred him to me. There was no logic to it at all. And to think that Mensa is based in Wolverhampton. I decided to cut short my visit and headed outside to the refuge of my car.

I had a lot to think about on the way back to London. And a long time to think about it, as there were the usual long hold-ups on the M1. Meeting the boyfriend had done more to put me off the Wolverine than the four years of failure with her had. If he was what she wanted in a man, she wasn't worth bothering with. Another sign that she had lost much of her allure was the fact that I was still in a good mood. The 3 points won during the afternoon seemed of far greater significance than my subsequent disappointment at her house. On the other hand, I still couldn't picture her face, so she must still mean something to me.

Perhaps I was being unfair to her, I thought. It wasn't her fault that she wasn't the girl I'd imagined her to be. Nor was it her fault that she loved her boyfriend, as she had presumably had as little choice in the matter as I had had when I met her. And the boyfriend may have had some good qualities; I may have been blind to them just as I often refuse to acknowledge the merits of opposing teams on a Saturday afternoon.

Should I let the whole thing drop once more? Or should I go charging back up to Wolverhampton on a magnificent white steed and offer to take her away from all that? It's all so complicated and confusing. I'm going to need some time to decide what to do next.

If only love were as simple and easy to understand as football, I could cope with it. Or am I over-complicating love just as some people over-complicate football? Possibly. After all, on the rare occasions I have tried to shake off the shackles of the male stereotype and talk about my feelings to colleagues at work, the response has been: 'Cut the crap, Kev, have you nailed her yet?' Ah, the route one approach, I presume.

I had a bit of a shock when watching *Match of the Day* back at the flat. After our first goal, they showed a section of the crowd celebrating. Look at that sad loser in the middle, I thought. Then I realised it was me. Thank goodness the programme doesn't run a Twat of the Month competition.

It was less of a shock to hear Gary Lineker and Alan Hansen in the studio again ruling out any chance of us carrying off the title. It seems that, however well we play, and however far in front we get (5 points now), we are still less likely to win the Championship than a hippo riding a gerbil is to win the Grand National.

Still, the bookies have now reduced our title odds to 10-1. The price was 250-1 at the start of the season. Pity I didn't stick a couple of quid on that. Or a fiver. Or a tenner. Or ... And the national papers are finally being fulsome in their praise. Take the *Sunday Times* (no, not necessarily every week – just read this bit): 'Marvellous. Breathtaking. Thanks for lifting us out of our seats. Norwich have decided the only way of making off with the Championship is by throwing caution to the wind and slugging it out with all-comers. It's brave and it's glorious.' Or the *Sunday Telegraph*: 'There is a bit of Brazil about Norwich ... and a dash of the Dutch too.' True, that reporter went on to say that City defended like East Stirlingshire at times, but we'll forgive him this time.

On Sunday evening, I was outside the block of flats where I live when another tenant (with whom I was previously only on nodding terms) came up and congratulated me on the way Norwich are playing. I didn't know he knew which team I support, but I suppose the inflatable canary in the window must have given it away. He turned out to be a Barnet fan, and we talked about football in the cold drizzle for a good twenty minutes. A very good twenty minutes, in fact. It's not often that football creates an instant, unexpected bond like this. It should, of course. But the infrequency of it does make it all the more enjoyable when it happens.

At work on Monday morning, I found that even my colleagues were treating me with new, albeit slightly grudging, respect. It was as if they had suddenly recognised a truth that I had known all along. When I told them about the hundred pounds I had won, they looked at me as if I had been blessed with some sort of divine wisdom. I didn't disillusion them.

Instead, I took the opportunity to go around and sarcastically ask all the Arsenal fans how their side had done on Saturday. I knew full well they had lost. This worried me afterwards. I mean, do supporters behave more irritatingly the more successful their team is? I hope I get to find out.

Saturday 5 December
Wimbledon (home)

I pulled a muscle in my leg during the week. I wasn't on a training run, though I should have done one this week as we didn't have a game last Sunday morning. I did it running for a train. I could see the headlines: 'Baldwin in big match injury scare'; 'Freak accident set to axe balding maestro'. Accordingly, I hobbled down the road and got the best treatment 69p can buy – a packet of frozen peas. It was a bit of an extravagance, I suppose, but the peas will always come in. I was all set to have a fitness test on Thursday, but I heard just in time that the game was off anyway. The pitch has, astonishingly enough, been declared unfit. Perhaps two bombs landed on it.

I wasn't the only one in the family to be incapacitated, though. When I arrived at Mum's on Friday night, I found her flat on her back on the floor. No, she wasn't paying the milkman. Her back had gone. What's more, it had gone so suddenly that it hadn't left a note to say whether it would be back for Saturday afternoon. It hadn't returned by Saturday morning, so I had to make the trip to the butcher's for Mum. 'Which one is Michael Fish?' I asked before I set off.

'Who?'

'The crap forecaster.'

'His name's Terry.'

It took a moment for the penny to drop. 'That's why he doesn't know anything about football,' I said. 'Terry Butcher!'

He realised who I was anyway when I asked to pay a couple of quid towards Mum's Christmas club. As soon as I gave her name, he tried to wind me up about the team in her place. When I refused to take the bait, he asked me to pass on a message to Mum instead. 'Tell her Wimbledon will win 2-0.'

From the butcher's, I went to buy my Christmas cards. This year, I have bought a load with a robin on the front. I've drawn on a black eye and added the caption: 'There's only one marked robin.' Geddit? Oh, never mind. I did see a card featuring a snowman wearing a yellow and green scarf being peed on by a dog. What's the betting that the Wolverine sends me that one?

Mum was still in pain when I got back from the shops. 'Will you be able to go?' I asked.

'Don't talk bloody silly,' she answered. 'Of course I'm going.'

I should have known. She's as bad as me for disregarding ill-health to see Norwich play. Though as I derive from her genes, it would be more accurate to say that I'm as bad as her. A prime example of this occurred a few years ago when Mum, Stephen and I were walking to Carrow Road on a bitterly cold afternoon to watch Norwich v Bradford City. We all had our hands in our pockets – but as we crossed the river bridge near the ground, Mum tripped on the metal 'hinge' where the bridge lifts up to allow tall boats to pass underneath. She didn't manage to get her hands out of her pockets in time, and toppled face-first on to the tarmac. Some people rushed to see if she was all right. Others rushed to see if the bridge was all right.

Mum had a cut lip, a bleeding nose, broken glasses, and one eye starting to puff up and turn black already. I didn't like the look of her at all. Mind you ... no, I won't say it. Yet despite all this, and the fact that she was severely dazed, she still stood and watched the whole game. Which, in the event, turned out to be a rather dull 0-0 draw.

When the neighbours heard that she had done this, they were astonished, even though they knew what she was like. She tried to explain that it had simply not occurred to her to return home or to go to a first-aid post for treatment. They assumed that the bump on her head was serious and started to criticise me instead for not bringing her home. But this had never occurred to me. If she had been really badly hurt, I would have called her a taxi, but as her injuries were merely disfiguring rather than disabling, I saw no reason why she or I should miss the game.

In any case, Mum used her black eye and cuts to her advantage in the days that followed, frightening people by pointing at her wounds and snarling, 'I got this down at the football.' The butcher gave her some meat to put on her eye, but she brought it home and used it in a casserole.

We left particularly early for the Wimbledon match because of Mum's bad back, my bad leg and the bad seats we had at the last home game. Stephen wondered whether our early arrival would improve his luck with the Golden Goal tickets. 'When are you going to sell me a winner?' he asked the man we always buy them from. 'I'm always a second or two out.'

The seller informed him that one woman had won £100 and £50 at successive matches. 'That's not fair. One of those wins should be mine.' Stephen formulated a plan to lie in wait for the said woman and, when she appeared, to push in front of her and buy the tickets she was going to have. However, Mum reminded him that we had come early to get decent seats, so we moved on.

We ended up sitting near two familiar faces. There was the Foghorn, though we did not spot him at first as we were sitting behind him. We only realised he was there when we found it difficult to breathe because he was sucking in the air from the whole stand before bellowing 'COME ON, YOU YELLOWS!' so loudly that earwax suddenly seemed an attractive proposition.

And Mum recognised a girl who used to work at the newsagent's across the road and who now does light gardening jobs with a friend. 'You can come and dig my garden for me,' said Mum. 'I've asked these two to do it, but they never get round to it.' Stephen and I rubbed our backs and claimed unconvincingly that they had come out in sympathy with Mum's.

'OK,' said the girl. 'We'll come round next week.' You hear a lot about business being done on the golf course, but this was the first time I'd seen a deal made in a football crowd. They didn't discuss a price, which was just as well since Mum didn't seem to be thinking straight, either because of her painful back or the painfully cold weather. 'There aren't many Tottenham fans here today,' she remarked.

'There wouldn't be,' I said. 'We're playing Wimbledon today.' I don't know how she could have confused the two. I mean, Norwich fans wouldn't be singing 'What's it like to see a crowd?' to Spurs supporters.

The standard of the game didn't make Mum feel any better. Wimbledon were living down to their reputation and making this the ugliest game I'd seen since – oh, their last visit, probably. Their methods could best be described as 'football interruptus'. They kept pushing up to the half-way line for offsides and pushing our players in the back when the referee wasn't looking. There were more high balls than in a planeload of giraffes, and more than once the ball was booted at close range into the family enclosure. The old joke about the ball having to be stretchered off injured in Wimbledon matches didn't seem too far removed from the truth. Ah, the beautiful game.

It says a lot when Wimbledon's most cultured and best-behaved player was one Vincent Jones. He was presumably on his least bad behaviour because he is appealing against a £20,000 fine and a six-month suspended ban imposed on him by the FA for his comments on a video entitled *Soccer's Hard Men*.

> For he dide telle, thogh pardoun he doth begge,
> How playeres raken studdes upon a legge;
> And eke how men do maken oother harme
> Whan that they tuggen hayres beneath the arme.
> The FA yaf nat bugerie for swich trickes,
> And smote hym as they were a tonne of brickes.
> Ageyns the fyne this Vinny hath appeeled;
> Woude that he were appeelyng on the feilde.
>
> Geoffrey Chaucer, etc. etc.

The referee seemed unable to cope with the organised mayhem going on all around him and lost control to the extent that he got even the simplest, clearest decisions wrong. The worst mistake was when a Wimbledon player rose a foot above Ian Butterworth (how?) to head the ball out for a corner, only for the git in green to give a goal kick. Mum wasn't the only one to stand up and offer the ref her glasses. She was the only one to shout, 'The referee's a lovechild'.

Norwich couldn't seem to get going at all, and the supporters gradually became as rattled as the players. Loud cheers rang out whenever a Wimbledon player was fouled or injured – a sure sign that the Dons had succeeded in determining the moral climate in which the match was to be conducted.

Half-time offered a brief respite to our battered sensibilities and gave us a chance to restore some feeling to our frozen hands by putting gloves on. You can't wear them when the game's on, as the crowd's applause would sound as vibrant as a granny plumping up the sofa cushions. Clapping normally helps to keep your hands warm in the coldest weather, but today there had been nothing at all worth applauding.

Things couldn't stay this bad in the second half, we thought – and they didn't. They got worse. After sixty minutes, Sanchez scored for Wimbledon, and it looked as if they might keep up their record of getting results against the top teams this season. So far, they have won only three league games – but these were away at Liverpool and Manchester United and at home to Arsenal. City didn't seem likely to score at all. Indeed, we almost went 2-0 down when John Fashanu, who had come on as a substitute, fired in a fierce shot that Gunn just managed to beat away.

Fashanu has been even less popular at Carrow Road than most returning ex-Norwich players. This is largely because he is still blamed for ending the career of John O'Neill after only 34 minutes of his City debut in 1987, but even before that he was disliked for his style of play. In fact, Mum loathes him so much that on one occasion her abuse of him attracted the attention of the Metropolitan Police. At a match at Plough Lane (it may have been the O'Neill game, now I come to think of it), she had been moaning about him solidly since the pre-match warm-up. When Wimbledon scored at the other end of the pitch, it was Fashanu who got the goal.

'Who scored?' asked Mum, who wasn't sure. I told her. 'OH, SHIT ON HIM!' she shouted – and a few steps down from us, two policemen swung round to see who was swearing. On seeing it was Mum, they looked at each other, raised their eyebrows, shook their heads and looked away again.

People often ask me if I worry about hooliganism at matches when Mum is there. I generally reply that, as long as I am there to keep her under control, no one should get hurt. And she hasn't pissed in anyone's pocket since I took her funnel off her. (It's only a joke, Mum.)

Fashanu has been doing his best to shake off his 'Fash the Bash' tag lately. After all, he has his career as a wholesome TV presenter to consider (though whether *Gladiators* can be described as wholesome TV is debatable). However, some of his challenges today would not have been suitable for broadcasting before the 9pm watershed. I assume he was wearing red boots so that any spilt blood would not show up.

Twelve minutes from time, we somehow managed an equaliser. The ball fell kindly for Robins after he had attempted a header and failed to make proper contact, and he happily thumped it in from six yards out. The sigh of relief around the ground was visible as well as audible, with everyone's breath steaming in the cold air. A point was probably as much as we deserved, and certainly more than we had looked like gaining, but in the final minute a low Fox cross reached Phillips at the far post, and he duly tapped it home. We all went berserk – including Mum, whose back had apparently been miraculously cured.

'I thought you couldn't move,' I said, tapping her on the shoulder. It was like watching one of those cartoon characters that runs off the end of a cliff and continues to run on thin air until he notices, or is informed, that he should not be able to do this – at which point he plummets into a ravine.

'Oh, yes,' Mum said, and gingerly sat down again. It had been a telling, if transient, example of how football can help you to forget your problems and ailments – though, of course, there are times when the game gives you more worries and concerns than you had in the first place.

In certain respects, this win was even more encouraging than the one at Aston Villa last week. Teams who win Championships have to be resilient and tenacious enough to pick up points when they are not playing well and the cause looks lost, and it would be hard to find a better example of this than the game we had witnessed here.

But perhaps the best aspect of the result was that it put us 8, yes 8, points clear at the top of the league. We heard by listening to other people's radios as we gleefully mounted Jimmy Hill (despite Mum singing 'We are top of the league') that all our rivals had lost. Even so, I still needed to see the table on Teletext before I could believe we were so far clear. Stephen still couldn't. 'Are you sure that isn't a misprint?' he asked.

Interestingly, I read somewhere during the week that Nantes are now 4 points clear in the French league. Like Norwich, they are unfashionable – and they play in yellow and green! OK, so that wasn't so interesting. Try these facts, then. We have already won more league games than we did in the whole of last season. And, last time, it took us until the end of February to accumulate as many points as we have now (39). It looks as though those cries of 'Safe by Christmas!' may prove to be astute forecasts.

The draw for the third round of the FA Cup was made on Sunday afternoon. Unfortunately, it was made on Sky, so Mum and I had to wait for it to come up on Teletext. Somehow, this doesn't have the same sense of occasion or nervous anticipation as listening to the draw on the radio at Monday lunchtime, with the hushed, reverential voice of the presenter introducing us to the mysterious and otherwise impenetrable inner sanctum of the FA headquarters, the tantalising clicking of the committee's balls increasing the tension more than a drum-roll could, and the calling-out of the numbers, when you would try and fail to guess which teams they corresponded to before their identities were announced. Anyway, we've been drawn home to Coventry. It could be worse. At least it's not Blackburn away.

Saturday 12 December
Manchester United (away)

Alex Ferguson, the United manager, frequently refers to Old Trafford as the 'theatre of dreams'. At present, however, the old Stretford End (to be renamed the West Stand when rebuilding is complete) most resembles the remains of the original Globe theatre that were discovered a few years ago. Still, any excuse for a bit of Shakespeare...

> O! How on Saturdays the ditch-drab lanes
> Of England's motorways are transform'd quite,
> When divers-colour'd scarves from windows waft,
> To sundry lords allegiance to avouch.
> Here, one from th'Orient of Leyton comes;
> There, one from Luton flies in esperance
> (Too fond, I fear) that they may Wolves unfang
> And leave them, sans teeth, to behowl the moon.
> From Wycombe too, though lowly of estate,
> An army pours; yet this is but a speck
> To that which from each corner o' the realm,
> United unto Manchester doth hie.
> Their blood-red favours do the road englut,
> That they seem arteries flowing to the heart,
> The seat of their affection and their passion.
> So fair and foul a sight I have not seen;
> Would that there were the like in yellow and green.
>
> *As You Leg It*

The oddest scarf I saw on the way to the game was in Altrincham. A car with an Ipswich scarf across the rear window had stopped outside a pub and the driver, wearing an Ipswich shirt, was getting out. Now, Ipswich were playing Manchester City... but in Ipswich. Could this man have travelled to the wrong place by mistake? Ha! Ha! Ha!

My progress to Old Trafford was straightforward enough until I approached the ground.

First Wretch: Gentle sir, a word, I thee entreat:
Dost thou for the match require a seat?
Me: No, i'faith.

Second Wretch: Thou art of judgement sound.
So buy instead this T-shirt for a pound.
Me: Ne'er, I say.
Third Wretch: Perchance a Santa hat
Thou wouldst fain acquire.
Me: And look a prat?
Fie! Importunate curs that dog my steps,
Base knaves with ill-won tickets overpric'd
And false apparel; nay, I'll not buy aught.
Take, I conjure, your wares and scuttle hence,
And on your very heads a pestilence.

The Merchants of Tat

You find touts and tat-sellers at most grounds, of course, but not as many as there were here. The sordidness contrasted markedly with the grandeur of (most of) the stadium. Visiting Old Trafford is always a highlight of the season and is one of the reasons why clubs want to be in the top division. Even during the summer, thousands of people visit the museum and go on guided tours.

Having said all that, I have to admit I've never liked Manchester United. I can't explain why; there doesn't seem to be a particular reason I can put my finger on. It's not because United have bought some of our best players, such as Bruce and Phelan. It's not because they generally beat us. In fact, our record against them is quite good. And if I were going to dislike any club on such grounds, it would be Manchester City. It's not because United fans wrecked Carrow Road in 1977. My antipathy began long before then. I can remember going to bed in tears the night they won the European Cup in 1968, as I'd wanted Benfica to win.

Perhaps my feelings towards United are merely another example of my general perverseness. With the obvious exceptions of Liverpool and Manchester City supporters, most of the country seems to hold United in affection, presumably through continuing sympathy after the Munich air crash of 1958. This happened well before I was born and thus could make no immediate impact on me, but it is possible that I have simply reacted against the subsequent wave of support.

Certainly, I couldn't help laughing when United threw the Championship away to Leeds last season after being in so strong a position that the bookies had stopped taking bets. I chuckled when I heard about the supporter who had a 'Man. Utd – Champions '91-'92' tattoo etched on his arm three weeks before the end of the season. I smirked when the 'arsonist' joke did the rounds, even though it wasn't really that funny. (In case you're the one person who hasn't heard it, it goes: What's the difference between Manchester United and an arsonist? An arsonist wouldn't throw away his last three matches.)

It was as if they were destined not to win the title, even though they thought they were assured of it ...

152   *Norfolk 'n' Good*

> Alex Ferguson: How now, you hags! Vouchsafe to me anon,
> Which club shall in the Championship prevail.
> First Witch: One who for United plays
> Shall the argent trophy raise.
> Second Witch: Manag'd be the team by one
> Whose last name doth end in 'son'.
> Fergie: These words do seem to victory portend,
> And yet I fear equivocation still.
> Third Witch: Know then that the captain hard
> Oft for Manchester hath starr'd.
> Fergie: Upon mine ears these foresights fall as balm.
> I'th'lists of battle none can do us harm!
>
> *All's Ill That Ends Ill*

Pity he forgot that Gordon Strachan was 'from United's womb untimely ripp'd.'

The facilities at the ground had been improved considerably since last season. Perhaps they're going to rename it New Trafford eventually. There was a new refreshment bar, new decor ... but the same old pies, which were so bland as to rate only $^5/_{10}$ on the Gourmand Scale.

Looking down on the pitch before the players came out to warm up, I noticed a lot of strange advertisements around the perimeter. It appeared that the game was being shown live in Scandinavia, as many of the hoardings were in Swedish. One in particular caught my eye: it said 'Marknadhuset'. Was this Swedish for 'Mark Hughes'? I hoped it wasn't an omen.

It was the appearance of Mark Robins that was most keenly anticipated. After all, we had signed him from United just before the start of the season, and the media had been building up his homecoming all week.

> Vermilion was the Robins breast from birth:
> With valour he his office hath fulfill'd,
> Was cherish'd by the fans withal; and yet
> For Ferguson's designs he was not meet
> And unto Norwich cheaply sold straightway.
> In teeming foison did his goals spring forth,
> While fallow lay the vanguard of the Reds.
> Most dolorous was the plaint that then ensured,
> From those who Fergie's judgement did dispute.
> And though he did protest, 'O! 'Tis not so!'
> More crimson grew his visage with each goal.
> Would Robins's former deeds now be forgot
> And he incur the general mock before
> Old Trafford's vast calumniating hordes?
> Or would they do him reverence as of old?

The answer presently they did declare:
'There's only one Mark Robins' fill'd the air.

Much Ado About Robins

Such a welcome from the United fans was impressive and heartening, though I hadn't really expected anything less. The regard they had for Robins was evident from an incident I heard about just after the start of the season. Apparently, Robins's father, who as I mentioned is a high-ranking police officer, heard a knock at the front door one evening and was confronted by a tough-looking skinhead wielding a bottle. To his surprise, it turned out to be a bottle of champagne, and the skinhead asked him to pass it on to Mark with his best wishes.

The only unfortunate aspect of the warm reception accorded to Robins was that it reduced the chances of him scoring. If you recall, the success of a player on his return to a former club is inversely proportional to how much the supporters there thought of him. Still, I was confident he would score at least once and that we would win. In fact, every Norwich fan I know had been convinced for weeks that we would pick up 3 points here.

Despite the small allocation of tickets we had been given for this game, the Norwich contingent made a lot of noise, with several loud renditions of 'On the ball, City'. The mention of the word 'City' didn't seem to go down too well with the United fans, but even so they remained as quiet as a long pause in a Pinter play.

Perhaps their ardour had been quenched by the rain that was inevitably pelting down:

> The quality of weather is not fine;
> It pisseth as a hosepipe upon the earth beneath.
> In Manchester is jocund day unknown,
> As Phoebus' chariot were broken down
> And ne'er by th'AA man could be repair'd.
> In fiery climes Red Devils ought to dwell,
> But here the rain doth make a wat'ry hell.

The Tempest

At the old Stretford End, which has no roof as yet, the United fans had been given clear polythene covers as they entered the ground. Goggles and snorkels might have come in handy as well.

City began the game brightly enough, but after only ten minutes, Ian Crook pulled a muscle in his calf. Rather like me, in fact. Should I send him my packet of frozen peas? He couldn't move at all, and as his immobility immediately handed United two clear chances (thankfully missed), he had to be replaced by Gary Megson. The latter didn't do badly, but we really missed Crook's ability to change the angle of attack and unlock defences with long, accurate passes. We didn't seem to be getting anywhere at all.

> This cunning Fox, whose silken dalliance
> Upon the wing defences hath beguil'd,
> Was hounded and immur'd within his lair.
> ('Forsooth,' quoth one, 'our Ruel rules not.')
> E'en his playfellow Sutch, for such is he,
> Could not, alack, his iron shackles shed.
> 'Gainst Pallister, the tow'ring citadel,
> And marble-constant Bruce (as Judas known),
> Had Beckford and Mark Robins scant success;
> Save once, when Providence the leather orb
> Unto the boot of Robins did supply.
> It were a goal, had not the Danish foot
> O'th'Reds custodian dash'd it from its path.
> The Norwich fans did void their rheum in woe
> And rail'd at cruel Fortune's latest blow.

The Taming of the Canaries

Just before half-time, United missed two golden opportunities to score. One of them fell to Eric Cantona, who was making his home debut, though up to then he had been invisible. A case of 'Où est Cantona?' rather than 'Ooh aah Cantona'. More worrying, however, was the fact that the Norwich players had started to argue with each other, in marked contrast to the good humour that had been evident at Aston Villa.

During the break, I bumped into some fellow members of Capital Canaries. One handed me a piece of paper which turned out to be a photocopy of an article written by the chairman of our committee for the local paper in Norwich. (How did Mum miss it?) In his piece, he talked of the difficulties involved in following City from London and stated that 'to see all the games, you need an understanding boss, a good car and a lot of money'. Well, I've got a car anyway ...

He went on to mention me by name and revealed how much it had cost me to get to Carlisle. Yes! A hat-trick! Having featured on the radio and TV already this year, I'm now in the papers! I wonder if I'll start getting fan mail to go with my new-found fame. Perhaps I'll get a free ticket to a match if anyone at the club saw the feature. Then again, perhaps I won't.

I also saw Jon, to whom I'd given a lift before the Middlesbrough game. Then, he had told me about someone who spent even more money than me to get to Carlisle. Now he outdid me again. I was half-way through telling him about the hundred quid I'd won at Villa Park when I noticed he was doing a goldfish impression with his mouth and trying to interrupt. It turns out that a City fan who comes to games from Norway put £10 on the score being 3-2 to us. He'd only got odds of 33-1, but even so he'd won over three times more than me. It seems that every time I think I've done something unique, there is someone who has gone one step further.

Even Jon had won a lucky £13 by predicting that Phillips would score the first goal that day. Did any Norwich fans lose bets there? I'm beginning to doubt it. I wouldn't be surprised if Ladbrokes don't open their kiosk when we visit Villa Park next year.

Norwich began the second half well – but fifteen minutes into it came the decisive moment of the game.

> Narrator: As swift as lightning from the firmament,
> Calamity befell the ill-starr'd Sutch.
> From in betwixt his legs the ball did squirt
> And offer'd up a morsel of a chance,
> The which Mark Hughes did greedily devour;
> This Mark, unmark'd, with such celerity
> Dispatch'd the sphere into the City net
> As to confirm the 'Sharp' upon his chest.
> Bryan Gunn: Out, damned ball! Out, I say! O shall my sheet ne'er be kept clean?
> Narrator: The clamour of United varletry
> Did cleave the air; the Norwich fans thereat
> In green and yellow melancholy sat.

A Tragedy of Errors

'Hughesy, Hughesy,' chanted the relieved United fans. Actually, it sounded more like 'Who's he?', but I assume they would know who the scorer was. This was the first time the home fans had sung during the game, and they soon felt confident enough to display the breadth of their repertoire. 'United, United ...'

Quite a little dialogue then developed, though this could hardly be termed Shakespearean:

> Norwich: Do you know another song?
> Do you know another song?
> United: One-nil, one-nil, one-nil, one-nil ...
> Norwich: Sing when you're winning,
> You can only sing when you're winning ...
> United: You're not singing any more,
> You're not singing any more ...
> Norwich: On the ball, City ...

While this was going on, I was concentrating on the game. I was still convinced we'd score – after all, we hadn't failed to do so in the league all season. The team pressed forward more and more, though this left the defence increasingly exposed, and only a series of desperate last-ditch tackles kept the score at 1-0.

There has been speculation in the last fortnight, incidentally, that the Swedish international defender Patrik Andersson may sign for us. This would be good news, I think, though Stephen is not so sure. 'We can only play three foreigners in European competition, and we've already got Gunn, Bowen and Phillips,' he pointed out.

Even with one minute to go, I was still sure that we wouldn't lose. Then the referee blew for time. Surely there had been a mistake? 'Oi, come back!' I wanted to shout. 'You can't leave, we haven't scored yet!' But it was all over.

United had had more of the play and more chances, but it wouldn't have been that great an injustice if we'd got a draw. If Sutch hadn't made that mistake, or if Schmeichel's boot hadn't deflected that shot from Robins – two incidents that lasted just a fraction of a second – everyone would be saying what a fine, battling performance Norwich had put up. As it was, *Sports Report* on Radio 5 began: 'Twenty-five years ago, Manchester United won the league title, and it looks like it could be their year again as today ... ' For goodness sake! It's still only December, and we're still 5 points clear! And we're 6 ahead of United! There isn't that much of a gap between Charles and Di.

Mind you, this defeat now makes our next match very important – though I'm not sure it could be any more important than it already is. 'Nine days to Ipswich, there's only nine days to Ipswich ... ' They beat Manchester City 3-1 – a result which increased both the delight and the gloom at Old Trafford when it was announced.

For once, we were able to leave the ground straight after the game. In previous years, we had to wait so long that Godot turned up. The players left for a short break in the Canary Isles. An appropriate destination, really. I'm thinking of booking up for the Virgin Islands next summer.

I didn't bother to stop off in Wolverhampton on the way back to London, entertaining though it would have been to rub in Wolves' 2-1 defeat at home to Luton. I still haven't decided whether to send the Wolverine a Christmas card or not.

> He's mad that trusts in the tameness of a wolf.
>
> *King Lear*

Hang on a minute – that quotation was genuine.

After Saturday's visit to the grandest stadium in the Premier League, our Sunday team made the glamorous trip to the home of West Barnes Reserves for our cup replay. I couldn't play, as my leg was still bad. Or should I say 'crook'? I couldn't even run the line, though I'm pretty good at that. Whenever I've done it in the past, both sides have sworn at me in equal measure, which suggests that I've got it about right. The most frustrating aspect of the job is that the referees generally assume that all the linesmen are biased and often ignore you when you are furiously flagging for offside.

It was the first time I'd watched the team from the touchline for ages. Apart from the usual chronic lack of calling (except for the odd mumbled 'Man on' a nanosecond before the player on the ball is trampled into the mud by some pachyderm), they weren't bad. More worrying was the fact that everyone else thought I was having my best game for weeks. 'Fewer mistakes than usual, Kev.' 'More mobile, too.'

As at Manchester, the match turned on one mistake – but here it was made by the referee. His name was Jim Callaghan. The political version would have done better. There is also a referee in our league called G. Fawkes, but he hasn't taken one of our games yet.

Five minutes from the end of normal time, the score stood at 2-2. Then Jolly Jim awarded a penalty against us for handball when no one had come close to touching it (least of all our keeper). The opposition didn't appeal; in fact, the ref had to call them back as they trotted to the half-way line to wait for a goal-kick. One of our players complained so bitterly that he was sent off. Unfortunately, the ref was still able to make out the sounds 'f ...' and 'c ...' despite sundry hands being slapped over the abuser's mouth as his team-mates tried to drag him away.

With some embarrassment, our opponents converted the penalty, then scored again with literally the last kick of the game as we pushed forward for an equaliser. Not that the goal would have been allowed if we had scored. I discovered after the game that the referee had let slip beforehand that he couldn't let it go to extra time as he had to get away early to attend a christening.

We gave him $2/10$ on the match report – one for turning up, one for getting changed. We also had to give him his £15 match fee as we were the visiting team. 'He's done well today, with that fifty quid we gave him before the match,' said the West Barnes manager. I think he was joking.

Ah, well, we can concentrate on the league now.

Monday 21 December
Ipswich Town (home)

The shortest day of the year, and the biggest night. This was our first league game against Ipswich for nearly eight years, and I'd been looking forward to it more than Christmas. I've actually wanted Ipswich to get promoted for the last few seasons so that we could have this fixture again.

In recent years, we have only played them in the meaningless Full Members' Cup and in pre-season friendlies (ha!) for the Hospital Cup – so called because that's where half the supporters end up. No, that's not true. We don't have much trouble at Norwich. There were only a few arrests at Carrow Road last year, and they were mainly when supporters tried to climb the gates at the end of last season – the stewards managed to force most of them back in to watch the game. One or two idiots come out of the woodwork when we meet Ipswich, but the rivalry is nowhere near as bitter and vicious as that between, say, Manchester United and Liverpool. The only time I've experienced any trouble at the hands of Town fans was when I went to school in Felixstowe for six months at the age of 8 and I got chased in the playground.

To whisper the truth, I don't dislike Ipswich that much. Yes, I know I've made all sorts of rude remarks about them up to now. And I am always desperately keen to beat them and finish higher in the league. But we have more in common with Ipswich than with any other club, whether we like to admit it or not. I even wanted them to beat Arsenal in the 1978 FA Cup final. Mind you, it does seem appropriate that they are sponsored by Fisons. And why is there a carthorse on their badge?

The local media had been building up anticipation for ages – but it would be wrong of me to claim that the dismal performance of the Norwich Supporters' team on Sunday morning was down to the Ipswich game playing on our minds. Rather, it was because half the team had stinking hangovers from various Christmas parties the night before. We were playing Newcastle Supporters so, given the reputation of Geordies for heavy drinking, you'd think they would have been in a worse state. But either they don't get invited to parties or they're much better at holding their beer. Whatever the case, they thumped us 5-0 – and it could have been worse.

Mum felt queasy all Monday. To stop her fretting around the house, she went to the butcher's to get her Christmas goose (!) but, of course, she ended up talking about the game there. No prizes for guessing the butcher's prediction of the score. I don't think Mum went round the pubs looking for Town fans so she could sing 'Come and have a go if you think you're hard enough' – but I can't be sure.

Stephen was also tense when he arrived at Mum's before the game, though he didn't agree with this being designated a 'Category A' game, which meant high ticket prices. 'But everyone wants to see this one,' I said. 'It's a sell-out.'

'That's as maybe,' Stephen replied. 'But Ipswich can't be called one of the big clubs. This should be a 'C' game, like with Oldham or Wimbledon.' He said he had a bad feeling about the game. I did too, because of …

Kevin's Alternative Laws of Football (No. 6)

'Whenever Ipswich and Norwich meet in the league, the game will be won by the team that are lower in the table.'

With Norwich top, Ipswich were necessarily lower. The fact that we were unbeaten at home this season offered little comfort. Who was more likely to knacker our record than our neighbours?

Karen didn't know what to expect at the game, as this would be the first local derby she'd been to. However, she did get an idea of the passions that are aroused when her mother-in-law came round in the afternoon and pleaded with her not to go. Karen, you will remember, is eight months pregnant, and the worry was that the excitement might be too much for her.

'They'll have to stop the match if you start.'

'Oh yes, I can just see it now,' said Karen. '"Norwich 4 Ipswich 0, match abandoned after 85 minutes because one of the spectators went into labour."' Karen refused to miss the game – though she almost didn't get into the ground. Even without the blankets and hot water, she had real trouble trying to squeeze through the turnstile. We thought we might need to round up some big lads to give her a shove or find a crane to winch her over the top, but at last she made it by herself.

'Do you like being big and fat?' Stephen asked her.

'No'. Karen replied. 'Do you?'

As the match was being televised by Sky, we again had to put up with the awful prancing around on the pitch before it began. This followed the usual format, except that Bart Simpson and the troupe of girls wore Santa outfits and danced to a Christmas medley before exhorting us to perform the 'Canary wave' – aka the Mexican wave, aka the Sad People's wave. The Ipswich fans didn't join in and were roundly booed, though for once I thought they had the right idea.

The two sets of supporters started singing to each other, though the songs were not exactly Irving Berlin or Cole Porter:

> Who's the shit of Anglia?
> Ipswich. Ipswich.
> Who's the shit of Anglia?
> Ipswich is their name ...

The Ipswich supporters' version of this isn't too hard to work out.

> We hate Ipswich and we hate Ipswich,
> We hate Ipswich and we hate Ipswich.
> We hate Ipswich and we hate Ipswich,
> We are the Ipswich haters.

> Oh Ipswich Town (Oh Ipswich Town)
> Is full of shit (Is full of shit),
> Oh Ipswich Town is full of shit,
> It's full of shit, shit and more shit,
> Oh Ipswich Town is full of shit.

Can you detect a theme emerging here? Uplifting, isn't it?

The Ipswich fans sang 'Shitty ground', as it was the first time they'd seen the new Barclay Stand. The upper tier was open, though it was full of Norwich fans for this game. In future, it is to be the away section.

Once the game began, the crowd became relatively quiet, though this was a sign of tension rather than lack of interest. I tried to shout several times but found that nothing came out. The players displayed their nervousness in other ways, chasing around frantically like headless chickens and sliding into tackles so late that they didn't make contact until the second half. The referee let everything go, probably because he thought that once he started cautioning players, he'd soon have a full book and an empty pitch.

Norwich had marginally more of the game in the first half, but Ipswich had the better chances, which is often the way with derby games. Steve Whitton had a one-on-one with Bryan Gunn, but to our relief his shot was saved.

Suddenly a message came over the loudspeakers, asking someone to call home urgently. I couldn't see anyone going anywhere. 'Would you go if there was a message for you?' Mum asked.

'Certainly not', I said. 'The only people who'd need to get in touch with me are you, Stephen and Karen, and you're all here.'

'What if you were at a game on your own?'

'I don't know. It would depend on who we were playing, the score, and how close it was to the end of the match.'

Ian Butterworth didn't come out for the second half, and we fell to pieces at once. The Swedish defender Andersson is not joining us now, incidentally. He's been offered a better deal by Blackburn. After ten minutes, we conceded a goal from a corner – a carbon-copy of the one Ipswich scored against Aston Villa in the Coca-Cola Cup last week. If City hadn't been sunbathing in the Canary Isles, they would have seen it on television.

For the first time in the evening, there was a hint of trouble. A small group of Ipswich supporters at our end leapt up and cheered. At this, various thick-necked and pea-brained individuals got up and moved towards them until stewards blocked their path. 'If you won't get them out of here, we will,' grunted one member of Densa.

It is true that the Ipswich supporters should not really have been in our section, but they weren't causing any harm. And it was understandable that they should be there, as Ipswich had been given only 1,600 tickets for the game. They are giving us the same number for the return match just after Easter, so I may well end up having to sit among the Ipswich fans if it's the only way I can get in.

Eventually, the stewards persuaded the Brains Trust to go and sit down again without further trouble – though Karen (who was sitting with Stephen some way away from Mum and me because we had to sit in specific seats for this game) told me later that an Ipswich supporter sitting just in front of her had been punched early on. There was one sitting next to her as well, but having seen what had happened to the other fan, he merely whispered 'Yes!' under his breath when the goal went in and left it at that. The next day, it was reported that there had been sixteen arrests at the game. This is sixteen too many, but none of the incidents was too serious, thankfully.

The mood of most of the home supporters after the goal was divided evenly between resignation and panic. Even with thirty minutes to go, the two men next to me were muttering, 'Fancy losing our first home game of the season to this lot.' Others just screamed at the team to play even faster and hoof the ball forward as hard and as quickly as possible.

Unfortunately, this is just what they did. As in the FA Cup semi-final against Sunderland last season, hopeful long balls were thumped towards the strikers but brought not even a hint of success. We needed an individual flash of inspiration from somewhere, but no one could provide it. Robert Fleck was the sort of player who could, but tonight he was sitting in the stand watching. It was a pity we couldn't sign him on loan for the last quarter of an hour and bring him on.

'They haven't got a bloody clue' and 'They're rubbish tonight' were just some of the comments around me. You'll notice that the team was now being referred to in the third person rather than the first. This was similar to the subtle shift in pronouns commonly employed by parents when talking about their children. It's 'Will you deal with your son, please?' when the little horror's playing up, but 'Isn't my son clever?' when he does something right.

The Ipswich fans became more and more confident as they realised that their defence was having no trouble dealing with our approach. We were taunted with the obligatory 'One-nil, one-nil' and 'Blue Army', though I'm not sure whether the latter was a declaration of their identity or a comment on the mood of the Norwich supporters. In keeping with the season, the Town fans then sang:

> Jingle bells, jingle bells,
> Jingle all the way.
> O! What fun it is to see
> Ipswich win away.

The City supporters were hardly in a mood to adapt Christmas carols, though our feelings could have been summed up by 'Deck the ground with wreaths of holly' or 'O come all ye mournful, pissed off and indignant'.

For some reason, all the clocks in the universe went straight from 9:10 to 9:30. In the last two minutes, Norwich were still pressing forward, but Ipswich broke away and scored again. The Town fans went wild. One idiot even ran on to the pitch and tried to put his blue and white bobble hat on the head of one of the players, but was arrested for his pains. The City fans went home. There was the odd chant of 'We are top of the league', but it sounded very hollow. The fact that we were still 4 points clear was irrelevant for the time being.

The Sky fireworks were every bit as infuriating as I had suspected they would be after a defeat. It was as if they were celebrating Ipswich's victory and laughing at us. Not that the Town fans needed any help. Choruses of 'We beat the scum 2-0' followed us all the way up Jimmy Hill, which seemed twice as long as usual and almost vertical – especially to Karen who, of course, was climbing for two.

'Well, the butcher was right about the score,' said Mum.

'Even a broken clock shows the right time occasionally,' I replied, which almost ranks as a philosophical remark from me. Nothing else was said on the way home. We all felt sick. Losing to Ipswich was like being kicked in the guts. Or having your home burgled. Or seeing your favourite pet run over by your neighbour. Twice. And the thought of our assailants/burglars/pet killers laughing at us all the way down the A140 just made it worse.

I'm glad I don't have to go back to work until January. I'm even gladder I don't know any Ipswich fans personally. Though Stephen does. He's had a £50 bet with one on which team finishes higher in the league this season. I think he's going to lie low for while.

'There always seem to be disasters just before Christmas,' Mum often says. 'There'll be a lot of unhappy families.'

She's never been more right.

Saturday 26 December
Tottenham Hotspur (home)

Merry Christmas? Ho bloody ho.

As Elvis once sang, it was a 'Blue Christmas'. Or as James Brown never sang, 'Waaagghh! I feel shite, I thought that I might.'

Yes, I know it's childish to sulk about not getting what you want for Christmas, but I'd set my heart on 3 points from the Ipswich game. The presents I did get were OK, though I didn't get anything to do with the club. As Mum put it, 'What do you get the man who has everything?' Well, everything I want, anyway. I don't want a tie or a bedside lamp from the club shop just because they are yellow and green and have the club badge on them.

The only item I have thought of acquiring from the club shop lately is a new team shirt. Yes, I do actively like it now. The only reason I've refrained from buying one is that it might break the spell and send the team plummeting down the table. Similarly, I daren't change the message on my answerphone, which is still *The Canaries* by the 1972 promotion squad. I can imagine the TV interviews now. 'So, Mr Walker, how do you account for your team's alarming slump over the last two months?'

'It's all because Kevin Baldwin of London changed his answerphone message in the middle of the season.' Ridiculous? Probably. But it's not worth taking the chance.

I got quite a few Christmas cards. More people than usual remembered me this year, presumably because Norwich are doing so well. I got one from Doc Martin, whose wedding I went to back in September – though he forgot to tell me his address in London, so I couldn't send him one back. I did send a card to the Wolverine in the end, as an interim measure while I try to decide what to do about her. It had a picture of a wolf (well, Wile E. Coyote from the Road Runner cartoons actually, but it's near enough) about to be hit on the head by an anvil-shaped present. It seemed appropriate. I didn't get a card from her, though. Perhaps she's made my decision for me.

I've been hoping this wouldn't be a traditional Christmas as far as football is concerned. We never do well at this time of year – in fact, you could count the number of points we've picked up over the last two Christmases on the fingers of one foot. Is this because the players are displaying an excessive amount of goodwill to all men, believing it better to give points than to receive them? Or is Bernard Matthews giving them free turkeys so they all get bloated?

I knew one thing would be different, at least. This season, the league's computer gave us a home fixture on Boxing Day. We've had to make the trek across to Manchester on the last three. Or was it the computers making us travel all that way? I have been reliably informed that our chairman specifically requested away fixtures for Boxing Day. This was doubtless to save on police costs – but he may also have been worried about the danger of Carrow Road being blown up. Boxing Day matches are always the smelliest of the season. With all the nuts, figs, dates and stuffing that everyone has eaten the day before, phenomenal amounts of methane are produced in the stands, and it would only take one person lighting a Christmas Castella at the wrong moment to blow the roof off and send it into orbit.

The match against Spurs looked like being enjoyable despite this, however. They are an attractive team, it's not too far for their fans to travel – and they wouldn't be bringing Gary Lineker along this time. He's a nice enough bloke, I know, but he always bloody scored against us.

Before we went down to Carrow Road, Stephen put on the new trainers I had given him for Christmas. 'I wonder how long it'll take to teach this pair the way,' he said. When we got there, it seemed that everyone had been given new trainers, coats and sweaters the day before. The ground looked like a giant Debenhams window display. My scarf looked new too, but this was because I'd been scrubbing it furiously since Monday night. (See home match v Everton.)

Once again, Mum and I had to sit apart from Stephen. We were surrounded by the same people as at the Ipswich game. 'Looks like we'll be keeping each other warm all winter,' winked Mum's neighbour, a gent of roughly the same age as her. Oh Lord, I think she's pulled. Stephen had to sit next to two old gits who, he said later, were every bit as miserable as they looked – and not just because of the Ipswich result. He was on his own today, as Karen had to visit the in-laws. I don't suppose she'll come again for a while, with the dropping of the next sprog now imminent, but we could soon be bringing her eldest daughter along. She's nearly 6 and recently expressed an interest in coming to a game (after only ten minutes of arm-twisting – she was much easier to persuade than her mother), so we've joined her up with Junior Canaries. Another victim, ah-ha-ha!

There were new visitors to the ground for this game. When the teams came out, the photographers' cameras were pointing not at the tunnel, but at the directors' box. At first we thought that this was because Graham Taylor and Lawrie McMenemy, England manager and assistant manager disrespectfully, were sitting there. Their presence is such a rare event that you could understand a fuss being made about it. Maybe the club sent them a road map each for Christmas.

It turned out later that Captain Mark Phillips was there with his son. It must have been his day for the kids. But how did they get tickets for the match? Are they members? Did they queue? Did they bollocks. If they were related to David Phillips, they would surely have come along before. As it was, I could imagine them looking down at the pitch, scratching their heads and wondering where the horses and jumps were.

It was a pity Prince Charles hadn't come along too. He could have given his views on the construction of the new Barclay Stand. Bearing in mind his concern for tradition, I hope he would argue the case for retaining standing areas. If Princess Di had come along too, she and Charles could have sat in separate sections and made rude gestures at each other.

Before the game started, everyone rose to their feet – not because of the royal presence, but for a minute's silence in honour of Ted Croker, the former FA secretary who died on Christmas morning. Unfortunately, with the loudspeaker system at Carrow Road being so poor, the announcement was not clear at all, so several people were under the impression that we were mourning the 3 points so tragically lost on Monday evening. Someone a couple of rows behind me had to ask his neighbour what had happened. 'Ted Croker croaked,' was the less than respectful reply.

The silence itself was not silent. The fans inside the ground were all quiet, but a conversation at the foot of the steps leading up to the seats between a steward and a fan (who seemed to be hard of hearing and understanding) could be overheard by everyone.

'Hold it there a minute, mate,' said the steward.

'Why, what's going on?' The steward spoke in a quieter voice from this point on, so we could not hear what he was saying. Trouble was, neither could the man he was talking to.

'You what? Who died? Who's he? Well, can't I go up anyway? Why not? Go on, I know where my seat is …' Then the minute was up, and he was able to come up and take his seat anyway.

The match began with a huge roar, as it always does after a minute's silence. It is as if the crowd is trying to make up for lost shouting. Once the game got underway, though, the ground fell relatively quiet. There was nothing wrong with the football. As usual, Spurs came to play an open game. There was plenty of excitement as chances came and went at both ends. And there was not the same throat-and buttock-clenching tension that we had felt on Monday evening.

The reason for the subdued atmosphere was that, for the first time, the away fans had been allocated the upper tier of the Barclay. This meant that the Norwich and Spurs supporters at that end could not actually see each other – and how can you shout at someone you cannot see? I also suspect that the new stand has been acoustically designed so that the shouts of the away fans cannot be heard around the rest of the ground. There were plenty of Tottenham fans at the game, and I'm sure they couldn't have been quiet for the whole ninety minutes, but we couldn't hear a thing from them at the other end.

Yet this does not explain why the home supporters were so muted. Even when Ruel Fox was fouled just inside the Spurs area and a free kick was given just outside, not much fuss was made. Perhaps many were suffering in the same way as our Golden Goal ticket-seller who, when asked why he was looking so pale, muttered quietly, 'It's the last time I touch that peach wine.' Perhaps others had kids and wanted some peace and quiet after the mayhem of the previous day. Either way, the lack of vocal support at the ground at the moment is rather worrying. Even the local press remarked on this in an article headlined 'The Silence of the Fans'. Here, you don't think it has anything to do with the ground being all-seater now, do you? No, of course not.

The score was still 0-0 at half-time. We had had more possession, but there had been too much hesitancy and elaboration as we approached the Spurs box. We had certainly been far too direct against Ipswich, but now we were going too far the other way again. And why were no chances falling to Mark Robins? Earlier in the season, everyone was talking about his uncanny ability to 'be in the right place at the right time'. Is he now in the wrong place at the right time? Or the right place at the wrong time? Or the wrong place at the wrong time?

During the interval, the announcer talked to a woman in the crowd who is soon to marry a club steward she met through a lonely hearts column in the local evening paper. He'd brought her along to her first game today. Was this so that she could appreciate and share in a major part of his life, just as when I first dragged Karen along? Or was he perversely introducing his prospective wife to his first true love so that he could compare them?

'Here, you ought to put an advert like that in the paper,' Mum said, predictably. I began to wish I was sitting on my own so that Stephen could put up with this instead.

'What would I put in the ad, then?' I asked. '"Attractive, witty man with full head of hair and dislike of football seeks woman who loves a compulsive liar"?'

'Yes, that would do,' she said enthusiastically.

'I don't think so,' I sneered. 'I'm not that desperate yet.' Well, not for a week or two, anyway. I mean, the Wolverine's card might have got lost in the post.

The second half produced the same strange combination of entertaining football and a crowd at half-volume. Spurs scored with a free kick after an hour, but the referee disallowed the goal, declaring that the kick had been taken too quickly. Alan Shearer's free kick against us in the Coca-Cola Cup match at Blackburn had been taken more quickly, but that goal had been allowed to stand. Still, I wasn't complaining on this occasion, though several of the Spurs players did.

Our best chance fell to Chris Sutton a couple of yards out. It seemed that he must score, but a mysterious force-field on the Tottenham goal-line kept the ball out. Or was it Erik Thorstvedt's knee? Final score: 0-0.

On balance, we just about deserved to win – but we didn't. This is rather concerning. It has often been said that it is the sign of a good team to win when playing poorly. What does it signify when a team doesn't win when playing well? Oops.

The overriding feeling as Mum, Stephen and I made our way home was one of unfulfilment – and not because we had all stuffed ourselves with rich food on Christmas Day and had now been denied the feast of goals we had hoped for. True, we had kept a clean sheet at last. We had brought the run of defeats (all two of them!) to an end. But if a team aspires to win the league, it should be able to beat teams like Ipswich and Spurs at home. Moreover, both of these games took place after our main rivals had played and slipped up. We have had two glorious opportunities within a week to stretch our lead at the top and failed to take either.

Oh no, are the old doubts back again? I've been criticising the national media for casting aspersions on Norwich's chances of winning the title, but now it appears that my own misgivings were lurking just below the surface all the time. No, I mustn't give in to them. After all, I don't expect the team to. Perhaps it was the beer talking just then. Well, the beer fumes at the ground, anyway. Or another symptom of post-Ipswich trauma.

Monday 28 December
Leeds United (away)

I had vowed that it would be a cold, cold day before Mum and I set foot on a Club Cabbage coach again. Well, it was, and we did. I thought the roads between Norwich and Leeds might be icy and didn't want to risk the car unnecessarily.

The potential was undoubtedly there for yet another case of 'Once bitten, twice mauled', but in the event things were much better this time. Perhaps Mum and I were just lucky: there were four coaches making this trip and, for once, we picked the best one. There were no smells, apart from the occasional whiff of Vick and cough sweets wafting past. No one ate cheese and onion crisps, and though someone across the aisle opened a packet of dry roasted peanuts, I wasn't close enough to smell the cow fart that is always sealed in for some reason.

The man supervising the coach warned that anyone with turkey sandwiches or hand-held computer games would have them confiscated and thrown out of the window. I think we can guess what Christmas in his house was like. 'What about hand-held turkeys?' a voice asked.

'No, nor them either.'

Unusually, there was a liberal smattering of *Independents*, *Guardians* and *Telegraphs* on board. I even saw someone perusing a visitors' guide to Nepal. Perhaps there is intelligent life in Club Cabbage after all.

Balloons and streamers decked the ceiling. The coach was nice and warm – a little too warm if anything, as I was sitting directly above a heater. Everyone was in a jolly, playful mood, exemplified when someone from the back of the coach came to put some rubbish in the litter bag at the front and was directed to the supervisor's bag that contained his sandwiches.

Some things didn't change, however. Once again, we stopped off at the Unhappy Eater, which looked gaudier than ever with Christmas lights and tacky decorations added to the dayglo signs. Even though it had only just turned 10am, several supporters headed straight for the bar to start knocking back pints to show how hard they were. And some of the men were just as bad.

As we approached Leeds, I wondered what sort of reception we would get. It was OK last season, but then it was the last match and Leeds had already won the Championship, so all the home fans were in a party mood. For years, though, Elland Road was a frighteningly hostile place to visit. Mum once gave me a present a week before we were due to play here. 'You might find this useful,' she said. It turned out to be one of those do-it-yourself wills from WH Smith.

I never did fill it in. I couldn't decide who to leave my things to, nor what I would like to have sung at my funeral. 'On the ball, City', I suppose. 'Abide with me', possibly – except that Mum always bursts into tears when she hears it. She says it was her mother's favourite hymn, but it may also be because she gets upset that we don't get to Wembley very often. What else? 'When the greens go marching in'? 'Onward Norwich City, marching as to war/ With the green and yellow going on before'? 'And did those feet in ancient times/Play for the team in yellow and green?'? Perhaps a chant of 'Cheerio, cheerio' as the coffin slips through the curtains in the crematorium wouldn't be out of place.

I wouldn't want my ashes to be simply scattered over the pitch at Carrow Road; I'd like them to be put to more use. They should be kept near the goal for the Norwich keeper to throw in the eyes of an Ipswich striker during a derby game just as he's about to head the ball into the net.

At last we caught sight of the ground – but what was this? A new stand had been built along one side of the pitch, and it was absolutely enormous. It looked as if someone had misread the dimensions on the blueprint and built it 50 per cent too big. 'I wish I'd bought some shares in a company that makes plastic seats a couple of years ago,' said one man on the coach. 'All these new stands around the country that have got to be all-seater – the seat-makers must think it's Christmas.'

'Er – actually, it is Christmas,' one of his mates pointed out.

Inside the ground, Mum and I made a beeline for the refreshment kiosk, as we had obviously not eaten at the naff caff on the way. We each had a meat pie, but were regretting it by the second mouthful. The filling appeared to be a mixture of recycled meat (i.e., someone else had already eaten it) and muddy slush, flavoured with more salt than a Siberian mine. It scored $1/10$ – and the one was for the foil container.

Just then I bumped into one of the few fellow Norwich supporters in the Norwich Supporters' Sunday team. Steve had driven over from Grimsby, where he'd spent Christmas, with his Celtic-supporting brother-in-law and his father-in-law, a Grimsby fan. 'Have you seen us play before?' I asked.

'I saw Norwich against Wimbledon last year,' Steve's father-in-law replied.

'In that case, you haven't seen us play,' said Mum.

'Ah, you must be the hooligan we've all heard about,' said Steve. I covered my eyes, but looking through my fingers I could see Mum giving me one of her 'What have you been saying about me now, you little git?' stares. I changed the subject before Mum demonstrated what a hooligan she could be. We all tried to think of players who had appeared for Norwich and either Celtic or Grimsby. We didn't get very far. We only came up with Jim Bone, who played for City and Celtic in the '70s, and Kevin Drinkell, who joined us from Grimsby in 1985. 'You had Dave Beasant on loan a couple of months ago, though,' I said to Steve's father-in-law.

'He hasn't played for you, has he?' he asked.

'Well, he is an old Norwich favourite,' I said. 'He won the game for us at Stamford Bridge this season.'

Steve revealed that he'd been in the Norwich directors' box a few weeks ago. Apparently, his father writes to Chairman Chase every other week to tell him where he's going wrong, and the latter had invited him to come along to a game with a guest. 'Chase was all right, really,' said Steve. 'He ran around getting autographs for the kids and making sure they enjoyed themselves.'

'Huh,' I grunted, being unwilling to acknowledge any evidence that contradicted my view of the chairman. 'Sounds like PR flannel to me.'

'He did say one interesting thing,' Steve went on. 'He claimed Blackburn had just offered three million pounds for one of our young players.'

'What? And more to the point, who?'

'He wouldn't say. Chris Sutton's the only one we think it could be.'

'Three million?'

'So he reckoned. He even said, "Can you imagine having that much money in your front room?"' I suddenly had a mental picture of a front room wallpapered with tenners and armchairs built with bundles of twenty-pound notes. Could this be what Chase's house is like?

In the end, I had to conclude that Steve's story, or Chase's claim, had to be taken with as much salt as had been put in the pies that Mum and I had recently not eaten. If it were true, Chase would surely have snatched Dalglish's hand off.

As soon as we had taken our places on the small terrace that Leeds had allocated us, I met another friend, though this time by design. Charlie is my oldest friend – or rather, the friend I have known longest – but since he and his wife moved to Scarborough three or four years ago, I have rarely seen him and he has rarely seen Norwich. In fact, this was the first game he'd been to since the semi-final at Hillsborough last season. I got him a ticket for that game as, apart from the fact that he is my best mate and that I am godfather to his eldest son (christening presents: an inflatable canary and a Norwich scarf and moneybox), I still regard him as being a City supporter of longer standing than me. Despite the fact that he hasn't been able to watch City regularly for some time, he's probably seen them play more times than me. He had a season ticket at Carrow Road throughout the 1970s when I often couldn't afford to go.

These days, he has to settle for the TV, radio, papers and phone calls to me after every game. I'm sure he thinks the Clubcall number and mine are one and the same. For once, though, his wife had granted him an exeat for the afternoon so that he could see the team in the flesh.

I was particularly anxious that we should play well today, not just to strengthen our position in the league, but for the sake of my credibility as a match reporter. Having described to Charlie every week how well we were playing (except in the game against you-know-who), I now hoped that the team would live up to the expectations I had raised in him.

The official pre-match entertainment wasn't up to much. There was just a small group of thin, awkward-looking young girls dancing on the far corner of the pitch. 'They aren't the Canary girls, are they?' asked Charlie.

'Maybe,' I said. 'Perhaps they were given a free transfer here. Or Nigel Pleasants [the Leeds company secretary, formerly at Norwich] might have brought them with him.' Fortunately, there was more fun to be derived from other sources. A Norwich player booted a ball into our enclosure for us to knock around in the air – but this didn't last long, as when the ball landed on the perimeter track of the pitch, an orange-jacketed steward refused to throw it back to us.

'Merry Christmas, you miserable bald git!' yelled a man near me.

'Is he talking to you?' Mum asked me. She clearly hadn't forgotten about my defamatory remarks about her after all.

In the match programme, there was an advert for 'Leeds United's European Diary'. 'Bloody short diary that must be,' remarked Charlie. Then there was an advert for club merchandise, most of which was being modelled by Eric Cantona who left for Manchester United a month ago. One picture had the caption 'Not available' slapped across it. It wasn't clear whether this referred to Cantona or the tracksuit he was wearing.

Some T-shirts on the page were emblazoned with Cantona's name and picture as well as the club badge. Who on earth would want to buy one now? The only way to shift them would be to alter the first vowel of his name. (Think about it.)

'They could always fold the shirts in the wrapping so you can only see the badge,' Charlie suggested.

'They couldn't do that, could they?' Mum interjected.

'It wouldn't be the first time it had been done,' said Charlie. 'Remember that scarf I once bought?' I did. In the early 1980s, he had bought a cut-price scarf from a vendor in Carrow Road and only discovered when he unwrapped it at home that it bore the legend 'John Bond's green and yellow army'. Bond had left for Manchester City several months before.

The other noteworthy feature of the programme (and you couldn't help remarking on this) was the number of times the Leeds supporters were praised. References to their wonderfulness were to be found on pages 2, 11, 29, 30 and 33. This flattery may have a particular purpose. It seems to be one way in which the club is trying to improve the behaviour of its followers; through being told constantly how good they are, the fans are encouraged to be well-behaved. To be fair, the policy seems to be working. The Leeds fans were much less hostile than they had been in the past. The only abuse they came out with all afternoon was directed at Mark Robins. 'What are they shouting?' asked Charlie – which surprised me, as I thought that living in Scarborough would make understanding the Yorkshire accent a simple matter.

'You're just a shit scum bastard,' obliged Mum. Presumably this was because Robins had joined us from Manchester United, Leeds's rivals for the Championship last season.

The Norwich fans were sufficiently emboldened to offer a few taunts in return, which in the past would have been asking for trouble with a capital punishment. 'Strachan, Strachan, shut your mouth' was repeated as the said player persisted in moaning and complaining to the referee. I'd never seen him in such an argumentative mood; it was as if all those bananas he reputedly eats to give him energy had finally gone to his head. This was followed by a rendition of 'Coming Home' from Dvorak's New World Symphony, which might seem incongruous if you didn't know – though, of course, you did – that this is the theme from the Hovis commercials and that those humming it were, *ipso facto*, mocking Yorkshire, albeit gently.

Less gentle was the sneering chorus of 'Where's your Froggy gone?'. 'Remember they used to put up "Ooh aah Cantona" on the scoreboard last season?' said one of a group of lads in front of me.

'They had to, to help the crowd remember the words,' replied one of his mates. Don't blame me, Leeds fans, I'm only reporting what they said.

The match began at a frantic pace, but after a few minutes ... it got even faster. Both teams seemed desperate for a win (Leeds had lost 3-1 at Blackburn on Boxing Day) and were chasing around manically trying to close each other down early to prevent the other side from settling into a rhythm. After ten minutes, though, there was a pause when Ruel Fox was brought down as he sped towards the Leeds goal and we were awarded a penalty. It wasn't clear for some time that a spot kick had been given – indeed, Mum didn't realise until half-time that we had had one. As her view was blocked by a tall man to her right, she thought it was a free kick outside the area. Furthermore, Mark Bowen shaped to take the kick as if he were trying to swerve the ball around a wall from thirty yards, with a predictable outcome. He almost decapitated the steward to the right of the goal.

It was virtually an action replay of his penalty miss at Anfield in October. After the game, he said that he would never take another penalty. No one tried to persuade him to reconsider.

The rest of the half was played at the breakneck speed at which it had begun. Charlie was horrified at the effect of the new back-pass rule, which he had not seen in operation before. 'I did warn you,' I said, happy that he shared my view.

I was more pleased that he confirmed my opinions on the relative merits of the players. He agreed, for example, that John Polston is a hugely underrated defender, that Ian Culverhouse reads the game very well, and that Ruel Fox was not as positive when attacking as he could be – and had been earlier in the season. He was also able to put the current line-up into some sort of historical context, comparing the goal-poaching skills of Mark Robins with those of Ted MacDougall and contrasting the occasionally over-elaborate Mark Bowen with Colin Sullivan, a rather more straightforward full-back in the '70s. I had seen these players too, of course, but Charlie can picture them more vividly than members of the present team.

The surest sign that we were playing well in the second half was the quietness of the Leeds crowd. There was only one chorus of 'Leeds Leeds Leeds', an old club song that inexplicably topped the pop charts in Japan last year, plus some whistling when Rob Newman lay on the ground, apparently to waste time. I wonder if they felt ashamed when they found out he'd broken his ankle. I hope this injury won't affect his other career as a member of the Mary Whitehouse Experience.

Our two best chances fell to Robins. He rolled one shot just past the far post (I thought he miskicked it, but Charlie disagreed) and had the other kicked off the line. (I thought he dallied over his shot, but the highlights on *Match of the Day* proved me wrong again.) 'This is just like watching Celtic,' said Steve's brother-in-law. I took this as a compliment until he added, 'We can't score either.'

The game finished 0-0, but getting a point at the home of the champions wasn't a bad result. And we played quite well, without reaching the peaks of a month ago. Charlie certainly enjoyed it. 'I wish I could come more often,' he said. 'It's a lot less nerve-racking than listening to it on the radio.' See, we agree again!

The journey home was passable. The driver announced that, unfortunately, the dayglo dining establishment we had called at earlier would be closed by the time we got there. Mum clenched her fist and hissed, 'Yesss!' We stopped at Ferrybridge Services instead, but the restaurant had hardly any hot food. 'We weren't expecting anyone tonight,' said the woman behind the counter. Eh?!

We've now reached the half-way point of the year, the time of Janus when we can look back at what we have achieved so far and forward to what we hope to achieve in the next few months.

Never mind the Queen. This has been an *annus knobhardicus* for all Norwich fans. I certainly didn't imagine at the outset that we would be 3 points clear at the top by the time we had played all the other teams in the league. Come to that, I don't suppose anyone at the club thought that by Christmas they would be rushing out a video called 'Flying High', showing all the early games of the season.

All we have to do now is the same again, and the title's ours! Hang on a minute, though. What am I saying? 'All we have to do'? It's still a momentous task. I shouldn't weigh the team down with my recently-acquired expectations. Just as long as the video of the second half of the season isn't called 'Blasted out of the sky with a twelve-bore shotgun' ...

Saturday 2 January
Coventry City (home) – postponed
FA CUP THIRD ROUND

In the bleak mid-winter,
Frosty wind made moan,

Earth stood hard as iron,
Water like a stone;
Norwich bought a blanket
To keep the ground all soft,
But Keith Hackett tried it
And said the game was off.

I hate last-minute postponements. You get keyed up for a game (and Third-Round Saturday is one of the most exciting days of the season), and nothing happens. It's as painful as starting to pee and stopping before anything comes out.

The postponement also means a midweek replay, which I could do without. We have several midweek matches coming up in the next couple of months, and I can see this causing a problem or ten at work. They should have got Chairman Chase to stand in the centre circle and talk. All that hot air would have thawed the pitch within half an hour.

Still, at least we got a win on the pools panel. And I didn't make a long journey before discovering the game was off, unlike the bemused and disappointed Coventry supporters I saw outside the ground when I popped down to buy my ticket for next week's game at Sheffield Wednesday.

How would I fill my afternoon now? There wasn't much point in visiting the sales. Every year, they begin on a day when Norwich are playing away, so by the time I get down to the shops, there are just a couple of shirts looking all forlorn on their hangers. And you can't buy them, as you realise that everyone else in the city has looked at them and decided they are crap. I went for a haircut instead – but as this didn't take long, with me having so little hair to cut, I spent the rest of the afternoon looking through newspapers from the 1959 FA Cup run.

Mum had been talking about the run again during the week. Like many Norwich supporters of a certain age, she mentions it quite often – and as with people who go on about the war all the time, this can be tiresome. Yet when you look at the events they talk about, you realise why they do. The story of how a Third Division team reached the FA Cup semi-final and lost in the replay may not sound remarkable on the face of it. Other Third Division sides have got that far, if rarely. I only appreciated the magnitude of the achievement when Mum dug out the old newspapers a few years ago. Then I saw that this was no ordinary Cup run; this was an epic journey. These were not faded old newspapers; they were precious pieces of fragile parchment – like the Dead Sea Scrolls, only more important. I felt my heart racing and a cold sweat came over me as I traced the story.

When the campaign began in November 1958, there was no hint of what was to come. Norwich, who had almost gone out of business eighteen months previously, had not won at home for almost two months. They even trailed at half-time in the first-round match against Ilford from the Isthmian League before they eventually pulled through. In the second round, they needed a replay to scrape past Swindon, also of the Third Division. Then they were drawn to play Manchester United. The brilliant 'Busby Babes'. Gregg, Foulkes, Viollet, Quixall, Charlton. The team who had just won eight First Division matches on the trot. No one expected City to win, but they thrashed United 3-0. The adventure had begun.

Epic tales such as Homer's *Iliad* and Virgil's *Aeneid* mean little or nothing to most people nowadays but, in Norwich, the legendary exploits of the 1959 team provide a more vivid and relevant modern equivalent. Where Hercules took on and defeated the Nemean lion, the Hydra, the Erymanthian boar and the Cretan Bull, Norwich overcame the might of Manchester United, Cardiff City, Tottenham Hotspur and Sheffield United. Where Hector was wounded but fought on, the City goalkeeper Ken Nethercott played the last half-hour of the first match against Sheffield United with a dislocated shoulder. He never played a competitive match for the club again. There were great journeys (to White Hart Lane, Bramall Lane and St Andrews) and stirring battles until the gods finally turned against us, when Errol Crossan's goal against Luton Town in the first semi-final match was disallowed for reasons that no one in Norwich can understand to this day.

What I find most moving about the story is the fact that everyone in Norwich recognised at the time that they were witnessing something extraordinary, magical even. Many legends seem to be built up after the event by a gradual process of embellishment and dramatisation as the tale is retold. Obviously, a certain amount of this has occurred with the 1959 Cup run – for example, a song entitled *The Ballad of Crossan and Bly* was later composed in honour of the team's twin strikers – but there was clearly an awareness of the momentousness of the campaign while it was still in progress. (This, after all, explains why Mum kept the newspapers from the period.) Apparently, the whole city went football-crazy. The city council ran into severe financial problems because so many people were spending their rent and rate money on following Norwich in the Cup.

Nothing the club has achieved since (including two League Cup wins and two Second Division Championships) has been able to eclipse the feats of the '59 team. We have reached the FA Cup semi-final twice more in the last four years, but neither of those runs captured the imagination in quite the same way. Not least because most of the ties were at home against teams below us in the league – or, in the case of Sutton United in 1989, from a different league altogether. To outdo the '59 side, the present Norwich team would need to win the FA Cup by beating the likes of Arsenal, Liverpool and Manchester United away from home with ten men, each with one leg tied behind their backs – or by dropping a couple of divisions first, which frankly I'd rather they didn't do.

Reading through the newspapers of the time again, I still felt the old bottom lip wavering when I read about the defeat in the semi-final replay against Luton. Billy Bingham scored the only goal, and Mum's never forgiven him for it. What really struck me this time, however, was the way City's chances of success were constantly being written off by everyone outside Norfolk. This was just about understandable, with Norwich being in the Third Division then. But over thirty years later, with the club now well-established in the top flight, nothing seems to have changed on that score.

The papers this week have carried lists of honours awarded by the Queen. I see Gordon Strachan was given an OBE. It must stand for Often Bleats Endlessly. Mike Walker didn't get anything, though he'll be up for canonisation if we do win the league this season.

I saw Charlie again on 31 December (New Year's Eve to some) as he and his family had come down to Norfolk for a few days. His wife was soon subjecting me to the usual interrogation about the rarity of my visits to see them in Scarborough. She does not seem to understand how I can travel all over the country to watch Norwich play, yet am unable to find the time to go and call on them – though, in fairness, I have never managed to offer her a satisfactory explanation.

'Come on, give me a date so I can put it in my diary now,' she insisted. 'When are you coming to stay?'

I thought for a moment. '8 May,' I concluded.

As she scurried off, satisfied, to find her diary, Charlie whispered, 'Middlesbrough away?' I nodded. Charlie gave a discreet 'thumbs-up' sign.

I had to drive back down to London through freezing fog on Saturday night. I didn't want to, but I had little choice as I had the nets for the Sunday-morning match. We all take it in turns to bring the essential equipment. One person will bring the nets, another the balls, another the kit, another the half-time oranges, another the *Sunday Sport* to laugh at in the dressing-room.

The professionals don't have to do all this, of course. They're just mollycoddled. Have you ever seen the players of a Premier League team struggling to put up goal-nets with frozen fingers in a biting wind five minutes before kick-off? Mind you, it may be just as well they aren't given these added responsibilities. I can just imagine the announcement: 'Ladies and gentlemen, we regret that the kick-off for this afternoon's match has been delayed by an hour, as Ruel has left the kit at home.'

We all turned up at the ground, but the referee took one look at the pitch and declared it too hard and rutted to play on. I wish he had looked at it the day before and saved me the trouble of travelling down in the fog. He would also have saved me from the stick I took for my new haircut. I was greeted with 'Vinny! Vinny!' when I showed up and a rendition of *Deeply Dippy* as we made our way back to the car park. Perhaps I might have had my hair cut a little too short this time. It's not that I wanted to be a skinhead; I was just taking revenge on my hair for leaving me. As if to say, 'Well, bugger off if you're going.'

The draw for the fourth round of the FA Cup was made on Sunday afternoon. If we get past Coventry, we'll have Spurs at home. Hmm. Could be worse.

Sunday 10 January
Sheffield Wednesday (away)

The week got off to a rotten start, what with having to go back to work on Monday. My boss seemed to have made a resolution to try to bear a closer resemblance to a human being. 'How are Norwich doing?' he asked in as friendly a manner as he could manage. Then he blew it. 'Did you see them over Christmas?'

Did I see them? What a prat. He hasn't got a clue. I wonder what he'll have to say if he notices me leaving early on Wednesday afternoons over the next few months. I'm certainly not going to miss any games with the season we're having. Sod the consequences, recession or no recession; this could be the best chance we ever have of winning the league.

On Tuesday morning, a Christmas present turned up. Much later, and I'd have wondered if it had been posted early for next Christmas. It turned out to be from the Wolverine. 'OK, Kevin, here's the deal,' read the gift tag. 'If Norwich win the Championship this season, you can have a ceremonial burning of this present. But if they don't, you have to wear it around Norwich for a day (uncovered).'

What could it be? A Wolves scarf? A Wolves shirt? Unbelievably, it was even worse. It was a T-shirt that had been specially printed with the legend 'Blackburn 7 Norwich 1'.

Even the present she sent for my birthday last year wasn't this bad. On that occasion, she gave me the Wolverhampton Wanderers board game, the aim of which seems to be to get all four sides of your ground open before the turn of the century. For added realism, each player has to sit fifty yards away from the board. (No, that won't mean much if you haven't been to Molineux in the last ten years.)

I rang her in the evening to have a go at her. 'Come on,' she said. 'You have to admit that I put some thought into it.'

'Yes, bloody malicious thought,' I raged. 'That's not the sort of thought that counts. And it was late.'

'I wasn't able to pick it up until Christmas Eve. You don't sound very grateful.'

'Grateful? You're the one who should be grateful.'

'Me? Why?'

'Because I haven't come up and throttled you with this bloody thing. I would have done if you'd had the Ipswich score printed on it.'

'So will you wear it if Norwich don't win the league?'

'No I won't. Why would I want to wear something that says "My team are crap"? In any case, I'd probably get beaten up if I wore that around Norwich.'

'Why? They'd realise you weren't from Blackburn when they heard your accent.'

'No, but they might think I was an Ipswich fan taking the piss. I've a good mind to have a ceremonial burning of it now.' And I will burn it. Honest. I just haven't got round to it yet.

The conversation moved briefly on to other subjects, such as the Wolverine's impending redundancy (which I was sorry to hear about) and her boyfriend's gout (which I wasn't), but inevitably it returned to football. It turns out that both of us have a strong feeling that Wolves and Norwich will meet in the FA Cup this year.

'I'll get to meet your Mum at last,' she said. Oh no! I can do without the two of them greeting each other with a simultaneous 'I've heard so much about you.' I don't think that Mum would want to meet her now, though. She's been encouraging me to make more of an effort with the Wolverine, but once I told her about this T-shirt, she changed her tune completely.

'That's just being nasty,' she said. 'She's no good, forget her.' I'll try, Mum, I'll try.

The match with Sheffield Wednesday had been moved to Sunday afternoon for the benefit of our friends at BSkyB. Once again, this meant I was left kicking my heels on Saturday afternoon and unable to kick anyone else's on Sunday morning. The fact that we were to play on a Sunday did, however, put me in mind of all the parallels that can be drawn between football and religion. Some similarities have been pointed out many times, of course. The followers congregating at the place of worship every week, singing songs to their idols, either in prayer or praise, the partaking of wafers and alcohol as part of the ritual (in this case, crisps and beer rather than bread and wine). Football, like religion, has been called the 'opiate of the masses' – though it does seem today that there are powerful figures in the game who would prefer it to be the designer drug of the privileged few.

Yet there are plenty of other parallels if you look closely. In both cases, being an adherent involves an act of faith that has little to do with logic or pragmatism. I went to see Billy Graham at Villa Park a few years ago and felt he should have been taken off at half-time. He tried to use pragmatic reasons to persuade people to follow God and ended up sounding like an afterlife insurance salesman. 'When the time comes for you to shake off this mortal coil – not too soon, we pray – make sure your future is protected with a fully comprehensive Acme faith policy. Just a small weekly outlay will guarantee you that retirement cloud of your own that you've always dreamed of. And just think of the alternative ... '

Then there are the conflicts, occasionally violent, that take place between members of different sects and factions when they should really be brought together by a spirit of mutual respect and understanding. This in turn can lead to people who might like to get involved in football or religion being put off when they see the sort of people who are already followers, even though these trouble-makers are invariably a tiny minority.

Football grounds often resemble churches in that there are generally rows and rows of empty seats, but when there is a big occasion and the TV cameras turn up (though without Thora Hird in the case of football), the place is packed out.

At Norwich, there is a further similarity in that the team frequently moves in a mysterious way.

But by far the most important parallel is the way in which both football and religion give a structure and a purpose to a life which is essentially chaotic. In both cases, the structure is artificial – man-made, you might say – but it is no less valid for that ... though football is perhaps the more valid of the two, as at least the Norwich team clearly exists. Well, usually.

It had been rumoured a couple of months ago that the club would be laying on another plane trip for this game, but nothing came of it in the end. Mum, Stephen and Karen had the task of finding somewhere to watch the game on Sky instead, while I drove up from London as usual. I allowed plenty of time for the journey, and as there was an unforeseen lack of delays, I arrived at Hillsborough ridiculously early. I was inside the ground at 2:30pm, which wouldn't have been ridiculous except for the fact that, because of Sky, the game was to start at the bizarre time of 4pm.

I bought a meat pie ($^6/_{10}$ – OK, but a bit dry) and sat down alone (apart from the police and stewards) to watch the huge ground start to fill up. It *was* like being in a church; it was cold, damp and almost deserted. Yet when full, as it was for our FA Cup semi-final against Sunderland last season, it is a marvellously vibrant stadium.

Ah, the semi-final. What a memorable, moving, miserable day that was. Memorable and moving for the singing of 'You'll Never Walk Alone' with the Sunderland fans before the game, the laying of flowers at the end where so many Liverpool fans had died at a semi-final three years before, and Karen's presence at an away game for the first time. (Disappointingly, none of these events received much coverage in the media at the time.) Miserable because we lost 1-0. To a goal that should have been disallowed for offside, though we played appallingly anyway.

I hoped that the players wouldn't still be haunted by the defeat that day, but I feared they might. After all, here I was thinking about it. This wouldn't be our first game here since the semi-final (we had lost 2-0 to Wednesday in the league a couple of weeks afterwards), but it still wasn't out of my system. In fact, if you mention the name 'Hillsborough' in Norfolk, most people's first thought will be of the disastrous performance against Sunderland rather than the Liverpool tragedy. It was difficult to imagine that the latter could have occurred just below us in the West Stand (formerly the Leppings Lane End). The infamous steel fences had gone, there were seats where the terraces had been (for once I could appreciate why this had been done), and stairs leading up to the top tier where we were.

Mercifully, we were spared the usual Sky pre-match fireworks and frippery. Have they got the message at last? Or have the dancing girls got the flu through having to prance around in all weathers? Instead we were entertained by a man wearing an owl costume and a Sheffield Wednesday strip. When he tripped over and his head rolled off, he got one of the biggest cheers of the afternoon.

By kick-off time, there were around a thousand Norwich fans in the ground – a decent turn-out considering the distance from Norwich and the fact that the game was being televised. Judging from the conversations (and smells) of the people around me, several had rushed up to Sheffield straight after playing football in the morning.

One voice stood out among all the others. It sounded like a cross between John Major and a train-spotter – same thing, really, I suppose – and belonged to a man just behind me who was subjecting his hapless neighbour to a nerd's version of *Twenty Questions*. 'Where have you travelled from today? What was the traffic like? Did you stop anywhere? What did you have to eat? Did you come to the semi-final last year? Why do you think we lost? Have you seen any Italian football on the television.? What do you think of Gazza? Do you prefer anoraks with big hoods or with ones that zip into the collar? Can I be your friend? ... '

The question 'Why don't you shut up?' was not far from my lips, but the man being interrogated got up and left him sitting there with no one to talk to. He said he was just going to get a cup of tea, but wisely he never returned. Still, it was interesting to hear someone else mention last season's semi-final, even if he was a spanner. I clearly wasn't the only one brooding about it.

Unfortunately, my fears that the players might be similarly affected appeared to be entirely justified. There seemed to be a marginal drop in self-belief in the team. Marginal, but crucial. After all, good deeds alone will not secure a place in the Kingdom of Heaven; absolute faith is essential. The defence was hesitant, and there was a lack of conviction up front that we had not seen since last season.

There may, of course, have been other reasons than the memory of the semi-final for this. Mum had rung me on Saturday morning and told me to go and buy the *Daily Mirror*. 'You should see what Ian Crook's been saying,' she said.

The article wasn't hard to spot. 'We're no champs, says Ian' ran the headline. It got worse. '"I don't think we will win the title," he said. "I don't expect us to be top by the end of the season. Nobody at Norwich does."' True, his words may have been twisted or taken out of context. It wouldn't be the first time a tabloid has done this. But even so, they did reveal a negative attitude at the club which is even more distressing than that of the national media towards us, to which the players are often the first to object. This attitude has been present at Norwich for some time. Only last season, two players (Bowen and Sherwood, if my memory serves me correctly) remarked casually on the radio that we are a side who will always win a few, then lose a few. Mike Walker has done his best to get rid of that outlook this season, but at the moment it seems that, like stubborn weeds on a garden path, it will take several treatments to eradicate altogether, if ever.

The Norwich crowd were very quiet. On reflection, a church congregation would have done more singing. 'Blessed are the yellows, for they are so good it is unbelievable' or 'Come unto us if thou thinkest thyself hard enough', perhaps. Then Mark Robins, the saviour who had come among us to heal the sick and lame, was carried off with a suspected broken ankle, and our spirits sank even lower. Wednesday dominated the rest of the first half, forcing Gunn to make save after save and having a goal disallowed – but just when we thought we might hang on until the break, they scored. Gunn could only parry a long-range drive from John Sheridan, and Nigel Worthington thumped in the rebound.

I met Jon, the fellow Capital Canary, at half-time. He looked even more morose than me. 'I said I'd never come here again after the semi-final,' he muttered, shaking his head in total resignation. It did seem that everyone was preoccupied with that game.

The City contingent made more noise in the second half, but the tone was one of desperation rather than encouragement. Impassioned pleas of 'Come *on*, Norwich' were followed by great groans when the players' efforts came to nothing. The only enthusiastic applause was given to the referee, though this was out of sarcasm on those rare occasions when he awarded us a free kick. He did have a poor game, but when supporters concentrate their attention on the ref rather than on their team it is generally a sign that they fear the worst and are trying to console themselves with the notion that their fate has been preordained by an all-powerful malevolent spirit. Still, there were no cries of 'What a load of rubbish' directed at the players; they have given us too much this season to be abused so abruptly. We'll give them another couple of weeks.

In the last quarter of an hour, we created two excellent chances but missed both. We all knew, however, that on the balance of play we should have been three or four down by then anyway. Everyone trooped out, not uplifted and illuminated by glory, but as solemn as if we had been told we were lost souls heading straight for damnation.

Apparently, the deepest depression ever recorded by the Met Office was located between Scotland and Iceland this afternoon. Huh. If they'd had a barometer in the West Stand at Hillsborough, they'd have found one to beat it.

When I got back to the flat, I rang Mum to see if she was as dejected as I was. As it turned out, she wasn't, because she and Stephen hadn't managed to see the game. They had spent most of the afternoon driving around Norwich looking for somewhere with a satellite dish, but all their friends were out and all the pubs were shut. Even the bar at Carrow Road was closed. Should I blame Sky, the licensing laws, or the club? Best to be on the safe side and blame everyone.

Surprisingly, my colleagues at work were almost sympathetic the next day. Some suggested that we might do better just out of the spotlight that always falls on the team at the top. (We are now third behind Manchester United and Aston Villa.) Unsurprisingly, the national press stuck the boot in. *Today* was the worst. 'Norwich title bid exposed' gloated the headline. 'Norwich City's Championship credentials look about as genuine as a dodgy Rolex. They ... have been exposed as fakes.' This was offensive enough, but then the reporter stooped disgracefully low. 'Norwich might not even end the season as the top team in East Anglia.' I don't think there's any call for that, really.

Wednesday 13 January
Coventry City (home)
FA CUP THIRD ROUND

After Sunday, I decided that drastic measures needed to be taken to win this match. I always make a point of not wearing anything the same colour as the opposition's kit (jeans are classed as neutral for this purpose), but now something more had to be done. So it was that I turned up to work in a yellow coat (hi-de-hi!), green jumper, yellow shirt, green socks and pants and yellow shoes.

Despite my intentions for the evening being so obvious, I managed to sidestep the boss, weave down the stairs, and play a neat one-two with the receptionist at around 4pm. The journey thereafter was not so straightforward. The traffic in North London was so heavy, it took an hour to travel ten miles. While stuck in the jam, I heard on the radio that high winds had overturned a lorry on the northbound carriageway of the M11 and this was causing a long tailback. It looked as if I wouldn't make the game – at my rate of progress, I would reach Norwich at around quarter to four in the morning.

Once on the M25, however, I went screaming all the way up to Norwich. Screaming 'Out of my way, you bastards', mainly. As I neared the centre of the known cosmos, I heard Chairman Chase being interviewed on the local radio. Unlike me, he didn't admit to being a miserable bloke. Instead, he was expressing his opposition to the idea of a mid-season break and supporting the idea of installing undersoil heating at Carrow Road. What was this? He was actually saying things I agreed with. He can't be feeling well. Or I'm not.

Apparently, the reason undersoil heating hasn't been put in before now is that improving the toilet facilities was a priority. That's fair enough, I suppose, though I never use them. Perhaps I ought to pay a visit to see if Chase has made them all-seater too.

I arrived at Mum's fifteen minutes before kick-off. Unfortunately, the house is twenty minutes from the ground but, running downhill with the wind behind me, I managed to get there just as the teams were coming out. Mum and Stephen had saved me a seat, which was just as well since our stand was packed. The away section was also full, probably because Coventry had laid on free coach travel for their fans to compensate them for their wasted journeys ten days before. The resulting atmosphere was so loud that I had trouble making Mum and Stephen hear why I was late.

The volume of Mum's voice meant that she had much less trouble in telling me about Karen's condition. In fact, the whole of the River End soon knew that the baby was 'engaged' (this was the first time I had heard Mum use the word without giving me a meaningful stare) and could be born at any time. What would Mum do if a message were broadcast telling her to rush home? 'I'll have to go,' she said, ' ... unless we're one up with five minutes left.'

The game was of poor quality from the start because of the conditions. It was very windy, which usually means the ball should be kept on the ground, but the wetness of the pitch made a short-passing game impossible. You couldn't see any puddles, but every time a player made a sliding tackle, a wave of Old Spice proportions was created.

In the circumstances, it was just as well we had Chris Sutton and Darren Beckford up front, as both are tall and strong enough to act as target men. In any case, Lee Power had been ruled out for making the wrong sort of runs in training. (To the toilet.) Coventry's twin strikers came in for more attention from the home crowd, however. Mick Quinn, a recent signing from Newcastle, was greeted with cries of 'Sumo! Sumo!' and 'There's only one Mr Blobby' whenever he touched the ball. The Coventry supporters did not deny the, er, stockiness of his physique, but strove to emphasise his qualities with 'He's fat, he's round, he's worth a million pounds'. Our old friend Robert Rosario was taunted with donkey noises and calls of 'Can you get us tickets for the final, Rosie?' – a reference to his ban from receiving any for having previously let his allocation fall into the hands of the touts.

'He hasn't improved, has he?' said a man nearby.

'Well, he must be doing something right,' came a reply. 'They've made him captain.'

'They've never.'

'They have.'

'Bloody hell. I've never thought of him as captain material. Hair-oil monitor perhaps, but not captain.' You could see what he meant about Rosario's hair. It looked as if he had just been for a dip in the slick off the Shetlands.

The fact that Coventry had two glorious chances to score in the first ten minutes could not be attributed to the talents of Quinn and Rosario. Rather, it was because the Norwich defence was again flapping around like a loose tarpaulin in a high wind. 'You're even worse than the Villa' came from the Coventry section, which was rich considering how we had completely outplayed them not so long ago.

'Come on, City. Get stuck in, City,' Mum pleaded.

'Can you be a bit more specific?' I said. 'They're City as well. You don't want to encourage Coventry by mistake.'

Spurred on by the subsequent chorus of 'Come on, you yellows', which could not be misinterpreted, Norwich came more into the game. Both teams were now fired up by the special atmosphere which always surrounds FA Cup-ties. In fact they were too fired up, and the late challenges and off-the-ball elbowing and pushing were threatening to get out of hand. 'Sort it out, Hackett!' bellowed Mum, who needed little incentive to abuse her least favourite referee of all time.

Suddenly, an announcement came over the loudspeakers. 'We have a message for a Norwich supporter in the River End.' Oh no! Karen must have started to produce the new Norwich supporter! Mum was half-way to the exit when she realised it was a false alarm. The message turned out to be for someone who had come into the ground with his mate's ticket in his pocket. His mate had been standing outside waiting for him for twenty minutes.

Sutton was having an excellent game up front, working tirelessly to make something happen. This was in marked contrast to Beckford, who seemed to be waiting for a simple chance to present itself to him a few yards out. Curiously enough, though, this is precisely what happened three minutes into the second half, and Beckford prodded the ball past Ogrizovic (or, as Mum calls him, 'Ogizro ... Ozvigo ... the Coventry goalie') to score our first goal in 499 minutes of football. I discovered later that this had been the club's longest spell without a goal for 66 years. When I asked Mum if she remembered that barren spell, she asked if I would like my tea over my head. I took that as a 'no'.

When Mum opened her Golden Goal ticket after Beckford had scored, she discovered that her lucky number was only four away from winning a new watch. For some reason, Stephen didn't seem very sympathetic.

After the goal, Norwich grew more confident and made several more chances. Bobby Gould, the Coventry manager, grew more irate and was made to sit up in the directors' box by Hackett. Fortunately, his team did not show the same passion, and we held on reasonably comfortably for a 1–0 win.

The game had hardly been a glorious spectacle, but then successful Cup runs often have humble beginnings. The important thing was that we had won. I hoped that this marked the end of our bad spell for the season. The traditional Christmas trimmings had been taken down eight days before; our traditional Christmas run of poor form was now over too.

'Your clothes worked then,' said Stephen. 'You'll have to stay unchanged for the rest of the season now.'

'He'll hum a bit come May if he does,' said Mum. 'He'll have to have a block of seats to himself.'

We fairly bounded up Jimmy Hill, oblivious to the awful weather in our happy mood. 'I think I do well to keep up with you youngsters,' said Mum.

'With us what?' I asked.

'Youngsters,' she repeated.
'What?' I asked again.
'Youngsters! Are you going deaf or something?'
'No, I just like hearing you call us that.'

For some reason, *News at Ten* led that night with the story of US aircraft bombing Iraq. I don't know why – the end of our goal drought seemed far more important to me. TV news programmes are always getting their priorities wrong like this. At least with newspapers, you can start at the back page and read them in reverse. When ITN finally got to the FA Cup results, the main story was Bolton's 2–0 win at Liverpool. This was excellent news, and not just because of the malicious pleasure of seeing the Mighty Reds being the victims of a giant-killing act. It meant that our fourth-round match would be televised live on BBC1 instead of Wolves'. Ha! Ha! If Wolves had been playing Liverpool as everyone had expected (tickets have apparently been selling like hot sex in Wolverhampton), their game would have been shown. Wolves v Bolton is thought by the BBC to be less appealing than Norwich v Spurs, so we're on! At last, a chance to show everyone what we can do.

Incidentally, I noticed in the paper this week that Dave Beasant has gone to Wolves on loan. I hope he plays to form – it would give me an early opportunity to get my own back on the Wolverine for that ruddy T-shirt.

When I got to work on Thursday morning, I found that the boss had been on the warpath again. My desk was covered with notes. '4:30pm. Where are you?'; '4:40pm. Could you pop into my office?'; '4:50pm. I NEED TO SEE YOU URGENTLY!' There were variations on the theme until 6pm.

He had cooled down somewhat when I saw him. 'I was looking for you last night,' he said.
'So I see. What was it about?'
'Oh, I managed to sort it all out myself in the end.' In other words, he hadn't really needed to see me at all. 'I suppose you'd gone to see Norwich.'
'Of course.'
'Well ... well ... just let me know when you're going next time.' I'd better, I suppose. But what about the time after that? And the time after that? And the time after that?

Saturday 16 January
Coventry City (home)

Football is full of ironies. Do you remember how at the start of the season I was teased at work by a Notts County supporter who couldn't remember our new manager's name? How he referred to Mike Walker as Mike Hedgehog? This week, Neil Warnock was sacked as manager of Notts County and replaced, though only on a caretaker basis for the time being, by the club's youth-team coach – one Mike Walker! I paid our resident fan a visit. 'Two Mike Hedgehogs, there's only two Mike Hedgehogs ...,' I sang. Unfortunately, he had no recollection of what he said five months ago and is now convinced that I am stark raving mad (whereas before he only suspected it).

I visited Karen on Saturday morning. There's still no sign of the baby (apart from the enormous bulge, naturally). This is causing a certain amount of concern, as Karen may end up being in hospital when the Cup match is on TV. 'Can you bring your miniature TV back with you next weekend just in case?' she asked. I said I would, but I can see this causing some confusion if she's watching the game in the delivery room ...

'Oooh! Aaarrgghhh!! Ohhh!!!'
'What's the matter, madam? Would you like some more gas?'
'No, we've just hit the bar.'

Stephen looked very smug when he came round to Mum's for lunch. He said he'd found a new source of inside information from the club. Mum and I looked at each other, worried that he might be seeing the woman in the club shop again, but our fears were unfounded. He'd bumped into John Deehan, Norwich's assistant manager, in a chip shop. Nice to see they're all on a healthy eating programme at the club. Mind you, I don't suppose it matters too much if Deehan eats at the chippy. It's us players who have to stay in peak physical condition.

Stephen wasn't able to lord it over us with any juicy bits of news from the dressing-room, however. They had just had a general chat about confidence and morale. Apparently, it's still very high, which is good news, though Deehan said that the best team spirit he has ever known at any club was at Norwich in the early '80s, when he played alongside Keith Bertschin, John Devine and Mike Channon. They were always playing practical jokes on each other, such as the time when all the clocks and watches at the training ground were put ahead by two hours to make Channon think he would miss the afternoon's race meeting at Newmarket.

Despite Wednesday night's win over Coventry, I wasn't too confident that we would beat them again in the league. If anything, this was because of Wednesday's win ...

Kevin's Alternative Laws of Football (No.7)

'When two teams play each other in the league and Cup in the same week, whichever team wins the first game will lose the second.'

This law was proved recently when Gillingham won at Colchester in the FA Cup, then lost at home to them in the league three days later. Even with the weather being much better and Coventry having several injuries, I felt distinctly uneasy.

Not surprisingly, Coventry had far fewer supporters with them than on Wednesday night. The fans had had to pay to travel this time, and their performance in the Cup wouldn't have persuaded any waverers that it would be worth it. Yet the Norwich turn-out was even more disappointing. Yes, there's a recession on and Christmas is just over. Yes, we've been going through a bad patch. True, Coventry are not the most glamorous team in the league. True, there is the big Cup match against Spurs next weekend. But a team third in the league should not be playing in front of whole blocks of empty seats, especially when admission to this game was as little as £6 (£3 for juveniles and OAPs). I can't help thinking back to those years when we were languishing in the middle of the old Second Division. It seemed then that everyone in the city would have given their non-rattle-waving arm just to see Norwich in the top division, let alone in contention for the league title, but now the team's position seems to be taken for granted. Perhaps people are fed up with seeing the team promise so much, yet fail at the last – but this is no excuse, as supporters should turn up in numbers to try to ensure that the team doesn't fail.

Several of the fans who did bother to come to this game had their minds on other things. Many were pressing radios to their ears to listen to the commentary on the England v France rugby international, while others craned their necks to watch it on the TVs in the executive boxes. 'What do they think they're doing?' I complained.

'They obviously like rugby,' said Mum. 'Not everyone is interested in football and nothing else, you know. Anyway, it's only the same as you taking that little radio to the doctor's wedding to keep up with the football scores.' I pointed out that there was a subtle but critical distinction to be made here. Rugby is crap and football isn't.

I loathe rugby for all the years I was forced to play it at school. Not that I really played it. Charlie and I had an ongoing competition to see who could go more games without touching the ball. We both became experts at predicting where the ball was going, then moving to the other side of the pitch. Charlie once managed to keep a clean pair of hands for eight games; my best run (six) came to a painful end when the teacher in charge realised what I was doing and hurled the ball at me.

We would much rather have played football, but this wasn't an option at our school. The other major sports were hockey (which wasn't too far removed from football, but the sticks seemed an unnecessary encumbrance to me) and cricket (the sporting equivalent of Mogadon). All those wasted years. Just think, if I'd been able to play football throughout my formative years, I might have been a professional today. Well, semi-pro. Well, semi-decent. Well, maybe not.

Many of the fans in the lower tier of the Barclay Stand had another preoccupation. The club stewards had been instructed to clamp down on those supporters who still insisted on standing instead of sitting. This stand-up protest against the all-seater policy has been going on all season, but now the chairman has decided to put a stop to it. He claims to have received complaints from spectators who say they cannot see because of others standing in front of them. I find this hard to believe, as those who insist on standing make sure that they arrive early and occupy places at the back. Besides, it is hardly a dangerous practice. And in any case, everyone at that end stands up when Norwich attack. Mr Chase would doubtless deny it, but his actions suggest that he regards the continued defiance of this group of fans as a personal affront.

Whatever the motivation, the fact was that, for the whole of the first half, we were treated to the shameful spectacle of some of the club's most loyal and vociferous followers being ejected from the ground for the heinous crime of standing up. Not for fighting or vandalism or obscene chants. For standing up. To argue that, if the fans do not like the rules, they should not come is to fail totally to understand them. If you are a true supporter, as these people are, you have to be there. Protesting by staying away isn't an option.

Some fans left quietly, but others were more reluctant. One took off his yellow and green scarf and hurled it away in disgust. Two supporters who had come up from London, I heard later, paid to get back in and sat quietly in a different part of the stand but were spotted by a steward who promptly threw them out again. Those who remained in the ground showed their solidarity with those expelled by applauding them and chanting 'If you all hate seats, clap your hands' as well as that timeless classic 'Chase out!' We hadn't heard that for months, with the team being top of the league and cheap flights to sun-kissed Oldham being offered, but the old resentment had clearly not disappeared. The prospect of the club's season degenerating amid a series of bitter disputes and recriminations was now real and worrying.

The team didn't seem too distracted in the first half. We went one up after fifteen minutes with a low shot from Sutton which rounded off a wonderfully clever passing move involving Crook, Phillips, Bowen, Fox and Uncle Tom Cobley and all. We would have scored several more but for that accursed hesitancy in front of goal which we still hadn't shaken off completely. Yet after half-time – during which the electronic scoreboard announced that the 1993 Norwich City calendar now cost only £3.50 in the club shop, whereas it had been £.50 (?!) – the game changed dramatically.

A bizarre sequence of events led to Coventry being awarded a penalty. A weak back-pass from Bowen was intercepted by John Williams, Gunn came careering out of his goal like a driverless truck with no brakes hitting an ice patch and almost knocked him on to the roof of the main stand, the ball ran across the penalty area, and Sumo Quinn tapped it into an empty net. The Coventry players naturally claimed a goal, but it turned out that, in the millisecond between the pile-up and the goal, the referee had blown for a penalty. In that case, Coventry argued, Gunn should be sent off for assault and battery on a player who had a clear goal-scoring opportunity. The new rules were quite firm on this; he had to be dismissed. However, he escaped without even a booking. How could this be? Surely not because the referee was called Gunn ...

'Sorry son, you'll have to go off.'

'Oh, Dad ... '

'Look, it's the rules.'

'I'll tell Mum about you when we get home.'

'Now then Bryan, I don't think there's any need for that ... '

'I will, I will.'

'Oh all right, you can stay on. But if you do it again, you'll be sent to bed early without any tea.'

To our enormous pleasure, Bryan Gunn saved the spot kick, and Quinn thumped the rebound against the bar from point-blank range. If we had been denied a goal in these circumstances, we would have been furious, but after all the penalties we have missed this season and the lack of luck we have had in recent weeks, any moral scruples we had were forcibly ejected from our minds by the orange-jacketed stewards Relief, Desperation and Schadenfreude.

Coventry could have been demoralised or fired up by this. Unfortunately for us, they chose the latter reaction and, just two minutes later, they sliced open our defence and Quinn exuberantly hammered the ball home. The goal opened all the unhealed sores again. The players lost their way once more, some fans started moaning at them, other fans started moaning at the fans who were moaning, and the stewards demonstrated again that their courses in advanced officiousness hadn't been in vain.

A dispute arose when Norwich were awarded a free kick near the half-way line. The ball was on the goal-line in front of the River End with no players anywhere near it, so in view of the ball-boys' and girls' customary inertia (either because they are awe-struck at being so close to the hallowed turf, or because they are bone idle), a Norwich fan nipped on to the pitch, booted the ball towards the centre of the pitch so that the game could be resumed, and returned to his seat. He earned applause from the crowd – and a telling-off from one of the stewards. 'Jesus Christ,' bawled a man a couple of rows in front of me, 'can't we do anything in this place any more?'

It appears not. There was a notice in the match programme requesting supporters not to welcome the team on to the pitch by throwing handfuls of torn-up paper into the air, as the pieces are hard to pick up. Honestly, the club sounded just like those killjoy vicars who don't allow confetti to be thrown outside their churches after weddings. Even seaside boarding houses don't have this many petty rules. What next? 'Quiet please' signs being put up? Matches sponsored by the Noise Abatement Society?

Despite two more injuries (Crook hobbled off, Polston was carried off), we managed to hold on for the draw. My seventh alternative law of football had been broken in this case, but only because of the welcome error by Bryan's dad. We had returned to the top of the league with this point, but you would never have guessed it from the faces of the City fans leaving the ground. We all knew that we had dropped 2 points rather than gained 1, and that our stay at the top would probably be short with Villa playing on Sunday and Manchester United on Monday night.

Was it all my fault for not wearing the same clothes as on Wednesday? (They were still in the wash.) Whatever, I got the blame for the Sunday side's performance the next morning. While I was travelling to Hillsborough last week, the team won 2–1. This week we lost 6–1. 'It must be down to you, Kev, you're the only change.'

I tried to argue that the result owed more to the quality of the opposition (top of the division, beaten only once all season), but in vain. My cause wasn't helped by a terrible miss in the first half. Unchallenged, and with only the keeper to beat from fifteen yards, I sliced the ball ten yards wide.

'Never mind,' Mum said when I rang her later. 'Even the professionals miss badly sometimes. And at least you didn't have ten thousand people calling you a useless tosser.'

'Ten people was bad enough, mother,' I replied.

Villa hammered Middlesbrough 5–1 on Sunday afternoon to move ahead of us again. And Wolves scored twice in the last seven minutes to beat Birmingham 2–1. Damn and blast.

Sunday 24 January
Tottenham Hotspur (home)
FA CUP FOURTH ROUND

Karen's baby still hasn't turned up. 'Can't you have it induced?' I asked her, thinking that this merely involved using a megaphone to shout 'Come out, we know you're in there' or 'Hurry up, the big game's tomorrow'. Karen then told me what inducing a baby actually involves. I'm glad I wasn't eating at the time.

I spent the whole of Saturday getting tense for the Cup match. I spent the best part of the evening (well, perhaps 'best' isn't the right word) on the toilet. The next time someone says I'm full of crap, I'll be inclined to agree with them.

This was a big occasion. We were to be live on BBC1, so at last everyone would see why we've been having such a good season. I told everyone at work to watch and set the video even though I was going to the game. I would certainly want to see it again. After all, Norwich–Spurs matches are always good. Even when we lost in the quarter-final of the Rumbelows Cup at White Hart Lane last year, it was an outstanding game and an electric evening. There was bound to be a cracking atmosphere at this Cup-tie too, I figured. It would be one of those occasions when it seems as if the whole of Norwich is packed inside the ground. And when we won, the whole city would celebrate.

It's not like living in a city such as Liverpool, Manchester, Sheffield, Birmingham or London, where there are several teams. In these, the loyalties of the inhabitants are inevitably split. If Sheffield Wednesday win a game, there are as many people in Sheffield who curse the fact as there are who rejoice in it. When Arsenal win the Championship, the percentage of Londoners who are happy about it is relatively low.

In Norwich – in Norfolk, indeed – there is only one professional team to follow. You get the odd Manchester United or Liverpool fan, of course, but they don't exist in great numbers. In fact, the second largest faction in Norfolk would have to be those grumpy sods who support whichever team Norwich are playing that week, without actually following any team in particular. Mum's butcher is a prime example of this type, though there are many others who enjoy it when Norwich lose so that they can write long letters to the local papers saying how awful City are.

In the late '70s and early '80s, when Bobby Robson was in his heyday at Ipswich (I know it seems hard now to believe that he ever had one, but he did), many of these miserable individuals temporarily became Town followers. 'ITFC' started appearing on walls, though it never took long for 'SH' to be added in front. They've faded away in recent years, but will they soon be making a reappearance?

Being born in Norwich to a Norwich-supporting family, there was never any question who I would follow. In the past, though, I have wondered who I would support if I had been born in London. Spurs, for their entertaining style of football? West Ham, for the same reason? Temperamentally, I would probably be best suited to Fulham. They aren't very successful, but their supporters have a wry sense of humour and are able to laugh at themselves. Well, it saves others the trouble. If I followed Barnet, I would be able to have a good moan about the chairman as I do now.

But it's pointless speculating about it, I now realise. I simply wouldn't have a choice. I would be drawn towards a team by other members of my family, the area I lived in, friends, or even by accident. One girl at work follows Arsenal simply because her father gave her a couple of Esso World Cup coins in 1970 that happened to feature two Arsenal players.

It has been suggested to me (by people who understand nothing about football, admittedly) that I should transfer my allegiance to a London team now that I live in London. What a ridiculous idea. I simply couldn't do this, and I have always been deeply suspicious of anyone who does switch their support. David 'Kid' Jensen used to support QPR when he really was a kid, but now you can't listen to him on Capital Radio in the afternoons because he's shouting 'Eagles!' every five minutes. More relevant to this match is the example of Sir John Quinton, a very large toupee in Barclays Bank and the Premier League, who used to support Norwich and is now a Tottenham fan. I do fear for football when a turncoat is allowed to occupy such a prominent position in the game.

When I arrived at Carrow Road, wearing the yellow and green clothes that had proved so successful in the Cup match against Coventry, it wasn't as if the whole city was there after all. Judging from all the empty seats, most people had decided to stay at home and watch on TV. They hadn't been saving up for this game as I had hoped; if anything, this turn-out was even worse than that for the Coventry league match. Only 15,000 were here, and that included 3,000 Spurs fans. It was disgraceful. I heard some complaints that the prices were too high for this game, but for once I wouldn't blame the club. The prices were the same as for the league match against Spurs on Boxing Day, and you would think that tickets for such an attractive tie would be snapped up at once. If we got to Wembley, you can be sure that all the stay-away supporters would expect tickets.

Perhaps the name of the ground should be changed. What would be an appropriate name for a large construction by a river with lots of empty space to be filled? I know. How about Canary Wharf?

Disappointing though the crowd was, I was in an expectant mood myself (though not as expectant as Karen, obviously). I was cheered by the news before the kick-off that Wolves were losing 2–0 to Bolton in their game, which had started at 2pm, and prepared to chant 'Wolverine, Wolverine, can you hear us on the box?'

The first half carried on from where the Boxing Day game had left off. Both sides played some attractive football, with Norwich having slightly more possession but Spurs creating the better chances. Unfortunately, events in the Barclay Stand continued from the last Coventry game. There were more ejections for standing, and this time fewer fans were prepared to leave quietly. One required half the Norfolk police force to carry him out. Chants of 'Chase out' greatly outnumbered the choruses of 'On the ball, City'.

This was hardly helping the team, but even so we looked increasingly likely to score as the half progressed. I was quite happy at half-time – and very happy when I heard that Wolves had lost. Mum and the Wolverine won't be meeting up this year, which is just as well as it would only cause me trouble.

Within the first five minutes of the second half, it was as if two bombs had gone off without warning in an unsuspecting neighbourhood. Sheringham (ironically, the name of a peaceful resort in Norfolk) scored twice in two minutes to leave the City supporters in shock and our team damaged beyond repair. The Spurs fans in the Barclay went berserk, as you would expect ... but so did the ones in the South, City and River End Stands. They had supporters all over the ground, in areas which were supposed to be for home fans only. How could this be? They couldn't all be guests of Norwich supporters; they were not scattered around in ones or twos, but sitting together in groups. I suspect that they bought their tickets from touts.

I am not against the idea of fans mingling. I have watched matches with opposing fans (e.g., at Crystal Palace), and it would be nice to think that fans would no longer have to be segregated in the future, though this is probably an impossible dream. But what I do find offensive is opposing fans infiltrating the home supporters and taunting them. The Ipswich fans had not done this before Christmas, but here the Spurs fans were crowing like the cockerel on their club crest. The potential for trouble was obvious, yet the police and stewards took no action. They were content to let the situation develop, while at the other end Norwich fans were still being thrown out for doing nothing more than standing at the back. It was crazy.

We had forty minutes left to save the game. We had come back from being two goals down more than once this season – but this time the players did what they had done in the second half against Ipswich. They panicked. Time and again, long, aimless balls were thumped forward to give Tottenham possession. Norwich played like a poor Sunday-morning team. Like ours, in fact.

For the first time this season, the team's yellow and green strip suggested cravenness and naivety. Or was it camouflage? The players seemed invisible compared to Tottenham's, who were buzzing with confidence and playing some excellent football. The only Norwich player to stand out was Gunn, who single-handedly kept the score down with some fine saves.

Tell a lie, there was one other hero – and an unlikely one at that. When Jeremy Goss was substituted, the crowd disagreed strongly with the decision (feeling that Beckford, Phillips or Fox should have been taken off) and gave him a standing ovation. This was an amazing turnaround in his popularity; it was not so long ago that he was the target of much abuse. The reason for the change was that he had at least made an effort in this game, which was more than most of the team had appeared to do.

The substitution didn't work. In fact, things went from bad to worse. The Norwich supporters looked on in horrified silence at the shambles. I now wished that the match wasn't being televised. What on earth would the millions at home be making of this? Would Karen now be suffering from pre-natal depression? Perhaps I shouldn't have laughed at Wolves.

It was so quiet that a Spurs fan a few rows behind could be heard mouthing off. 'You're giving them a lesson in football, Tottenham.' 'Come on, Spurs, we can have a dozen here.' His comments were all the more offensive because they were true. They would have incited trouble at many grounds; it was just as well that Norwich fans are generally peaceful. One woman (no, not Mum, though I did have to turn round and check) eventually told the bigmouth to shut up or clear off, but was calmed down by other Norwich supporters who told her that he wasn't worth getting upset about.

Normally when your team is losing, time seems to run out very quickly, but here it just dragged on and on. It was almost a relief when the final whistle went, as we had only lost 2–0.

The feeling of utter dejection really hit me as we made our way back to Mum's. I realised that our name wasn't on the Cup, but on something else (just below the name 'Armitage Shanks'). The trite maxim 'There's always next year' offered no comfort – if anything, it made me feel even worse as I thought how long we would have to wait to make amends. It was this year that mattered – and we had failed.

> We're not on the march, we're Walker's army,
> We're not going to Wem-ber-lee.
> And we won't shake 'em up,
> 'Cause we won't win the FA Cup,
> 'Cause Norwich aren't the greatest football team.

> Que sera, sera,
> Whatever won't be, won't be.
> We're not going to Wem-ber-lee,
> Que sera, sera.

So much for my yellow and green outfit.

Mum, Stephen and I said very little back at the house, though we couldn't resist looking at Teletext to see who we would have played in the next round if we had won. We would have been at home to Villa or Wimbledon – so we wouldn't have faced Wolves after all. I drove back to London later that evening on autopilot; all I could think about was how badly we had played. As I neared the flat, I saw several cars with miniature Tottenham kits hanging in the window, and it struck me again that I am living in the wrong place. I loathe London so much.

I couldn't face watching the match again on video, even to hear what was being said about us. I could guess. I hoped that a good night's sleep would help me feel better. It wasn't and it didn't. When I awoke the next morning, I felt OK as I drowsily established where I was and what day it was – and then the awful reality hit me. Shit. We had lost.

Things got worse at work. Time and motion studies have proved that productivity falls when a worker's football team loses at the weekend. This is not just down to a drop in morale; it is because other people keep coming along to pour on the scorn. Last week's drops of sympathy had evaporated, presumably as I had told everyone to watch us on television. 'We thought you were shit, we were right, we were right' – this was just the reaction I had feared. Like the rest of the country, my colleagues had been left wondering how on earth Norwich could be so high in the league.

I was subjected to wisecracks all Monday (and much of Tuesday). 'Norwich City FC? We know what the FC stands for.'

'Did you see that programme of funny cock-ups on TV yesterday?' 'What, *You've Been Framed?*' 'No, *Match of the Day.*'

'It's nice to see Norwich doing a lot for the disabled, Kev.' 'Yes, it is a good stand, isn't it?' 'No, I meant putting them in the team.'

I was phoned every half an hour by a Spurs fan downstairs who kept singing 'Spurs are on their way to Wembley' – and I suspect that he was also responsible for the pictures of Teddy Sheringham that were sent to me in the internal mail with the caption: 'We're on our way to Wembly your not.' With spelling and grammar like that, the sender would be better off on the way to an adult literacy class.

I didn't even receive any sympathy from the Arsenal fans. They seemed to hold me personally responsible for not beating their great rivals. Talk about being kicked when you're down. I wonder if the players realise the consequences of their actions. They play badly and the supporters get all the stick.

Everything seemed to be mocking Norwich that day. There was a cartoon in the *Guardian* on the subject of Michael Heseltine's position as head of the Board of Trade being in doubt as a result of the controversy over his pit closure plan. One of his aides was shown pointing to an unconscious bird in a cage in his office and saying, 'The canary's passed out, Mr President.' I couldn't decide whether this was a side-swipe at us as well.

I phoned Charlie in the evening, and we talked for three-quarters of an hour about what had gone wrong and what should be done about it. We didn't discuss anything else, as nothing else seemed as important. Charlie thought that the defeat was his fault. He had concentrated hard on the game in the first half, when everything was fine, but he missed the first five minutes of the second half to look after his two kids and returned to the television to find City 2–0 down. It was as if the goals had been conceded because he hadn't been paying attention. Honestly, he's as daft as me.

I then rang Brian, the manager of the Sunday team, to find out how they had got on without me. They lost 4–0. Ha! I couldn't be blamed this time! Brian did say, however, that the team had played well and created enough chances to win the game. Is he trying to tell me something?

Wednesday 27 January
Crystal Palace (home)

After I rang Charlie and Brian on Monday evening, I had a growing feeling that everything was changing for the better. First, Arsenal drew with Leeds in their FA Cup match, which means that they will have to travel to Yorkshire next week instead of coming to Carrow Road – so I won't have to sneak out of work early two Wednesdays running. On Tuesday night, Blackburn missed the chance to leap above us to the top of the league when they lost 5–2 at home to Coventry. Mike Walker won his first match in charge of Notts County. (Is it the same person? I mean, you never see them together.) I also heard that Thursday's Capital Canaries committee meeting had been postponed, which gives me more time to come up with excuses for our continuing poor form.

On Wednesday morning, Mum rang to tell me that Karen had given birth at last – and it's a boy! He is to be called Jamie Robert. Funny, I can't think of anyone connected with the club who is called Jamie. Where did Robert come from? Robert Fleck? Robert Chase? Aaagghhh!

Another welcome piece of news was that my boss was to be out of the office from lunchtime. 'You ought to get Norwich to arrange a game for this evening,' said his secretary.

'Consider it done,' I replied.

I left earlier than usual for the game, though not early enough to visit Karen in hospital. Some people at work thought it astonishing that I should travel so far to watch Norwich play, rather than to see my sister and new nephew. It didn't strike me as odd. In fact, it didn't strike me at all until they mentioned it.

Mum couldn't go to this game, as she was helping to look after Karen's other offspring. When it was time to set off for the ground, however, she became very jittery. 'I wish I was going tonight,' she said.

'Let's wrap the little ones up and take them with us, then,' I suggested. Mum hesitated for a moment, but concluded that this would not be fair on them.

Stephen didn't come either. He had to be at an early-morning meeting at his firm's head office in Wales the following day, so he stayed at home to do his paperwork, pack a suitcase and grab some sleep. Tch! What a part-timer! And Karen didn't come in his place, though I don't know why. It's not as if she's pregnant now.

As I walked down to the ground, I tried to remember the last time I had been to a match there on my own – and couldn't. It was rare enough for either Mum or Stephen to miss a home game, but I couldn't recall an occasion when both had been unable to attend. I felt very lonely, which may seem odd considering that I go to most away games without them. It must have been because our rituals had been affected. I bought only one packet of Polos instead of the usual three, and there was no laughter at my insistence on using the pelican crossing instead of dodging the traffic as everyone else does.

Yet as I reached the ground, I had the feeling that everything was going to be all right. The familiar sights and sounds were comforting, and the away fans had been moved back into the South Stand. It was as if normal service had been resumed. The reason for this change was that Norwich fans in the lower tier of the Barclay Stand had been showered with spit, cigarette ends and (I believe) the odd seat by Coventry and Spurs supporters sitting in the upper tier at recent games.

It may not sound too serious. A bit of gobbing could be dismissed as an early teething problem. (Hmm, I'm not sure that was the most apposite phrase, but you know what I mean.) What you have to realise is that spitting is a considerable escalation in crowd trouble at Norwich. And if you've ever been spat on, you'll know how disgusting it is.

The only time I have ever been caught up in trouble involved spitting. It happened in the mid-1970s when I was 14 or 15. I was walking through Norwich city centre with Charlie and a couple of other boys on the way to school one Saturday morning when we were approached by nine or ten Newcastle fans of about the same age. They had travelled down on the overnight train and had clearly been drinking all the way. One of them saw something sticking out of my rucksack and grabbed it; it was a slide-rule I'd borrowed from Stephen. They gathered round and looked at it in puzzlement, scratching their heads as if they were a long-lost tribe seeing a camera for the first time. I had a real dilemma – should I risk a thump from them for trying to get it back or risk one from Stephen for not getting it back? I decided that I might as well retrieve it if I was going to be thumped anyway, so I marched up and snatched it back. I wasn't thumped. I was kicked in the shin instead.

The Geordies followed us all the way to school. We didn't dare run, as we knew they would love a chase. Instead, they produced packets of chocolate biscuits which they proceeded to chew until soggy and then gobbed them down the back of our trouser legs. By the time we got through the gates, it looked as if we'd all shat ourselves. Look, you're not supposed to be laughing at this. You're meant to be appalled and revolted.

The behaviour of some of the Coventry and Spurs fans was disappointing and disturbing. Everyone talks about how much the behaviour of football supporters has improved recently – and it has – but it appears that unpleasantness hasn't been totally eradicated. There is no room for complacency. I agree that if people are treated like animals, they will tend to behave like them, but here the away fans had been treated well and still responded badly. For once, I could understand what Chairman Chase was trying to do. He had extended the hand of friendship, and it had been spat on.

The Norwich fans had been given the upper tier of the Barclay again. Just as well the seats hadn't been arranged to spell 'TWATS SIT HERE'. As this had been a last-minute decision, City supporters were offered free tickets for that section. This may also have been to try to drag people back after Sunday's disaster.

I felt confident about this game as the teams came on to the pitch. As I said earlier, everything had been going right for me this week. But in the very first minute, Palace took the lead. Ian Culverhouse was outpaced on our right side, and the cross was turned in by a completely unmarked Chris Armstrong. The home supporters fell as quiet as they had on Sunday. Some looked up to the executive boxes to see if anyone was watching *Coronation Street*. After ten minutes, though, we equalised with a wonderful goal. A free kick was flicked across the edge of the area by Phillips's head, and Lee Power (in for the dropped Beckford – will we ever see him again?) powered the ball into the net.

Then something rare and magical happened. The match, the whole evening, rose to a higher plane and became an indescribable experience. Did I just say 'indescribable'? One of the aims of this book is to dissect these feelings, so I'd better have a go.

The first point to make is how profoundly moved I was. This was – and I hesitate to use the phrase – a 'deep emotional experience'. The reason for my hesitation and inverted commas is that this phrase is a stick that Charlie still uses to beat me with. It goes back to an essay on football that I wrote at school when I was 12. I described watching football as a deep emotional experience and, when I had to read my essay out to the class, Charlie almost died laughing.

The problem lay, I think, in the word 'deep'. Watching football is an emotional experience, but generally a superficial one. You get to express joy, anger, frustration – most of the basic emotions, in fact – but these feelings come and go in a moment; intensely felt, but superficial none the less. Only very rarely does football offer what might reasonably be termed a 'deep emotional experience'. It happens once or twice a season if you are lucky.

Or unlucky. There are profoundly painful times caused by football, of course. The worst I can remember was when we were relegated to the old Second Division in 1985. Coventry, you will recall, had to win their last three games to stay up and send us down – and did. Their last game was on a Sunday morning against an under-strength and under-motivated Everton team, and they thrashed the new champions 4–1. Sunday dinner at Mum's was terrible (no, Mum, I'm not referring to your cooking). Mum was in tears, Stephen's bottom lip was wobbling – something I'd never seen before and haven't since – and I just sat there like a zombie, shaking my head. The feeling lasted for weeks, literally. And the whole city was affected. The devastation caused by this one match was largely down to its consequences – we had been relegated – but we had been hit by a massive psychological blow in that we had been convinced that we were safe only a couple of weeks before. On top of all this, the Heysel disaster denied us the place in Europe that we had gained by winning the Milk Cup in March that season.

This evening's match against Palace, however, was an uplifting experience. If I had to encapsulate its essence in one word, it would be birthdeathresurrectioncosmicdefiancetimelessness. (If the Germans can stick several words together to make one long one, why can't we? We are in Europe now.)

I recently read somewhere that birth and death are two aspects of the same thing. At the time, I thought this was pseudo-intellectual, pretentious bollocks – and in fact I still do, but on this evening I became acutely aware of how life is transient, yet is constantly being renewed. People come and go, yet their spirits (or other people's memories of them, if you like) live on. And football is always there too.

The birth I had in mind was that of Karen's new son. I thought of how we would bring him along to Carrow Road one day, just as we are going to bring her eldest daughter soon. The family tradition would be maintained.

There was a death in the crowd during the first half. A man collapsed in the South Stand, and the medical staff on hand were unable to save him. The match was not disturbed, though. Again, it was only pointed out to me at work the next day by people who are not football followers that everything usually stops if someone is dying. Here, the ambulancemen pushed the unfortunate spectator all the way around the pitch instead of straight across it so that the game could continue. Other spectators glanced over to see what was going on, but by and large they concentrated on the match.

This incident, plus the fact that I was sitting on my own in the crowd, prompted me to consider what it would be like if Mum and Stephen were dead. It was the first time I had ever considered the possibility of their mortality. Oh, I know Mum is always saying that she wants to see me married before she goes, but I have never taken this prospect seriously. Now that I did, it didn't feel so bad. I'd better explain that quickly before I'm cut out of the will.

It felt as if Mum and Stephen were with me in spirit. Which, of course, they were in that I knew they were listening to the local radio commentary. But whenever there was an incident on the pitch, I knew exactly what they would have been saying if they had been with me. Stephen would be hurling abuse at the linesman for missing a shirt being pulled or a ball crossing the touchline, and Mum would be shrieking every time the opposition attacked. We have watched football together for so long, I could hear their comments in my head. Presumably, it would be like this if the worst ever happened.

On this night I understood that, if I were ever left on my own, football, Norwich City and Carrow Road would be my support and comfort. The atmosphere enveloped me and reassured me that there would always be a place for me here. I hope I will never be on my own, of course; I trust that Karen and her family will come along in the future if I never have a family of my own.

Birth. Death. And there was a rebirth going on here too. Three days after we had been killed off in the FA Cup by Pontius Venables's men, the team had risen again and ascended to glory. Or, if you would prefer a non-religious image, the Canaries were doing a remarkable impression of a phoenix. The performance in this game was fabulous. The confidence, sharpness and style from the start of the season returned, and we scored four goals – as many as in our previous nine games. All were marvellous.

Power's strike was quickly followed by an excellent header from Sutton. Early in the second half, Phillips raced down the left, crossed to Fox at the far post, and he pulled the ball back for Goss to hammer it past Martyn from five yards. Goss was enjoying his own resurrection after being substituted against

Spurs. He was even being referred to by some in the crowd as 'Gozza', though I'm not sure whether it was thought that he shared Gazza's skill or his ability to belch into a microphone. In the final minute, Power collected the ball on the half-way line, made straight for goal and slid it in at the near post. It was an exceptional effort, yet Power acknowledged it only with a modest, understated wave to the crowd. The only error that Norwich made after the first minute was when a soft goal was presented to Geoff Thomas on the stroke of half-time. Unusually, hesitation by Gunn was to blame, but earlier he had produced three saves that bordered on the miraculous.

The team's rebirth was mirrored by the crowd's – or did each inspire the other? Now that the away fans had been moved and an end had been brought to the spitting, it was as if a tacit agreement had been reached that, in return, there would be no more stand-up protests. True, the fans in the Barclay were still worse off than last season as they were still lumbered with these unwanted seats, but there was a general acceptance that continuing the protests would distract the team in this important game. Everyone got behind the players, and once again 'On the ball, City' rolled around the ground.

There was a strong element of defiance to the evening. For one thing, we were defying the elements. The weather was cold and windy, and the drizzle swirled around like mist – yet City's football shone through this and made the drizzle seem like dry ice on a stage.

We also defied the referee. At times, it felt as if we were battling against the dark forces of evil to prove the ultimate power of our goodness.

> To err is human; to persist, a sign
> Of one who would be ref (or run the line).
> A scurvy, scuttling pest, a bug of dirt,
> Whose shrivell'd heart is blacker than his shirt,
> He little knows the laws (his father, less)
> And reaches each decision with a guess.
> Ignoring tackles when the ball has gone,
> Yet whistling when he ought to wave play on.
> Though granted powers, weak; though seeing, blind;
> He vents his petty spite against mankind.
> He should the scales of Justice bear aloft,
> But keeps his hand on something small and soft.
>
> Alexander Pope, *An Essay on Referees*

The referee for this game was Vic Callow – who isn't callow at all. He's been around for years. So why was he so poor? I think it must have something to do with the place he comes from – not, as some suggested, a village just outside the small town of Wedlock, but Solihull. I worked in Solihull for four years, and it is one of the oddest places I have ever been. It seems to be populated almost exclusively by teenagers with too much money and middle-aged women who cake their faces with make-up to try to disguise their fading looks. No wonder it's sent Mr Callow a bit funny.

As well as defying the weather and the ref, we also defied the so-called experts of the national media who had been writing us off and declaring that the Championship was now a two-horse race between United and Villa. And we defied all those who had given me such a hard time since we lost to Spurs on Sunday.

Birth. Death. Rebirth. Defiance. Artistry. Three points. They were all part of my ... my ... my deep emotional experience. Stop laughing, Charlie. How else can I describe it? It was overwhelming. Transcendent. It seemed as if everything was connected, and this evening was the equation that made sense of all the different elements. This was the only true reality. The cares of work, my petty boss, my lack of success with women, were all so far away that Jodrell Bank couldn't have picked them up. They didn't matter at all.

When I talked about the game at Sheffield Wednesday, I compared football and religion. One parallel that I didn't stress then was that both can offer spiritual fulfilment – and, on occasions, ecstasy. They provide what feel like true values and make all else seem ephemeral. I walked home from the Palace game in the rain and was splashed as the cars passed me, but in my euphoria I hardly noticed. If I had, I would have felt cleansed. Once or twice, I even punched the sky with both fists as I made my way back.

I realise that all this may sound fanciful and overblown, but any supporter who has experienced feelings like this will know that I am not exaggerating. (Any football follower who hasn't experienced this must be following the wrong team.) When you try to explain it to someone who doesn't go to football, though, you just sound as weird as those people who come up to you and suddenly start telling you how God wants to come into your life. We had one of these types in our tube carriage the other day. He tried to get everyone to come along to a prayer meeting. I said I'd love to come, but Tuesday lunchtime was already booked for ritual goat-slaughtering.

My transcendent feeling evaporated as soon as I reached Mum's. I was back to everyday life. Mum had cooked me some tea (featuring sweetcorn and peas, which made an attractive yellow and green pattern on the plate) and was soon making her usual apologies for her non-existent mistakes.

Mum now thinks that she and Stephen should stay away from Carrow Road as Norwich clearly do better without them. Yes, like they're really going to stay away – especially after seeing the goals on television later. Mum watched them again and again on video. Not that I'm complaining, you understand.

We're still 33-1 for the title. The odds are very tempting considering how we played against Palace ... but no, I daren't.

Saturday 30 January
Everton (away)

I phoned Karen on Friday after she'd come out of hospital. 'Well, wasn't it wonderful news?' I enthused.

'Yes, we really wanted a boy,' she replied.

'No, I mean beating Palace 4–2.'

FIFA announced the birth of another brainchild this week, but I sincerely hope this one doesn't survive. The father is Sepp Blatter – or is it Blätter? The latter would be more appropriate, being the German word for 'leaves'. The man is clearly out of his tree.

His latest idea is for throw-ins to be replaced by kick-ins, which is even more ludicrous than the new back-pass rule. It will encourage the persistent thumping of high balls into the area, which will further reduce the amount of skill in the game and destroy the flow and rhythm of a match. Instead, we will have continual mayhem in the penalty areas. Free kicks and corners will no longer have the same value or excitement. And, apart from anything else, such a change would completely knacker the introductory verse of 'On the Ball, City', which begins: 'Kick it off, throw it in … '

I assume that Blatter thinks this rule change will create more goals and thus more excitement. Fans like goals and penalty-area action, it is true, but only to a point, and not to the exclusion of everything else. If too many goals are scored, they will be devalued, just as a currency is if too much money is printed. Goals are special and celebrated accordingly because they are so hard to come by. They can come as a climax after a sustained spell of pressure, or completely out of the blue. Compare this with a sport such as basketball, where the teams trundle up and down the court all game and where it is the final tally of points that matters, each individual basket being relatively unimportant and soon forgotten.

Drastic changes such as the introduction of kick-ins (or the widening of goals, which was another daft suggestion a couple of years ago) would also invalidate past achievements, just as changing the design of the javelin every five minutes has rendered records in that athletic event almost meaningless.

If Blatter thinks that football supporters will be in favour of kick-ins, he is sadly mistaken. Yet I suspect that we are not his chief concern. It seems to me that he is prepared to butcher the game for the sake of people who do not know the first thing about it; in other words, the mass TV audience in the United States. It's one thing awarding the next World Cup finals to the USA to try to sell the game to the country, but selling the soul of the game to do it is another. There was even talk at one stage of dividing matches into quarters to provide more commercial breaks. Thankfully, that idea was dropped – but the fact that it was considered at all is very worrying.

FIFA certainly doesn't have a monopoly on stupidity, however. This week, ITV lost a lot of credibility in supporters' eyes when it was announced that this season's Coca-Cola Cup final will kick off at the odd time of 5pm, so that a Rugby Union sevens competition can be shown earlier in the afternoon. Postponing the final of an important football competition in order to televise rugby is bad enough, but when the rugby teams are eight men short ... words fail me.

Then there are the silly ideas put forward by some fans. The offside law is frequently said to be in need of drastic reform (you may recall that the pillock I sat next to at the home game against Chelsea mentioned this). But apart from formulating a clearer interpretation of the phrase 'interfering with play', it seems fine as it is to me.

The law is an integral part of the game. True, the persistent use of the offside trap may make the game seem boring. But excellent organisation is needed to operate it effectively every time. And it can afford the attacking team tremendous opportunities. When fans berate the opposition for using the offside trap all the time, they should really be criticising their own team for being stupid enough to keep falling for it. It can be beaten using simple intelligence. Either a midfield player takes the ball through by himself, or players have to make well-timed runs from deep positions while the forwards come out with the defence. If either method works, the attacking team immediately have a one-on-one with the keeper.

Even great players can talk twaddle about rule changes. Last summer, Michel Platini suggested that tackling should be banned. Norwich seemed to be experimenting with this idea during the Spurs game last week, but such a unilateral test had the same inevitable result as driving around Britain on the right-hand side of the road to see what motoring on the Continent must be like.

The drive from London to Liverpool this Saturday didn't seem any shorter than usual, though there was plenty to look at on the way. I saw several Portsmouth fans trying to hitch a lift at the Toddington Services near Junction 12 of the M1. Presumably their transport had broken down, and they had decided to abandon it to get to their game. A quick glance at the paper showed that Portsmouth were playing away at Barnsley, which is quite a distance from Toddington. I wonder if they made it. A little further on, I saw the Wimbledon team coach travelling to Coventry. I didn't see a supporters' coach, but then that was hardly a surprise.

I stopped for a cup of tea at some services just outside Liverpool and found the place packed with Norwich fans and Sunderland supporters who were travelling to Tranmere. Anyone unfamiliar with the two clubs might have feared that there would be trouble, since it was Sunderland who defeated us in the FA Cup semi-final last year. There was never the remotest possibility of this happening, however, as there has always been a special – though inexplicable – bond between the two sets of supporters.

The best example of this was at the Milk Cup final in 1985 (which we won 1–0). This is still referred to by many as the 'Friendly Final'; there was a sixty-a-side football match between the City and Sunderland fans in the Wembley car park beforehand, and many fans swapped scarves and addresses. Yet the friendship goes back much further. Mum has told me that, whenever Sunderland fans used to arrive in Norwich by train first thing on a Saturday morning, cafés used to open early especially for them – a service which was not provided for the followers of any other clubs. I bet the Sunderland supporters didn't show their gratitude by gobbing soggy chocolate biscuits over mild-mannered schoolboys.

Once in Liverpool, I started looking around for omens that might indicate how the match would go. The only thing that caught my eye was a sticker in the rear window of a car in front of me at some traffic lights. It showed that the car had been bought from a dealer called Baldwin in Warrington. That had to bode well. On the other hand, the sticker was blue and white – Everton's colours. Hmm.

I managed to get into the main car park in Stanley Park this time. It cost a pound to get in ... and £1.50 to stop some young hoodlum from slashing the tyres and scratching the paintwork. I didn't want to pay the little shit, but what choice did I have? Same old Liverpool. Yet I have to say that I have always found visits to Everton far more pleasant than going to Anfield. It is much less hostile, and the Everton fans are less arrogant than their red brethren. It would be nice if Everton signed a black player or two, though. Why are they the only club in the top division never to have fielded one in the first team?

I gave the 'scran vans' outside Goodison Park a miss and bought a pie inside. (7½/10 – a bit tough, but tasty.) I didn't manage to catch any of the toffees being thrown to the crowd by women walking around the pitch. If anyone else had started slinging sweets around, they'd have been ejected at once. Looking around, I noticed one or two Sunderland shirts in our section. Were these some of the fans I had seen at the services who had decided to come and watch us instead? Surely not. I concluded that the wearers of the shirts were Norwich fans who had done a swap and settled down to read the programme.

That didn't take long, as there was nothing worth reading. The Everton programme used to be the best in the country, but it has really gone downhill. The only thing that amused me was an inadvertent joke: Howard Kendall praised his team's 'fighting qualities' in their recent Cup match against Wimbledon, but when the two teams met in the league last Tuesday, there was a big scrap on the pitch. That can't have been what the Everton manager had in mind.

I looked up from the programme and saw that a couple of hundred Sunderland fans had now joined us. I guessed correctly that their game at Tranmere had been called off. The police didn't know how to react, being unaware of the friendship that exists between the fans, and made them all sit at one side of our section.

It soon became clear that the police had nothing to worry about. The Sunderland fans chanted 'City, City' and the City fans 'Sunderland, Sunderland'. There were no references to last season's semi-final. The only awkward moment came when the Wearsiders sang 'There's only one Terry Butcher' (he joined them earlier this season), and the Norwich supporters responded with 'Ipswich reject'. This minor disagreement soon passed, however, and the mutual appreciation began again.

This went a long way towards restoring my faith in the ability of rival fans to get on with each other, which had been shaken somewhat by the recent spitting incidents at Carrow Road. The police were impressed enough to allow the supporters to mingle, and there was soon a great atmosphere at our end of the ground. There were more songs than usual, and these were punctuated by the thunderous sound of feet stamping on the wooden floorboards. I wonder if we could sign up some of the Sunderland fans to help us in an end-of-season push for the title.

The Everton team came on to the pitch to the old *Z Cars* theme. Why? What's so stirring about the music from a 1960s police series? It sounded as silly as the old *Robin Hood* theme that Nottingham Forest have run out to for years. Mind you, it's given me an idea. Whom would I have to bribe to arrange for the *Steptoe and Son* theme to be played when Ipswich run out?

If Norwich were to take the field to a TV theme, I suppose it would have to be from an Anglia programme. *Survival* would have reflected our ambition at the start of the season, though *Tales of the Unexpected* would be more appropriate at the moment, as you never know how they're going to play from one game to the next. Then again, our chairman's policy regarding our best players could be conveyed by the theme from *Sale of the Century*. 'From Norwich, it's the swizz of the week!'

At present, the Norwich players are emerging for the second half at Carrow Road to Queen's *Another One Bites The Dust*, which has been pretty accurate so far this season. (Queen songs have always been popular choices at football clubs, with *We Are The Champions* and *We Will Rock You* being very common. To my knowledge, though, no club has gone for *I'm Going Slightly Mad*.) It's certainly better than the song that was used last year. This was a number recorded by a local group that featured the refrain 'Doin' the Canary'. Unfortunately, most visiting teams did. I shudder to think what song the team would have recorded if we'd reached Wembley in the FA Cup. *The Birdie Song*, perhaps?

When Norwich came out here at Goodison Park, I realised I had a problem – the bloke sitting next to me. There were signs up that warned supporters to 'commit no nuisance', but a nuisance is just what he was. He had a scarf tied to his wrist (very 1970s), and when he clapped or punched the air, the scarf flicked into my face. I would have moved away, but with the arrival of all the Sunderland fans, I couldn't see anywhere to move to.

It didn't stop there. The match had not been in progress long when he showed what a numbskull he was. I have often wondered where the false information about other matches that often spreads through crowds comes from. (This tends to happen more towards the end of the season when the scores in other matches can determine the fate of your team.) Does it spring from stupidity, malevolence (i.e., people deliberately telling lies) or mishearing? If my neighbour was anything to go by, stupidity was the sole factor. He had a radio pressed to his ear throughout the game, yet he still informed me after a few minutes that Manchester United had gone 1–0 up at Ipswich. It took half an hour for him to realise that it was Ipswich who had scored. Later on, he told me that Southampton were beating Villa 3–0, but on the way back to London I heard that the final score was only 2–0.

He was also slightly out with all the chants. When Gary Megson was acclaimed with 'General, General', he was shouting 'Gazza, Gazza'. When everyone else was teasing the Everton keeper with 'Neville, Neville, what's the score?' he was asking 'Southall, Southall, what's the score?' These were only minor differences, it is true, but they all added up.

The reason for asking Neville Southall the score was that we took the lead after sixteen minutes. Sutton seized on a piece of poor control by Judas Watson, took the ball on a couple of strides and drove it in off the far post. It was no more than we deserved, as we had been playing every bit as well as we had against Palace on Wednesday.

The pillock next to me went berserk, sending my newspaper and programme flying and lashing me with his scarf and uncoordinated, flailing limbs. The Sunderland fans pointed at the home supporters and sang 'Going down, going down', which was more than a little odd considering that Sunderland are in the division below us already. The Everton fans looked more puzzled than they had earlier on first hearing 'Blaydon Races' coming from the Norwich section.

The Norwich followers sang 'One-nil, one-nil' to the tune of *Hi-Ho, Hi-Ho, It's Off To Work We Go* rather than *Amazing Grace*. Who had decided to make this change? Is there a composer and arranger in our midst who organises all this?

> I wrote the old 'Come on, you yellows' song,
> I wrote 'You thought you'd scored but you were wrong'.
> I wrote 'One-nil, one-nil' and 'You're shit – aaghh!'
> I write the songs, I write the songs.

Did you realise, incidentally, that Barry Manilow didn't write the original version of *I Write The Songs*? I think he's got a bit of a nerve to keep singing it.

Norwich continued to play some wonderful football and left the Everton players chasing shadows for most of the game. The news that United and Villa were losing cheered us even more. It isn't often that Norwich fans want Ipswich to win, but this was one occasion when we did. The news that they had taken a 2–0 lead over United was joyfully announced to the team, though care was taken not to give Ipswich any credit or praise. 'Two-nil, the scum are winning two-nil ... ' This was followed by a chorus of 'We are top of the league' and a song about Alan Hansen on *Match of the Day*, the general thrust of this being that his sex life involves only one consenting adult.

With fifteen or twenty minutes left, the score was still only 1–0 to us and Everton realised that they still had a chance of getting something from the game. We found ourselves having to defend more and more – and, ten minutes from the end, we survived a loud (and, I have to say, justified) appeal for a penalty. Megson made a desperate challenge on Tony Cottee just as he was about to shoot, missed the ball completely and tripped him up. I was amazed to see the referee wave play on, though there was some justice to his decision. For one thing, he was the referee who had booked four of our players at Anfield earlier in the season, and this helped to make up for it. For another, this made up for the penalty that was wrongly awarded to Everton when we played here in the 1988–89 season and which denied us the win our performance had merited.

Despite this let-off, I knew that the danger was still not over according to:

Kevin's Alternative Laws of Football (No.8)

> *'When a team is only one goal down with five minutes to go, however poorly they have played for the previous 85 minutes, they will have at least one clear opportunity to score.'*

It was this law that gave us a 1–1 draw here last season, when Phillips equalised in the last minute after a dire performance.

Sure enough, three minutes into injury time, Cottee connected perfectly with an overhead kick and it looked a certain goal. Yet somehow Gunn flung himself to his right, got a fingertip to the ball and touched it on to the post, from which it rebounded into his arms. It was the best save I'd seen in years.

For the first time ever, I'd seen Norwich win at Goodison Park. Behind me, a woman was prodding her partner in the ribs, saying, 'You can't say I'm a jinx any more!' Confirmation that Villa and United had both lost (in the latter case, I was to discover, the Ipswich keeper Clive Baker had made a point-blank save from Mark Hughes in the last minute) meant that we were top of the league again!

How did the national media respond? How do you think? *Today* said little about us this week, while the *Sun* remarked that the donkeys might yet win the carrot. The nerve! Reading other papers, however, I discovered that this was based on a tongue-in-cheek comment by Bryan Gunn. Really, Bryan, you shouldn't encourage them. I know you were being ironic, but that falls well outside the understanding of most tabloid reporters.

On Radio 5 on Monday evening, Jon Champion came out with the most disgraceful remark. He asked the Aston Villa coach whether he thought the Championship was now a two-horse race between them and United. How could he ask such a thing when we are at the top of the table??

Returning to Saturday evening, I listened to *Six-O-Six* presented by David Mellor on the way back to London. I wouldn't say the show was toe-sucking good, but it wasn't bad either. During the programme, a Spurs supporter rang in to complain about the toilets and stewards in the Barclay Stand at Norwich. He thought the bogs were too small and the stewards too big for their boots. It obviously hadn't occurred to him to tackle both problems at once by peeing on the stewards.

When I got back to the flat, I read through the Norwich papers that had arrived from Mum that morning. There were plenty of letters about the team, as there always are when anything has gone wrong. The trouble with writing to the papers about a team like Norwich, however, is that by the time the letter is published, City's fortunes have often changed dramatically. The talk of 'mid-table mediocrity' now seemed unnecessarily pessimistic. Could it really be only six days ago that we had played so abysmally against Spurs?

There was one funny letter. A correspondent offered his services as a goalscorer and only revealed at the end that he was 61 and awaiting a double hip operation.

On Sunday morning, by another of those coincidences that football is always throwing up, we had a match against Sunderland Supporters (aka Wearside Wanderers). Well, I say 'we', but I was only a substitute for this game. Brian only told me after I'd given him a lift to the park. He could walk home, I thought.

It seemed a bit unfair that I should be on the non-existent bench considering that I am one of the few genuine Norwich supporters in the Norwich Supporters' team, but being a good club man (i.e., a doormat) I put up with it. I even agreed to run the line.

After five minutes, I gave one of the Sunderland players offside when he put the ball into the net and received the usual abuse. Two minutes later, he scored a legitimate goal. 'Was that offside? I don't think so,' he sneered at me. I gave him a sarcastic smile in return. Shortly after, we went 2–0 down. Ha! The team's no good without me, I thought. Then something extraordinary happened. Our team ran riot and scored nine – yes, nine – goals. That's more than we ever score in the pre-match kick-about, which usually involves the keeper being bombarded with four or five balls at once as every other player tries to blast them into the net, this being the only chance we are likely to have to do so all morning.

The final score was 9–4. I was brought on with 25 minutes to go when the score was 5–3. I laid on two goals, but I'm not sure this will get me back in the starting line-up next week. I fear that I have now become the team's 'supersub'. All the same, I was in a good enough mood to give Brian his lift home.

Before I did, I noticed someone in the Sunderland dressing-room wearing a new Norwich shirt. It was the striker who had had a go at me for giving him offside! It turned out that he is a Norwich fan, but he plays for the Sunderland team as they are mates of his. It seems that Norwich supporters are to be found everywhere but in the Norwich Supporters' team.

Oh – I almost forgot. I acquired a nasty cut on my head on Sunday morning. For once, my lack of hair was useful as I was able to show off my wound and look macho. Because it was small and curved, everyone assumed it was a stud mark that I had picked up when bravely diving for a header. I didn't disabuse them of this. After all, it's not very cool and macho to overbalance in the shower and hit your head on the tap.

Saturday 6 February
Arsenal (home) – postponed

Yet another Saturday with no game, but at least football was the cause this time, rather than the demands of television or Graham Taylor. Arsenal had to play Crystal Palace in the Coca-Cola Cup this weekend, so once again I had to find another way to fill my day.

I decided to travel back to Norwich for the day, my conscience pricking me a little for not going to see Karen's new baby before now when I'll travel any time, any place, anywhere to see the team play. I took the baby a present to make up for this – a yellow and green bib from the club shop bearing the words 'The best dribbler at Carrow Road'.

'Oh, not already,' moaned Karen's husband Chris.

'Well, you can't be too careful,' I said. 'With him being a boy, a lot of his clothes will be blue and white. We don't want him to be psychologically scarred so he ends up following that other lot down the road.' Chris wasn't convinced. When I left, he was encouraging Jamie Robert to throw up over the bib. Wait till he sees what I've bought their eldest daughter for her 6th birthday on Wednesday.

It does seem that my obsession with football is growing stronger, not weaker, with age. Even I was a little concerned when I realised that the only things on TV that made me laugh out loud this week were two football jokes. For the record, the lines in question were 'It sounds like "Shit on the Villa", sir' in *The Detectives* and 'Duck, everyone, this could go anywhere' in *Drop the Dead Donkey*.

There have been some amusing football stories in the papers over the last week. Manchester United have unveiled a new second strip – which turns out to be yellow and green. I bet Alex Ferguson went to see a fortune teller to find out who would win the league this season. She looked into her crystal ball and said, 'I see a team in yellow and green', at which Fergie ran off to get a new kit made in these colours.

Remember those 'Cantona' sweatshirts that were advertised in the Leeds programme some time after he was transferred? It said in the *Daily Mirror* this week that they've been sent over to Romanian orphans. They should go well with the 'Free Nelson Mandela' T-shirts, 'Bush and Quayle 92' caps and Yugoslavian national team tracksuits.

Lee Power made the local papers after he was caught speeding in his car. That's twice within a week that his pace has earned 3 points.

I picked up a programme for the local cinema in London during the week. It announced that Mike Newell would be coming along later in the month to talk about directing such films as *Dance with a Stranger* and *Into the West*. I don't know how he manages to fit all that in with playing up front for Blackburn. If there's a question-and-answer session at the lecture, I think I'll go along and ask whether Alan Shearer's injury is clearing up.

Saturday afternoon's results didn't go our way. Manchester United beat Sheffield United 2–1 after being behind for an hour, while Villa beat Ipswich 2–0. Wolves lost 2–1 at home to Brentford, but even this didn't raise a smile. I haven't spoken to you-know-who for a month now. Perhaps I'm finally over her.

At least I'm back in the Sunday-morning team. And, for once, my presence from the start didn't prevent us from securing a point. We drew 2–2, which was particularly creditable as we played the last half-hour with only ten men. OK, nine if you count me.

Our left-back was carried off with a broken leg and deposited at the side of the pitch where he was covered with as many coats and sweatshirts as we could muster to keep him warm while we waited for the ambulance to arrive. 'Will you be all right like that, Russell?' we asked.

'No I won't,' he said.

'Why, what's the matter?'

'I can't see the pitch. Will you turn me round so I can watch the rest of the game?'

Russell remained remarkably cheerful considering his situation, even making bequests as the two ambulancewomen wheeled him away like a joint of meat on a restaurant trolley. 'I leave you my boots, you my shin-pads, you my Ralgex...' I don't think I'd have been composed enough to do that. My comments would have been more along the lines of 'AAAAAAAAAAGGGGGHHHHH!!!!!!' My allegiance to Norwich City isn't my only yellow streak.

Wednesday 10 February
Southampton (away)

I seem to be leading a charmed life at work at the moment. Once again, my boss was out of the office all Wednesday, so I had no trouble leaving for the game. I strolled out of the building at quarter past four and took the tube to Acton in West London, where I'd driven the car first thing in the morning to make my journey to Southampton quicker and simpler.

Having parked about ten minutes from the ground, I looked around for a phone box. It was Karen's eldest daughter's 6th birthday, and I hadn't had time to call her from work. 'Did you like the present, Joanna?' I asked. I'd sent her a Norwich hat and scarf.

'Ooh, yes,' she said. 'They're just what I wanted. I can go to the football now!' Karen said she'd hardly taken them off all day, even at school. She'd also been sent a card from the club (as she's a junior member) and she was equally pleased with that.

'I'm just going to see Norwich play now,' I told Joanna.

'Can't I come?' she asked.

'Not really. I'm in Southampton.' The silence at the other end told me that she didn't have a clue where this was, but if she starts following football seriously (and it doesn't look as if she'll have any choice), her geographical knowledge will soon improve.

The evening was cold enough to warrant wearing my yellow and green ski hat, but I've not been inclined to put it on since someone said it reduced my IQ by twenty points as soon as I did. Instead I settled for a hot meat pie ($^6/_{10}$) and squeezed into my seat. It was narrow, there was no leg-room, and I was between two people who had thick jackets on, but I suppose being huddled together like this meant we were able to share each other's body heat. The lack of room wasn't the only problem with my seat ...

Kevin's Alternative Laws of Football (No.9)

> *'Where there is a pillar in the section of a stand allocated to Norwich fans, the seat behind it will always be given to Baldwin K. of London.'*

This happened at the cup match at Blackburn, you will recall.

There wasn't much worth seeing on the pitch in the first half here. Norwich played like a Dream Team – i.e., they were all asleep. I've rarely seen a team so idle and uninterested, unless you count our Sunday side when half the players have been out on the beer the night before. They all messed themselves in fear whenever Matthew Le Pissoir got the ball.

We were two down after 24 minutes, the first a header from a corner (a Robins own goal? If so, it was his first goal since early December), the second a tap-in from Micky Adams, who looked yards offside to me as I looked across the pitch. Even Adams glanced up and was surprised to see that the linesman wasn't flagging.

It was the only time in the first half that the Norwich fans made any noise, and that was only to hurl abuse at the officials. The people sitting around me were moaners of taxi-driver standard. I think I've mentioned before that we have a few of these at Norwich, but they don't usually turn out for away games in such force. Perhaps they have a club of their own – the Dour, Unhappy Moaners Brigade, or DUMB for short – and this was their annual outing. They didn't get behind the team at all and spent the evening mumbling into their coats.

'Crap. Absolute crap.' 'They're rubbish, the lot of them.' 'How did they get so high in the table?' Not with backing like this, I thought. 'Culverhouse is having a stinker.' 'Don't give the ball to him, he'll only ... oh no.'

Now I'm not averse to a bit of moaning myself, as you will have gathered. There is a need for honesty and criticism in all relationships. Blind devotion is downright unhealthy; an attachment that exists with a full awareness of the other party's faults is much truer and stronger. But where football is concerned, I do try to keep my grouses away from the grounds.

Perhaps it is the fact that I too am given to grumbling that made the moaners all the more irritating. People are often quickest to condemn faults in others that they know they have themselves. At any rate, I was pleased when one of the old gits in the row behind me got cramp in his leg and was in agony for the rest of the half.

Ian Culverhouse was having a poor game for him, as had been remarked, but perhaps this was because the match programme had called him John Culverhouse. Over 300 appearances for the club, and they still get his name wrong. Similarly, Chris Sutton had been rechristened Mel. Do other teams have to put up with this? Would the Southampton programme talk about Phil Gascoigne, Gerry Lineker or Derek Cantona? I think not.

Mel – sorry, Chris – wasn't affected by this mistake as he wasn't playing. He had dropped out of the team at the last minute, leaving Power and Robins up front. This should have been an interesting combination, but for reasons probably not even known to themselves, the rest of the team reverted to the tried-and-failed tactic of hoofing hopeful high balls towards them. This has rarely proved successful for us and stood no chance of working here, seeing that Power and Robins would still have been smaller than the Southampton central defenders if one had stood on the other's shoulders. According to the radio, Mike Walker is hoping to make two new signings soon. The sooner the better, on this showing.

At half-time I bumped into Steve from the Sunday-morning side. (The chap I saw at the Leeds game with his brother- and father-in-law. This time he had come along with his mother and father.) 'You could play in that midfield at the moment,' he said. 'I should bring your boots with you next week.'

I told him about Russell's broken leg, as he had missed Sunday's game. Brian had rung me on Monday night to tell me the latest news, which was not good. Russell's leg has been operated on, and he's had a metal pin put in his shin. 'Of course, that means he's doubtful for next Sunday,' I said.

Actually, it's not clear at this stage whether he will ever play again. His leg will be making metal detectors at airports go berserk for the foreseeable future. Then again, I'm able to play with this metal plate in my head, and I feel perfectly haddock sheepshank carburettor wibble wibble arooga!

As soon as the second half began, it was evident that the City players had had a verbal hot poker applied to their metaphorical backsides. We poured forward and had more shots on goal in five minutes than in the previous forty-five. Robins hit the outside of a post after the Southampton keeper Flowers ('Hello, hello, Wolves reject ... ') had parried a drive from Power. Power then hit the bar with a shot that bounced down and was kicked away. Did the ball cross the line? I wasn't sure, but as every other Norwich fan was claiming it had, I joined in the general clamour. Unfortunately, the linesman wasn't Russian and the goal wasn't given.

Flowers made several good saves after that, and Butterworth had a header cleared off the line, but we had no luck at all in front of goal. We could have played all night and still not scored. I thought of Ken Brown's remark after we lost 1–0 at Chelsea a few seasons ago: 'With our luck one of our players must be bonking a witch.'

I kept telling myself, 'Right, if we score in the next minute, we can still win this.' But ten minutes from time, Southampton beat our offside trap (or motionless back four, depending on how you look at it) and clinched the match. Dell Boys 3 Plonkers 0. Thank you and goodnight.

I see that Bryan Gunn has just been recalled to the Scotland squad. He'd better look after himself now. All this bending over to pick the ball out of the net could put his back out like last season. On the subject of goalkeepers, Dave Beasant has left Wolves after his loan spell. Poo. There goes my plan to send the Wolverine a pair of gloves with 'Teflon non-stick' labels on the palms.

The Norwich crowd was utterly deflated. We couldn't even raise one of our songs of defeat, such as 'We came, we lost, we couldn't give a toss' or 'If you're all pissed off, clap your hands'. The whole evening had been irredeemably bleak. It was the antithesis of the Palace game two weeks ago. Then, the occasion had been rich in excitement and significance. Now, my mind and body were quite numb. The south coast air was still, apart from the odd shouts of 'You'll never win the league' and 'You're so shit, it's unbelievable' from the home fans. The fact that Southampton have never won the title – and are way below us in the table at the moment – was conveniently overlooked. But I was too cold to feel angry at the taunts and the first-half performance. That only came later when I'd warmed up.

This was the sort of evening that football fans supposedly have to endure in order to savour the true sweetness of success. Maybe. But such rationalising is only possible after the event. When you're at an unremittingly awful game, all you are mindful of is what an unremittingly awful game it is. And don't give me any of that rubbish about enjoying being miserable. You often hear (well, I do anyway) comments like 'He's only happy when he's not'. Even if such people do exist (Paul Merton, Jack Dee perhaps?). I'm not among them. If I'm being miserable, take it from me, I'm miserable. Perverse I may be, but not to that degree.

I got back to the flat at around eleven and rang Mum to give her a match report. She couldn't understand why the team's attitude should have been all wrong. 'The players said in last night's paper that they were going to treat every game as if it were a Cup final,' she said. Huh. They'd treated tonight's game like a cup of coffee, putting their feet up and having a snooze.

One possible explanation was forthcoming the following day. A couple of fellow Capital Canaries rang to ask if I knew anything about a rumour that was circulating, the gist of which was that there had been a dust-up between some of the players in the hotel before the game. It was the first I had heard of it. Could there be any truth in it? It would certainly explain why the players had seemed so distracted; on the other hand, unsubstantiated stories are always flying around, frequently spread by that shadowy figure, 'a man in the pub'. Perhaps this was another piece of misinformation from that pillock who sat next to me at the Everton game. At any rate, I think I'll get Stephen to ask John Deehan about it if he sees him in the chippy again.

Saturday 13 February
Nottingham Forest (away) – postponed

No game again! This is our tenth idle Saturday of the season so far. We were due to play Forest, but they're still in the FA Cup. We've only got three matches this month, but in March we have seven in twenty-two days. Surely this could have been arranged better somehow.

This Sunday was St Valentine's Day – or, as I usually refer to it, Fat Chance Day. I got twice as many cards as last year ... but what's two times nought?

Then again, I didn't send any. No, not even to the Wolverine, since you ask. I made that mistake four years ago. I made the card myself, with a picture of a referee brandishing (after I'd doctored the photo) a red heart. The caption was

'The dreaded red card', which I thought was quite clever, since the word 'dreaded' acknowledged that this declaration of affection might be unwelcome to her and would thereby defuse any awkwardness that might follow.

I don't know whether she was horrified when she received the card or not. She never mentioned it at all, but she must have known who had sent it, given its style and subject matter. I haven't bothered sending her anything for St Valentine's Day since – though I was tempted once to send her some yellow and green daffodils.

Wolves won at Peterborough on Saturday afternoon. Boo! More to the point, so did Villa at Chelsea. They are now 5 points ahead of us. True, we've got two games in hand, but I'd rather have the points.

Things went no better for our Sunday team, though one way and another it was an entertaining morning. On the way to the match, Brian and I passed Madame Tussaud's at quarter to ten and saw that long queues were forming already. 'What's the big attraction about going to see a load of wax dummies?' Brian wondered aloud.

'Don't ask me,' I said. 'I travelled all the way down to Southampton to see some on Wednesday night and I still couldn't tell you.'

In the dressing-room, everyone was talking about the programmes that had been on Channel 4 the night before to mark St Valentine's Day. There had been a naked chat show and interviews with people who enjoy being dominated and humiliated. 'We ought to get them to come and play for us, then,' someone suggested.

'Yeah, and we could advertise by putting cards in the phone boxes around Soho. "Severe thrashings and muddy balls", that sort of thing.' I'm not sure about this. We'd only have to change the team kit to yellow leather thongs and green nipple clamps.

One member of the team did inflict some pain on himself before we went out on to the pitch, though this was inadvertent. He was spraying some Ralgex on to his thigh, but accidentally hit what in football circles is euphemistically referred to as the groin. I've never seen him run around so much, though.

We played the same team as last week, but with a different result. This time we lost 4–0. I guess we missed Russell in defence more than we thought we would. OK, OK, so I was his replacement. But it wasn't my fault. I was nowhere near their forwards when they scored ... or was that where I went wrong?

Still, I learned a new shout during the game. Sunday-morning football has a language of its own – 'Easy ball, Tone', Drop one, Eddie', 'Go line', 'Touch, Andy' – but I had never before heard the exhortation of one of our opponents to a team-mate to mark one of our side more closely: 'Get up his Gary!' It turned out that this was rhyming slang. Gary Glitter = well, you work it out.

It wasn't a good weekend for any teams wearing yellow and green. Newcastle lost in the last minute of their FA Cup match at Blackburn wearing their change strip. And, on Sunday afternoon, Manchester United wore their new one for the first time at Sheffield United. Nice kit, shame about the team.

They lost 2–1, and Bruce missed a penalty. I enjoyed watching this on TV – until it occurred to me that United, like Villa and us, can now concentrate solely on the league. Drat.

Saturday 20 February
Manchester City (home)

The good news: I won't have any problems getting out of work to see all the midweek matches we've got coming up. The bad news: I've lost my job. From next Friday, I'll be one of Major's millions. Bloody Chelsea fan.

Ultimately, I suppose my dismissal wasn't that much of a surprise. I always suspected that it might happen one day; it was the timing more than anything which took me aback. Everything seemed to be going so smoothly. I thought I was leading a charmed life, with my boss being away on the last two occasions I've left early to watch the team. Why is it that life takes such unexpected turns? This is just like the time I ran into trouble after going to the home game against Carlisle when nothing had been said after I was half a day late getting back from the away leg.

I said then that football was more important than work. And, a few weeks ago, I said that nothing would stop me from seeing every game until the end of the season. The boss could do his worst. If it was a bluff, life has called it. The boss has done his worst. There is now nothing to stop me from seeing every game.

They say a principle isn't a principle until it costs you money. You can add 'or your job' to that. Not that my sneaking off to watch Norwich was given as the specific reason for my being 'let go'; 'it's just not working out' was what I was told. It must have had something to do with it, though. When I was being told that I had to leave, I was hoping for the chance to wheel out one of my favourite jokes. I wanted my boss to say, 'You think more of Norwich City than you do of this company', so that I could reply, 'I think more of Ipswich Town than I do of this company'. But it didn't happen and never will now. Life rarely provides us with such clear-cut scoring opportunities.

Here, I wonder if the players realise the sacrifices that we fans have to make to follow them. Probably not. But that's probably just as well. They wouldn't be able to move with all that weight on their shoulders.

Fortunately, I have some savings to keep me going for a while, which is just as well as there doesn't seem to be much point in looking for a job straight away. We've got so many midweek matches coming up (the return match against Ipswich is the latest to be moved to a Monday night) that I would just be walking into more problems. I mean, it wouldn't look good on my first day to book seven or eight afternoons off in the next two months. My best bet would be to try to find a new job as soon as the season ends, and then work hard to build up a reservoir of goodwill during the summer on which I would be able to draw when I need time off to follow the team in Europe. Yes, I'll worry about job-hunting later. For now, I'll take each game as it comes, Brian.

If we do win the league, I will know that everything has happened for the best. If we don't win it – well, I will still have enjoyed the attempt.

In the circumstances, it was good to be able to go back to Norwich for the weekend. This was our first home game in almost a month, which prompted the joke on the local radio on Saturday morning that Messrs Chase and Walker were putting up direction signs around the ring road to remind people how to get to the ground.

I paid another trip to the hairdresser's, which struck Karen as being rather unnecessary. 'What are you going so soon again for? Are you having highlights put in or something? Here, how about a neon sign saying "Here it is"?' Hmph.

The place I go to isn't like most hairdressing establishments. I always thought barbers were supposed to chat to their customers. You know what I mean. 'So' – snip, snip – 'are we taking a holiday this year, sir?' – snip, snip – 'who do we fancy to win this afternoon?' – snip, snip – 'want some johnnies for a Saturday shag?' At this place, though, there are three who just argue among themselves. Still, it's very entertaining. The owner of the shop is Italian, and this morning he was taking a lot of stick from the other two. 'We gave your lot a hiding the other night, didn't we?'

'Hey, whaddya mean?'

'England. San Marino. Six-nil, six-nil ... '

'I'm not from San Marino. I'm Italian.'

'San Marino, Italy – same difference.'

'Yeah? Well, how come your Platt and Gascoigne often can't get into their teams in Italy? We've got better players than them. You watch us against Portugal next week. And the Lord help Norwich if they ever play Milan in Europe.'

After this little outburst, attention turned to one of the other two who claims to support Liverpool, even though he's never been to Anfield. He was the one from the shop who went to the 7–1 defeat at Blackburn, so perhaps that put him off following City for good. 'If I lived in Liverpool, I'd go to Anfield all the time,' he said.

'Sure you would,' grinned the others.

The third says he supports Norwich, but whenever I have talked to him, he hasn't seemed to know a lot. 'You wouldn't go down Carrow Road if you were free on a Saturday afternoon,' the supposed Liverpool fan said to him.

'Yes I would.'
'How come you never go to any midweek games, then?'
'I'm usually busy.'
'Haaa!'

Having had my loose end trimmed, I went round to see Karen and her tribe. She kept up her daft suggestions for my hair from the brief phone conversation we'd had earlier that morning. 'Why don't you have the Norwich badge shaved into your hair at the back?' Oh yes, what a great idea. I think I'll have 'NCFC' tattooed on my forehead as well, while I'm at it.

I asked Karen if she wanted to come to the Arsenal game in a couple of weeks, but she said that Junior still wasn't sleeping too well, so she'd better give it a miss. I looked into his cot and discovered that, just as I had feared, he was wearing a Babygro that was blue with white sleeves. Aaagghhh!

While I was there, Karen gave me back the Wolverhampton Wanderers board game that I had passed on to her some time before. 'We finally played it the other night and it's a load of rubbish,' she said. It's quite realistic then, I thought. 'Look', she went on, ' "Unsuitable for children under the age of 36 months due to small parts". It should say "Unsuitable for anyone over the age of 36 months due to small interest value".'

That's not all it said on the side of the box. The game was made in Ipswich, which explains a lot.

As Mum, Stephen and I made our way to Carrow Road that afternoon, much of the conversation was naturally on the subject of me losing my job, but eventually we moved on to more important matters. 'Have you seen John Deehan in the chippy to ask him about that rumour of a punch-up?' I asked Stephen.

'No,' he replied, 'but the man in there says Deehan reckoned he was happy with the performance at Southampton last week.' What? He must have had money on a home win, as I can't see there was anything else to be happy about.

At the turnstiles, we have another brush with fame. A TV crew was filming people coming into the ground. Stephen grinned and waved at the camera. Mum and I didn't, in case we broke it. We recognised a presenter from the BBC in Norwich, so I suppose the film will be shown on there some time.

With cameras in mind, we took particular notice of all the stills photographers gathered behind the goals. It's easy to tell who they think will win; they go to the end where they anticipate more goals. Usually, this means the away team's goal, but at Norwich the photographers from the national press generally swarm around Bryan Gunn. Yet for once this was understandable here, as Manchester City are – as I believe I mentioned earlier – our chief bogey team.

The game began in an uneventful fashion, mainly because of the wet and windy conditions. Two wet and windy supporters in front of me took to amusing themselves by trying to knock each other's cap off. After half an hour, however, the gloom was suddenly lifted as Norwich scored twice in a minute.

Getting one goal against Manchester City is unusual for us, but to score two so quickly emphasised the freakishness of it all. Robins trickled the first in from two yards out, while the second was a terrific rising drive from Power to round off a fast, incisive move involving Bowen, Phillips and Fox which began at the edge of the Norwich penalty area.

I now knew how the Spurs fans had felt when they scored two quick goals here in the Cup match. Mum started to get out of hand. 'He's not saying much, is he?' she remarked loudly, pointing at a man with a light blue hat sitting quietly nearby. Regrettably, this was only a taste of what was to come.

Half-time arrived, and we noticed the appearance of a large figure of fun in the family enclosure. No, not the chairman. Postman Pat. This wasn't Carrow Road's first link with children's TV, of course. 'Tales of the Riverbank' aptly describes the ground's location, though I'll leave you to decide who Ratty is. The team looked a rag, tag and bobtail outfit at the end of last season. And it was good of the club to offer the Woodentops gainful employment as stewards at the Barclay end.

The second half was only forty seconds old when the wrong City scored. The Manchester fans burst into a chorus of 'Blue Moon'. One idiot ran on to the pitch to celebrate, but was soon grabbed and led away. The fan singled out for scorn by Mum earlier turned round and looked meaningfully at her.

The Blues were lifted by the goal, just as we would have been if we could have scored as quickly in the second half at Southampton, and the pressure on our defence was increased by a series of free kicks awarded by the referee for unfathomable reasons. He was even worse than the one at the Palace game (see Alexander Pope, Wednesday 27 January). Or is it that I am becoming more blind and biased as the title race hots up? Whatever the case, I wasn't alone, judging by the comments being yelled around me. 'Have you got this down for an away win on the pools, ref?' 'At least be honest and put a blue shirt on.' 'Kick his labrador, Norwich.' 'Is your rule-book in Braille? I bet he has to feel players' faces before he books them.'

Mum obliged with her usual cry of 'The referee's a love-child', but really came into her own in the last quarter of an hour. There wasn't any singing at the time, just the usual crowd noise. Suddenly Mum yelled out 'Come on, you yellows' on her own – and 2,500 voices on the lower tier of the River End joined in, followed by the crowd at the other end of the ground. Stephen and I killed ourselves laughing at Mum in her new-found role as cheerleader. 'What song are we doing next, then?' asked Stephen.

Norwich were defending frantically at this stage. We had some of the luck that had eluded us at Southampton when David White miskicked from two yards out and Gunn, already lying on the ground, gratefully grabbed the ball. It may seem strange that you can spend much of a game, to which you have been looking forward and for which you have paid a fair amount of money, willing the final whistle to come, but that was the case here. Watches were checked every few seconds, fingernails were chewed ... and people started making for the exits! Why?

I've never been able to understand how anyone can do this when the result is still in doubt. What's the point of coming to a game if your main concern is to get away quickly at the end? It's like reading a whodunnit and not bothering with the last page. It's particularly annoying in an all-seater ground, as entire rows of people have to stand up to let one person out.

On this occasion, those who left early missed a treat. In the last minute, the referee was kicked in the mouth (though I'm not sure whether it was a Norwich or Manchester player that did the deed). As he rolled around on the ground, the crowd accorded him the sympathy he deserved. 'Get up, you time-waster, you're all right'. 'I hope you're not adding this on – your injury time doesn't count.' 'Perhaps that'll knock some sense into you.' 'Let him die, let him die, let him die.' On top of all this, there were a couple of girls who couldn't have been any older than 13 shouting, 'Kick him in the bollocks!' As soon as the ref got to his feet, he whistled for time, probably through the new gaps in his teeth.

As we made our way out, Mum ended the afternoon with her *pièce de résistance*. Looking down over a railing, she saw that Stephen was already making his way down the steps that lead beneath the stand. She called to him – and as he looked up, she pursed her lips and produced a bubble of spit. Honestly. Taunting, leading the songs, gobbing – is this the sort of behaviour one expects from a woman of 69? Still, it's better than being housebound or bedridden, I suppose. And at least she doesn't punch the air and grunt, 'Ooh! Ooh! Ooh!' when we win a corner. Yet.

The fact that we had won and broken our jinx against Manchester City was a reassurance that losing my job didn't matter that much. And as we sauntered up Jimmy Hill, I was reminded of the advantages of my new status. Two men in front of us were discussing whether their work shifts would allow them to see the midweek games against Arsenal and Villa. I just smiled.

The news back at the house wasn't so good. Villa and United had both won, United coming back from 1–0 down at home to Southampton with two goals in the last eight minutes. And I just missed out on winning the pools. It would have been the perfect weekend to win – though any weekend would be pretty good. Admittedly, it wasn't the treble chance I nearly won, but the ten homes. Norwich (surprisingly, as I rarely touch them on the coupon), QPR, Cambridge, Luton, Brighton, Fulham, Stockport, Barnet and Walsall all did their stuff. Scarborough let me down, only drawing with Rochdale. I wonder if Charlie paid one of his rare visits to the ground and put a curse on my chances.

I shouldn't be too greedy, though. I have won the pools seven times before. You wouldn't have heard about this, as I always put a cross in the 'no publicity' box – though perhaps the fact that my biggest win to date is £43 has something to do with it too. My average win is around £1.50.

The first time I won, I actually lost money. I got the five aways up and, on checking the papers, I found that the previous week's dividend was around £50. I told my mates, who suggested I should get the drinks in. I bought a round for five pounds (this is going back a few years, you understand) – and a cheque turned up on the Thursday morning for 75p. Typical. I didn't bother to cash it, but framed it and hung it on the wall.

Match of the Day was a further irritation. Despite our win, the title race was presented as a Villa-United shoot-out. 'That might not have gone down too well in Norfolk,' grinned Des Lynam. Too right, you moustachioed ...

Our Sunday-morning game was the return against the Sunderland Supporters at Wormwood Scrubs. It was bitterly cold, and some of our team made for the café near the changing-rooms to buy hot dogs covered in onions. They smelt revolting. (The hot dogs, not the players ... oh, I don't know, though.) How could they eat them? Unless the after-effect of the onions was intended to create space in the opposition's penalty area, of course.

Our opponents were so late that the referee called the game off, awarded the points to us and went home. The Sunderland lot weren't happy, but we were. I knew that it had been a good move for one of our players to give the referee a lift home last Sunday morning.

The pitch was very poor in any case, as if a spate of tunnels from the prison next door had caused widespread subsidence, but as we had all turned up (eventually), we thought we might as well play a friendly anyway. After ten minutes, I thought this was a great idea as I scored my best goal ever. It was a perfectly-struck left-foot shot from 25 yards, if not further, that flew in like a guided missile.

Look, don't be so sceptical. I know this is what I claimed when I scored with that scrappy tap-in earlier in the season, but it really happened this time. You can ask anyone who was there. On second thoughts, you'd better not. Everyone else thought it was a mishit cross, which it wasn't. It bloody wasn't, honest. Oh, sod you all.

Soon after, we went 2–0 up. Then the drawback of allowing one of the opposition to referee the game became apparent as they got two penalties and one offside goal. Suddenly, the friendly was not so friendly. 'Here, you hit me in the face.' 'If I had, you'd be out cold, you whingeing little prat.' What a delightful way to spend a Sunday morning.

There were no showers afterwards, as the boiler had broken down. This meant I had to go to Tesco's to do my shopping all smelly. I thought it best to keep on the move so that I didn't turn the milk bad or put the other customers off. 'I say, darling, check the sell-by date of that trout, would you? Something smells a bit off to me.'

No one believed the story about my goal afterwards. Mum didn't, and nor did my colleagues at work. On Monday morning, the tale was repeated more frequently than items on the BBC's *Breakfast News*, but in vain. I wish someone had been at the game with a camcorder. I'm never likely to do it again.

Sunday 28 February
Blackburn Rovers (home)

Now here's a turn-up for the books. I was half-way through my cornflakes on Wednesday morning when the phone rang. It was one of the girls from work. 'Are you watching BBC1?' she asked. 'There's going to be a special report on your team.'

I already knew this, of course. The report was the reason for the cameras at the turnstiles last weekend, and Mum had phoned me on Monday to let me know when it was going to be shown. But that wasn't the point here. 'Thanks for telling me,' I said. 'But how did you know my number?'

'I rang the office and got someone to look it up.' She went to all that trouble just to tell me that Norwich were going to be on TV? Could this mean that she … ? No, surely not. Oh sod it, I thought, it's worth a try. I'm now taking her to the QPR game next week. Perhaps I will leave work with some happy memories after all.

I can't see me missing much else. I won't be able to sit and read all the papers in reception on a Monday after we've won, it's true. Nor will there be any more jolly banter such as occurred later on Wednesday. I took two videotapes to work to watch at lunchtime – one showing the *Breakfast News* report on City's title chances, the other featuring Tuesday night's episode of *Dream On*. 'You ought to label them both "Dream On",' said one bright spark. Oh yes, I'm really going to miss comments like that.

Still, one colleague – a Newcastle fan – did come and tell me this week that he thought Norwich's treatment by the national media was disgraceful and that he hoped we would win the league. That was nice. And he didn't spit chocolate biscuit on my trousers, which was a bonus.

The special TV report wasn't too offensive, by the way. Stephen didn't feature in it, as Mum and I had feared. They only showed the feet of the people coming through the turnstiles and I couldn't spot his trainers. Mind you, Chairman Chase was on screen for quite a time. And there was a patronising remark from the studio presenter about 'country cousins'. And the final shot of the film showed a foot stamping a Norwich match ticket into the mud. Come to think of it, the report was quite offensive really.

The day before I left work, we had a big fire. Billowing black smoke, fire engines, the lot. 'Well done, Kev,' several people said. I must have the look of an arsonist, as the Wolverine accused me of starting the fire in the stand at Molineux last season. If I had been responsible for either incident, though, I'd have made a far better job of it. (By connecting the firemen's hoses to the petrol tanks of the fire engines, for example.)

It was an appropriate way to mark the end of my time there – and a much more entertaining affair than a big leaving do would have been. I didn't bother to organise one as I was returning to Norwich on Friday night, but I wouldn't have had time in any case. My departure was so sudden that many people won't realise I've gone until they notice the lack of Norwich posters pinned up. I did tell one of the girls downstairs that I was leaving on Friday afternoon, but even then there was a distinct lack of comprehension. 'Why are you going?' she asked.

I swung my foot to signify that I had been booted out. 'Oh, you've been signed up by Norwich!' she exclaimed. Good grief.

I went down to Carrow Road on Saturday morning to buy two tickets for the QPR game. It took a while, as I had to wait behind a blind chap who wanted tickets for Wednesday night's game at home to Arsenal. The delay was caused by the fact that he wanted tickets for the Arsenal section. Still, if you follow them, it's probably an advantage not to be able to see.

I had a quick look around the club shop and found a Norwich City board game. It turns out to be just like the Wolves one (made in Ipswich!), only in different colours. Would it be very unimaginative to send one to the Wolverine for her birthday in a few weeks? Probably, but I'll keep it in mind as an option.

When I got back to Mum's, I took another look at the QPR tickets and imagined myself sitting next to my new friend next week. Only then did I spot that I wouldn't be if we used these tickets. They were five seats apart. Was this a sign that our relationship is doomed before it begins? I would have to change the tickets, but the box office was now closed for the day. I would have to do it after the Blackburn match the next day – but how was I to manage this without telling Mum and Stephen what I was doing? I didn't want them to find out I was taking anyone, or I'd be subjected to the usual interrogation.

On Saturday afternoon, United and Villa both won again. We're now 8 points behind. To think that we were once 8 ahead. Our home match against United is the latest to be switched to a Monday night by Sky. This is getting out of hand. How on earth are the Manchester fans going to get across to Norwich for the game at that time? It will be almost as hard for the Norwich fans who live in London. Most will make it, I would guess, but not without a lot of difficulty.

Sunday afternoon's four o'clock kick-off, again a result of Sky's interference, presented a different problem. I was so full and tired after Mum's roast dinner that I didn't want to leave my armchair. A 3pm start wouldn't have been so bad, as I wouldn't have had time to get so comfortable. Besides, it was freezing outside. I put two T-shirts on under my clothes (not including the one the Wolverine sent me for Christmas, you understand) and gave my IQ-shrinking ski hat its first airing of the season. I was still cold, but at least the sky was clear and bright blue as we walked to the ground.

Walking down the hill, we noticed that one of the houses perched precariously on the slope was now up for sale. 'Why don't you buy it?' Mum asked me. 'It'd be handy for the football.'

'What would I buy it with?' I replied. 'In any case, I don't want a house that looks as if it's going to slide down the hill.'

'It would be even handier for the football then,' Stephen pointed out.

At the bottom of the hill, we bumped into a group of Blackburn fans who were all wearing horned Viking helmets. I've no idea why, but at least they made my ski hat look almost sensible.

Inside the ground, we had a nasty shock. On top of the injuries to Crook, Newman and Goss, we were now without Butterworth and Megson. Apparently, they pulled muscles over the weekend. The team had a makeshift appearance, with the centre of midfield now occupied by Phillips, who isn't really suited to the position, and David Smith, an inexperienced youngster who has only just recovered from injury himself. It was just as well for us that Blackburn had been hit by an injury too. Alan Shearer was still out, and will be for the rest of the season.

You will notice that I referred to Shearer in the third person just then. Nothing unusual in that – but have you noticed that he does this himself? He's been on TV this year saying things like 'Alan Shearer isn't affected by a large price tag' and 'Alan Shearer just wants to score goals'. Does he talk like this at home as well? Does his wife ask, 'What does Alan Shearer want for his tea?' to which he replies, 'Alan Shearer would like spaghetti bolognese, please'? Come to that, when they got married, did he say, 'Alan Shearer does'?

This is by no means the only odd use of language in the football world, of course. One of the most annoying habits is the incomprehensible use of the plural, as in 'We want to be up there with the Liverpools and the Arsenals'. I'm sorry, but as far as I know, there is only one of each. Similarly, people often say that a promising young player may one day rank alongside 'the George Bests and the Bobby Charltons'. Are they referring to other beings in parallel dimensions? Or are there several men who look alike and share the same name? Now there's a thought. Perhaps Bobby Charlton shouldn't hold the England goalscoring record. Perhaps those 49 goals were scored by three or four different people. And maybe George Best was really three people who kept leading each other into trouble.

'Hello, George, how are you?'

'Fine, George. And yourself?'

'Hey, look. There's George. Yoo-hoo!'

'Hi, George. Wotcha, George. Fancy a drink?'

'Cheers, George. Coming, George?'

'Well, I ... '

'Oh come on, George.'

'OK, Georges, I'm coming.' On the other hand, this may all be a load of rubbish.

While I'm on the subject, though, another irritating and over-used phrase is 'With all due respect to X ... ' What this actually means is 'With no respect at all to X ... ' It's just a way of slagging off the opposition with impunity. I once knew someone who continually got away with the most outrageous insults by the simple method of appending the phrases 'No offence, mind' or 'Nothing personal', e.g., 'You're acting like a complete arsehole – no offence, mind.' Could football fans pull off this trick? If one set of fans sang 'You're so shit it's unbelievable – nothing personal, though', would the opposing supporters reply with 'Fair enough, you're entitled to your opinioin'? I can't see it somehow.

The companion phrase to 'With all due respect ... ' is 'I don't want to take anything away from the other side, but ... ' Just as the phrases 'I'm no prude, but ... ' and 'I'm not a racist, but ... ' invariably preface blatantly prudish or racist remarks, this generally precedes a long list of excuses which deny the opposition any credit whatsoever.

What else? Ah yes, what on earth does 'early doors' mean? (As in 'Norwich may be top, but it's still early doors'.) And why do people refer to the pitch as 'the park'? I can understand it where Sunday-morning football is concerned, but you don't see too many slides, roundabouts or people walking dogs at Anfield or Old Trafford. What do managers mean when they say that they are going to go to a ground and 'set our stall out'? Are they trying to bring some more money into the club by selling hats and scarves in the street outside? And why do they say 'If we didn't think we had a chance on Saturday, we wouldn't bother turning up', as if non-appearance is a legitimate option? Has there ever been a game called off because one team decided after due consideration that they didn't stand a chance and stayed at home? If so, I've never heard of it.

Sorry to go on like that, but I did want to get it off my chest. Back to the Blackburn game.

During the five minutes the players spent back in the dressing-room just before the start of the game, the conditions changed completely. Suddenly the heavens opened, and we were in the middle of an arctic blizzard. Naturally, the wind was blowing all the snow into our stand. The girl sitting just in front of Stephen put the hood of her duffle-coat up. 'Damn, there goes my ashtray,' he said.

The Sky cameraman on the crane above the South Stand was in the most exposed position. Oh dear. What a shame. Still, he should have counted himself lucky. If we'd been playing Wimbledon, they would probably have started taking pot-shots to knock him off.

As the teams came out to the ironic strains of the Test cricket theme, followed by Sam Cooke's *Wonderful World*, three lads near us greeted them by throwing handfuls of torn-up Yellow Pages into the air (see, they're not just there for the nasty things in life), but the effect was completely lost in the blizzard. The paper stuck to everyone's coats and hair (in the case of those fans with hair, of course) and went all soggy.

The pitch had changed colour so quickly that the referee was carrying an orange ball. Presumably there had been a bit of frantic ferreting in dusty cupboards to locate it. 'I don't know why, but orange balls always look a lot heavier than white ones,' I said.

'You should have seen the leather ones we used in my day,' said Stephen. 'When they got wet, they weighed a ton. And if you headed the laces ... ' I was surprised at him admitting to this. It was a pity Karen wasn't here to make the most of it.

Before the game, there was a minute's silence in memory of Bobby Moore. Well, there was supposed to be. Unfortunately, it went the same way as the tribute to Ted Croker on Boxing Day. Someone outside the ground shouted, someone else shouted at them to shut up, someone else shouted at the person shouting 'Shut up!' to shut up, and it degenerated from there. Meanwhile, all the players stood around the centre circle and turned the same shades of blue and white as the Blackburn shirts. 'This weather will suit Blackburn,' said a voice behind me. 'It's always like this up there.' This might have been a little inaccurate, but it did indicate the air of pessimism around the ground.

Little noise was made in the first half, except for the obligatory abuse of Tim Sherwood and the unbroken voices of all the schoolchildren in the ground. The list of school parties at the match went on for ages. This is all very well, it's good for our future support and all that, but it seems that fewer and fewer people are paying to come into the ground these days. The high-pitched squeals of 'Norwich, Norwich' cannot help sounding thin and weedy and underline the current lack of vocal support.

Of course, the weather and the quality of the game didn't exactly encourage singing. The players weren't wearing the right footwear for one thing – but then I'm not sure that ice skates are allowed. The best two chances fell to Blackburn. Our lot fell over before they made any.

Things scarcely improved in the second half. 'You're supposed to pass to the other ones in yellow shirts,' yelled one man in frustration. Ruel Fox appeared to be tripped in the Blackburn area at one point, and the crowd howled for a penalty, none more loudly than Mum. 'Actually, I couldn't see if he was tripped or not,' she confessed as she sat down again, 'but it was worth a try, wasn't it?' It was a pity the ref, a Mr P. Don, didn't see it.

If City had a game-plan, it must have been to let Bobby Mimms in the Blackburn goal get frozen through inactivity, then catch him unawares with a late shot. The first part of this plan was executed brilliantly. It was just a shame we couldn't manage a late shot.

The match finished at 0–0. At least we hadn't been P. Don this time – and I do remember saying after the 7–1 defeat at Ewood Park that I would have been grateful for a drab goalless draw instead. All the same, this result wouldn't help us to keep in touch with Villa and United.

As we left the ground in subdued mood, I remembered that I needed to change the tickets for the QPR game. What could I tell Mum and Stephen? 'I've just got to nip into the box office,' I said, deliberately vaguely.

'Why?' asked Mum. Damn. 'I thought you got your QPR ticket yesterday.'

'I did. I – er – thought I'd get one for the game at Sheffield United today.' Actually, I bought that the day before, but Mum didn't know. 'You go home and I'll catch you up.'

'No, go on, we'll wait outside for you,' Mum said. Damn again. Keeping my back to the window, I discreetly passed the two tickets to the man behind the counter and he swapped them for two others. Nothing was said when I came out of the office, so I think I got away with it.

By the time we got back to Mum's, all three of us were virtually sprinting down the road to get to the toilet first. Why is it that cold weather shrinks your privates but makes your bladder swell? Mum claimed to be the most desperate, so Stephen and I let her go first. She then abused this courtesy by turning the bath and wash basin taps on full to make us dance around even more outside the door.

I received a similar level of consideration from my work colleagues – sorry, former work colleagues – the next morning. They rang to tell me, with considerable glee, what the match report in the *Sun* said. So much for an end to the banter. Apparently, our title challenge was described as being as long-lasting as a DIY wardrobe.

It is said that if you gave an infinite number of monkeys with typewriters an infinite amount of time, they would eventually come up with the complete works of Shakespeare. That's as may be, but I am beginning to think that you could give all the tabloid football journalists an infinite amount of time and they still wouldn't come up with a decent report.

Wednesday 3 March
Arsenal (home)

Mum says that, since she retired, she's never been so busy. Because people think she has nothing to do all day, they keep finding jobs for her. I'm beginning to find the same is true for me now that I'm out of work.

On Monday, I was called by Brian, our Sunday football manager. 'I don't feel too good,' he groaned. 'Can you go to the league meeting tonight?' Obliging soul that I am, I duly made my way down to Wimbledon's old home at Plough Lane. The monthly meetings take place in Nelson's nightclub under the main stand. You may well have seen the place on TV, as it was the scene of a stabbing a few years ago and was featured in an ITV series on murder. I should point out that the incident took place at a party, not at a league meeting. The club secretaries don't get that worked up about the allocation of pitches. The knife was found behind one of the terraces – but, worryingly, it wasn't the only one the police found there. This apparently widespread use of weapons would explain the unnerving notices at the entrance to the nightclub warning visitors not to carry knives or drugs.

The evening wasn't the jolliest I've ever spent. Apart from the dingy surroundings, I found myself in the middle of possibly the most world-weary people I have ever met. The long faces were understandable. It's no fun being a club secretary, what with trying to find eleven, let alone thirteen, players every week, chasing people up for not paying their subscriptions, organising pitches at short notice, finding a referee when none has been allocated, and trying to raise money for new kit. The league committee sitting behind their rickety trestle tables didn't seem any happier with life, especially the secretary who had to keep banging his gavel in exasperation every time the deep mutterings around the room grew too loud.

I wonder why all these people take on their offices when all they get is headaches and hassle. At the same time, I'm relieved and grateful that they do, otherwise we wouldn't get to play on Sunday mornings.

The only time the committee members came to life was when the subject of fines was mentioned. So excited did they become that I suspected they must be traffic wardens or wheel-clampers during the day. It turns out that the league has enough funds raised by fines to clear the national debt and still have a knees-up afterwards. Yet the committee still seems to want to do better in this area. One member told a story about an incident in a neighbouring league when a team had a suspended player running the line at a game (an offence in itself, it seems). During the match, the referee overruled him. A row followed, and in the end the linesman thumped the ref. Eight charges were brought against him and three against his club, with the fines totalling £340. At the mention of this figure, the other committee members shook their heads in wonder and envy.

On Tuesday, I got a call from Jon, the supporter to whom I'd given a lift before the Middlesbrough game. He now wanted a lift to the Arsenal game, as the trains have suddenly become ridiculously expensive. On arriving at Liverpool Street Station on the way to the home game against Crystal Palace, he was told that he couldn't use a Saver ticket and would have to pay over £50 instead of around £25. Not having the money, he couldn't go. 'That's a shame,' I said. 'It was a marvellous evening.'

'Oh, rub it in, why don't you?' he replied, with the tetchiness of someone who had already been told this several times before.

I agreed to give him a lift. After all, it would help me decide exactly when to travel back to Norwich now that I don't have the demands of work to decide for me. We discussed a wide and varied range of topics on the journey.

Politics. There was apparently a big row in the Capital Canaries ranks a couple of weeks ago because two non-members attended a club lunch before the Manchester City game. I'm glad I didn't bother going. Then there is another member who is jeopardising cheap (cheap!) rail travel for the London branches of all football supporters' clubs by taking his petty complaint about the lack of tables in new train carriages to echelons of BR management that up to now have been unaware of the subsidised travel enjoyed by thousands of fans every year. (Oops – I hope no senior BR managers are reading this.)

Europe. We talked about which countries we would like to visit when Norwich play there next season. Jon favoured Bulgaria, as the drink is so cheap. 'Not that that will interest you, I know, Kev.'

'I don't mind as long as we qualify. And as long as you don't ring me at the last minute to see if I can give you a lift to Sofia.'

Music. There was a new composition from the home fans at Southampton which I hadn't heard because I was up in the seats. It concerned Portsmouth's star striker:

> Whittingham is illegitimate,
> He ain't got a birth certificate,
> He's got Aids and can't get rid of it,
> He's a Pompey bastard.

Such friendly rivalry.

The environment. Was that awful smell half-way up the M11 caused by that muck-spreader over in the field or by Jon's lucky underpants escaping from his bag in the boot? He hadn't had a chance to wash them since Sunday's game. It turns out that he has even more superstitions than me, the oddest being that he has to eat an apple before entering the ground. Taking one inside to eat later always brings disaster.

Business strategy. We discussed whether Norwich would be better off using a sweeper system with so many midfielders injured at present. This discussion didn't last long, however, as we both thought we would, so that was that.

Arsenal had their own injury problems before this game. Bould, Adams (who needed several stitches after practising his heading on a pavement last week), Smith, Merson and Hillier were all ruled out. Ian Wright, on the other hand, made a surprising reappearance. He is known to be a quick healer, notably when he returned soon after breaking his leg to score twice for Crystal Palace against Manchester United in the 1990 FA Cup final. But as all the newspapers said he would not play this evening, and with Arsenal having a big FA Cup match at Ipswich at the weekend for which I thought they would want to save him, I really didn't expect to see him at Carrow Road.

The general groan that went around the ground when his name flashed up on the scoreboard before the match showed that other Norwich supporters feared his presence as much as I did. Even more eloquent, in a perverse way, was the abuse and jeering which greeted his horrid miskick in front of the Norwich goal in the first minute. A few people adapted the lyrics of the Nike commercial in which Wright is currently appearing: 'Can I kick it? – No you can't.' When he then received the yellow card after patting the referee's cheek (on his face – he'd have got a Valentine card at worst if he'd patted the other sort), I thought he would certainly be substituted to avoid the risk of him being sent off. Unfortunately for us, he wasn't …

While this was going on, the Norwich players seemed to be trying to make their former team-mate Andy Linighan look good in the Arsenal defence by aiming as many high balls towards his head as possible. It came as a huge surprise when we took the lead, especially as Ruel Fox scored with a header. I know he did this against Everton at the start of the season, but I thought that was his quota of headed goals for the decade.

At half-time there was a lottery for two nights in an Istanbul hotel. The prize was won by a Norwich fan who said he was getting married soon. 'Yeah, very likely,' Stephen said. 'I bet he just said that to try and get two weeks out of them.' This struck me as unnecessarily cynical, but I began to question the trustworthiness of the winner when he said the wedding was on 17 April. Who would choose to get hitched on the weekend of the return game at Ipswich?

The crowd (14,500 or 19,000 depending on which newspaper you bought the next day, but more likely the former given all the empty seats) was very quiet in the second half. There were the odd jeers of 'We beat the Arsenal 4–2', but generally there was so little noise that Stephen could hear Mum shouting five rows away. Even with Mum's voice, this should not be possible.

Once again, we had to watch the game separately because we had to sit in specific seats. This in itself is a reason for the lack of shouting and singing at the moment. When we had the terraces, the noisiest fans would congregate in certain places and keep each other going. Now that they are forced to sit apart, they are spread too thinly to maintain any momentum.

Admittedly, the team's performance wasn't particularly inspiring either. The effort could not be faulted, but the team reminded me of those cartoon characters who hold on to a wall by their fingertips and then slide slowly down, leaving grooves all the way. The midfield players seemed to be moving haphazardly in different directions like the wheels of a supermarket trolley. Surely, to use a third simile in as many lines, the whole house of cards that was wobbling so alarmingly was about to collapse.

Actually, it didn't. Arsenal's constant pressure, especially from corners, produced few clear chances – and when they won a penalty, Gunn brilliantly saved Wright's kick after standing slightly to one side of the goal and encouraging him to go for the bigger target. At this, I began to think that Arsenal were never going to score. When Kevin Campbell began warming up on the touchline, I was convinced that he was about to replace Wright. However, fate and George Graham (in no particular order) were merely teasing me. Campbell replaced Limpar and, eight minutes from time, he crossed for Wright, who couldn't have been left more alone if he had Legionnaire's Disease, to score the equaliser. 'Ian Wright, Wright, Wright,' chanted the Arsenal fans, to the tune of *Hot Hot Hot*. 'Oh, shit, shit, shit,' I muttered.

I even cursed Chelsea for Wright's goal. As I saw it, they were largely responsible. If they hadn't beaten Arsenal with a late goal on Monday night, George Graham might not have been so anxious to get a result against us and might have rested Wright for all or part of the game.

Fox created and missed a good chance in the last minute, and the game ended with the score at 1–1. It was a fair result, I suppose, but right now we could do with a few unfair victories. Gloom descended on the majority of the crowd. We all knew how important this game had been. As it was, we had now used up our games in hand over United and Villa and were still 4 and 6 points respectively behind them. Had we really been 8 clear once? 'They've blown it,' I heard someone say as we trudged out of the ground. I hated him for saying it, but I couldn't help feeling he was probably right.

Is this how the title is to slip away from us? Gradually, unspectacularly, with an under-strength team battling out draws in front of mediocre crowds? It's similar to the way in which the magic can go out of a relationship. There are no cataclysmic catastrophes. Things seem to be going OK on the face of it (our record over the last six games reads: won three, drawn two, lost one), but one day you stop and realise that something you had has disappeared along the way. In this case, what might have been was demonstrated when Arsenal and Blackburn were beaten this week by Chelsea and Everton, who have been playing dreadfully of late.

It was nice not to have to get up at 5:30 in the morning to drive back to London. I didn't go back until the afternoon – and I wouldn't have returned at all that day if I hadn't already paid for my ticket to the APFSCIL dinner-dance.

APFSCIL, possibly the clumsiest acronym I have ever come across, stands for the Association of Provincial Football Supporters' Clubs In London. Looking around the room at the Oval cricket ground (couldn't they have found a more appropriate venue?), I decided that it ought to stand for A Pretty Feeble Showing, Convened In Lounge Suits. Only 150 people had turned up. I know that a lot of people are unemployed at the moment – boy, do I know – but I'd have thought that more would have come along to listen to Barry Fry, the Barnet manager, and Jack Taylor, the referee in the 1974 World Cup final.

Barry Fry was – how can I put it? – emotional and plain-speaking. All right, he'd had a few and kept saying 'fuck'. Still, he did keep stressing how important supporters are (contrary to the recent remarks made by his chairman, Stan Flashman), which not surprisingly went down well. Jack Taylor described everyone he referred to as 'totally unique' (as opposed to slightly unique, presumably). He disapproved of all-seater stadia and the rescheduling of matches for the benefit of TV viewers, so he was OK by me too (despite being a Wolves supporter).

The best part of the evening, however, was the chance to sit round a dinner table and talk about football without having people not interested in the game making over-dramatic yawning gestures and trying to change the subject. On our table, we talked a lot about former Norwich players. There was general astonishment that Nottingham Forest have just bought Robert Rosario to solve their goalscoring problem. Rosario (the name of one of the female characters in *Eldorado*, I recently discovered) has scored only 27 league goals in ten seasons! This was taken as the final proof that Brian Clough is off his trolley.

There was general amusement that Tim Sherwood had been sent off against Everton the previous evening. We talked about Louie Donowa's potentially lethal tackle from behind on Trevor Putney (then of Ipswich) in the Milk Cup semi-final second leg in 1985, for which he should have been sent off but wasn't. And we discussed John Devine, who was booed almost as much as Tim Sherwood at times during his career with Norwich in the early '80s. Someone advanced the theory that when the crowd boos a player, the criticism is actually directed at the manager who selected him. Hmm. Perhaps. But I don't suppose that would make the player on the receiving end feel any better.

During the evening, I discovered that, once again, I have been outdone by another member of Capital Canaries when I thought I had achieved something unique. Sorry, totally unique. Just as it turned out that someone made a greater effort to get to the game in Carlisle and someone else won more money than me at Aston Villa, it now transpires that another Norwich supporter lost his job before I did this season. Furthermore, the reason for his dismissal was more clearly connected with football. He worked for a bus company and took one without permission to the Ipswich match just before Christmas. He was found out and fired on the spot. Will I ever be the first to do anything?

It also seems that Mum is by no means the rowdiest woman of a certain age to be found at football matches. One man told how he and his wife had followed Fulham during their FA Cup run in 1975, when they were both in their 50s. At one game, someone behind them started to criticise Bobby Moore, then Fulham captain. 'Don't you say nasty things about Bobby,' the man's wife said, thumping him with her handbag.

A woman at our table mentioned that she had been to watch Sunderland at Charlton a few Saturdays ago. Her support had met with a certain amount of scorn, though. 'Bloody hell,' a Sunderland fan had said. 'We send five hundred to cheer your lot at Everton, and who do we get in return? You.'

What really made it a good evening, however, was the presence of two representatives from the club: Peter Mendham, a former player who now has the job of building up close links with local schools; and John Faulkner, once a centre-half with Leeds and Luton, who is now the reserve-team manager at Carrow Road. I was a little apprehensive about chatting to them, as it seemed I would be sailing dangerously close to breaking my policy of not talking to the team in person, but in the event they proved to be straight-talking, interesting and good-humoured. We got to find out a few things that are going on behind the scenes, were put straight about things which we thought were going on but aren't, and tested out some of our pet theories. Here then are ...

Fifteen things you didn't know about Norwich City. (Or perhaps you did, but I didn't.)

1) Peter Mendham used to sleep with Justin Fashanu. That is to say, they used to share a room on away trips. 'Is he still going out with Bet Lynch?' someone asked.
    'No, it was in the Sunday papers that he wants someone younger who can give him children.'
    'Like Tony Powell?' Powell, in case you didn't know, played for City in the '70s but now (again, according to the Sunday papers, so it's up to you whether you choose to believe it) lives in the USA as a transvestite or transsexual or something. Whether he is TV or wireless, though, he is possibly the finest Norwich player ever to pull on a dress.
2) Kevin Drinkell regularly used to defy the club's ban on visiting licensed premises in the 48 hours before a game. He used to go to the pub to play pool and have a few beers and cigarettes. It didn't seem to affect his performance though.
3) Steve Bruce used to prepare for matches by doing as little as possible during training sessions. He would compensate for this through sheer gut-busting effort on Saturday afternoons, which explains why his face always seemed to be as red as the shirt he now wears. I suppose this means I can say I train as hard as a professional, even if the level of my commitment on the pitch leaves something to be desired.
4) John Faulkner said he would put his house on Andy Johnson, a young player who is currently in Australia with the England squad for the Youth World Cup finals, making it to the top. This is heartening news for the future.
5) There have apparently been several approaches from big clubs regarding Chris Sutton. Mike Walker has said that the next time someone enquires, he'll ask £5 million for him. This strikes me as being rather dangerous. Blackburn would probably pay that.
6) Darren Beckford does not have a future with the club. John Faulkner reckons that, even at 45, he could mark him out of a game. However, Beckford is not, as I had heard, moving to Millwall.
7) Talking of false rumours, there doesn't seem to be any truth in the story that went round about a punch-up in the hotel before the Southampton game. 'That's nonsense,' said Faulkner. 'Where on earth did you hear that?' Oops. Wrong again.
8) Someone else mentioned that he had heard that one player had allegedly got a girl pregnant and paid her to go away and keep quiet about it. This was met with 'I don't know anything about that' – not exactly a categorical denial, but it brought the matter to a close.
9) Though the club has been inactive in the transfer market this season, it isn't through lack of interest or effort. A lot of time is spent every day trying to think of players we could buy to strengthen the team, but the

suitable players are not available and vice versa. It is not clear how involved Robert Chase is in these discussions, but it sounds as though he insists on knowing about every single thing going on at the club.
10) John Faulkner reckons that the crowd at Carrow Road is even quieter than at Luton. Strewth. I didn't realise it was that bad. He would like to make the atmosphere at the ground less laid-back. I see his point, up to a point – but changing the character of a county overnight doesn't seem a feasible proposition to me.
11) The main problem with the team at the moment is that, while the players are talented, too many of them are unable to raise their performance in big games. It used to be the case that Norwich would only play well against the better teams, but that seems to have changed in the last few years.
12) The team was sick with disappointment after Wednesday night's draw against Arsenal. This was good to hear. Fans often accuse players of not caring as much as they do, but this clearly isn't true with our team at the moment.
13) John Faulkner conceded that supporters often have a better idea of who should be substituted than the manager. Quite an admission for a member of the coaching staff.
14) The reactions of the fans are taken into consideration when deciding on team selection and tactics. Mike Walker seriously considered using a sweeper system against Blackburn but thought that the crowd would consider this to be too negative. It needn't be, of course.
15) Peter Medham has been told by Robert Chase that his job is safe for the next five years. 'You mean he's given you a vote of confidence?' I asked. I think Peter's a bit worried now.

I didn't stick around for long once the disco started. Some 95 per cent of those present were male, and I didn't fancy dancing with them or with a chair. As I don't drink, I was able to drive home, thereby avoiding the irritation of yet another taxi driver telling me about how he once had a trial for Brentford. Either Brentford have an astonishingly thorough scouting system, or the drivers are telling porkies. I wonder which.

Saturday 6 March
Queen's Park Rangers (away)

Truth will out, they say, and so it proved with my 'date' for this game that I had tried to keep quiet from the rest of the family.

When I got back from the dinner on Thursday night, there was a message from Mum on my answerphone. She asked if it would be all right for Stephen, who was working in London on Friday, to stay overnight at my flat and come to the game with me on Saturday. Effectively, she wasn't asking me; she was telling me. It was too late to phone Stephen to put him off, and he would be leaving for London before I got up in the morning. In any case, what would I say to him? I had no choice but to tell him when he arrived on Friday evening that I had already arranged to take someone (or, to give her a name now that her existence has been revealed, Jane) and had bought seat tickets.

Stephen was understanding about it and said he would go and stand on the terraces. 'I remember taking someone on a date to the football,' he said. 'I said we'd have a meal and then go on to a club. We bought some chips in Valori's on Timberhill, ate them sitting on the wall outside, and then went down to Carrow Road. It was a good evening, that.'

I met Jane on Shepherd's Bush Green at two o'clock. She had arrived there first and was standing not far away from a group of noisy Norwich supporters drinking outside a pub. I worried that she might be worried about the sort of people she would be mixing with at the game, but she thought they were very funny. 'Every time a Rangers supporter walks past, they keep showing off their Norwich shirts and laughing at them,' she said.

She seemed excited about coming to her first game. 'I even watched *Football Focus* to get in the mood.' Yet she still didn't know exactly what to expect – even from me. 'The others at work said you probably turn into a psycho killer at football matches.' I tried to reassure her that I don't, but all the same I resolved not to shout too loud. Well, not too often, anyway.

'Is Norwich supposed to win today?' she asked – and simply by using the strictly-correct singular tense of the verb rather than the plural, demonstrated her unfamiliarity with the peculiarities of the football world. It is a different world, after all. During the course of this book, I have offered some of my alternative laws of football, but it seems to me that, within the boundaries of football grounds, alternative laws of science apply. For example:

1) Time does not pass at an even rate. It speeds up markedly when your team is losing, but drags excruciatingly when they are a single goal ahead. Scientists such as Stephen Hawking talk theoretically about how time changes as you approach a black hole, but Hawking would be able to experience this for himself by visiting the Abbey Stadium in Cambridge where he lives, especially as this has been a black hole for football for the last couple of years.

2) Newton's first law of motion states that a body will continue in a state of rest, or of motion at constant speed in a straight line, except when this state is changed by forces acting on it. However, this does not apply if your name is Anders Limpar or Jürgen Klinsmann and you are in the opposition's penalty area. Not that they are the only players to fall myste-

riously to the ground without anyone touching them, of course. One possible explanation is that the earth's gravitational pull is several times greater than usual in eighteen-yard boxes.
3) $E=mc^2$, apparently. According to this, the greater the mass of an object, the more energy it has. Hmph. Anyone who has seen Mick Quinn play will probably disagree.
4) Pythagoras's theorem needs to be revised a little for football grounds. At Norwich, it should state that the noise at the Barclay end is equal to the sum of the noise on the other three sides.
5) Newton's third law of motion: 'To every action, there is an equal and opposite reaction.' Not from Gary Lineker, there isn't. And when it comes to luck and refereeing decisions, I've always been sceptical about the theory that they even themselves out over the course of a season. I've known times when it has seemed that every member of the Norwich squad has killed an albatross by smashing a mirror over its head.

All things considered, QPR's ground was a good place to take Jane for her first game. You are close to the pitch, the view from the away supporters' seats is good, and the stadium is compact and enclosed. It feels a bit like sitting inside a biscuit tin. The attendance wasn't bad, though it was difficult to see just how many Norwich fans had turned up as the standing area is below the seats. The weather was bright and much warmer than it had been of late, and buoyed by the surroundings I was able to adopt an air of confidence of which I am rarely capable and which Jane had certainly never witnessed before. Norwich may have been playing away, but in a sense I was at home. I was dealing with Jane on territory that was very familiar to me.

I was able to inform her about the Norwich players and the tactics we were likely to employ; I told her that we were tending to hit hopeful long balls to our diminutive strikers Fox and Robins; I pointed out the changes to the line-up in the programme before they were announced; I warned her about the ridiculous prices at the refreshment bars. In short, I impressed her with my knowledge, experience and judgement. At least, that was the idea.

The Norwich team emerged from the tunnel, preceded by two young mascots. 'I see what you mean about small strikers,' Jane said. I think she was joking.

Once the game started, so did the long balls. My pre-match analysis was proving to be spot-on, but this gave me no satisfaction at all. It wasn't even improving my standing in Jane's eyes, as she didn't seem to be picking up on the tactics being employed. She was just enjoying watching the ball ping around.

More worryingly, so was our defence. With John Polston's late withdrawal through injury, we had at last reverted to a sweeper system – but even with five at the back, no one seemed able to get anywhere near Rangers' Les Ferdinand. After twenty minutes, he was left completely unmarked as he nodded his first goal from six yards out. A quarter of an hour later, he picked up the ball on the half-way line, ran straight past the City defenders who let him through as if it were National Courtesy Week, and thumped in his second.

It was proving to be rather easier to keep quiet next to Jane than I had anticipated. Similarly, the standing Norwich contingent found little to sing about, though there was a loud chorus of 'You're just a bunch of wankers' at one point. I don't think this was directed at the players. I asked Stephen later what was going on down there, but he wasn't sure whether the chants were aimed at the police (who apparently removed two or three people from the crowd) or at the photographers from the national press who were jeered with cries of 'Scum!' later on.

Recently, it has seemed that the Norwich players have to lift the supporters, when it should be the other way round. Quite unexpectedly, this happened here five minutes before half-time, when a quarter-hit shot from Robins trickled slowly over the line. I leapt to my feet and yelled. I'm not sure what Jane did; I think she just clapped politely, but I'm afraid she wasn't the subject of my attention just then. (Does this reveal the true extent of my interest in her, or merely confirm how blinkered I am with regard to football and Norwich?) She didn't take to being a supporter as quickly as Karen, but then my sister must have been naturally disposed to it through her genes.

At last, a chorus of 'On the ball, City' rang around the ground. 'What song is that?' asked Jane. I explained that this was the Norwich club song, written early this century and (I believe) the first song to be specifically written for a football team. And a fine song it is too, as a cursory analysis will reveal.

>Kick it off ...

A neat use of ambiguity here. Does this signify the start of the song, of a match, or both? At any rate, the use of the word 'kick' at the very beginning gives the song immediate impact and momentum. One thing worries me, though. Why are Norwich kicking off and not the opposition? Have the others just scored? Or have Norwich lost the toss? If we had won it, we would surely have chosen ends – especially at home.

>... throw it in ...

This clearly refers to City's age-old practice of hitting a high diagonal ball to a player on the wing from the kick-off, which generally results in a throw-in to one side or the other.

>... have a little scrimmage.

The early stages of a match can often be scrappy. Managers often talk of 'earning the right to play', and the necessary early battling is clearly what is being alluded to here.

Keep it low ...

Self-explanatory, really. A phrase emphasising Norwich's continuing determination to play neat passing football rather than hopeful 'up-and-under' stuff. Though not in this game.

... a splendid rush ...

Well-deserved praise for the team's ability to launch swift, incisive counter-attacks. Again, not today.

... bravo, win or die.

A slightly problematic remark, this. 'Win or die' suggests that results are the be-all and end-all, but this has never really been the case at Norwich. The attractiveness of the football is just as important. Perhaps we should treat this phrase as a reflection of the exaggeration and excitement evident in the language of many fans at football matches. 'Bravo' seems to be an acknowledgement of an early promising move which has come to nothing.

On the ball, City ...

A statement of fact, or an exhortation to greater efforts? Again, the composer has cleverly left this open.

... never mind the danger ...

A perceptive line showing the awareness that we are at our best when concentrating on our own game rather than worrying about the potential threat of the opposition, or 'showing them too much respect', to use the common football parlance.

... steady on ...

A necessary corollary to the previous line. Ignoring danger should not mean being reckless and impulsive. Instead, a degree of composure and thought is needed when constructing an attack or exploiting an opening.

... now's your chance ...

At last, a chance to score is created. The fact that it has taken ten lines of the song to materialise reflects how much time and effort it has taken to make. In retrospect, the call to 'steady on' is all the more meaningful; such a hard-won opportunity should not be thoughtlessly frittered away.

... hurrah! We've scored a goal!

The word 'hurrah' may seem a little dated and quaint now, but it does convey the almost child-like joy experienced when the ball hits the back of the net. Similarly, 'we've scored a goal' is a simple statement of fact – a statement of the obvious, indeed – to mark the attainment of our aim. Yet there is a note of caution here too, possibly echoing the pessimism to be found among some City followers. Yes, we may have scored a goal, but it does not mean that we have won the game, nor that we are about to win a trophy. It is a victory, but only a minor one at present.

There are more verses to the song, but they are no longer sung.

At half-time, Jane ignored my warnings and went off to the refreshment bar for a cup of hot brown water. I had a look at the match programme and found it to be the best I've come across all season. It was informative, amusing, and the contributors' affection for their club was obvious (one received an award on the pitch to mark his 500th consecutive home game). Once or twice, though, the enthusiasm did overreach itself: 'I don't know of a Rangers fan who is not glued to their programme working out the possibility of yes, you've guessed it, European football.' Really? Looking around the ground, it didn't seem that way to me. There was also an unfortunate choice of words in the programme's tribute to Bobby Moore: 'Football is the poorer for his passing.' My teammates on Sunday mornings have made similar comments about my distribution.

As the second half began, I hoped that we were about to see a comeback to match those at Arsenal and Chelsea earlier in the season. Unfortunately, it wasn't long before an air of desperation set in both on and off the pitch. City resorted to shooting hopefully from long range, but for all the head-clutching of the players after each attempt, none of them looked remotely like going in. The supporters resorted to criticising Daryl Sutch, who was admittedly having a poor game, and the decision to take off Lee Power instead. John Faulkner's remark the other night that the fans often have a better idea of who should be replaced than the manager was illustrated perfectly.

With ten minutes to go, Rangers scored again and the game was up. What a match to bring Jane to, I thought. My misery was increased by the news coming through at the end that Manchester United had won away at Liverpool. Our Championship hopes had finally disappeared. As we left the ground, I heard other Norwich fans discussing whether they would prefer United or Villa to win the league now that our chance had gone.

I had hoped that this book would not turn out to be a story of hopes raised, then dashed. This is the typical experience of football supporters – especially Norwich supporters – but it is not the tale I wanted to tell here. All the same, it looks as if that is the story I have been given.

Jane, however, was disgustingly cheerful. I can just about see why now that I look back. She had sampled the atmosphere of a match for the first time and seen four goals, a bout of pushing and shoving involving most of the players, and a bone-crunching collision between Sutton and Ferdinand just below us. She was also pleased that England had beaten Scotland at rugby that afternoon. As if that mattered.

At the time, though, her chirpiness served only to infuriate me. Didn't she understand that our season was now over? I had intended to ask her if she'd like to go for a meal somewhere, but I changed my mind. Apart from being irritated by her good mood, I was aware that inflicting my bad mood on her would do me no favours at all. I knew I wouldn't be able to hide it even if I tried.

'I'd really like to come again,' she said. I tried to work out whether she meant it or not. 'When are ['are'! She's learning!] Norwich playing in London again?' What a dilemma. Our next game in London is at Wimbledon in a fortnight's time, but that's generally a fixture for the die-hards. It's always an awful game, and the crowd is always pathetic. Besides, Mum's coming down that weekend. Do I really want to subject Jane – or myself – to Mum's subtle, and sometimes not so subtle, questioning? I'll have to think about this one.

Our Sunday-morning game this week turned out to be two games. To get all the matches finished before the goalposts are taken down in the parks, the league has turned some games into 'double-headers'. This means that two matches, both of thirty minutes each way, are played between the same two teams on the same morning. How long before the Premier League introduces this measure? It's a daft enough idea to appeal to them, after all.

We drew the first game 2–2 – and would have won if the referee had spotted the 'hand of God' punching the ball into our net in the first half. Still, the point brought our tally for the season to 12, which is twice as many as we got last year.

We lost the second game 5–1, but I experienced an even more embarrassing fall than that of the team. I started this match as substitute and stood watching by a roped-off cricket square on one side of the pitch. After five minutes, two players came charging towards me trying to win the ball. I decided to take evasive action, took a couple of steps back – and fell backwards over the ropes. Everyone roared with laughter. Two kids of 9 or 10 who were watching their dad play pointed at me and shouted, 'He fell over! He fell over!' I regretted a couple of weeks ago that no one had a camcorder to capture my goal. This week, I was grateful. Otherwise, I'd have been prime Jeremy Beadle fodder.

There were other funny goings-on on the next pitch. Three girls of around 20 stood behind one goal and yelled, 'You're shit, aarrgghh!' every time the keeper took a goal kick. You expect this at professional matches, but it sounds very odd in a park on a Sunday morning with no one else watching.

In the afternoon, I had three interruptions as I watched the Manchester City v Spurs Cup match on TV. Though none was as long or as serious as the one caused by the pitch invasion at Maine Road. It looked as though the idiot who ran on to the pitch when Manchester City played at Carrow Road recently had brought his equally thick mates with him. First Mum, then Karen rang to ask who this girl was that I had taken to QPR. Well, it didn't take long for that to get around. Then Jon rang to say that he wouldn't want a lift to Sheffield United on Wednesday. He's written off our chances of winning the title as well.

Predictably, the national press did too. Again. The *Guardian*: 'It is perhaps best to say goodbye to Norwich for this season: thanks for the memory, for the way you play football, and here's hoping you can win a cup next year to keep your spirits up.'

I can't find it within me to condemn this attitude as patronising or negative as I usually would. How can I, when I've given up hope myself?

Wednesday 10 March
Sheffield United (away)

More phone calls on Monday. At this rate I'll soon be having delusions of popularity. First the Notts County fan from work (I mean ex-work) called about a story in one of the papers. Norwich have reportedly made an approach for three County players. 'You see,' he said, 'it must be the same Mike Walker in charge of both teams. He's just trying to switch players between the two.'

Then Jon rang to ask if I could give him a lift to the Sheffield United game after all. 'Why the change of heart?' I asked.

'I thought I'd give them one last chance,' he said. 'And if it does turn out to be the start of a miraculous surge to glory, I want to be there to see it.' I said I'd be happy to take him, so he planned a strategic migraine for Wednesday afternoon. I must say I miss the thrill of sneaking off work to see Norwich play. Like sex, it's not so much fun when the element of illicitness is removed. I tried leaving my coat in the car and slipping out of my flat with my collar turned up, but it wasn't the same.

We hadn't travelled far towards Sheffield when Jon asked me who I'd been sitting next to at QPR on Saturday. Good grief! Can't I keep anything quiet from anyone? I filled him in on the background – and then he revealed that he's been seeing someone lately. 'I finished with her last week, though,' he said. 'I realised there wasn't much point in going on with it, as I never got to see her with all the matches, not to mention playing for the Capital Canaries' pool team, quiz team ... ' Ah, the things we do (or don't do) for football.

'What on earth's gone wrong with the quiz team, by the way?' I asked. At a routine Capital Canaries committee meeting on Monday night, it had emerged that they have been having an even worse time than the Sunday football team this season. Played eight, won none, drawn one, lost seven. 'Don't you fancy turning out for us?' asked Jon.

'No, I bloody well don't!' I said. This may sound an unnecessarily rude reply to a perfectly reasonable question, but I am determined not to allow myself to get dragged into all that.

The Home Counties Football Quiz League may sound perfectly innocuous, even fun, but it is not. It is a strange, dark underworld from which few people ever return to tell the tale. It is a place where tailoring has not evolved since the days of John Collier, and where the passing of time is only marked by the annual publication of the *Rothmans Football Yearbook*. It is populated by failed train-spotters – anorak-clad strangers to shampoo, with packed lunches and seal-like laughs – though even among these sad creatures there is a hierarchy of sorts. Tales are told of legendary figures such as Mad Eddie from Blackpool, who has committed the whole of the yearbook to memory. He has given up watching matches as they get in the way of his swotting – which sounds akin to giving up having sex because it doesn't leave enough time for looking at mucky books – and even takes two weeks off work to prepare for the league's individual quiz night.

These are the sort of people who make a big deal of visiting every ground in the Football League. Then they go to all those in the GM Vauxhall Conference. Then the Diadora, Beazer Homes and HFS Loans Leagues. They reduce football, a rich, potentially beautiful game, to a collection of empty facts and meaningless statistics. They delude themselves that knowing these cold, dead pieces of information has some merit, that it is a sign of intelligence. Jean-Paul Sartre suggested that hell is other people. I suspect that quiz fiends were the people he had in mind.

If you are wondering why I should be so virulent in my condemnation of the quiz world and its inhabitants, the reason is simple. Just as the most militant anti-smokers tend to be ex-smokers, I am all the more scornful because I used to be a regular member of the Norwich Supporters' quiz team.

I was good, too. I have a decent memory and I devised all sorts of ways to help me remember obscure facts. For example, if I was ever asked to name the ground and manager of Dumbarton, I would think along these lines: 'Dumbarton' sounds like an insult ('You dumb barton!'), as does 'Boghead' ('You boghead!'), while 'Boghead Billy' has a nice alliterative ring to it. From this, I would be able to answer, 'Boghead Park, Billy Lamont.' Unfortunately, I used this example to explain to my team-mates how I was able to remember things and was called 'Boghead Billy' from that moment on.

We were promoted as champions two seasons running, but mercifully I realised what I was doing to myself before it was too late. I had worried that the only book I ever opened was the *Rothmans*, but I knew it was time to give it all up when I found myself looking longingly at the parkas in Milletts' window.

If I were asked today to name Darlington's only ever-present player last season, the cup-holders in Albania or the venue of the 1957 European Cup final, my answers would be 'Who gives a toss?', 'Bog off' and 'Get a life'. And they would be the correct ones.

Jon had another question for me as we headed up the M1. 'Who do you want to win the FA and Coca-Cola Cups this year?' I replied that I wasn't bothered since Norwich had been knocked out of both. He then pointed out that, if either Arsenal or Sheffield Wednesday win both cups, the third-placed team in the league would qualify for the UEFA Cup. Hmm. This means we could be in the extraordinary position of supporting Arsenal later this season.

'If Arsenal have to win the FA Cup for us to get into Europe and they lose the final, I'll be more pissed off than any Arsenal fan,' said Jon. I'm not sure that Arsenal supporters would agree with that, but I see his point.

We stopped at a service station for twenty minutes, during which time Jon did his best to make sure the tobacco industry wouldn't be too badly affected by No Smoking Day. I bought a packet of fruit pastilles – and the first two in the packet were yellow and green. Could this be an omen?

Jon thought the worsening weather was a bad sign, just as someone near me at the Blackburn game had feared that the freezing conditions would favour t'team from t'North. By the time we reached Sheffield, his pessimism had transmitted itself to me. The ground looked dark and forbidding as we passed it. Once again, I had greatly over-estimated the time it would take to drive from London to Sheffield, and we had arrived so early that no lights had yet been turned on. I thought of our less than successful visits here in the last two seasons. Bramall Lane? Buggerall Lane, more like. Furthermore, this was where Bryan Gunn sustained the back injury which kept him out for much of last season.

While Jon went to rectify the alcohol deficiency in his bloodstream, I waited for the turnstiles to open. Waiting outside a pub for opening time is supposed to indicate a dangerous dependence on drink. Is waiting outside a football ground a symptom of a different sickness?

'You get a prize for being the first,' said a cheery woman steward when I was finally allowed in.

'I just hope I'm not the last,' I said. She laughed, but I wasn't being entirely frivolous, bearing in mind our result at QPR. I bought a pie (hot but tasteless – $5/10$) and went to take my seat in the stand. 'You can sit where you like tonight,' said another steward.

'I'll try and squeeze in somewhere,' I replied, looking around at the rows and rows of empty seats.

'I hope you lot are going to be more pleasant than the Man. United fans we had here in the Cup the other week,' the steward went on. 'They were all sweetness and light when they were 1–0 up, but as soon as they went behind they became the most miserable, whining lot you've ever seen.'

'I don't suppose the Spurs fans were a bundle of laughs here last week,' I said. Tottenham had lost 6–0.

'Not exactly. It was a good night, though. We had to put a ball-boy in the back of the Spurs net.'

A couple more City fans turned up. One went to sit right at the back of the stand. 'What are you doing up there?' asked his mate.

'I'm getting ready to catch one of Ian Crook's shots,' came the reply.

The ground suddenly filled up five minutes before kick-off. As at QPR, it was hard to tell how many Norwich fans had made the trip as the standing area was directly underneath the seats. From the taunts of 'Worst support we've ever seen' coming from the home fans, though, I would guess not many had turned up. I didn't see anyone I knew from London, and Jon met only three on the terraces. The lack of late-night trains back to London must have been the main reason for this, though the general loss of heart on Saturday had clearly deterred most people from seeking other ways to get to the game.

It was a surprise to see Darren Beckford on the bench. He had taken Lee Power's place there, as the latter had tonsilitis. At least, that was the reason the club gave for withdrawing him from the Republic of Ireland Under-21 squad. Power may well be unavailable for selection again in the near future. Remember he was banned from driving for speeding? Just a few days into his ban, the police saw him driving to the training ground – I don't know whether or not he has a sponsor's car with his name splashed all over it. The court is considering a custodial sentence. I wonder if it's possible to come up with a team of players who have been inside during their careers. Tony Adams, Terry Fenwick, Jan Molby and Mick Quinn spring to mind at once. We need a keeper, though. Is there one who has been put away for handling things he shouldn't?

'Is Beckford our reserve keeper this evening?' I asked the man beside me. He gave me a funny look, but when Bryan Gunn put his back out here last season, it was Beckford who came off the bench to take his place. With the possible exception of the game against Everton when he scored a hat-trick, it was the best he ever played for us. He inspired choruses of 'Darren Beckford's green and yellow army' and even 'England's, England's number one'. Such popularity seems a long while ago now.

The first half of the match was probably the worst I have seen all season. Both teams were guilty of dreadful passing, appalling ball control and a woeful lack of imagination. I tried yelling some encouragement, only to discover that I had a parrot on my shoulder. Every time I shouted, a man just behind me (late 30s, shell suit, white socks) shouted the same thing, a slight reshuffling of the words being his only stab at originality.

'Come on, Norwich, win this ball!'

'Win the ball, Norwich, come on!'

'Take him on, Foxy, take him on!'

'Yes, take him on, Foxy!' This got on my wick after a while. I should have whispered 'I'm a tosspot' to see if he would yell it out loud, but I didn't think of this at the time.

The score was still 0–0 at half-time. 'Fancy coming all this way to see this crap,' said a steward, which was a fair assessment of the game so far. All the same, I began to feel that this might just be our night. Drab weather, an awful game, a sparse following – these were unlikely circumstances in which to relaunch a campaign to glory, but given the team's penchant for doing the unexpected, this was precisely the sort of place they would do it. This gut feeling was supported by the fact that at least the defence was looking solid. Polston and Sutton had not allowed Brian Deane a hint of a chance, while Mark Bowen was getting his own back on Franz Carr for the roasting he gave him when playing for Nottingham Forest in their 6–2 win at Carrow Road two years ago. A night when the chant 'You'll never beat Mark Bowen' had to be amended to 'You'll always beat Mark Bowen'.

Ten minutes into the second half, Daryl Sutch was replaced by David Smith. Suddenly, everything clicked into place. The team acquired a definite shape and, with it, control of the game. Five minutes after coming on, Smith won the ball, fed it to Robins who produced a perfect diagonal twenty-yard pass for Fox to run on to, and he fired the ball into the corner of the net from the edge of the area. Yeeeaahhooo!!

'We're gonna win the league,' sang the Norwich supporters for the first time in ages. 'You're gonna win – well, not a great deal in our opinion,' replied the sceptical home fans in their bowdlerised version.

Soon after, Norwich had the chance to make the game safe, but Fox shot wide when he should have passed to Robins who was unmarked in front of an open goal. Consequently, the last ten minutes of the match felt like twenty (as explained in the last chapter), and my high footballing principles went out of the window. 'Get it in the corner and stand on it!' I shouted.

'Stand on it by the corner flag!' squawked Polly Parrot.

At last, the referee blew the final whistle. We had won! Was this a turning-point in our season? Or could the team merely be toying with our hopes again? It was impossible to tell. All I knew was that I now felt intensely guilty at writing off our chances last Saturday.

Back at the car, I discovered more good news. Villa had only drawn at home to Spurs. United had lost at Oldham the night before, so we had made up a lot of ground. In the circumstances, Jon wasn't at all bothered that I drove around Sheffield city centre twice before I managed to find my way back to the motorway. 'Take as long as you like,' he said cheerfully.

'If we'd lost, you'd have been saying, "Pull your finger out, you useless prat".'

'No, I wouldn't. I'd leave that sort of remark to the Sunday football team.' Like I said, news travels fast.

We got back to London just before one in the morning. (It would have been sooner, but we stopped off at a service station again. It's funny how weedy chants of 'Yellow army' sound when there are only two of you and the café is deserted.) I decided to watch the highlights of the Villa game before I went to bed and was glad I did. They were hilarious! Villa should have had a hatful of goals, but Dean Saunders hit the post twice and had a shot cleared off the line

– or was the ball over the line? It certainly looked like it from the camera behind the goal, but the referee Keith Hackett ruled that it hadn't.

'I've changed my mind about Hackett,' Mum said the next day. 'I think he's all right now!' Until now, he has been her *bête noire* in the *vert*.

She had listened to the commentary on our game on the local radio station, but it seems that the reporter didn't know much about football. 'In the second half, he said that Sheffield had won a corner and Crook was about to take it.'

Still, at least the local media are continuing to give us some coverage. The *Guardian* devoted two lines to the match – and one of those talked of the 'host of chances' missed by the home side. Did the paper have a reporter at Bramall Lane? The only national recognition we've been given all week was when Mark Robins's bum featured on the picture board in *A Question of Sport*. It's not much, but it's something.

Saturday 13 March
Oldham Athletic (home)

Ever since I bought Karen's eldest daughter Joanna a Norwich hat and scarf for her 6th birthday last month, she has been pestering Karen to let her go to a match. She was told to wait until the weather improved but, with the sudden mild spell last weekend, she renewed her pleas and Karen agreed that she could come to the Oldham game.

By a stroke of luck, it turned out that she would be able to get in for nothing. To boost what might otherwise have been a poor attendance in view of Oldham's lack of glamour and our indifferent results before Wednesday night, the club decided to offer two free tickets to all season ticket-holders. Though this was not an original idea (Aston Villa have also been offering cut-price tickets to attract bigger crowds recently), it was a very welcome one. After all, it is far more encouraging for the players if the stands are full – and at this stage of the season, it is worth the club losing some money to achieve this.

The only slightly dodgy side to this initiative was the offer of free tickets and chocolate to mothers and children in the upper tier of the Barclay Stand. Call me over-cautious, but I was always told to beware of people trying to lure you into unfamiliar places with sweeties and the promise of a good time.

I went down to the ground to collect Joanna's ticket on Friday. While I was in the box office, I saw Lee Power getting out of a car outside – from the passenger's side this time. Then, on the way back to Mum's, I saw Darren Beckford going into a council housing office. Why was he going in there? Does he have a council house? Perhaps the wage structure at the club is even tighter than I thought. 'Maybe he's trying to arrange an exchange with someone in the Oldham area,' Mum suggested. It now looks as if Beckford may be transferred there soon.

Joanna came to stay at Mum's on Friday night to make sure that we wouldn't forget to take her. 'Can I go as well?' asked Lisa, the next oldest in Karen's brood.

'No,' replied Joanna. 'You'll have to wait until you have a hat and scarf.' She seems to think that these are compulsory for all supporters.

She had similar notions about singing in the crowd. 'Does it matter if I don't know all the words?' she asked.

Joanna was subjected to the teasing that was inevitable given her obvious excitement. 'You should take your football boots,' Mum's neighbour told her. 'You might get a game.'

'I haven't got any boots,' said Joanna worriedly.

'That's all right,' he said. 'You can borrow my old ones, but you might need to stuff some newspaper in the toes.'

Stephen and I told Joanna that we'd lost her ticket, only to get told off by Mum when Joanna's bottom lip started quivering.

We arrived earlier than usual at a sunny Carrow Road – and it was just as well we did. Far from being the quiet, gentle introduction to football that we had planned for Joanna, it was bedlam. It was like a huge birthday party, with mums and kids everywhere. And, as with all kids' parties, there were several in a bad mood, as all the tickets had gone by 2:30. Doubtless their parents had promised that they would be able to see the game, and now they had been disappointed.

We hurried inside and found somewhere to sit. We sat much closer to the pitch than usual, partly so that Joanna would have a decent view, partly to protect her delicate eardrums. 'Don't let her sit anywhere near the Foghorn,' Karen had asked us. It was not just our low position that meant that we saw the game from a different angle, however. Joanna also helped us to see things in a new way.

She produced a string of questions about aspects of the game which were so familiar to us that we never thought about them. 'What are those lines on the pitch for?' 'Why isn't there any grass in front of the goal?' 'Why can that man pick up the ball when the others can't?' 'What's that noise?' (It was an air horn.) When she asked who those men standing around the ground in orange jackets were, Mum had to stop me from giving my explanation.

One of her questions did reveal a remarkable level of perception for one so young. 'Who are those people?' she asked, pointing up at the faces in the executive boxes. 'It's a shame they can't afford to come in with us so they have to look through the window.' She's right, they are missing out, being cooped up in their fish tanks. Out of the mouths of babes ...

Fortunately, there were some questions she didn't ask, e.g., 'What does "offside" mean?' 'Will you take me for a wee-wee?', 'Can we go home now?' and 'What the fucking hell was that?'

She spent some time before the match practising her reading on the adverts around the ground (again, I'd never really noticed them) and then with the programme I had bought for her. I wish someone had bought one for me at my first match. Then I might be able to remember which one it was. I vaguely remember a 1–1 draw at home to Charlton in December 1967, but I'm not sure whether that was my first game. After some persuasion – well, coercion – I borrowed the programme back from Joanna to find out the arrangements for getting tickets for the Ipswich match after Easter. Apparently, they're going on sale immediately after the Manchester United game. Is this wise? There'll be a hell of a stampede at the final whistle. Surely there must be a safer way, though I'm not sure what this might be.

I had wondered whether queueing overnight for tickets might be required. This is what Ipswich fans had to do to get tickets for the match at Carrow Road back in December. 'It wouldn't be very nice having to sit outside the box office all night,' Mum had said.

'Oh, I don't know,' I said. 'I'd come and bring you a flask of tea at around midnight.'

As soon as the match got underway, Oldham looked assured and dangerous. They had clearly been lifted by their midweek win over United. 'Come on, City!' yelled Mum – and two little boys in front, who like Joanna appeared to be at their first match, turned round and looked in astonishment at this mad old woman.

Soon after, Joanna joined in with a chorus of 'Come on, you yellows' for the first time. 'Isn't it noisy here?' she said. I suppose it was, compared to anywhere else she had ever been, but for a football crowd it was still far too quiet. It seemed especially so considering that the ground was almost full. Most of the newcomers clearly didn't know how they were supposed to behave. Indeed, I heard afterwards that one regular fan in the Barclay who was shouting his support was told by a woman to be quiet. Did she think that football was like tennis, snooker or golf? If you ask me, these sports would be a lot more interesting if the spectators were allowed to shout.

After twelve minutes, Norwich scored with a bizarre own goal. A shot from David Phillips hit an Oldham defender on the head and the ball looped over the keeper into the net. Everyone stood up – so Stephen, realising that Joanna wouldn't be able to see much apart from a row of backsides, grabbed the hood of her coat and hauled her up so that she could enjoy the sight of the ball in the net, the players congratulating each other, and the cheering crowd.

Joanna seemed rather pensive after this. 'What is it?' Mum asked.

'Does anyone here like the blue team?' Joanna wanted to know. She obviously has a well-developed sense of sympathy. We'll have to do something about that. Mum pointed out the small group of Oldham fans sitting at the other end of the South Stand. Joanna, reassured that the blues had some supporters, resumed cheering for Norwich.

Oldham continued to play well, while we didn't look anything like as solid as we had on Wednesday night. 'I heard that they're on £45,000 a man to win the league,' said Stephen. 'You'd think they'd be pulling their fingers out for that kind of money.'

Just before half-time, Mark Robins put the ball in the net again. I had already seen the linesman raise his flag for offside but, unfortunately for Joanna, Stephen hadn't. Once more, the poor girl was hauled unceremoniously into the air.

Joanna came out with more questions in the second half. 'What does the manager do?' 'How many people are here?' This was soon answered by the electronic scoreboard. 'Are those boys supposed to be up there?' She was referring to some lads who, having failed to get in, had clambered on to the top of a poster hoarding outside the ground. This question was answered when they soon disappeared, presumably ordered down by the police. I hoped that Joanna wouldn't be ordered out of the ground by the police and stewards for standing up throughout the second half.

At one point, Bryan Gunn came over towards us to collect the ball. 'Look, it's Jim Robinson in *Neighbours*!' said Joanna. She seems to have inherited an ability to see tenuous resemblances to soap characters from her mother. Karen reckons that John Polston looks like Andy McDonald in *Coronation Street*, but I can't see it myself.

'Have you got a favourite player?' Mum asked Joanna.

'Yes, I like Foxy,' she replied. I'm not sure whether this was because he is the favourite of Mum and the majority of the crowd ('Ru-el, Ru-el'), because he is playing so well at the moment, or because he was the only black player in the team today and therefore the easiest one to pick out. At any rate, he was a good choice.

Oldham continued to dominate the midfield, but couldn't break down our defence. Towards the end, Norwich made a few more good chances, but 1–0 was the final score. It hadn't been a great match, but it hadn't been that bad either. Joanna had certainly enjoyed it, anyway. Hopefully most of the other newcomers enjoyed it enough to want to come again, though there won't be many more opportunities this season. It's only mid-March, yet we have only one more home game on a Saturday (Liverpool on 1 May) – and I wouldn't be surprised if that gets moved as well.

Joanna had no trouble with the daunting Jimmy Hill on the way home, as I gave her a piggyback ('You didn't do that for me after the Ipswich game,' Karen complained later) – though she had to duck sharply once or twice to avoid being clobbered by overhanging branches. 'What did we win?' she asked. 'Do we get a prize?' I don't know whether you've ever tried explaining the concept of points and league tables to a 6-year-old, but it isn't easy.

Her enthusiasm was undiminished when she got back to Karen's. 'We won! We won! Can I go again?' she shouted as she rushed in.

'You've certainly done a good indoctrination job there,' said Karen.

'Will you buy me a hat and scarf so I can go?' asked Lisa, presenting herself as the next candidate for brainwashing. Karen can't really disapprove of my influence, though. She asked me this weekend if I would like to be godfather to their baby son. I'll be only too happy to ensure that he doesn't stray from the path of righteousness.

'Don't forget to watch *Match of the Day* tonight,' I reminded Karen. 'We should be the main game.' That's what we'd been told at the ground, anyway. And with United and Villa playing each other on Sunday afternoon, what other game could they show first?

Everton v Nottingham Forest. Oh well, we'll certainly be on next, I thought. We weren't. They showed Middlesbrough v Liverpool instead. I just about remained calm, but it wasn't easy.

Since the Sheffield United game, I have been trying to persuade myself that I shouldn't get so upset about our coverage in the national media. They obviously aren't going to change, and in any case their scepticism may work to our advantage. Yet when I read in the *Observer* on Sunday morning that we 'are still absurdly in the Championship race' despite 'looking more like relegation candidates', and when I saw in Monday's *Guardian* that 'one of the horses in the race is riderless, a minor menace to the two contenders', I almost blew my top again. Would they say such things about us if we happened to be called 'Liverpool'? They used to grind out plenty of unconvincing 1–0 wins in their heyday, and this was acclaimed as a sign of their greatness.

Our Sunday-morning game was a much more light-hearted affair. The defence played as if it had been sponsored for Comic Relief. Our best striker had pulled a muscle, so he went in goal and turned out to be just as dangerous in front of our goal as the opposition's, generously dropping crosses at the feet of inrushing forwards. I'm not sure how we only lost 3–0.

Back in the dressing-room, someone asked if I had a hair brush he could borrow. Oh yes, like I never go anywhere without one for my long, flowing locks. Then everyone else cleared off, and I was left with the dirty kit, all the balls and the goal-nets. It's just as well Mum's coming down next week so she can help me carry everything. I wonder if I should tell her to bring her neighbour's boots with her.

Villa and United drew in the afternoon, which was the result I had wanted. Actually, I had also been hoping for a mass punch-up with several sendings-off and points deducted by the league, but you can't have everything, I suppose.

Oh yes, and the Wolverine rang in the afternoon. The first time she's called in ages, and I almost forgot! It was a dull sort of conversation really – though now I come to think of it, she was fairly complimentary about Norwich. She admitted that she wants us to win the league. Yes, she laughed at the prospect of us meeting AC Milan in the European Cup next season, but she did say she was supporting us.

I would have read a lot into this not so long ago, but I was left strangely unmoved. Has the spell been broken at last? (OK, I've thought this has happened before and I've been wrong, but it's got to happen some time.) Or is it because my hopes have been raised with Jane?

Wednesday 17 March
Nottingham Forest (away)

Mum said she wanted to go to this game. I'm not sure whether the main reason was to support Norwich or to boo Brian Clough, but I drove back to Norwich so that we could travel to Nottingham together.

For Mum's benefit rather than mine, we had Radio Norfolk on as we left the city. 'And here's one from Cathy Dennis,' said the DJ. 'Hey, she comes from Norwich. I wonder if that's an omen for the match tonight.' Now I may be given to seeing omens everywhere before a match, but choosing to play a record by a local singer and then suggesting that this is significant in some way is surely stretching things a bit far.

As we drove through the Norfolk countryside, the yellow and green fields were resplendent in the March sunshine. I didn't see this as an omen for tonight – merely as a sign that Mother Nature supports us. There was no Forest red around, though the way some cars were overtaking, it was only through luck that the A47 wasn't covered in it.

We approached the Unhappy Eater. 'Shall we stop here?' I asked. Mum replied with a glare. I didn't see any supporters' coaches or cars in the car park. In fact, there didn't seem to be many Norwich fans on the road either. What had happened to all the new support that had filled Carrow Road on Saturday?

'It's not like the time we played Derby in the Cup,' said Mum. (FA Cup fifth round, 1984.) 'We came along this road then. Every car was full of Norwich supporters that day.' She went on to recall how she had seen a removal van with Norwich fans tied to the wall bars inside by yellow and green scarves.

When we reached Grantham, though, everything changed.

> I wandered lonely as a cloud
> That floats on high o'er lakes and lands,
> When all at once I saw a crowd,

A host of Norwich City fans;
In vans, in cars, in twos and threes,
Their yellow scarves dancing in the breeze.

William Wordsworth, *The Daft Afield*

We arrived in Nottingham at quarter to seven and parked about half a mile from the City Ground. It has changed a lot since I last saw it. The large open terrace has gone, though from an away fan's point of view this is no bad thing. The fences and the floodlight pylon in the corner used to make it very difficult to see. In their place, there is now a grand, sweeping all-seater stand. Well, it looks grand on television. When you're in it, it seems rather small.

Mum said the new toilets were the best she'd ever seen at a ground. Pity the meat pies tasted as though they'd been left over from last year ($^4/_{10}$). The announcer reading out the team changes was scarcely up to scratch either. Who are Bob Walton and Jeremy Gross? Still, it was good to hear that John Polston was playing. His wife is expecting a baby any day now, and he has been given permission to go to the birth if she goes into labour on the day of a game.

I've no idea what I would do if my wife were due to give birth on the day of a Norwich match. ('My wife'? Mind those flying pigs.) I hope I would have the foresight to time the conception so that the child would pop out during the close season, but if circumstances dictated otherwise, I would be in a real dilemma. I suppose my decision would depend on the relationship I had with my wife, the opinion of the doctor or midwife, and the importance of the game in question. If I did miss the birth for football, I certainly wouldn't be the first father ever to do so; I've heard a few tannoy announcements of newly-acquired parenthood over the years.

I wouldn't presume to tell Polston what to do in his situation. Every person has his or her own scale of values. However, I can say what I would do if I were a player in a team that stood a chance of winning the Championship. I would play.

I am not just saying this because I am obsessed with Norwich City and football (though, of course, I am) – this is a question of self-fulfilment, of self-definition. Everyone has ambitions in life. Few ever get the slightest chance to achieve them. Even fewer actually manage it. If you have a chance to fulfil your life's ambition, you should seize it – especially in football, where careers are so short. If I had the chance to define myself as a Championship-winning footballer, I would take it.

Many people say that having children is the greatest thing that anyone can achieve. I am afraid I am rather cynical about this. I accept that I am speaking as someone who has not experienced the joys of parenthood, but it seems to me that those who dote most on their offspring are those who realise that they will never reach fulfilment in their own lives. Their aspirations are transferred to their poor, unsuspecting children who, when the weight becomes too great to bear, will in time load them on to the shoulders of their own children. Sorry, but I felt it needed saying.

The match programme featured several former Norwich players, though I'm not sure whether this was deliberate or coincidental. The front cover showed Andy Linighan, and the centre spread featured that goal machine Robert Rosario (unfortunately not playing for Forest in this match, so their chances of scoring were considerably increased). The most unlikely reference came in the programme's 'Focus on Youth' section, in which a young keeper who is being released in a few weeks' time was interviewed. He was asked to name the three foreign players he would buy if he were a Premier League manager with unlimited funds at his disposal. Two of his choices were Peter Schmeichel and Marco van Basten, which were reasonable enough, but the third was Henrik Mortensen from Denmark. Did he mean the Henrik Mortensen who spent two seasons at Norwich and showed little except for the ability to dive spectacularly in the opposition's penalty area? Who left the club with such a bad injury that it was said he would never play again? I can see why Forest are getting rid of this youngster. He clearly knows nothing about football.

I didn't see any City fans from London, presumably because there was again no late train back after the match. Still, there were hundreds of new ones from Norfolk, swelling our numbers to a couple of thousand at least. Mum and I found ourselves sitting among the noisiest fans, who bellowed deafeningly into our ears. It was great – except that Mum objected to several of their songs. Songs like 'Bring on the champions' and 'We're gonna win the league'.

'They're asking for trouble', said Mum. I knew what she meant. She was obviously thinking of ...

Kevin's Alternative Laws of Football (No.10)

'The chances of a team winning the league or going to Wembley are inversely proportional to the number of times their supporters sing about it.'

There are various corollaries to the above law, of course. Singing 'One-nil, one-nil' greatly increases the likelihood of the opposition equalising. The chorus here at the City Ground of 'Going down, going down' must have boosted Forest's chances of staying up. There is a precedent for this. In the 1983-84 season, Ipswich were struggling near the foot of the First Division when we played them at Easter. The Norwich fans poured into Ipswich railway station singing 'Going down' – and not only did we lose the match, but Ipswich's form picked up as ours slumped and they went on to finish above us.

Television 'experts' are just as prone to making predictions that are quickly made to look ridiculous. At last summer's European Championships in Sweden, Jimmy Hill said after two matches that Denmark had no chance of winning the tournament and that they were just making up the numbers. Their success was assured from that moment on. Similarly, England's exit was certain as soon as the BBC showed a provisional group table at half-time in their game against Sweden, based on the scores at that stage of the evening's matches. England were top – but 45 minutes later they had conceded two goals and were packing their holdalls to come home.

Why should it be that assumptions are so often proved wrong in football? Some believe that it is because the mysterious, divine forces that govern the game are offended by the insolence of mere mortals. Some believe it is Sod's Law. My view is a mixture of the two: I think the game is governed by sods.

As if to confirm Mum's worst fears about the chants, the match began with Forest on the attack. An astonishing torrent of abuse and vilification poured forth from those around us: 'Make a tackle, Crook, you wanker'; 'Get your mind on the fucking game, Polston' (not much empathy with his situation in evidence there); 'You're a wimp, Robins'; 'Come on, Phillips, you bloodymothershitfuck' (I think I got that down correctly). Whose side were the intelligentsia on anyway?

It was only when Nigel Clough shot over the bar that this vitriol was directed towards Forest, with the predictable taunts of 'Daddy's boy' and 'What the fucking hell was that?' At this, the police decided that they had had enough and moved in to have a word with the offenders. They met with the usual 'I ain't done nuffink' response and were subjected to a few muttered comments as they went away again (the football fan's equivalent of bravely sticking up two fingers behind a teacher's back at school).

Shortly after, the same thing happened again. 'Are we in fucking Grimsby or what?' said someone behind – a reference to some trouble there in 1986 which Norwich supporters have always maintained was instigated by the police. 'I always wondered what happened to the SS,' said someone else.

The situation might have got out of hand but for a female steward whose good humour helped to defuse the tension, and the fact that Norwich started to get on top on the pitch. Phillips shot just over the bar, then Crook missed from five yards out. This brought more abuse from the panel of experts in the row behind, but most of us were encouraged that these chances had been created.

I'm not sure what to make of the interventions by the police, principally because I am ambivalent about swearing at football matches. It's difficult to offer a definitive view, as swearing can be expressive or offensive, funny or depressing depending on the tone, the sentiments being voiced, the context, the person doing the swearing, and whether it is an isolated comment or a chorus of thousands. On the whole, I don't care for swear words in songs but, in individual remarks, they are generally OK as long as they are not used in every sentence. I think this is probably because they sound so stupid and unimaginative when a lot of people are shouting them in unison.

Many clubs seem to be trying to stop all swearing inside football grounds, but this strikes me as unnecessary and unachievable. If there are any adults whose delicate sensibilities are likely to be offended by others using rude words, they should stay off the streets, get rid of their television and radio, cancel the papers and avoid all books. Those who wish to promote a 'family atmosphere' should realise that there is a fair amount of swearing in most families. There is in ours, anyway.

I can understand some people being concerned about exposing young children to this sort of language. Not because there is anything inherently evil in swear words. As I see it, the reason for discouraging children from swearing is that it can become too easy an option and leaves them less articulate. The odd Anglo-Saxon word can be wonderfully powerful, but only as a carefully-used weapon in an armoury. Still, there are family enclosures where most of the spectators are children. And most children seem to know all the words at an early age in any case.

Forced to make a decision (and I usually have to be forced before I will), I would have to say that the actions of the police were quite in order in this case. They only intervened when the swearing became persistent and annoying, and even then they settled for having a quiet word. In any case, their actions should not have come as too much of a surprise. Swearing has been an issue at the City Ground ever since Brian Clough put up 'Gentlemen – no swearing please' signs a few years ago. History does not record whether signs saying 'Brian – no bloody sexism please' were produced in response.

'Come on, City, we want one before half-time,' shouted Mum. I wasn't sure that we did. Conventional wisdom has it that scoring just before half-time is a great psychological boost, but I think it is often better to go in at 0–0 (as we did at Sheffield United last week). There is no temptation to sit back on a lead, and the opposition and their supporters are not so fired up for the second half. Just as I was thinking about this, however, we did score. Crook took the ball on for thirty yards into the Forest half before releasing Robins with a perfect through-ball which he fired in off a post.

Mayhem broke out around us. Mum and I jumped up, but were sent flying. I was thumped on the back of the head as those behind us leapt around. Once again, choruses of 'We are top of the league' and 'Going down, going down' rang out as the teams went in for half-time.

As our accidental assailants headed downstairs to discharge their ex-lager, Mum had a look through the programme and I chatted to my other neighbour about our midfield. It still didn't seem to be quite right. Should Smith or Woodthorpe be replaced by Gross – er, Goss? Should Mike Walker change a winning team? This was a tricky one. After some discussion, we agreed ... that we were glad Walker had to make the decision and not us.

He didn't make any changes – and, within five minutes of the restart, my neighbour and I were criticising him for this as Forest swarmed all over us. They had obviously been given one of Cloughie's famous team talks in the dressing-room. ('You 100 per cent, you 100 per cent ... ') It looked like being a very long half.

When City did manage a counter-attack, Phillips headed wide of an open goal. Mum and I feared – and heard – the worst. Mike Walker finally decided to make a substitution, though not the one we had anticipated. Mark Robins was taken off – and, unbelievably, was criticised by the group behind us as he left the pitch. 'He doesn't do a lot, does he?' 'Can't hold the fucking ball up at all.'

How unfair can you get? He had worked hard all game and had scored a very good goal. True, he is not an imposing target man. Nor does he have all of Robert Fleck's deft touches around the box. But he sticks the ball in the net with a regularity which Fleck could not match and which we have needed for years. I hope this talent isn't going to be belittled with the result that he ends up leaving the club.

Robins's replacement, Power, shot just wide and we all groaned again, but then at last there was a concerted effort to get behind the team. It soon paid off. Fox won a corner ('But he kicked it out,' said Mum. 'Oh, who cares?' I replied), Crook took it, Mark Crossley in the Forest goal pointed at it passing overhead as if he were following Halley's Comet, and Power tapped it in at the far post. 'Yeeesss!!' I shouted. 'Ooouucchh!' shouted Mum, whose fingers had been nipped against the back of her seat by the revellers behind.

There were still twenty minutes left, but the Forest fans started to leave to the inevitable cries of 'Cheerio, cheerio'. They'd obviously seen all this before. They took their team's spirit with them, and Crook scored a third goal with a shot that deflected comically off a Forest defender's bum. Mum looked relieved that her earlier worries about the chanting had proved unfounded.

Our friends behind sang the well-known conga ditty 'Let's go fucking mental', followed by 'We're all going on a European tour' (to the tune of *Yellow Submarine*). The Forest stands looked very empty.

During the last five minutes of the game, we enjoyed the unusual luxury of calling to the players for a wave while the game was in progress. Mike Walker didn't oblige when his name was chanted – but when 'Bryan, Bryan, give us a wave' was directed at Bryan Gunn, Brian Clough gave us a wave as well. Even Mum had to concede that this was very good-humoured in the circumstances. At the final whistle, the Norwich players hugged and congratulated each other as we cheered and applauded them to the echo. I certainly hadn't expected us to win 3–0 here – nor, by the look of it, had the players. This hadn't been the best performance of the season in terms of quality (the game at Aston Villa was better), but the commitment and determination of the players could not be faulted.

We were top of the league again, just a week after being 7 points behind, and for the first time you could sense a real belief among all the supporters that we could go all the way. Yes, there had been a lot of talk about it all season, but now it felt as though we were coming off the final bend of the race in front with the finishing tape in sight at last. We poured noisily out of the ground singing 'On the ball, City' – but there weren't many people around to hear it. Most of the Forest fans were at home on their second cup of tea by then.

An ecstatic convoy weaved its way back towards Norfolk. The chip shops in Grantham did a roaring trade. Mum and I tried to listen to what was being said about us on Radio 5, but it was a bit difficult to make out – not because the reception was poor, but because the presenters were choking on their words in the studio.

We arrived back in Norwich at midnight. Mum's neighbours were still up, waving at us as if we'd scored the goals ourselves. We waved back in triumph as if we had. We felt special, having been to the game, but it was good to see the enthusiasm spreading. Perhaps this was the night when the whole city would get behind the team at last.

We watched the all-too-brief highlights of the game on tape before turning in. Alan Hansen, again singled out for abuse at the match, admitted that it was a good win, but you can tell he still doesn't believe we have a chance. Even when (NB!) we win the title and he is shown the final league table, he will probably still refuse to believe it. And he wears too much make-up in the studio.

Saturday 20 March
Wimbledon (away)

As soon as the phone rang at Mum's on Friday evening, I knew who it was and the reason for calling. Sure enough, it was Jane who had decided not to come to the Wimbledon game after all. She said she was busy. Huh.

'Would you like to do something else next Saturday?' I asked. Not that I was offering to sacrifice a match. I was well aware that we don't have one next week. She replied that she was going away next weekend. Would she like to come to the game at Spurs on Good Friday? No, she was going home. Hmm. What could have brought about this change? It can't be anything I've done or said, as I haven't seen her since the QPR match. Or did I do anything wrong there? Perhaps she took my caveats regarding the Wimbledon game the wrong way. Oh well, that's that – as confirmed by the fact that I didn't get a birthday card from her on Saturday morning. I think Mum was more disappointed about that than me.

I did get a card from the Wolverine, though fortunately there was no present (bearing in mind what she sent me for Christmas). 'Best Wishes', she put at the bottom. Such warmth.

Most of my birthday cards had some reference to football, despite the fact that I have now reached the grand old age of 32. For example, the one from Karen and family said: 'What's the difference between *Match of the Day* and a toilet pan? Men never miss *Match of the Day*'. Charlie sent me a Danny Baker football video. I suppose I'd better watch it. Another friend sent a book called *How To Thrive On Rejection*, with a note confirming my first suspicion that this was a reference to my continued failure with the Wolverine.

I had thought that I would be spending my birthday very quietly at Wimbledon, as the attendance is usually dismal whenever we play there. It is said of some grounds that the level of support is worth a goal start to the home team. At Wimbledon, it's worth a goal start to the away team. Our Sunday side tried to book Selhurst Park for our games this season, but Wimbledon objected on the grounds that we would probably attract bigger crowds than them.

In the event, I was accompanied by thousands from Norwich. After Wednesday's result, the club decided to lay on 25 free coaches for supporters. Mum and I travelled down by car, however – partly so that I could call in at the flat before the game to open all (or, as it turned out, both) of the birthday cards that had been sent there, partly because Mum was staying over to watch me play football the next day. A special Mother's Day treat, if you like. Stephen drove down to the flat separately, as he wanted to get back to Norwich for Saturday night.

The journey down wasn't exactly straightforward. Norfolk County Council had chosen that morning to start a series of roadworks on the A11. Is there an Ipswich fan in the Highways Department who realised that two out of every three vehicles leaving Norwich at around 10am would be going to the game? Then there were the bad drivers who thought it was Dodgem Day. If you happen to drive a silver Rover, reg. no. F453 WPW, perhaps you might like to try using your mirrors when you overtake on a dual carriageway.

Mum wasn't behaving any better inside the car, offering rude answers to the questions on Dave Lee Travis's pub quiz on Radio 1. The worst example was when she suggested that DSO stood for Dick Shot Off. I was relieved when it was time to turn to Radio 5 for the commentary on the Manchester derby. We attracted some odd looks at a set of traffic lights when City scored and we yelled and shook our fists. Pity United equalised just as we reached the flat.

After a few rounds of toast (I remembered what the pies were like at Selhurst Park earlier in the season), we all set off for the game together. It took ages. Every traffic light on the way to South London was red. In my paranoia, I began to suspect that our progress was being monitored by traffic cameras above the streets, with a couple of policemen in the control centre killing themselves laughing every time we had to stop. It was just as well Jane wasn't coming to the game. If she had been, I would have had an awkward decision to make: should I go and pick her up and risk missing the start of the game, or leave her waiting and carry on down to the ground? I really don't know what I would have done, which probably indicates that a relationship with her would have been short-lived.

We eventually reached the ground at quarter to three. I dropped Mum and Stephen off so that they could buy tickets while I found somewhere to park. By the time I'd run the half-mile back to the ground in the warm sunshine, I was sweating like a pig. (Oops, sorry officer, didn't see you there.)

It was heartening to see so many Norwich fans inside the ground – and yet I couldn't help feeling a little resentful. I know I shouldn't have done, but I was a bit put out that all these people were treading on my toes. In previous years, this game had been a test of dedication; only the truly committed would turn up. Now everyone was here. Perhaps what was really worrying me was the thought that I might miss out on tickets for our remaining away games if all these new travellers got the taste for it. I know this was petty and selfish of me, but since I'm trying to be honest here, I thought I should mention it.

Everyone was in a cheerful mood as a result of the weather, our recent form ... and the free coach trip, of course. As the players ran out, they were greeted by a barrage of balloons and a blizzard of paper shreds. Even though our record away to Wimbledon has been generally poor, there was a great feeling of confidence that we would sweep to victory here.

It didn't take long for this mood to be dispelled.

> The mynutes ypaste noumbred barely eyghte,
> Yet Vinny Jones was overmuchel late.
> Ful lustily he smote a Norwich ladde
> And cleft in tweyne yonge Woodthorpes shinne-padde.
> The chalenge did moore harme than koude a knyfe;
> When Jones doth marke, he marketh men for lyfe.
>
> Geoffrey Chaucer, etc.

But I could have told you, Vincent, this game was never meant for one as cynical as you.

This incident changed the whole match, though not in the way we wanted. All the Norwich fans hoped that the early yellow card earned by Jones would make him and the rest of the Wimbledon team behave. Instead, the yellows became frightened at what might happen to them and kept their distance for the rest of the match. Smith, who I believe was supposed to pick Jones up, was as anonymous as his name suggests and didn't get within five yards of him after the assault on Woodthorpe. There was no blatant violence after that, but there didn't need to be. Norwich had been intimidated enough by Jones's early challenge and Wimbledon's reputation, of which they were occasionally reminded by a push in the back or a pull on the shirt.

It wasn't exactly a shock when Wimbledon scored, but the quality of the goal was. John Fashanu (boo!) pushed the ball between Polston and Culverhouse and ran on to it to deliver a perfect cross for Holdsworth to head past Gunn. Groan.

City tried to reply at once, and Fox burst through the Wimbledon defence. Just outside the box, though, he was hauled back from behind. Surely it was a sending-off offence ... but no, the card was yellow again. This confirmed to Wimbledon that the referee didn't mean business, and the niggly fouls became more frequent (and more often than not were unnoticed and unpunished).

So much for my birthday horoscope in the *Daily Mirror* which Mum had pointed out to me. It said: 'You are sensitive to your surroundings and appreciate beauty.' Ha! There wasn't much beauty in these surroundings to which I could be sensitive. I don't believe in all that astrological twaddle, you understand – though some people have thought it significant that my star sign is Pisces, the wet fish. If I'd been born ten minutes later, it would have been Aries, the thrusting ram. Could it be that Mum's impetuosity has scarred me for life?

After half an hour, we were 2–0 down. Most of the Norwich crowd gave up there and then, falling very quiet. Every mistake prompted muttered criticism. 'What the bloody good is that?' a man behind me moaned ungrammatically. Some fans started to criticise their fellow supporters. When a rare song could be heard from the home fans, a lone City voice shouted, 'Keep the noise down, there are people trying to sleep at this end.'

The Norwich players looked very sorry for themselves as they trooped off at half-time. I felt even sorrier on hearing that Villa were 1–0 up. The only good news was that Mum hadn't arranged for my birthday to be announced on the scoreboard as she had threatened.

Things didn't improve in the second half. Vinny Jones was still, incredibly, controlling the midfield. One fan wished that he had had to pay to travel down on the coach so that he could ask for his money back. Others began a chorus of 'Do you want to win the league?' This seemed to be directed at the team, but could have been aimed with equal justification at the thousands of City fans still looking on in silence.

Mum, Stephen and I tried to make some noise to get behind the team, but provoked only sniggering from some lads nearby. As in the first half, the quiet was emphasised by the fact that we could hear both of the Wimbledon supporters singing. Thus we were treated to 'What's it like to be outclassed?', 'You're worse than Crystal Palace', and 'You're in the wrong division'. It is particularly galling to be taunted by Wimbledon fans. What do they mean, 'outclassed'? 'What's it like to be elbowed off the ball?' would be more accurate. I don't know how these fans can justify the use of such ugly tactics to themselves. Most of them seem to be schoolkids. Perhaps they have not yet developed a full understanding of the concepts of right and wrong.

Ten minutes from the end, we went 3–0 down. Game over.

Well, not quite. With five minutes to go, a shot from Phillips seemed to be pushed round the post by a defender, and the referee awarded us a penalty. He was immediately surrounded by protesting Wimbledon players and, the next thing we knew, he had changed his mind and given us a corner instead. We all went mad, as this looked like intimidation. Vinny Jones's broad grin made us even angrier. It turned out later that Phillips had told the referee that the keeper had saved his shot. This was a refreshing and admirable thing to do – though given Wimbledon's level of respect for the laws of the game, he would have had some justification for keeping quiet. Perhaps he realised that the penalty would not affect the result anyway – and our goal difference this season is already beyond saving. On television that night, however, it did look as if a defender had pushed the ball away after all.

As the final whistle was blown, we all left, depressed and upset. It was just as well Jane hadn't come to this game. Even the news that Wolves had lost to Cambridge in the last minute failed to make me smile.

As we travelled back to the flat, there was talk on the radio that, following last week's pitch invasion at Manchester City, anyone coming on to the pitch who shouldn't be there may be fined £1,000 in future. 'On that basis, all our lot should have been fined today,' said Stephen.

I felt awful in the evening. This was not directly attributable to the result – I had picked up a bug a couple of days before – but the match couldn't have helped. It was just as well I hadn't bought any theatre tickets. Mum and I had considered going to see the stage version of *Misery*, but I don't think I could have faced any more that day even if I had been in good health.

I'm not sure whether Mum suspected that I was just making an early excuse for the football on Sunday morning. She had wanted to come and see me play for ages. After all, she hadn't seen me in football kit since I was in my junior school team when I was 11. I'd been trying to put her off, especially after she put me under more pressure a couple of years ago when she said that she was disappointed that I'd never become a professional footballer. Well, sorry. Perhaps if there had been a bit more sporting ability in my DNA ...

I had no chance of living up to her expectations. However, it became clear that she wasn't going to be put off, so I had to try to lower her expectations before her visit. I warned her about my lack of pace, my poor ball control, and the fact that I usually shut my eyes when I go for a header. I made myself out to be much worse than I am in the hope that she would be impressed when she saw me play. After all, I am really not that bad, in spite of my constant self-deprecation throughout this book. I am of slightly above average ability, which I have always found immensely frustrating. I have never had any musical or artistic ability, so these areas were written off very early on and have never bothered me. But I am just good enough at football to wish that I were better. My brain generally knows what to do on the football field; the trouble is, my feet often can't do it.

Mum might not have been expecting so much if our team didn't play in full Norwich kit. She would doubtless be visualising me as a Norwich player. I must admit that I indulged in this fantasy the first few times I played for the team, but it wasn't long before reality intruded. A few heavy defeats soon dispelled my cosy illusion.

I knew Mum would get her journey's worth this Sunday morning, as we had another 'double-header', this time against the bottom team in the division who had won only one game all season. As we waited outside the dressing-rooms for the rest of the team (displaying their usual punctuality), we noticed among the other people milling around some lads wearing Wimbledon shirts. 'Boo!' said Mum.

'Oh no, don't start any trouble here,' I said. Of course, these lads turned out to be in the team we were playing. They chanted 'Wimbledon, Wimbledon' and 'Three-nil, three-nil' at us, but the wind was taken out of their sails when they were informed that most of our players don't support Norwich.

I was terrible in the first hour-long match, partly because I was trying too hard to impress Mum, partly because I still felt ill, even though I had dosed myself up to the eyeballs with aspirins. Just as well we don't have dope tests in Sunday football. Mind you, they'd probably discover we all are. Despite all this, we won 4–0.

We thought the second game would be a doddle and relaxed. This helped me to play better, but the rest of the team fell to bits and we lost 5–2. It got to the stage where we were taking shots on goal from the kick-off, which is a sure sign of desperation. I told Mum to stage a one-woman pitch invasion to get the game abandoned, but she said she couldn't afford a thousand pounds for the fine.

It was a poor way to end our season, but not an inappropriate one. Our final league record was: P22 W5 D4 L13 F41 A66 Pts14. Still, this is better than last year.

Mum offered an astute analysis of the team's failings after the game (not enough talking, players holding on to the ball too long), but I wanted to know what she thought of me. 'You were OK,' she said. Then, after a pause, 'It's just, well, ... '

'What?'

'When you run, you remind me of Marcel Marceau doing his "walking against the wind" act. There's lots of effort, but you don't seem to get any-where.' Serves me right for asking, I suppose.

Before I finish this chapter, I have to mention the national media again. I wasn't going to comment on our coverage this week, but events have left me with no choice. On *Match of the Day*, Mike Walker said that our chance of winning the title had now gone. It was obvious that he had his tongue in his cheek when he said this, but the Sunday tabloids took him seriously! Further proof, if any were needed, that most football journalists can't tell when some-one is taking the piss out of them.

Then, in Monday's *Guardian*, David Lacey said that the Championship was not a two-horse race. Nor was it a three-horse race. He claimed that it was being contested by two horses and a mule. Does anyone know where I can get my hands on a shotgun?

Wednesday 24 March
Aston Villa (home)

I apologise in advance in case this chapter doesn't seem too coherent. I haven't been in full control of my senses or my powers of expression since this game finished.

I had been feeling odd in the days leading up to the game, though for different reasons. After the games on Sunday morning, my mystery illness had got worse and worse. My head ached, my body ached, and I had a convulsing cough that made conversation almost impossible at times. My condition was complicated by rectal hyperactivity through nervousness from Tuesday morning onwards.

The latter complaint was hardly surprising. I knew how important this match was for us. Defeat would put us 5 points behind Villa having played a game more, with little time to close the gap again. Furthermore, I'd been telling people for weeks that Villa (and United) still had to come to Carrow Road, as if it were a trump card up our sleeves. The time had finally come to play it.

The local media in Norwich had also been building up the tension and excitement. The news on Anglia TV showed a woman on Norwich market singing 'On the ball, City' – except that she sang 'Never mind *your* danger'. 'Your'? The Norwich evening paper sent a reporter on to the streets to canvass opinions from the public on our Championship chances. Again, people were chosen who didn't know much about football. One man said he didn't rate City's chances as the London clubs were too strong for them. Has he looked at a league table lately? Or does he think Villa and United are London teams? I don't entirely blame the interviewees for these mistakes being broadcast or printed, though. A lot of responsibility lies with the media. Why do they never talk to the right people?

The nervousness grew worse throughout Wednesday. At tea-time, my right foot was tapping so hard that the whole table was shaking – and even then I didn't realise what I was doing until Mum pointed it out. It was an awful feeling. And yet, at the same time, I was grateful to be experiencing it. It was a sign that the game was of significance, which I didn't think it would be after we lost 3–1 at QPR. And the anticipation of a big game like this was infinitely preferable to the debilitating fear and tension we suffered at the end of last season when we were desperate for points to stay up.

Mum, Stephen and I said little on the way to the ground. The usual cheery chat had been replaced by a serious mood. The same was true of most of the other supporters we saw. One or two nodded silent acknowledgements to people they knew, as if they were about to go into battle – which in a sense we were.

It was only as we neared Carrow Road that a hum of excitement developed. It was as if our nerves had been made audible. I wondered how the players were feeling. Could they keep their composure this time when they had been so quick to panic before (e.g., against Ipswich and Spurs)? I was certainly finding it hard to think straight, so overwhelmed was I by the desire to win.

The DJ's attempt to lighten the mood by playing the Singing Postman's classic *Hev Yew Gotta Loight, Boy?* didn't work. It sounded horribly incongruous. Reading the match programme offered no relief either. On virtually every page, someone was stressing the importance of this game.

I managed to concentrate for long enough to notice that the ticket arrangements for the match at Ipswich have been changed. Postal applications are now required. This avoids the danger of a stampede after the United match which had been worrying me; on the other hand, I am always nervous about applying by post. What if my letter is delayed or lost altogether? Or if the same happens to the tickets? At least they are put straight into your sweaty hand if you queue at the box office.

A separate notice announced that regular travellers to away matches could improve their chances of a ticket by sending in ticket stubs from recent trips. Now they tell us! I haven't kept any – in fact, you would have to be extraordinarily sad to do so. I could write and tell them that I have been to every away game this season – but anyone could say that. How do I prove it, short of showing them the manuscript for this book?

Time rushed past so fast that the start of the match almost caught me unawares. The referee blew his whistle – and the next 45 minutes were a blur.

The word that best describes this game is 'brilliant', but it's used so cheaply these days. 'Me and Tony had brilliant fun down the pub', for example. Or: 'This is a brilliant hot dog'. 'Brilliant' should be a special word, reserved for those rare occasions when the intelligence, creativity or whatever on display reaches levels way above the imagination, let alone the capabilities, of the average person. This was such an occasion.

Both teams performed with exceptional skill, speed, strength and subtlety. The passing and movement were mesmerising. If anything, Villa were the better team in this half. Our defence was stretched this way and that, but held together wonderfully. The large advertising hoarding visible at the Barclay end that bore the headline 'V. Smooth. V. Safe.' could have been referring to Polston and Sutton.

The courage shown by both teams was inspiring. Steve Bruce identified this particular brand of courage after the Manchester derby last Saturday, pointing out that it takes a lot of nerve to keep the ball on the ground and play composed passing football when there is a lot at stake and passions are running high.

As at the home game against Crystal Palace, the rain gave this match an epic feel. It glowed under the floodlights and made the stadium seem incandescent. It is difficult to recall particular incidents as I was swept along like everyone else – though now I think of it, Saunders had a couple of good attempts for Villa and had an excellent header disallowed for offside. The V-signs which greeted this showed that the home fans feared him every bit as much as they had Ian Wright. Gunn saved a Yorke header at point-blank range and, at the other end, Fox, Megson and Robins went close.

I don't remember hearing any of the customary wisecracks around me, if indeed there were any. Everyone in the 20,000 crowd was too busy challenging for every header and making every tackle to act the comedian. In any case, there was too much noise to hear individual comments. I have lamented the lack of vocal support at Carrow Road in recent weeks, but it seemed that everyone had been saving their voices for this game. There was a terrific din – and I mean terrific.

The first half flew past; as with films, the fewer times you check your watch, the higher the quality of what you are watching. The teams left the pitch to a standing ovation from all parts of the ground. We were all left with just enough breath to turn to our neighbours and say what a fabulous game it was. I didn't hear a single negative comment, which must be some sort of record for the River End. The consensus was that Villa were the best team we had faced this season but that this was the best we had played too. The performance at Villa Park had been excellent, but this game was far more important and far more intense.

During the interval, a draw was made on the pitch for a satellite television system. A seat number was picked and the winner was invited down. This reminded me of the time in 1989 when I was awarded a prize on the pitch at half-time in a home game against Aston Villa. To this day, it is the only time I have ever set foot on the hallowed turf.

The story started some months before when Mum bought one of the club's lottery tickets and spotted a competition on the back. 'Here, you should have a go at this,' she said. 'It'll be right up your street.' You had to make as many words of four letters or more as you could from 'Trevor's Cycles', the shop that was providing the prize – a small moped. 'What do I want a moped for?' I asked.

'You can give it to Karen if you win,' Mum said. 'Chris can use it to go to work on, which will free the car for Karen to use during the day.' So it was that I spent every spare moment for three months at the library just round the corner from where I worked, scouring the twenty volumes of the Oxford English Dictionary. I found obscure Old English and Middle English variants of the most obscure words – and eventually came up with a total of around 4,000. I shan't list them all here. I didn't keep the list, and I'm certainly not going to go back to the library and do it all again.

The club ruled out several hundred words as I had used the possessive form of many of them – despite the fact that there is an apostrophe in 'Trevor's Cycles'. I had even done some research to find out when this was first used in the English language. But I still ended up with 3,101. The next best total was around 800 words, so I was invited to collect my prize on the pitch at Carrow Road. (Apparently, one little old lady went into Trevor's Cycles a week after the closing date and asked if she could enter anyway as she'd tried very hard and come up with ... 28 words. I believe she was rushed to intensive care after she was told how many I'd got.)

The club's commercial manager said an odd thing when I met him. 'You don't look like one of our usual lottery winners,' he told me. Hmm. What did this mean? At the risk of sounding immodest, I can only assume he meant that I seemed more intelligent and was not part of the beer, fags and string vest brigade who he considered to be the natural target market for his lottery. Mum thought this too when I told her and was so offended that she has rarely bought a lottery ticket since.

I managed to get through the presentation without any chants of 'You sad bastard' or 'You're so dull, it's unbelievable' – or a chorus of *Funky Moped* from the Villa fans, for that matter – and took it round to Karen's after the game. She and Chris looked at it in silence. 'Is that it?' she said eventually. 'Chris can't be seen riding around on that wanky old thing.'

'Wanky new thing,' I corrected her. But what was I to do with it? I had a car, as did Stephen, and Mum had a bike she was quite happy with. I decided to give it to Karen and Chris anyway, and a week later they sold it on and put the money towards some kitchen units – which, after all, cost even less to run and don't require a helmet.

I became a minor celebrity for a while through all this. My picture appeared in the next programme, and a piece on me in the local paper called me a 'wordsmith'. What a start to my literary career. I can just see my entry in *Who's Who* when I become a famous author: 'Kevin Baldwin began his glittering path to the Nobel Prize by making 3,101 words out of the letters in "Trevor's Cycles".' Did other writers begin this way? Did Jean-Paul Sartre set out by making words out of 'Les vélos de Trevor'? I don't think so. Even so, several people stopped Mum down at the shops and said, 'Was that your boy who won the moped? Ooh, he did well.' Some people are easily impressed.

Before the second half of this game against Villa, the words of 'On the ball, City' were flashed up on the scoreboard for the benefit of anyone who might be unsure of them (e.g., the woman in the market). Unfortunately, the scoreboard operator was no more accurate than she had been: 'KICK IT OFF, THROW ITN ... ' ITN? Why? It's the BBC that keeps giving us a hard time.

It was always going to be difficult for the second half to be as good as the first, and it wasn't. It was better. The intensity of the contest was incredible. It was more dramatic than drama, more poetic than poetry. The players put the lie to John Faulkner's suggestion that they were unable to raise their game on big occasions, while the crowd surrounded them with a wall of noise on each side.

After an hour, a few gaps began to appear in both defences. Gary Megson only had the Villa keeper to beat, but the latter saved his shot. Then Garry

Parker ran on to a through-ball, rounded Gunn, left John Polston on his backside with a neat turn and, with the goal at his mercy ... hit the outside of a post. It looked as if Villa would never score – but then, I had had the same thought in the recent game against Arsenal.

The vocal support increased, with chorus after chorus of the club song rolling round the ground. Almost everyone joined in. My voice, which had been so croaky for the previous few days, had been miraculously (though temporarily) restored and all my aches had disappeared. Those who couldn't speak for excitement munched on their fingernails until they looked like the Venus de Milo.

With ten minutes to go, the passion was almost unbearable – and I noticed someone leaving early! How could he do this? I wouldn't have left if I'd been told my house was on fire. I was just thinking that he should have his membership withdrawn, as he was patently unworthy of it, when he was given the ultimate punishment. With nine minutes to go, Norwich scored.

At the time, I wasn't sure how it came about. After a goal, I am usually able to produce an action replay in my mind at once, but this game had so hypnotised me that I only realised what had happened when I saw it on TV later. Crook took a corner, Megson's diving header was saved, and Polston booted the ball into the net from close range. NB, David Lacey, I said 'booted'. He did not head the ball as you stated twice in the *Guardian* the next day. I'm surprised Polston had enough energy to keep going for the whole match. His baby finally turned up last night.

As soon as the net bulged in front of us, pandemonium broke out around the ground – except in the block of Aston Villa fans. They remained completely motionless in one corner as everyone else leapt, waved, danced and screamed for joy. I felt as if fireworks were going off accompanied by a full orchestra and 21-gun salute in the middle of an earthquake. I threw my head back and produced a roar which started in the soles of my feet and came up through my whole body. Everything was in that roar – the joy at the goal, the release of the tension that had been building up for days, the fulfilment of my hopes for the game, the possibility of greater fulfilment at the end of the season, and the defiance of the sceptics, my previous employers, the Wolverine and anyone else who loathes me.

For the remainder of the game, the crowd whistled as loudly as possible, urging the referee to do the same. Eventually he obliged, and everyone went mad again – except for me. With a presence of mind that astonishes me even now, I rushed out of the ground to get into the queue for tickets for the Spurs game on Good Friday.

As it turned out, there wasn't a queue, and I was out of the box office before Mum and Stephen got out of the ground. We joined the happy tide of Norwich supporters flowing up Carrow Road, though not before Mum had stumbled off the edge of a pavement. 'Have you been drinking?' a man asked her. 'I feel drunk,' she replied – as we all did. We floated up the hill, borne up by the songs that were still emanating from the ground.

Only at the top were we hit by tiredness. Suddenly, we all felt as if we'd played ninety minutes ourselves. Mum became curiously reflective. 'Just think of the Villa fans having to go all that way home now they've lost. Do you feel sorry for them?'

What? 'No, I don't,' I said. For one thing, they certainly wouldn't have had any sympathy for us if we'd lost. For another, I'd had enough of being on the losing side in big games. Sunderland in last year's FA Cup, Spurs in last year's Rumbelows Cup, Spurs in this year's FA Cup, Ipswich in the league at Christmas – it was definitely our turn now. Furthermore, Villa's hopes of the title had not disappeared as ours would have done if we had lost.

I don't suppose the Villa fans thought it had been a great game, even though it was undoubtedly the best I have seen in years. If the result had gone the other way – as it could easily have done if Parker hadn't missed that open goal – I probably wouldn't have done. But why waste time on such imponderables? We won! Even if we don't win the league in the end, I'll have the memory of the way we played this evening and of how it made me feel.

When we arrived back at Mum's, her neighbours were at their window raising a glass to us. We went in to watch the highlights on *Sportsnight* – and what a disappointment. The game looked scrappy (though plenty of people remarked to me afterwards that it looked very good), and it seemed as quiet as a morgue. How could this be, when my ears were still ringing from the noise at the ground? (Unless that's why it seemed quiet, of course.) But there was no way that TV could possibly convey what we'd just experienced.

The 'experts' now had no choice but to admit that we now have a great chance of the Championship. There are only six games left, for goodness sake.

I had a hard job getting to sleep that night through excitement and worry. What could I say in a letter to the club to convince them that I deserve an Ipswich ticket? I must have nodded off eventually, though, as I woke up next morning – only to discover that my voice had gone almost completely. When I rang Karen to tell her about the game, she thought I was a dirty phone caller.

Karen said that when she had told Joanna the result in the morning, she had shouted, 'Hooray! We won!' – only for her younger sister Lisa to echo her. 'No, you can't shout "Hooray",' Joanna told her. 'Norwich are my team.' Karen had to explain to her that Norwich City FC is not her exclusive property and that her sister is allowed to support them too. Kids.

Later in the day, it was announced that City had signed the striker Efan Ekoku from Bournemouth to replace Darren Beckford, who completed his move to Oldham a few days ago. We used to buy a lot of ex-Bournemouth players (e.g., Phil Boyer, Ted MacDougall, Mel Machin, John Benson). Indeed, it was once thought that the AFC in AFC Bournemouth stood for 'A Future Canary'. I don't know much about Ekoku, though. Will he fit into our playing style? Come to that, will he fit into our songs? I can't think of any rhymes for 'Ekoku' off the top of my head. 'Let's hope he is Efan good,' suggested Mum. I'll go along with that.

Saturday 27 March
No Match

For once, a free Saturday came as a welcome respite after eight matches in just 25 days.

In the morning, I went into Norwich to buy a tankard for Russell, the member of our Sunday football team who broke his leg a few weeks ago. This had been suggested and paid for by the Capital Canaries committee. I wasn't sure what to have engraved on it, though. 'Tough titty on breaking your leg' didn't sound too sympathetic. I wondered about 'We have the technology – we can rebuild him', but this proved to be prohibitively expensive. In the end, I settled for 'Man of Steel 1993' – a reference to the metal pin holding his shin together.

In the evening, Mum and I went to see *On the Ledge*, a new play by Alan Bleasdale. Mum was warned when she went to buy the tickets that the play contained 'strong language'. 'Oh, that doesn't bother me,' she said. 'I've heard it all at the football.' In the event, we were both rather disappointed. 'Call that pissing swearing?' said Mum at the end. I could see that the climax of the play was meant to be powerful and dramatic, but it paled in comparison with the Villa game on Wednesday night. Besides which, I felt that Bleasdale forfeited the sympathy of the audience by setting his play in Liverpool. OK, so this may not be a valid critical response, but it's the way I felt.

For the rest of the weekend, I enjoyed the chance to be able to stop and think for a while. You might think that I would have plenty of time for this anyway, not having the distraction of a job, but over the last month I have just been living from one game to the next.

I let our position sink in. Here we are, with six games to go, and we're still top! (Although we've played a game more than United and Villa.) Can we really be on the verge of achieving the unthinkable? In all the years I have supported Norwich, I have never really believed we might win the league before this year. I have hoped for it and dreamed about it, but only in the way you do when filling in your pools coupon. You try to imagine what it would be like to win, but don't believe it will ever happen.

'Why bother to support a team like that?' I have often been asked. One reason is that I have no choice in the matter, as I have already explained – though I suppose it's my choice to go and watch the team every week. But another reason is that different clubs have different criteria for judging success. If Norwich ever reach the FA Cup final, it will be seen as a huge triumph. Yet the fact that Liverpool won the FA Cup last season is seen as no big deal. Anything less than the League Championship is considered by them to be of minor importance. When a small team has a good Cup run or defeats a team from a higher division or league, that is considered to be success – and the feelings of their fans are every bit as strong as those of fans of a major club when they win a trophy.

If Norwich do win the Premier League, the achievement will be so far beyond our expectations as to defy comprehension. There will be unbelievable euphoria, and the memories of it will last forever. Yet it only occurred to me this weekend that such a victory would also change the terms by which the club judges success forever. All future seasons could become a disappointment if the achievement could not be repeated. In other words, after winning the league, things could only get worse.

Winning the title would also affect my personal relationship with the club. Until now, I have been able to see the club as an image of myself. We are both laid-back, friendly, generally fairly well-liked (at least not violently disliked by many), entertaining, but ultimately not as successful as we might be – possibly because, deep down, we don't really want it. We may even be afraid of it. These parallels are doubtless another reason for the strength of my feelings for the club. But, if Norwich do finish top, I will no longer be able to make such convenient comparisons. They will have outdone me, rising to a level of achievement I will be unlikely ever to match.

I have never considered before now that winning the title might have a negative side to it. Perhaps I should have done. After all, to quote Oscar Wilde, 'when the gods wish to punish us they answer our prayers'.

So does this mean that I no longer want Norwich to go all the way? Does it bogroll.

Monday 5 April
Manchester United (home)

Hello and welcome to 'That Was The Sporting Week That Was'.

Monday. Vinny Jones is given an indefinite ban by the FA for arriving ninety minutes late for a disciplinary hearing. Not the first time he's been late in making a challenge. Pity this didn't happen before we played Wimbledon. I just hope he's back to frighten United on the last day of the season.

Tuesday. David Phillips appears on *A Question of Sport* and helps Bill Beaumont to win. Yes, he was on his side.

Wednesday. Phillips and Bowen are only substitutes for Wales, but this is good news as it means they won't be injured or knackered for the United game.

Thursday. I get a call from one of my former work-mates. He says how well Polston is doing at the moment, scoring for us against Villa last week and for Denmark last night. I point out that Polston is English and that it was Flemming Povlsen who scored for Denmark. What a pillock – or was this a pathetic attempt at an April Fool joke?

Friday. Two tickets for the Ipswich game plop through Mum's front door. Yes!! The begging letter worked! Perhaps I can get a decent night's sleep at last.

Saturday. I put money on two horses in the Grand National – Laura's Beau and Esha Ness. I know nothing at all about horse racing, so I choose these two because their riders are wearing yellow and green silks. The race turns out to be the biggest sporting fiasco since … er … well, the biggest sporting fiasco ever. Several horses ignore the second false start and complete the course – and, sure enough, Esha Ness comes first. Typical. This is the first time that a horse I have backed has ever passed the post first (it usually unseats its rider in the paddock) – and the race is declared void.

Stephen finds this hilarious, partly because I have given him so much stick about his bad luck with Golden Goal tickets this season, partly because he has won £50 this afternoon. Ipswich's 3–1 defeat at Manchester City means that they cannot catch us now, even if they win all their remaining games and we lose all ours, so Stephen has won the bet he made with an Ipswich fan at the start of the season.

Sunday. Arsenal beat Spurs in the FA Cup semi-final to join Sheffield Wednesday, who beat Sheffield United on Saturday, in the final. This is very good news for Norwich, as it means the same two teams are in the FA and Coca-Cola Cup finals. As Jon pointed out a few weeks ago, if the same team wins both cups they will go into the European Cup-Winners' Cup, and the UEFA Cup place allocated to the winners of the Coca-Cola Cup will go to the team who finish third in the league. Confused? Well, take it from me, it's true. But let's hope we qualify for the European Cup anyway and avoid all the ifs and buts.

On the day of the United game, I was beset by nerves, just as I was before we played Villa. Any chance I might have had of putting the match out of my mind for a while was wrecked by a painter from the local council who came to do the outside of Mum's house. The colours are to be red and white. Not a good omen.

He spent nearly all day singing 'On the ball, City', wildly off-key and getting most of the words wrong. There was a brief respite when he launched into a chorus of *Let's Do The Timewarp* from the *Rocky Horror Show*, but he almost fell off his ladder when he got to the bit about pelvic thrusts, so he went back to the football song.

To give myself a break, I went to the bookie's to get my Grand National stake money back. But again I was reminded of the big match by all the boards and TV screens showing the odds being offered on it. I was tempted to put the money on a score (3–0 to Norwich at 28–1 looked good), but managed to resist.

The evening paper was dominated by previews of the match. In a special supplement, there was an interview with the United captain Steve Bruce. He was generous in his praise of Norwich, but I couldn't help wondering whether he had ulterior motives for this. For one thing, he wouldn't want to wind up the Norwich fans and players by criticising us. And for another, he wouldn't want to jeopardise the success of the soccer schools he runs in Norwich every year.

As Mum, Stephen and I walked down to Carrow Road, my nerves suddenly disappeared. I felt absolutely confident that we would win. United couldn't play any better than Villa had, I told myself. And United hadn't won any of their last four games.

The pre-match entertainment went just the way I wanted. The Red Devils failed to drop in, the music conked out during the Sky dancing girls' routine, and the crowd showed a commendable lack of interest in the exhortations to perform a Mexican wave. My mood seemed to be shared by everyone around me. A knot of supporters chorused, 'You're gonna get what Aston Villa got', and others nodded their approval.

The first action of the game gave us no reason to doubt that this would be our night. We might have had a penalty in the first couple of minutes when Robins was knocked over, and then Ian Crook curled a free kick just over the bar. No one was prepared for what happened next – not even David Phillips, despite his appearance on *A Question of Sport*.

United scored three goals in eight minutes. Three times they burst through our square back four, who stood there with their arms raised as if they wanted to be excused. Three times Bryan Gunn had to face players in red shirts coming straight towards him, and three times he was unable to prevent a goal. The Norwich players and fans were in shock. There had been such a big build-up to this game, and it was all over after twenty minutes. Apart from anything else, goals simply shouldn't come so quickly or easily.

A scapegoat was hastily sought, and the blame settled on the linesman. Well, the man with the flag had been blamed at Aintree on Saturday, for failing to stop the horses after the second false start. He was duly subjected to all sorts of abuse, even from Gunn. When he did raise his flag to signal offside shortly afterwards, he was given a sarcastic standing ovation by the River End crowd. I didn't join in: I seemed to be paralysed from the waist down – and in any case, it was impossible to tell from behind the goal whether the United players were offside or not. (I'm getting far too old and sensible.) Television showed later on that the linesman had been correct every time, which added embarrassment to the range of emotions felt by City supporters after the game.

When the goals went in, it became clear that there were United supporters in every part of the ground. Had they got in with tickets supplied by touts or mates? Or were they some of those pathetic souls who were born and live in Norfolk, yet claim to follow more 'glamorous' teams, though they only see them once a year when they play at Carrow Road? Whatever the case, there were a few ugly scenes as there had been during the Ipswich match. There were demands for them to be thrown out, but again the police and stewards took no action as far as I could see.

On the pitch, Norwich spent the rest of the half staggering around like a boxer trying to get to the end of a round to regain his composure and receive fresh instructions. There seemed to be no chance of getting back into the game, although there was a precedent for it. In the 1983-84 season, City were losing 3-0 at home to United, yet fought back to snatch a 3-3 draw. However, United's defence then was nowhere near as strong as it is now. Nor was their attack, come to that. The United fans knew the game was won and amused themselves by bowing in homage to Ryan Giggs whenever he came near them and shouting 'Hooray!' every time a United player touched the ball. It's not often you hear that in the first half.

Further confirmation that the game was up – as if any were needed – came when Gary Megson was felled in the United penalty area and the referee waved play on, to the predictable anger of the home crowd. 'Shall we go home now?' asked Mum at half-time. I said no – though I might have left early to queue for Ipswich tickets if the club had stuck to its original plan. I found out later that Karen and Joanna, who had gone to a friend's house to watch the game on TV, did go home at the interval.

A huge roar greeted the Norwich players as they came out for the second half, though I wasn't sure whether we were encouraging them to make a comeback or not to concede any more goals. A new theory to explain the scoreline had been developed by a group behind the goal at the River End. As the United keeper took up his position, he was asked, 'What'd you pay to win the league?' – a suggestion that the match officials had been slipped a few quid.

City proceeded to play with new heart and put together some good moves, even though United didn't seem too bothered. Efan Ekoku was brought on and gave their defenders some trouble. His name gave the crowd even more problems. What was the correct pronunciation? Most people eventually settled for 'Cuckoo' – which meant that we now had a Cuckoo, Robins and nine other Canaries on the pitch. Who are we going to buy next? Glenn Cockerill? Jonas Thern?

We got one goal back when Robins applied the 'law of the ex' after sixty minutes. The crowd tried to recreate the intensity of the atmosphere at the Villa game – and a terrific noise was sustained for ten minutes or so – but it subsided as the remainder of the match slipped by relatively uneventfully.

Apart from a couple of ugly incidents towards the end, that is. United brought Bryan Robson on to allow him to make enough appearances to qualify for a medal if they win the Championship. Within a minute, he had made a dreadful tackle which should have earned him a booking. Then he launched himself into a horrible late two-footed tackle on Ian Crook. I remembered why I had never liked him and had not wanted him to become the Norwich manager last summer. A tussle ensued, with all the City players pointing accusingly at Robson. Even Bryan Gunn appeared on the scene near the half-way line, which was a little foolish as his differently-coloured shirt made his involvement all the more obvious. Robson was eventually booked – though he should really have been sent off, as it should have been his second caution of the game. Paul Ince was also lucky to stay on the pitch, as he appeared to push John Polston in the face, but this went unnoticed.

When the final whistle went, we all left in silence. No one shouted angrily at the team. They had not played badly for 82 of the 90 minutes – but more to the point, we all felt numb. It was arguably the most important match in the club's history, and we had lost it because of a crazy spell lasting eight minutes. Eight minutes! I can make a Polo mint last longer than that. It was hard to believe it had happened. But it had.

When we got back to the house, we saw that Mum's neighbours had their curtains closed as if they were in mourning. I certainly was. 'I'm going straight to bed if you're going to moan for the rest of the evening,' said Mum – so I didn't say a word after that.

The national press revelled in United's win the next day. True, United had been very impressive, but there was a definite sense of relief in the papers that the yokel heroes had been put in their place. I tried to remain optimistic by reminding myself that United had faded badly after winning 3–1 at Norwich towards the end of last season, but my realistic/pessimistic side kept intruding. Could United go to pieces again? And could Villa falter as well? It seems unlikely that both will have a bad run over the next few weeks.

I drove back to London to sign on the dole, which didn't improve my mood. I had to fill in a form which asked where I'd like to work and how much I wanted to earn. Now £100,000 a year in Norwich would suit me, but I don't hold out much hope.

The only good thing about Tuesday was that no one rang to laugh because we had lost. I appreciated this consideration – or was it that nobody cared?

Friday 9 April
Tottenham Hotspur (away)

At half-time in the Marseille-Rangers game on TV on Wednesday evening, the phone rang. It was a journalist from the evening paper in Norwich who said he wanted to ask me a few questions.

I broke into a cold sweat. Was I to be named in an exposé of a sex scandal? Or identified as the ringleader of a vicious gang of bank robbers? Then I remembered that I was swagless and shagless, so these couldn't be the reasons for the call. It turned out that both Mum and Karen have nominated me for a feature the paper is running at the moment. A search is on to find City's biggest fan. But in what sense do they mean 'biggest'? If they're judging it according to waistline, Stephen should have been nominated instead of me. Still, I don't suppose for a moment that it will turn out to be me. As we have seen several times already this season, every time I think I have done something extraordinary (the trip to Carlisle, the bet at Villa, losing my job), I find that someone has gone one step further.

Anyway, I suddenly found myself in the middle of an interview, just as I had at the airport on the way to the Oldham game. My prime concern was not to condemn myself this time by saying what a miserable bloke I am – but I promptly fell into the trap again. Why do I keep doing this in interviews with the media? I seem to find it more difficult to go sixty seconds without lapsing into self-deprecation than most people trying not to say 'yes' or 'no' on *Take Your Pick*.

First I was asked why I support Norwich. That was easy enough. I told the reporter that I'd been brought up that way. 'Ah, you're a real dyed-in-the-wool fan, then,' he said. I wondered whether he was making some dubious reference to sheep – and, looking back, I think it must have been this which caused me to drop my guard. He then asked why I go to watch the team every week, and before I knew it I was explaining how it fills the gaps in your life when you are a sad person. Damn!

The usual journalist's questions (How do you feel? What are your thoughts for the future?) were combined when he asked me how optimistic I was about City's chances of winning the league. I didn't say we would win it; as you will have gathered by now, my loyalty is not blind. Then again, I didn't say we wouldn't win it; I didn't want to come across as pessimistic in the paper – and, of course, I was proved wrong when I thought our hopes were dead after the QPR game.

When he asked me about the difficulties involved in travelling to matches, I summoned my favourite BSkyB hobby horse from its stable and trotted out my usual criticisms for rescheduling so many fixtures. I bet that doesn't get mentioned in the article, though. Sky have been running quite a few adverts in the local press lately.

When Mum turned up at my flat with Stephen before the game on Friday morning, I took her to task for telling the paper all about me. She wasn't at all repentant; in fact, she took considerable pleasure in passing on the even more worrying news that they want to publish a photo of me and have been ringing her and Karen for help. Fortunately, there are very few pictures of me in existence. Our family has never been keen on photography, and I am naturally camera-shy. When I appear on *This Is Your Life*, it will be a bloody thin book. I just hope they don't send a photographer round the next time I'm at Mum's. All those featured so far have been made to look extremely gormless by waving scarves or giving 'thumbs-up' signs to the camera.

We settled down to enjoy some hot cross buns and watch the Laurel and Hardy films on BBC2. It was very cosy – just like the Good Fridays of my childhood, in fact. Perhaps we should have stayed in my flat, because the day went downhill fast after that. I'm still not sure why we were playing on Good Friday, by the way. There had been several complaints made about it, notably by the priest in the Catholic church opposite the Spurs ground. He wasn't concerned that the attendance for his own fixture that day might be affected; he just didn't think it was appropriate for the game to be played on a day that marks the crucifixion of one loved and worshipped by so many. In the event, it proved to be highly appropriate.

Stephen drove us all to the ground, as he claimed he knew a place to park that was closer than the spot I generally choose. And he did. It seemed a very handy place indeed. At the time. We walked to White Hart Lane past several chip shops, which were all open although it was only 10:45 in the morning. (The match was to kick off at twelve noon, a time as unfathomable as the fact that we were playing on Good Friday.) And there were people inside buying fish and chips already! Ugh!

Inside the ground, we found that we had seats directly behind a pillar. (See Alternative Law No. 9, away match v Southampton.) All the same, I felt good about the game. Yes, Spurs had beaten us soundly in the Cup. But we had more to play for here than Spurs, who I suspected would be deflated after losing to Arsenal in the semi-final last Sunday. And we had bounced back after most of our defeats this season, so the disappointment of Monday night should affect us positively rather than negatively, I thought.

Once again, I thought wrong. As soon as the match started, the large Norwich contingent was filled with horror and despair at the performance (or lack of it). I shouldn't have been too surprised. Just as we traditionally have a poor Christmas, we are usually bad for the last few games of the season. Back in December, I wondered whether the players had eaten too much turkey. Are we now to assume that they opened their Easter eggs two days early?

In the match programme, there was an advertisement for Tottenham's sponsors, Holsten Pils. Their current advertising campaign consists of a series of anagrams of their name, and this execution showed a bouncing football with the nonsensical headline 'PILLSEN SHOT'. Who is Pillsen? It wouldn't have taken too much foresight to show instead a picture of the Norwich team looking miserable with the line 'SHIT SPELL ON'.

I read the next day that Norwich had been using a sweeper system. This was news to me, as the defence simply looked a mess. Time after time, the back four/five were caught in possession, miscontrolled the ball, and put each other in trouble by trying to play intricate passes in the wrong areas. Things were no better up front. A hoarding alongside the pitch urged: 'Next time you score, use a condom.' There was as much chance of us scoring as ... er ... of me scoring.

After twenty minutes, Spurs scored. They won a dodgy free kick just outside the box and, in accordance with Alternative Law No. 5, Neil Ruddock thundered a shot into the net. This also made up for his disallowed goal from a free kick in the league match at Carrow Road on Boxing Day. Minutes later, we were 2–0 down. I suspect that Gary Lineker passed on the secret of how to score against Norwich to Teddy Sheringham before leaving for Japan.

The two quick goals visibly shook the City players. The barely-healed scars of the eight-minute nightmare on Monday were reopened. The Norwich supporters seemed unable or unwilling to lift the team, offering only a chorus of 'There's only one Tony Adams' (scorer of the winning goal in last Sunday's semi-final). This was petty, pointless, and particularly ungracious considering that the Spurs supporters had given a warm welcome to the former Tottenham players in the Norwich side before the game.

Spurs won another free kick just outside our area. 'Am I in your way?' asked a policeman standing in front of, but slightly below me.

'No,' I said, 'but I wouldn't care if you were. I don't want to see this.' As it happened, nothing came of the kick.

By now it was pouring with rain. In the evening games against Palace and Villa, the rain had added to the atmosphere, but here it just made the proceedings even more miserable. It was as if our hopes were being drowned like puppies in a weighted sack thrown into a river.

Half-time didn't come a moment too soon, but this proved to be just as infuriating as the game. Some idiot behind me started boasting about how he had hit a United fan in the Barclay on Monday night when the latter was celebrating a goal. He had been told to leave, but wasn't arrested. What an arsehole.

Looking around, I saw other people chatting, smiling, even laughing. How could they? Didn't they understand what was happening here? Why weren't they as distraught as me? They angered me almost as much as Mr Hard behind me.

Ekoku was brought on for the second half. "E'LL PISS ON T.H.,' we hoped, anagrammatically – but he didn't. It was hardly his fault, though, as he received precious little service. Meanwhile, the defending went from bad to worse.

At 3–0, we knew the game had gone – and, with it, any hope of winning the league. 'Where's your title gone?' chanted the Spurs fans. At 4–0, several City fans got up to leave. I noticed a few Capital Canaries among them, who were presumably off to drown their sorrows in a pub as they didn't have the excuse of wanting to make an early start back to Norwich. Mum and Stephen, to their credit, didn't suggest leaving early, though I could tell by glancing at their expressions that they thought their day had been wasted (OH, 'S ILL-SPENT). At 5–0, I was reminded of the 5–0 defeat we suffered at Arsenal in 1989. That game had also been played at an odd time on a bank holiday at the end of a fine season – and ended any lingering hopes we had of winning the league that year.

At last, far too late, the Norwich fans started singing, for the same mixed motives as at Blackburn when we lost 7–1. When Ekoku scrambled a late consolation goal, the noise increased. 'On the ball, City' – 'We're gonna win the league' – 'You're not singing any more' – 'We're going to Europe, you're not' – 'Where are Tottenham in the league?' – the songs came thick and fast. And yet they couldn't mask the terrible, almost terminal, disappointment at our failure here. (NO PTS IS HELL.)

This really did feel like the end. 'The dream's over,' said Stephen. Earlier, I advanced the theory that most failures in life are gradual and unspectacular. Whether or not that is true, this was definitely the cataclysmic version. The club had better tell the local bus company to stop taking the roof off that double-decker for the triumphant journey through the streets of Norwich. And that order for 'Champions' T-shirts can be cancelled too.

Mum tried to point out that at least we are not battling against relegation as we were this time last year – and as we thought we would be this year – but it didn't help. We'd got so close and now it was all over.

> Wish I drank so I could hit the booze,
> Wish I had a temper that I could lose,
> Wish I had a cat so I could kick it,
> Wish I had the nerve to burn my ticket.
> I'm fed up always turning the other cheek.
> I'll never go again ... until next week.
>
> *A Fan's Lament* (Trad., arr. me)

We walked back to the car in the rain and were absolutely drenched by the time we got there. The windows steamed up and refused to clear. Then the drawback of Stephen's chosen parking place became clear. We got stuck in a traffic jam – and I'm talking superglue here. It took over an hour to get back to the flat, when it normally takes five or ten minutes.

Although I was driving back to Norwich too, Mum had no trouble choosing who to travel with. 'I'll go with Stephen,' she said. 'I can't face you moaning for a hundred miles.' We went straight round to Karen's, as Mum had agreed to do some babysitting, and I found I was just as unwelcome there.

'You're not allowed in the house if you're going to go on about the game,' Karen said. I don't think this was a lack of understanding or sympathy on her part, or Mum's. I rather think that they were trying to put the defeat out of their minds and knew that my obsessive mutterings would keep reminding them.

Good Friday? You must be joking.

I simply didn't want to get out of bed on Saturday morning. I was beset by an awful lethargy – and when I did manage to haul myself down to the shops, I shuffled around Norwich city centre like an old man. I couldn't see where our next points might come from.

SO – PILLS THEN? No. You never know. Where there's life, there's hope. Or maybe there isn't. I sat by the radio all Saturday afternoon praying for a miracle – and, for a while, it looked as though we might get one. United were losing at home to Sheffield Wednesday, Villa were drawing 0–0 at home to Coventry, and Blackburn (in fourth place) were losing at Leeds. I began to wonder whether we might still have a chance of winning the title ... and then it happened. The Villa and Blackburn results were confirmed, but United equalised five minutes from the end of normal time. That was bad enough, but seven – yes, seven – minutes into injury time, they snatched a winner. I couldn't believe it.

What made this especially hard to take was the fact that Steve Bruce scored both goals. He it was who scored the 87th-minute goal against Ipswich in the semi-final second leg to take us to the Milk Cup final in 1985 – the most wonderful moment I have ever known. How could he now deal the final blow to our dreams like this? I drew an analogy with the Easter story earlier, but I don't recall Judas banging the nails in himself.

Wednesday 14 April
Leeds United (home)

The result of last week's interview with the local press reporter appeared in the paper on Monday. It was a bit disappointing, really. There were no 'World Exclusive' banners splashed across the page. And much of our conversation had been left out completely. There was no mention of my epic trip to Carlisle, nor of how I used to sneak out of work to go to matches. My criticism of Sky had, as I predicted, been omitted too. Instead, the article talked chiefly about my answering machine ('City fan Kevin has the answer'). It doesn't say a lot for my conversational skills when my answerphone is considered more interesting than me.

The feature also stated that I attend 'as many away games as [I] can'. Cheek! I've been to every away game this season (and last), and the paper makes me sound like a part-timer who'll wander down to Highbury or White Hart Lane if there's nothing worth watching on TV. I've a good mind to write to the Press Complaints Commission. Perhaps I could get an apology on the front page. Still, at least I wasn't described as a 'dyed-in-the-wool' fan as I'd feared. And there wasn't a picture of me either, which was good news for everyone.

The Villa and United results on Monday were a far more serious matter. Both won away from home to move 6 and 7 points ahead of us respectively – and Blackburn stayed on our tails with a 2-1 win over Ipswich. For once, Mum and I were shouting for Town as we listened to the commentary on Radio 5, but a fat lot of good it did.

I got a call from the Wolverine on Tuesday night. It wasn't unexpected, as it was her birthday ... and yes, I'd sent her a card. It was another of my homemade specials. A couple of years ago, I sent her one entitled 'Chances with Wolves', a spoof of the film poster with Steve Bull in the lead role – and last year I sent a brick as my contribution to the Molineux redevelopment fund. This year's effort suggested that William Shakespeare might have been the first-ever Steve Bull fan:

> The king's a bawcock, and a heart of gold,
> A lad of life, an imp of fame,
> Of parents good, of fist most valiant:
> I kiss his dirty shoe, and from my heart-string
> I love the lovely bully.
>
> *Henry V,* IV.i.44-48

She seemed genuinely touched by it and said again how much she'd wanted Norwich to win the league. Apparently, she went around kicking the furniture after the Manchester United game.

I asked what presents she'd been given. Her 'beloved' (her word – I couldn't tell whether there was a trace of irony present) gave her a pair of gardening gloves. Jesus.

I've let this situation drift again this year, despite my declared intention to resolve it one way or the other. To be honest, I had hoped that writing this book would force me to bring matters to a head; a dramatic climax in my personal life would counterpoint the dénouement of the football season very effectively. As it is, I have allowed week after week to slip by, punctuated by occasional phone calls in both directions, and things are as hazy and unsatisfactory as ever.

I could claim that Norwich's part in the Championship race has been the focus of my attention this season – as it has – but I wouldn't be convincing anyone, least of all myself, that this is an acceptable reason for avoiding the issue. It is my craven fear of ultimate rejection, compounded by my natural indecision, that has kept me from settling it. I feel like a mediocre mid-table team (Wolves!) who have failed to make a concerted push for glory, but are relieved to have avoided the dreaded drop. (In some cases, though, teams come back much stronger after they have been relegated.)

Will I ever do anything about it? The situation can't go on indefinitely, but

I'm not sure I'll ever be the one who ends it ... unless this book does it for me. If and when it's published, she's bound to want a copy, and that will sort things out once and for all. It's a cowardly way to do it, but then that's me. Yellow army, yellow army ...

There is a further complication. Jane rang on Wednesday. Mr Popular or what? I hadn't expected to hear from her again after she decided not to come to the Wimbledon game, but it seems that she's continued to keep an eye on City's fortunes. She mentioned how disappointing our result at Wimbledon had been in view of the fact that United had only drawn their derby game that morning; she knew that United's goals against us had come in the space of eight minutes; she knew how many points behind we are and how many games we have left. Does this new interest in football indicate an interest in me? I don't know, but I must investigate further the next time I'm in London (I don't seem to be there much these days). It's a welcome distraction from the dilemma with the Wolverine – but unwelcome in that it is yet another excuse for inertia on that front.

Not for the first time in my life, it was a relief to be able to put such concerns to one side and concentrate on a match. Nor was I the only one to be looking forward eagerly to the Leeds game. Ever since we played Oldham, Karen's eldest daughter Joanna had been asking to go again, and with this week being a school holiday, Karen said she could come to this one. Joanna was particularly excited about this, as it meant she could stay up well past her usual bedtime.

'Have you brought your torch?' I asked her during the afternoon.

'What torch?' she replied.

'Well, it'll be dark tonight, so everyone has to take a torch so that the players can see what they're doing.' She looked rather worried until Mum came in and told me off for teasing her. I needn't have bothered trying to put bizarre ideas into Joanna's head, though; she's got plenty of her own already. 'Who are the blues tonight?' she asked me. After some head-scratching, I worked out that she thought the visiting team at Carrow Road always had to wear blue, since Oldham wore blue the other week. Then, when we arrived at the ground in the evening, I asked if she'd like a programme. 'I've already got one,' she replied, believing that the match programme was the same every time. It only occurred to me later that this may indicate highly-developed critical faculties at an impressively early age.

I let Joanna have my usual seat next to Mum so that she could have a decent view. Did she realise what a sacrifice this was for me? I don't think so. I sat next to Stephen a few seats away and found myself with a Leeds supporter on my other side. 'Who's your friend?' asked Stephen, nodding in his direction. I hoped he wouldn't turn out to be a trouble-maker (the Leeds fan, not Stephen), as the atmosphere was very relaxed and jolly. It was almost as if everyone was relieved that the pressure of chasing the title was over – though we would have given anything for Norwich to have won the last two matches.

My only concern about the game was Leeds's away record this season.

Kevin's Alternative Laws of Football (No. 11)

'Any team with a long sequence of victories or defeats behind them will see it come to an end at Carrow Road,'

The positive aspect of the above law was amply illustrated in October 1990 when we became the first team to take a point off Liverpool in the league that season. The negative aspect was that Leeds were likely to win here in this game as they hadn't won away in the league all season.

My fears were increased after two minutes of the match, when Lee Chapman put Leeds ahead. Their supporter next to me gave a suppressed yelp, but no more. He didn't even react when someone abused Chapman, remarking that 'his wife used to shag Mr Bean'. However, my next thought was of the home match against Crystal Palace, the marvellous evening that Mum and Stephen had missed, which had begun with us giving away a soft goal in the first minute at the River End and ended with us winning 4-2. Could this evening be a repeat performance?

The answer proved to be yes, but the final score was arrived at in a dramatically different way. Last week, against Manchester United, we conceded three goals in eight minutes. This week, against Leeds United, we scored three in five: a header and shot from Sutton, a penalty from Phillips. It was as if the great and mysterious gods of football had decided to show us what the Manchester fans had experienced. It was as strange a feeling as conceding three quick goals, but infinitely more pleasant. Something similar happened earlier in the season, when not long after we lost to two Spurs goals in a minute, we beat Manchester City with two in a minute. It's that 'every action has an equal and opposite reaction' thing again.

To my great surprise, the Leeds fan next to me stood and clapped politely at every Norwich goal. This was sportsmanship beyond my comprehension – unless his Norwich-supporting friend who was sitting on his other side had told him of the unpleasantness when Ipswich, Spurs and Manchester United fans had manifested themselves earlier in the season. All the same, Stephen started jeering, 'You're not singing any more' – though he soon shut up again when he noticed that his Golden Goal ticket was three seconds out from the time of our second goal. I found this reassuring as well as funny; it was as if normal service had been restored.

I think I annoyed the Leeds fan more than Stephen did by yelling 'Come on, you yellows' in his left ear for most of the half, but he could hardly complain as my shouts were not directed at him. A few miles away, I discovered later, Karen was similarly annoying her husband. Having seen that we had scored three goals in quick succession, she checked the score on Teletext every thirty seconds for the rest of the game and completely spoiled the film he was trying to watch.

At half-time, with no further additions to the score thanks to the efforts of John Lukic in the Leeds goal, I went to see what Joanna thought of the game. Mum said she'd kept on shouting and jumping up and down, much to the amusement of those around her. 'Are you going to do that all game?' someone had asked her.

'Of course,' she replied, glaring at him uncomprehendingly. 'You have to shout to let the Norwich players know you want them to win.' Joanna had also been asking questions about the ball-boys and ball-girls and the mascot. Now there's an idea for the future.

The second half began badly. Leeds scored an admittedly excellent goal through Rod Wallace, and City proceeded to play statues for the next half-hour. The Yorkshire fans claimed to be the champions of Europe. Don't ask me why. They used to sing this when they were in the old Second Division, and it made even less sense then.

Twelve minutes from the end, however, Sutton rounded Lukic to complete his hat-trick, and there was a great roar of relief. The game was safe, my worries about Leeds's poor away record had been shown to be unjustified, and we had increased our lead over Blackburn. This 4-2 win had been a less emotional occasion than the 4-2 victory over Palace, but it was just as comforting.

Mum took Joanna out a few seconds before the final whistle to save her from the crush, but she said it was lovely to see everyone's smiling faces as they poured out of the ground. We skipped all the way home. Well, Joanna did, and the rest of us watched.

The BBC chose not to show the highlights of the match until 11:30, so we taped them for Joanna to watch the next morning. She looked rather quizzical when she did. 'What is it?' Mum asked.

'That man talking keeps saying "Fox".'

'Well?'

'His name's Foxy, isn't it?'

When she'd had her breakfast, I took her home and ended up discussing the selection of the England squad with Karen. As usual, I wasn't bothered who was picked, but Karen said she really wanted Chris Waddle to be recalled. I asked why. 'Because he's dead horny,' she said.

Since when has this been a factor in team selection? When Graham Taylor announced the squad later that day, did he say, 'After due consideration, I have decided to leave Waddle out because he isn't horny enough'? No, he didn't.

On Friday evening, Mum and I went to see Norwich play Leeds at Carrow Road again, only this time it was the first leg of the FA Youth Cup semi-final. It was the first time we'd been to watch the youngsters this season, though we'd been meaning to for some time as there are some particularly promising prospects among them.

It was an enjoyable evening, and not just because the weather was so warm. There was a big enough crowd to create an atmosphere, but that atmosphere was much more relaxed than usual. We wanted Norwich to win, but it wouldn't matter too much if they didn't. It was an evening for enjoying a good game and for trying to spot which players, if any, might one day make it to the first team.

It isn't easy to tell whether a boy of 18 will become a top player. Early promise is often unfulfilled, while ordinary-looking players may prove to be late developers. Even experienced judges can make mistakes: in recent years, City have released John Fashanu and Dion Dublin, both of whom have gone on to enjoy considerable success elsewhere. Both are big, strong, awkward strikers – and it may be the dread of making this error for a third time that has prompted the club to offer professional terms to the youth team's current big, strong, awkward striker Ade Akinbiyi.

Akinbiyi (or, as Mum kept saying, 'A bikini') put Norwich ahead after five minutes, but by half-time Leeds were deservedly 3-1 up and made it 4-1 midway through the second half. Despite this, the general mood was still jolly – and because there was less noise than usual, it was easier to hear other people's remarks during the game. When City's left-back sliced the ball into the crowd for the third time, someone nearby suggested that he must be getting special coaching from Mark Bowen. And when a Leeds player earned a booking for bringing down our tricky winger from behind, there were no furious cries of 'Off! Off!'; instead, I heard someone behind us tell his neighbour, 'I think that was Bryan Robson's tackle just arriving' – a reference to his crude challenge on Ian Crook eleven days before.

City had a late goal disallowed because the referee had given us a free kick a moment before the ball went in, so the final score wasn't an exact reversal of the one on Wednesday night. All the same, I found myself commenting to Mum as we left the ground that I was glad we had won the first game and lost the second rather than the other way round. As if you have a choice in the matter!

On the way back to the house, we bumped into two old friends of Mum's who mentioned that they had seen the piece about me in Monday's paper. Fame! I'm gonna last for five minutes ...

Monday 19 April
Ipswich Town (away)

Do you know the way to Ipswich Town?
I haven't seen their ground,
Not since the Town went tumbling down.

(Apologies to Bacharach and David)

This was the first time I had ever driven to Ipswich. On previous occasions – a long, long time ago – I had travelled down by rail or coach. I actually drove 265 miles before reaching Portman Road – not because I got lost, as I usually do when driving somewhere new, but because I had to go down to London early in the morning to sign on before returning to Norwich to collect Mum and take her to the game. I'm not sure it was worth all the hassle; the dole money will probably only cover the cost of the petrol I used driving to London and back.

There was a discussion about religion on Radio 5 as Mum and I travelled down the A140 to Ipswich. 'What do you think about God?' Mum asked me when a record was played.

'I think he'll probably keep the same team who played against Leeds,' I said. Mum groaned. I think she was actually expecting a serious answer.

A little later, Mum looked up at some tall, but still bare trees at the side of the road. 'It's going to be a hot summer,' she declared. 'The rooks are nesting high this year.' I wonder if there is any country folklore that indicates how the team will do, such as 'Red sky at night, Norwich are shite' or 'Crows on the mill, we'll win three-nil'. If there isn't, there should be.

We arrived at Ipswich's ground safe and sound (though only because I managed to persuade Mum not to stick her fingers up at Town fans on the way) at quarter past six. It looked a much dingier place than I remembered: grimy corrugated iron covered much of the exterior, and a rather tatty blue and white flag fluttered limply in the breeze. To think that the Ipswich fans had sung 'Shitty ground' at our place before Christmas.

We had to stand around for a while before we could get in, which surprised me. You'd have thought the police and stewards would have wanted to get the fans off the streets as soon as possible to avoid any confrontations. As we waited, we saw the most enormous woman walk past in an Ipswich shirt. It couldn't have been size XL. It must have been a Z (for Zeppelin), and even so the tensile strength of the stitching thread was being subjected to a rigorous test. 'Good grief,' said Mum, 'if I looked like that, I wouldn't want to come to games and show you up.'

'Mum,' I replied, 'if you looked like that, I wouldn't let you.' It turned out that Miss Ipswich was sitting in full view of the Norwich fans inside the ground. Mind you, she would still have been visible if she'd been at the other end. I can only assume that the rendition of 'Who ate all the pies?' (sung to the tune of 'Knees up, Mother Brown') was directed at her.

The Norwich contingent (only one or two of whom I recognised – who were all these others?) also sang 'Going down, going down'. This chant had not brought the defeat I feared at Nottingham Forest (contrary to Alternative Law No. 10, Corollary II), but it still worried me here. Similarly, although Leeds had not managed to end their bad run against us (contrary to Law 11), I had an awful feeling that Ipswich might. They hadn't won in the league for an unlucky thirteen games. I wonder if a Town fan imprudently changed his answerphone message in February.

The atmosphere was distinctly unfriendly. The City supporters all wanted revenge for the defeat in December, while the Town fans were gleefully rubbing it in, reminding us of the 2-0 result by holding up the appropriate number of fingers. Scorn was poured on Ipswich fans for failing to fill the ground ('Sell all your tickets, you couldn't sell all your tickets'), while they commented on our faded Championship hopes ('You're gonna win (very little) as usual'). I hadn't noticed such hostility at the match at Carrow Road, but that may have been because I was sitting well away from the main body of Ipswich fans; here, Mum and I were right in the middle of it all.

With all this chanting going on, the Sky 'entertainment' went almost unnoticed, though I did pick up on a couple of bizarre record choices by the club DJ. Shortly before the game, he played *All Because Of You* by Geordie and *Hi Ho Silver Lining* by Jeff Beck. It was odd enough that such old records should have been chosen – especially the obscure Geordie track from 1973 – but the really strange thing was that both of them had been played at Norwich just before the Manchester United game. Is the same DJ working at both grounds? If there is a double agent in our midst, I think we should be told.

The match was utterly gripping from the start. The intensity of the clash matched the intensity of the rivalry in the crowd; the players were every bit as committed and passionate as we were. And the best thing was that Norwich were soon on top. We didn't thump hopeful balls forward as we had in the last derby; we launched swift, sweeping attacks with excellent passing and control. We forced corner after corner and made the Ipswich defence look very shaky. Everyone in our corner of the ground belted out 'On the ball, City' as loud as possible to compensate for being so heavily outnumbered by home fans. Surely, with all this pressure and all this support, a goal had to come.

It did. To Ipswich.

Bryan Gunn, who has had an outstanding season, tried to clear a cross with his feet, but missed the ball completely and ended up on his backside, leaving Jason Dozzell with a simple tap-in. If any player should be forgiven a mistake, it is Gunn – but why did this have to happen here? Here, in front of these roaring, jeering, delirious Town fans?

After a moment's stunned silence, we carried on singing and the City players carried on attacking as if nothing had happened. We dominated the match to such an extent that I had to keep glancing at the scoreboard to confirm that Ipswich really had managed to get into our half once. Finally, three minutes before half-time, Crook curled a free kick into the Ipswich area, Sutton nodded it in, and we all went berserk. Justice had been done, revenge looked a certainty – and best of all, the Town fans looked horrified. For the first time in the evening, the scoreboard added the word 'City' to our name – an acknowledgement, I felt, of Norwich's superiority as a team and as a place to live.

Ipswich had a penalty appeal turned down in injury time (although the incident was at the other end of the pitch and someone stood up and blocked my view, I'm sure the referee was right), and we reached the interval on level terms. I don't think there was one Norwich supporter who did not feel confident that we would go on to win by several goals.

We were also unanimous in our contempt for the proceedings on the pitch at half-time. The sumo wrestlers were rightly booed off with cries of 'What a load of rubbish', while the Sky dancers who tried to boot footballs into the net and missed hopelessly were subjected to 'Are you Ipswich in disguise?'

The second half began – and I still can't fathom what happened in the next 45 minutes. Our midfielders stood off their Ipswich counterparts whereas they had been making immediate challenges in the first half. We over-elaborated and hesitated when attacking, though we had been so confident and direct before. Worst of all, the defence suffered one of its recurrent bouts of frailty.

The defending which handed Ipswich their second easy goal of the evening was criminal. The BBC should have shown it on *Crimewatch* rather than *Sportsnight*. Three or four players could have wellied the ball to safety; instead, the one Town player in the vicinity had time to fall over and get up again before putting it in the net. (Not the first time this has happened this season – see the away league game at Blackburn.) Then, for the third time in four games, we conceded another goal within two minutes.

The Ipswich fans went wild, all the more so because they were beating us. Our misery was all the deeper because we were losing to them. 'You'll never play in Europe', 'Let's all laugh at Norwich' – their jeering was as merciless as ours would have been if we were 3-1 up. It is horrible being on the receiving end of this treatment. I said earlier that there are moments of ecstasy that only football fans can experience; unfortunately, there is another side to this. (Isn't there always?) We also experience moments of unparalleled ... what? There's no one word for it. It's a mixture of humiliation, pain, anger, despair and helplessness. The proportions of each vary according to the circumstances.

Some Norwich supporters reacted by venting their frustrations on the team. 'Do you want to win?' screamed a man in front of me. Mike Walker was abused for not making immediate substitutions. Others reacted by threatening the home fans ('You'll be dead by ten to ten') and claiming to be harder. ('Ipswich run from Norwich'). This met with an equally mature response from the Ipswich sections, and the atmosphere became uglier than ever.

It was frightening to see the level of hatred that can be generated between two groups of people who do not know each other at all but see only 'the enemy'. It may well seem ridiculous to outsiders – but, of course, this phenomenon is hardly exclusive to football. It happens all the time, all over the world, in politics and religion. It depresses me greatly that such blind enmity will always be a part of life – and it worries me that I may be guilty of this to some degree. After all, my attitude towards different people is shaped to some extent by the football team whom they happen to support. On the other hand, rivalry adds spice and interest to life; it is only when it is exaggerated to unreasonable levels that it becomes dangerous.

Robins and Butterworth hit the post with headers, but these near-misses served only to underline that it was not to be our night. The last half-hour slipped away, and suddenly the game was over. The dejection of the City players showed just how much they had wanted to win.

The home fans gleefully chanted 'We beat the scum 3-1'. Some City fans replied with 'Milk Cup, Milk Cup '85', which helped me feel a little better for a moment or two. That victory still outweighs any other derby result.

We were kept inside the ground for a few minutes, supposedly to allow the police to disperse the Town fans outside. However, when we were let out, we found ourselves surrounded by jeering Ipswich supporters. The potential for trouble was obvious, so Mum and I hid our scarves and slipped unnoticed through the crowd and back to the car. Others, we discovered the next day, were not so lucky. Several were pushed around, abused and spat on. Well done, the Suffolk constabulary. The funny thing (well, not so funny, actually) is that both Norwich and Ipswich supporters have deserved reputations for being well-behaved. How come there's trouble when they meet?

Mum and I hardly spoke on the way back to Norwich. We were too shocked. How could we have lost? The match statistics on the scoreboard at the end showed how much pressure we had exerted; we had won eleven corners to Ipswich's two. We hadn't even lost to a good team, as Town's recent record proved. The euphoria we had experienced when we equalised only made defeat more painful.

Winning the Championship is now mathematically impossible. Alan Hansen and the national press were ultimately right to doubt us after all, even though we kept up our challenge far longer than anyone expected. Third place is now the best we can manage – and to get into Europe, we need Arsenal to beat Sheffield Wednesday in the FA Cup final. They beat them 2–1 in the Coca-Cola Cup final on Sunday.

Ipswich, conversely, are now virtually safe from relegation; the 'Going down' chants had had their predicted effect. Town's survival means that we will have a chance for revenge next season – but this thought provided no consolation as I drove to Mum's.

I had a terrible nightmare when I eventually managed to fall asleep that night. Everyone I know was in it – and all were wearing Ipswich shirts and laughing at me. The next morning, I couldn't stop myself from going over the game again and again in my mind. I constructed an alternative sequence of events, imagining how the game would have gone if Gunn hadn't missed the ball in the first half, if someone had cleared it instead of allowing Ipswich to score their second, if our two headers that hit the post had gone in. I stared at the result in the paper and pictured how it might have looked ... and then the reality of our defeat hit me again.

Mum took out her frustration on the garden; I wandered around the city centre in a daze. The weather was incongruously sunny – and the blue sky seemed to be offering a final taunt.

Dr Thomas Holmes, an American professor of psychiatry, once devised a rating scale to show the relative stress factors of various events in life. For example, the death of a spouse rates 100, divorce 73, being imprisoned 63, being fired at work 47 (ha!), moving home 20. Dr Holmes didn't include losing to Ipswich, but I'd guess it would carry a stress rating of around 359.

Two items in Tuesday's local paper caught my eye. A sub-head on the front page proclaimed: 'Fox "superb".' I thought this was rather odd. Ruel hadn't been that good at Portman Road. It turned out that the article was about Edward Fox, who is currently appearing at the Theatre Royal.

I also discovered belatedly that the youth team had won 2-0 at Leeds in the second leg of the FA Youth Cup semi-final. Despite this, they had lost 4-3 on aggregate. All in all, Monday night was not the greatest in the club's history.

Saturday 24 April
No Match

> Oh what a horrible morning,
> Oh what a horrible day.
> I've got a horrible feeling
> Nothing is going my way.

I've felt like this ever since Wednesday night, when Blackburn beat Villa 3-0 to move within 3 points of us with a game in hand and a far superior goal difference (isn't everyone's?). Not having a game this weekend (because of England's match against Holland next week) didn't give me a break at all; it merely prolonged the sick feeling in my stomach for several more days.

I tried to predict the likely outcome of Norwich's and Blackburn's remaining matches to assess our chances of holding on to third place in the table, but this offered no comfort. We are predictable only in our unpredictability, while Rovers' matches could go either way. They have to play Manchester United (away), Spurs (away) and Sheffield Wednesday (home) in the space of six days. Winning all of them appears unlikely on paper - but Spurs and Wednesday will have little to play for, and if Blackburn can stuff Villa, who's to say they won't get a result at Old Trafford?

We simply have to win our last two games to stand a chance of getting into Europe - and the club, realising this, is considering running a plane trip to our final fixture at Middlesbrough to encourage more supporters to go. Unfortunately, I won't be able to take advantage of this if it goes ahead, as I'm spending that weekend in Scarborough with Charlie and his family, as arranged at the end of December.

I spent this weekend in London, partly to pick up my mail (an unwelcome assortment of brown envelopes - I must start taking job-hunting a bit more seriously soon), partly because of a Capital Canaries committee meeting on Monday, but mainly to see Jane.

In the event, I didn't see her. She said she had already made other arrangements for the weekend. I should have rung her earlier in the week, I suppose, but after the Ipswich defeat I couldn't face calling anyone until Friday. Oh well. It might be a good idea to leave things until the season's over, when less of my time (and less of my mind) will be taken up by football.

There was one interesting snippet of information revealed at the committee meeting. The Capital Canaries chairman recently met Robert Fleck in a pub (surprise!) to pick up our Player of the Year shield from him. (Bryan Gunn has won it this year.) Fleck said that he expected to be sold by Chelsea soon, as he has had a less than successful season there, and also mentioned that he loves Norfolk and intends to return to live there some day. Hmm. Are you thinking what I'm thinking?

The main football story on Monday, however, was Brian Clough's resignation from his position as manager of Nottingham Forest. All sorts of people paid tribute to him on the TV and radio. They should have asked Mum what she thought about it.

Saturday 1 May
Liverpool (home)

I gave Jon a lift when I drove back to Norwich on Friday afternoon. Predictably, much of the journey was spent discussing the possibility of Blackburn pipping us for third place in the league. I'm not sure whether voicing our fears to each other did us any good; I suspect that any therapeutic effect this might have had was outweighed by the new worries we were left with as we both brought up concerns which had not occurred to the other.

For example, I wanted Villa to beat Oldham on Sunday afternoon so that United would have to go all out for the win against Blackburn on Monday night; Jon, on the other hand, feared that this might make United tense up and accordingly wanted Oldham to beat Villa to hand United the title so that they could face Blackburn in a relaxed, confident frame of mind. Not only was I still worried about the Villa-Oldham result, I was now worried that I didn't know what I wanted the result to be.

'Do Blackburn have to play Spurs at home or away?' Jon asked.

'They're at White Hart Lane next Wednesday,' I said.

'Hmm, I might go along to that and shout for Spurs.' I won't be joining him. I once went to a match between two other teams hoping for a result that would suit Norwich, and it was terrible when the outcome was the wrong one. It was the Coventry-Luton game in 1985, the second of the three matches that Coventry had to win to stay up and send us down.

'I went to the Coventry-Everton game that settled it all,' said Jon when I mentioned this. 'That must have been even worse.'

'Quite. So why risk going to see Spurs and Blackburn?'

'Well, I went to the Oxford-Arsenal game at the end of the '85-'86 season where the result sent Ipswich down, and that was a great day.'

Since Jon had mentioned Ipswich, I asked him what he thought of the atmosphere at Portman Road last week. Back in December, I said that the rivalry between Norwich and Ipswich was not all that bitter, but since the game there last Monday, I have been wondering whether I might have underestimated the animosity that exists. Perhaps I have been leading a sheltered life all these years. Jon reckoned that these derby matches were as acrimonious as any in the country.

'Oh. In that case, do you think this mutual loathing is innate, or do people fall into it because they feel it's an attitude expected of them as a true supporter of their club?'

'I'm not sure that really matters,' said Jon. 'Whether it's inborn or acquired, the feeling eventually becomes so strong that its existence is all that counts.' I tried to explain that it isn't Ipswich I hate, but the feeling of humiliation at losing to them. I'm not sure Jon went along with this, but then he works for a company based in Ipswich and has to put up with several Town fans in the office. (So why work there?)

On Saturday morning, my free taxi service was again in demand as Karen asked me to give her a lift to her all-day child-minding course. 'I don't know how I'm going to get through the day,' she said.

'What do you mean?' I exclaimed. 'You've got four kids already. This will be a piece of cake for you.'

'I don't mean that the course will be difficult,' she explained. 'I won't know how City are getting on during the afternoon. I'll never be able to concentrate.' She may not have been able to get to any matches lately, what with her new baby requiring a lot of attention, but she clearly hasn't lost any of her interest in football.

Nor has her daughter Joanna, come to that, and for that reason I'm not in her good books at the moment. I thought she was going to a party this Saturday and didn't get her a ticket for the Liverpool game. By the time my mistake had been pointed out, all the tickets had been sold. I felt guilty about this – but not guilty enough to let her have my ticket. I suggested to Karen that we should try to stop Joanna finding out the game was taking place, but somehow she had already found out about it. The realisation that she wouldn't be able to go again for another three or four months made me even less popular in her eyes.

My own mood wasn't exactly cheerful on Saturday morning. They say that tension affects different people in different ways. Sometimes it can affect the same person in different ways. On this occasion, I didn't sit on the toilet for two hours; I became as snappy and irritable as a crocodile with toothache. Mum and Stephen gave me a wide berth, though they did intervene as we walked to the ground to persuade me not to try asking a couple of Liverpool fans for money to mind their car.

The mood at Carrow Road seemed relaxed and summery, the team shirts being worn by many of the City supporters looking like Hawaiian shirts in the bright sunshine. I, perverse to the last, wore my yellow and green scarf.

The occasion, the last home match of the season, reminded me of the end of a school year. There was a prize-giving ceremony, with head boy Bryan Gunn receiving two Player of the Year awards (not including the one from Capital Canaries). Special treats were given out, with 250 footballs being kicked into the crowd. But above all, there was a sense of disbelief that the end had come. I thought back to all the midweek trips from London that I had made during the season. All that effort seemed a long time ago now.

The big difference between this and the end of a school year was that I used to be delirious when the summer term ended, but here I was sad that this would be my last time inside the ground for months. On top of this, I was still terribly tense, as if I were waiting for my examination results – a feeling which I only used to experience several weeks after the end of school.

The Norwich players were greeted by a standing ovation as they came out on to the pitch. It was thoroughly merited, of course, but rather spoiled by the fact that the club announcer had called for it. Such a gesture has to be spontaneous to be meaningful. There wasn't a great deal of noise after that, though I couldn't tell whether this was because people were sunbathing and couldn't be bothered to shout, or because everyone else was biting their fingernails like me. I only discovered the reason for Mum's quietness at half-time, when she revealed that, for the first ten minutes of the game, she hadn't been able to see the ball for a large black spot in front of her eyes. It seems that she'd been on the point of fainting for all that time, possibly because it was so warm, but she hadn't told me. This was very selfless of her – or did she realise that I probably wouldn't have done anything to help until the interval?

The Liverpool fans made as little noise as they had at Anfield. There was the inventive chant of 'Liverpool, Liverpool', but that was about it. Perhaps they were demoralised at the imminent prospect of Manchester United becoming champions.

Liverpool enjoyed a lot of possession during the first half, which worried me greatly at the time; it was only afterwards that I realised that they did nothing with the ball when they had it. City made more chances, the clearest being when Sutton ran on to a through-ball but was hauled down by David James, the Liverpool keeper, just outside the area. There were shouts of 'Off! Off!', as most Norwich supporters saw this as a professional foul, but the referee showed only the yellow card. I assumed that this was because he considered that Sutton was not heading directly towards the goal. Those around me had different ideas and made chicken noises at the ref for the rest of the half.

During the break, I had a look at the programme and learned that Ian Butterworth is to open a sports shop in Norwich during the summer. It's to be called 'Run, Kick and Jump'. I wonder if John Fashanu's thinking of opening one called 'Shove, Trip and Thump'.

There was also an article on the club stewards, in which one of them remarked, 'We still find people arriving late who expect to be able to sit with their friends as when people stood and they often used to wander around to chat to different people.' What? People wanting to sit with friends and talk to others? I trust that the stewards will use all the means at their disposal to stamp out such reprehensible practices.

The second half continued where the first had left off, with Norwich playing well and making more chances. It seemed as though the Liverpool players now thought their best chance of scoring was to throw themselves to the ground in the Norwich area and appeal for a penalty – though when Paul Stewart tried this, he earned only a mouthful from Rob Newman and a chorus of 'Same old Scousers, cheating again'. Both players were also booked.

In fact, it was Norwich who won a penalty, though in the most bizarre circumstances. John Polston challenged the Liverpool keeper James for a cross from a corner kick. James caught the ball, but promptly turned round and kicked Polston on the shin in full view of the referee. Amid loud laughter and choruses of 'Cheerio, cheerio', he was sent off – and, to our delight, the ref pointed to the penalty spot. Phillips stepped up and duly scored to atone for Bowen's missed spotkick at Anfield earlier in the season.

Carrow Road erupted – though the girl wearing a Liverpool scarf who was sitting next to Stephen burst into tears. This struck me as being a touch excessive. After all, the game wasn't that important for Liverpool. What on earth does she do when they lose a crucial game? When Stephen checked his Golden Goal ticket, however, he almost burst into tears. He was ten seconds away from both the time of the goal and a hundred pounds. His bad luck had continued to the very end.

In retrospect, we saw out the last half-hour reasonably comfortably, though it didn't seem so easy at the time. Ian Crook tried to lighten the mood by volleying a shot over the top of the Barclay stand – a phenomenal feat which he acknowledged by signalling a 'six' – but I would have felt much more relaxed if just one of the chances created by Ekoku (brought on as a sub for the last twenty minutes) could have been converted.

At last, after Alan Hansen's onanistic tendencies had been proclaimed around Carrow Road for the final time this season, the referee brought the game to an end. Mike Walker and the players were given another standing ovation – unprompted this time – for winning the game and providing us with a fabulous nine months. For most of the crowd, this was the last chance to show their appreciation. But for me, the season is far from over. There is still the game at Middlesbrough to come – and if we do hang on to third place, the outcome of the FA Cup final may send us into Europe.

After saying 'See you in August' to all those sitting around us, Mum, Stephen and I made our way up Jimmy Hill for the last time for three months. The sun was still shining, there was a carpet of pink blossom beneath our feet, and all was well with the world. I thought Mum would feel even happier at the news that Nottingham Forest had been relegated, but this did not seem to hold much interest for her now that Brian Clough has resigned.

I didn't ring Gary or Brian, the two Liverpool supporters I know, to gloat about the result. I haven't spoken to Gary since I lost my job, and there's no point in jeopardising my place in the Sunday team next season by antagonising Brian. And anyway, they'll know.

Sunday morning was spoiled by the Sunday papers. The match report in the *Observer* was almost exclusively about Liverpool, while Brian Glanville in the *People* concluded that our success this season indicated that the standard of the Premier League had been poor: 'The fact that as limited a team as Norwich has been there or thereabouts for so much of the season is a comment in itself.'

I predicted this sort of half-baked comment months ago, but I was still furious to see it in print. Come the great day, Glanville will be lined up against the wall with David Lacey, Alan Hansen, and the entire sports department of Radio 5.

Villa surprisingly lost 1-0 at home to Oldham on Sunday afternoon, which confirmed United as champions. I didn't feel anything at all about this; neither resentful because I've never liked United, nor envious because we might have won the title. The Championship no longer concerns me. What matters now is finishing third ahead of Blackburn.

I couldn't face the prospect of following Monday evening's United-Blackburn game on the radio, so I went to the pictures to try to take my mind off it. It didn't work, of course. I sat inside the cinema looking at my watch and wondering what was happening. As soon as the credits began to roll, I shot out of the door and dashed home. 'Go on, tell me the worst,' I said to Mum.

'No,' she replied. 'I've recorded *Match of the Day*. You'll have to watch that.'

'Look, you might as well tell me. I'll look it up on Teletext anyway.'

'All right, all right, calm down. United won 3-1.' Yesss!! I punched the air and kissed the dog. Or was it the other way round? We are almost safe now – and will be completely safe if Blackburn fail to win at Spurs on Wednesday night.

Saturday 8 May
Middlesbrough (away)

Since my strategy of avoiding all news of the United-Blackburn game on Monday produced such a happy outcome, I decided to pursue the same policy on Wednesday. I didn't go out this time, but watched TV at Mum's, somehow resisting the temptation to check the latest score on Teletext. I've no idea what we watched – as on Monday night, all I could think about was the game I was avoiding. I kept telling myself that Blackburn would be tired after Monday's match, that Spurs would want to win their last home fixture of the season, that they'd thrashed us 5-1 and would surely be able to deny Rovers victory.

At quarter to ten, I finally looked up the result. It hit me like a juggernaut. Spurs 1 Blackburn 2. Shit, shit, shit, shit, shit. They were only 3 points behind again. I had almost convinced myself that we would be safe in third place by now, and we weren't. I had looked forward to being able to relax and enjoy the game at Middlesbrough, and now I couldn't.

I worked myself up into such a state of anxiety that Mum began to fear that my few remaining shreds of sanity were crumbling away. I had a splitting headache when I went to bed – and it was still there when I woke up again at 2am. I couldn't get to sleep again as I was still consumed with worry about being caught by Blackburn. In the darkness of my room and in my half-conscious state, I could see how everything would go wrong on Saturday. Blackburn would beat Sheffield Wednesday easily, as: a) they are having a good run; b) Wednesday would not be exerting themselves with the FA Cup final next week; and c) Rovers would be out for revenge, as Wednesday beat them in the semi-final of the Coca-Cola Cup. We, on the other hand, would lose to Middlesbrough, as: a) they would be able to relax and enjoy the game, being relegated already; and b) the nerves of the City players would be as taut as piano wire.

I felt no happier in the morning. I looked at the league table and hoped that there had been a mistake in adding up the points, but of course there hadn't. If only we could have got one more point from somewhere – at Ipswich, for instance – we would now be safe and would even have a chance of pipping Villa for second place.

I rang the club to see if the plane trip to Middlesbrough was going ahead, as Mum and Karen were interested in flying up. I was told that it was, but that tickets would only be sold to regular Club Cabbage travellers whose names were on a list they had compiled. Neither Mum nor I appeared on the list, so Mum and Karen decided to stay at home, the possibility of a six-hour journey home after a defeat deterring them from travelling up by coach.

I drove up to Scarborough on Friday afternoon, by now in a terrible state. I looked drawn, my skin was punctuated with pimples, and I had hardly eaten in two days. (What you might call an F-for-Fear-Plan diet.) I couldn't see beyond Saturday's game; it was like the run-up to exams at school, when I could never conceive of life continuing after they had finished. What was I driving towards? Euphoria or devastating disappointment? I thought again that I could have been happy if Blackburn hadn't won at Spurs – and, for a moment, I envied the supporters of clubs a little further down the league who had nothing at stake on Saturday. I quickly realised, though, that our position was preferable and that I ought to be grateful to be in this nerve-racking situation.

I'm not sure Charlie was all that pleased that I had come to stay when he saw how stressed I was. He had been looking forward to seeing the team for only the second time this season, but now I was making him feel tense.

We didn't talk much on the way to the game on Saturday, though I remember that we both booed when a woman phoning in on Radio 5 to take part in a quiz revealed herself to be an Ipswich supporter. Still, she did say that she wished Ipswich and Norwich could both have been at the top of the league, as this would have been good for East Anglia. This, I thought, confirmed my original opinion that most City and Town fans are not fiercely hostile towards each other. All the same, I did think how funny it would be if Ipswich were to be relegated later that afternoon. It would require an unlikely combination of results, but it was possible. We would be deprived of the chance to exact our revenge in the league next season – but I could live with that.

For the last time this season, I looked around for omens of success. Charlie had a yellow jumper on, while mine was green – but, though this had not been planned, it was hardly a strange coincidence. More striking was the number of bright yellow oil-seed rape fields between Scarborough and Middlesbrough. And the clearest indication that fortune was with us was when we parked the car in a back street near the ground and discovered that it was called Norwich Road.

Ayresome Park (what does 'Ayresome' mean, by the way? Is it an adjective? 'You look particularly ayresome in the moonlight, Penelope ... ') has an unglamorous, old-fashioned air about it, but it is no less agreeable for that. Approached through narrow streets of terraced houses, it offers a reminder that football is essentially a game of the people, not of corporate sponsors or legislators who want to take it up-market. There are no imposing new stands or executive boxes. There is no electronic scoreboard, nor even a hand-operated A-Z half-times board alongside the pitch. There was no clock to be seen either. I did notice, however, a tatty sign offering Middlesbrough congratulations on reaching the Premier League. You'd think someone would have discreetly taken it down during the week.

The Norwich fans – around 1,500 of us, I'd say – were packed into a tiny open terrace and a few seats at one corner of the ground. Charlie and I found ourselves on the front row of seats, with our heads virtually at pitch level. This made our view bad enough, but there was also a steward in front of us who spent most of the match opening and closing a large gate to let the police and other stewards move around. Why? Where were they going?

The mood among the City supporters was mixed. Some were as tense as I was. Others had decided, out of confidence or defiance, that they were going to have an end-of-season party and enjoy themselves anyway. Balloons, beach balls, and even an inflatable sheep were tossed around. Several fans had come up from Norwich in fancy dress. The Pink Panther, Donald Duck and Robin Hood were there, and I also spotted a monk, an escaped convict and a man in drag (who looked a bit hard, so I didn't dare laugh).

The game was only a few minutes old when one of the lads behind me tried to start a rumour that Blackburn were already 4-0 down. Being too improbable to take seriously, this helped to ease my anxiety a little. And the team soon went one step better. Ekoku (in the team in place of Robins) was put through for the second time in the first fifteen minutes. For the second time, his shot was saved – but he thumped the rebound into the net and we all went wild, dancing around for joy.

The police moved into the Norwich sections, but soon realised that no one was causing any trouble and duly left again. The Middlesbrough police are actually OK. Once when I travelled up from Birmingham by train, they gave me a lift back to the railway station in a police van after the game – and no, I hadn't done anything wrong.

Norwich should have gone on to dominate the game, but inexplicably eased off and handed the initiative to Boro. They hit the bar as a warning and followed this up with a goal after half an hour when Gunn dropped the ball.

'You're not singing any more,' chanted the home fans.

'Any more, any more, any more,' came the reply.

A group of cheeky Middlesbrough fans, aged around 11 or 12, came over and sat in the seats on the other side of a low dividing fence. 'Ah hoape yuz doan't get into Europe,' said one, 'cause yuz woan't represent England very well.'

'At least we can speak the language, bonny lad,' replied a City fan behind me.

The team's performance over the last twenty minutes of the first half left me as worried as ever at the interval. Charlie tried to keep me calm, pointing out that a 1-1 draw would be good enough for us and that, with Blackburn drawing 0-0, we effectively had a two-goal cushion going into the last 45 minutes of the season. I think he intended the phrase '45 minutes' to seem short, but it sounded like an eternity to me.

Someone nearby suggested that we should all start whistling for the end of the match as soon as the teams came out for the second half. Before the referee did blow the final whistle, however, we had to endure a roller-coaster ride of emotions that left me feeling sick rather than exhilarated.

First, I felt desperately frustrated at the way Norwich continued to give the ball away and stand off the Boro players as they knocked it around. Mike Walker's half-time talk surely couldn't have been 'Take it easy and help yourselves to these cream buns, lads', but that's the way it was looking. I alternated between screaming for more effort and clutching my head with anguished cries of 'Jesus Christ, Jesus Christ'.

The few fragments of reasoned conversation concerned Andy Johnson, the young midfielder who was in our starting line-up for the first time this season. I mentioned John Faulkner's remark that he would stake his house on Johnson making it to the top. 'So how long has he been sleeping on the streets?' asked the man sitting on my left. This was rather harsh, but it was true that Johnson was finding it difficult to get into the game. Everything seemed to be passing him by, and it was generally agreed that he should be substituted.

'It's lucky we're only playing Middlesbrough today,' my neighbour continued. But even though it was 'only' Middlesbrough, we were clearly in trouble. Boro hit the bar again – and, as in the first half, this was the prelude to a goal. When Wilkinson's header went in, I was filled with horror. My worst fears had been realised. I could see the whole season's work going down the toilet. Our misery was compounded by the sneering and mockery of the young Boro fans only a few feet away. They must be junior members of the Middlesbrough branch of the Dangerous Sports Club. They got away with their jeering on this occasion as Norwich fans are very restrained, but I can think of several clubs whose followers would not have stood for this and would have rewarded them with a smack in the mouth.

Then the news filtered through that Blackburn had gone 1-0 up (scorer: Tim 'Rubbish' Sherwood – who else?). So much for our two-goal cushion. I was in a blind panic by now, as we didn't look likely to score at all.

Yet, extraordinarily, we did. Twice. In two minutes. When Ekoku nodded the ball home after Sutton's majestic header had hit the bar, there was enormous relief. And when Johnson – yes, the player I had wanted to see taken off – brilliantly volleyed us into the lead, the Norwich corner was ecstatic. In just three minutes, we had experienced the deepest despair and the greatest elation. Can anything other than football – and hard drugs, I guess – offer such extremes so close together?

I thought we had to be safe now – but the drama wasn't over yet. With fifteen minutes to go, Boro equalised again, and we were racked with worry once more. By now there was no pattern or shape to the game, as both sides frantically sought a winner. The only respite came when Newman hoofed the ball clean out of the ground.

The police came and stood in front of our section, which would have been a welcome sign that the match was almost over, except that we were so low down, we now couldn't see what was going on. 'Hey, we watch *The Bill* three times a week as it is,' yelled one man. 'We haven't paid twelve quid to watch it here.'

After we had apparently missed an open goal (though I couldn't identify the culprit because of a not-so-thin member of the thin blue line), and after approximately three hours and 57 minutes of injury time, the referee finally signalled the end of the match.

This was the cue for wild celebrations. I was surrounded by singing, dancing, clapping, beaming fans. I cheered and applauded too, but inside I still felt terrible. I was hoarse and exhausted after the ups and downs of the game, and though we had secured the point we came for, all I could think about was those three minutes when we were 2-1 down and we peered down into the abyss of oblivion. Was it because fear and terror make a greater impact on us than joy can? Or was this yet another indication of what a miserable bloke I am?

Mike Walker and the City players came over to us. Some threw their shirts into the crowd, while Bryan Gunn gave away his boots (poo!) and a pair of gloves. 'We're all going on a European tour' was sung again and again, until it was remembered that this was somewhat premature and 'Arsenal, Arsenal' replaced it.

Circumstances can prompt the most unlikely temporary allegiances. This was the first time I had ever heard Norwich fans voicing support for the Gunners. The season has now turned full circle. On the first day back in August, we joyfully celebrated a 4-2 win over Arsenal; now, nine months later, we find ourselves wanting them to win their last match. As I write this, I feel quite relaxed about the final – partly because I am so relieved that we did our bit by finishing third, partly because I feel more confident that Arsenal will win a European place for us than I would if we were in the final ourselves. (What an indictment of my team!) Come next Saturday, though, I'll probably be just as tense as I was at Middlesbrough.

Back at the car, Charlie and I listened to Radio 5 to hear what had been going on around the country. Oldham had managed to stay up, sending Crystal Palace down instead. I thought of my old Palace-supporting friend. Doubtless he would be saying how unlucky they had been as usual – though, for once, he probably had a point. I would have liked Palace to stay up for purely selfish reasons: it is much quicker for me to get to Selhurst Park than to Oldham. West Ham have been promoted, which is handy – but so have Newcastle, which will mean another long trek next season. There was little or no mention of our game in the national media, however. I was offended that a match that had been so important to me should be ignored, while the supposed managerial crisis at Liverpool received no end of attention.

Mum and Karen, I learned later, had spent most of the afternoon deliberately avoiding reports on the game. Mum went to the bingo and then for a wander around the shops (steering clear of TV showrooms), while Karen did some ironing wearing headphones connected to the hi-fi so as not to overhear the score accidentally. However, neither had been able to resist turning the radio on to listen to the last ten minutes of the commentary on a local radio station. 'I'm glad I didn't go to the game now,' Mum said. 'I think I'd have had heart failure if it was as nerve-racking as it sounded.' I confirmed that, for once, it was.

On Sunday morning, I was quietly unwinding and savouring our success when Charlie reminded me that, but for a couple of bad results recently, we would have been preparing to play Middlesbrough in a bid to win the title on Sunday afternoon. (Sky would have rescheduled the game.) 'Just think how nervous you'd have been then,' he said.

'I wouldn't have been as nervous as I was yesterday,' I protested uncertainly. 'We would have had everything to gain in that case, but yesterday we could only lose.'

'That's rubbish. You'd have gone to pieces if the title were at stake.' Who can tell? Perhaps we'll see next year.

Later, as I prepared to travel back to London, Charlie's wife asked when I was likely to visit again. 'It could be years', Charlie interjected. 'Now that Middlesbrough have gone down, he'll have no reason to come and see us.'

'Oh, come on,' I said. 'We might get drawn at Scarborough in one of the cups.'

Once I had arrived back at my flat, unpacked my things and settled down with a cup of tea, I was suddenly struck by the most obvious fact. All of our games were now over. I would not see the team play again for another three months. I had been so preoccupied with the Middlesbrough result that I had forgotten that it was our final fixture.

It has, of course, been a wonderful season. At the outset, I (in common with most Norwich fans) feared a dour struggle against relegation, but the team's performances have exceeded all our expectations. We have achieved our highest-ever final position in the league, finishing ahead of many 'bigger' clubs with far greater financial resources – oh, and Ipswich – and may yet be playing in Europe next season. Our hopes of winning the Championship were sustained until early April, and we should not feel that we have failed because the ultimate prize finally slipped away from us. To quote Robert Louis Stevenson, 'to travel hopefully is a better thing than to arrive'. Yes, it would have been marvellous to arrive, but we should thank the players and manager for allowing us to dream for so much of the journey. I suppose I have to give Chairman Chase some credit too, as he appointed Mike Walker and recognised that Robert Fleck was not essential to the success of the team – though there is still a stubbornly graceless part of me that feels that he made the correct decisions by luck rather than judgement.

There have been many memorable moments along the way: the astonishing comeback at Arsenal; the hilarity at Chelsea; the 'deep emotional experience' at home to Crystal Palace; the brilliant win at home to Aston Villa (even better than the one away). These will stay with me for ever. There were awful moments as well, of course (the Ipswich games, the Spurs games, the crunch game with United and the disaster at Blackburn), but they were heavily outweighed by the good ones – even though we did end up with a negative goal difference, the first time this century that a team has finished in the top three with one.

On top of the team's achievements, I have had great fun over the past months. There have been countless jokes in the crowd at matches, with supporters of other teams at work, with my team-mates on cold Sunday mornings in West London, and with the rest of the family almost constantly. Another member of the family has been introduced to the game, and there are still three more on Karen's child production line to be phased in over the next few seasons.

You will have noticed that I have made little or no mention of being herded around like animals, of random violence, of disgusting anti-social behaviour or of racist chants. This is not because I have edited out such incidents; there has simply been very little to report. I am particularly pleased about the lack of racist shouts, as they were worryingly common until recently, even with black players in our team. There were the spitting incidents when the upper tier of the Barclay Stand was briefly given to away supporters, and I heard of some trouble at the Ipswich games and the home match against Manchester United, but they are all I know of and I didn't even witness them myself.

I am not claiming that football in general is now free of trouble-makers; I realise that I am lucky to follow a team whose supporters are particularly well-behaved and who generally arouse little hostility among followers of other clubs. However, I have detected a markedly less belligerent attitude among football followers in the last few years. Even over the course of this season, the frequency of 'sheepshagger' taunts directed at Norwich fans has dropped dramatically. There seems to be a wider realisation that fans have more common interests and similarities than differences. Rivalries are usually expressed through humour rather than with boots and knives. Add to this more congenial atmosphere the improved facilities at most grounds (though the catering standards are still poor, regrettably), and you have to say that following a football team around the country has never been more enjoyable.

Lest you think that I have become a misty-eyed old fool at this late stage, however, I should point out that I am still as angry as ever about several aspects of our game. I am still against all-seater stadia (overall, I think there has been less atmosphere at Carrow Road this season because of the loss of the terraces). The back-pass rule is as ridiculous as it seemed back in August, yet FIFA are to go a step further and experiment with their even more stupid 'kick-ins' at a youth tournament. The influence of Sky television on the game has been dreadful. The extra money received by the club did not compensate for the tacky razzmatazz, the constant rescheduling of matches resulting in an unacceptable number of blank Saturdays, or the fact that so few people around the country have seen us play during our best season ever. It wasn't 'a whole new ball game' at all. The Premier League was just like the old First Division, dressed up with a whole new load of balls.

Finally, the attitudes of the national media towards Norwich were nothing short of disgusting. They ranged from patronising to dismissive to downright rude, with more than a dash of indignation at the effrontery of these 'Norfolk turkeys' for having ideas above their station. May the dung of a thousand camels land on all those concerned from a great height.

Following the team around has cost me an awful lot over the last nine months. I have travelled over ten thousand miles and spent – well, I've no idea how much exactly, but it must be well into four figures. And I lost my job. Yet I don't regret a bit of it. If I had the year again, I wouldn't have done anything differently – and how often can you honestly say that?

Saturday 15 May
Arsenal v Sheffield Wednesday
FA CUP FINAL

OK, so I do have one regret about last year. And yes, she lives in Wolverhampton. But perhaps it just goes to show that some things do not come to a clear and definite end as the football season does.

Then again, some things do. I saw Jane during the week and discovered that she has been going out with a lifeguard for a couple of weeks. A lifeguard! What can she see in him? Then again, having seen *Baywatch* ... It sounds as though she met him on that weekend when I tried to see her but failed because I was late ringing her as a result of my post-Ipswich depression. Once again, football has wrecked my love life before it has begun.

This wasn't my biggest concern of the week, though. As I suspected I would, I grew more and more anxious about the FA Cup final as the week progressed. I wondered whether I would find it all too much to watch the match live on television. Should I take myself off to the pictures for the afternoon? In the end, I decided that it would be cowardly to scuttle off to the cinema – not to mention pointless, as I couldn't relax when I avoided the United-Blackburn game in this way. I sat in my flat on my own, with the blinds down and the phone off the hook.

The City players apparently gathered to watch the match in a bar in the Cayman Islands, where they are currently on tour/holiday. During the week, it was announced that they have won this season's Fair Play Award for being the most sporting team in the Premier League. Despite this, I couldn't help wondering how clean their language would be if Sheffield Wednesday won the final.

As the game kicked off at three o'clock on Saturday afternoon, I told myself that our fate would finally be decided by five. This didn't make me feel any better, though. I've never been so tense watching a game that: a) was a load of crap; and b) didn't feature Norwich. (What makes me think that a) and b) are related?) I watched most of it through my fingers.

When Ian Wright scored for Arsenal midway through the first half, I leapt up and punched the air. I wish the ceiling in my flat was a bit higher. Well, a fist-shaped bit of it is now.

By half-time, I was starting to feel confident. We were now 45 minutes from Europe. Then the panel of pundits on the box said they couldn't see Arsenal conceding a goal, and I knew we were in trouble. Sure enough, Wednesday came out and dominated the second half, equalising on the hour. I hurt my foot kicking the sofa.

I could see our European place slipping away, but although Arsenal continued to sit back and gave the ball to Wednesday time and again, they somehow managed to reach full-time with the score still 1-1. Right, I thought, I'll definitely know our fate by 5:30.

No, I didn't. After thirty minutes of extra-tense extra time, the issue still hadn't been resolved. I felt exhausted – and now I will have to go through the same ordeal during the replay on Thursday evening. Oh God, what will I do if it goes to penalties? I'll be a gibbering wreck.

I didn't watch the Eurovision Song Contest on Saturday night. Apart from the fact that the songs are rubbish, I couldn't face watching Sonia play in Europe when I still didn't know whether we would get the chance.

Thursday 20 May
Arsenal v Sheffield Wednesday
FA CUP FINAL REPLAY

Agony, agony, agony. On top of the extra five days of waiting to see whether we would be in the UEFA Cup next season, there was a further delay to endure as the kick-off of the FA Cup final replay was put back by half an hour. This was because an accident on the M1 had delayed many of the Sheffield Wednesday fans travelling down to Wembley. 'Sod them!' I shouted at the television. 'Start the match before they get there!' It's frightening the way your sense of right and wrong can disappear when you are really desperate.

When the game did get underway at 8pm, it followed the dreary pattern of Saturday's encounter. Both sides played it tight and closed each other down relentlessly. There were a few less-than-legal challenges, the worst being when Mark Bright elbowed our old boy Andy Linighan in the face, apparently breaking his nose. 'Send him off!' I screamed at the screen, but the referee didn't hear me.

Arsenal started to get on top. Paul Merson shot weakly when he had been put clean through (provoking more abuse in my commentary box), but after thirty minutes Ian Wright gave the Gunners the lead just as he had on Saturday. Yeeesss!! I reacted just as I had on Saturday. Still, I don't suppose it will take much longer to repair two dents in the ceiling than one. Soon after, Alan Smith almost made it 2-0, but I realised in mid-air that he had hit the side netting.

Half-time arrived, and we were in the same position as we had been in the first game. Forty-five minutes from Europe. This time things just had to be different. I did my bit by not making a cup of tea and going to the toilet as I had last time – but as I sat there, parched and bursting, I saw my sacrifices being nullified by the 'experts' again saying how difficult it would be for Wednesday to get back into the game. They kept this up during the second half and, of course, Sheffield equalised. The fact that Waddle's shot took a deflection before flying into the net made the blow all the more cruel. I held my head in horror. Our future was in the balance again. Did Karen still think Waddle was 'dead horny'? I bet she didn't.

After that, it was all Wednesday. Bright missed a virtually open goal a minute later, and Arsenal went to pieces. They did, however, manage one decent chance five minutes from time when Merson shot, Chris Woods in the Wednesday goal dived to save it, and the ball disappeared under his body. It reappeared behind him and seemed to be trickling towards the goal-line, but Woods turned round and grabbed it in the nick of time. Blast.

Extra time again. It was now 10pm. I could hardly bear to watch by this stage – yet I couldn't bring myself to turn the TV off or walk away. Smith missed a good chance for Arsenal. Bright's head was millimetres away from connecting with a Waddle cross for Wednesday. In fact, he seemed to get closer to the ball every time an action replay was shown. The clock ticked off the minutes, and the prospect of a penalty shoot-out loomed.

The commentators discussed whether penalties were a satisfactory way to decide an FA Cup final. I didn't know about that, but I did know that they weren't a satisfactory way to decide our season. After all the games we'd played, after all the miles I'd travelled, the thought that the ultimate success of the campaign could be determined by such a lottery was appalling.

Before I had realised, it was the very last minute of the match. The clock in my room showed 10:32pm. Arsenal won two or three throw-ins on the far side of the pitch, and though they didn't manage to 'hoof the bastard ball into the box' as I entreated them, they did win a corner.

At this point, I said a prayer. It wasn't addressed to God specifically, but was intended for any divine spirits with an interest in football who might be listening. Nor did I put my hands together and close my eyes; I clenched my fists and hissed, 'Please let Arsenal score. Please let us be in Europe' – and then, egoistically – 'Please let something go right for me for once.' We had kept our hopes alive with two goals out of the blue at Middlesbrough; couldn't we have just one more here? I also thought of how Arsenal had won the league in 1988-89 with a last-minute goal in the final game at Liverpool. If they could do it then, couldn't they do it now?

The next few seconds seemed to happen in slow motion. The corner kick came over. Yes, it was a good one. No, Woods wasn't going to come out and catch it. Then I spotted Andy Linighan moving in for a header. He rose and connected firmly with the ball, despite his painful nose. Yes, the header was on target. Woods, another former Norwich player (how fitting that our destiny should be decided by two old boys), flung himself to his left and got a hand to the ball, though he didn't seem to stop it properly. There was a split-second of uncertainty which seemed to last for ever. Had the ball crossed the line or not? It only became clear when a Wednesday defender tried to hook the ball clear but succeeded only in hacking it into the roof of the net.

I levitated magically off the sofa and jumped around the room, knocking over a table and sending a mug of cold tea flying against the wall. Yelling loud enough for Mum to hear me in Norwich, I fell to my knees and threw my arms up like the soldier in the poster for the film *Platoon*. We were in Europe! We were in Europe! And a former City player had put us there! Was this another example of Robert Chase's astonishing foresight/luck? Did he sell Linighan to Arsenal three years ago knowing that this was going to happen?

I looked around me at the mess I had made of the room and hoped that my landlord wouldn't decide to pay me a surprise visit in the next few days.

The game restarted – and there was just enough time for one last panic attack by Wednesday and for me. They won a corner, and I feared the worst. Were we to be denied after all? That would be the cruellest blow. The cross came over ... but it was cleared! There's a bald git jumping on the sofa, he thinks it's all over. It is now!

I picked up the telephone and, before the caption confirming the final score had disappeared from the TV screen, I was shouting down the phone at Mum and she was shouting back. Somehow she had known it would be me calling. 'I take it you're happy,' she said.

We were both too short of breath to speak for long. And what was there to say apart from 'YEEEEEAAAAAHHHHHOOOOO!!!!'? For once, I regretted not being a drinker – but even if I were, it was now too late to go out and celebrate. Quarter to eleven on a Thursday night – what a strange time for everything to be settled.

I just sat there for a couple of hours with a stupid grin on my face (apart from the odd bout of dancing around the flat singing 'We're all going on a European tour' and 'Europe, Europe, here we come') and tried to let it all sink in. We'd made it. And although we had had to rely on Arsenal to clinch our place, we deserved it – not just for the past season, but also for the number of times we had missed out before. We qualified by winning the Milk Cup in 1985 but were denied the chance to play by the ban on English clubs following the Heysel disaster, and since then we have finished fourth and fifth in the league – positions which used to be good enough to bring qualification in the years before the ban when England had four places in the UEFA Cup.

I travelled back to Norwich on Friday to savour the mood in the city and share in the celebrations with the family. I lapped up all the coverage of our success in the local papers and on the local news programmes, wherein Arsenal's achievement in winning two trophies was considered to be significant only in that it had helped us. I felt that I should do something to commemorate the occasion, so on Saturday morning I went down to the club shop and bought ... a team shirt! It seemed an appropriate choice, since the change in my attitude towards the design mirrored the change in my expectations of the team since the start of the season. I just hope the club doesn't bring out a new shirt before the start of next season.

Saturday afternoon was dreadfully dull. For the first time in nine months, I had no football to watch or think about. What made it worse was the knowledge that I have another twelve or thirteen weekends like this to endure before next season begins. You would think that all the free Saturdays we had during this season would have prepared me for this break, but I fear they haven't.

Yes, summer is here. And how I hate it.

> Sumer is icumen in,
> Lhude sing O pu!
> Waspes stingeth, cricket lingreth
> And haye fevere tu.
> Sing: Bu-hu!

It's the longest, bleakest period of the year. How on earth am I going to fill it? Even I can't spend three months dreaming of Europe.

There will be a few internationals and play-off matches on the box over the next couple of weeks, but these will hardly interest or satisfy me. Nor will I get worked up about the Australian matches on the pools coupons. Unless I win, of course. But how can you take them seriously when the teams have such silly names? I bet that even the fans of the teams are too embarrassed to use them in songs ...

> We hate Nunawading,
> We hate Wanneroo,
> We hate bloody Mooroolbark,
> But Dandenong we love you!

See what I mean?

There is talk of the team parading through the city on an open-top bus and being given a civic reception to mark the season's achievements. That should be a good day if and when it happens. And it shouldn't be long before a video showing the highlights of the season is on sale. I'll probably wear the tape out before August.

The fixtures for next season will be out fairly soon – and the draw for the UEFA Cup takes place in mid-July. Here, I still haven't got around to checking whether my passport is still valid. I haven't used it for years. I'd better sort that out quickly.

I suppose I could spend some time this summer knocking the rust off my foreign languages – and perhaps learning the rudiments of some new ones. It would be nice to be able to shout, 'You're a blind git, ref', 'Here we go' and 'Mike Walker's green and yellow army' in the majority of European tongues before we play on the Continent.

Of course, finding a new job should be my priority. And this would appear to be the best time to do it, without the distractions of football for a few weeks. But City gaining a European place has presented me with a new dilemma, albeit a welcome one. Should I try to find a succession of short-term jobs arranged around my trips abroad? Or should I look for another permanent position and risk getting the push again after a couple of months when I announce, 'Right, I'm off to Estonia for three days. See you on Friday'? There is no question of me missing the trips. I've waited too long for them. And for all I know, this could be the only time we ever play in a European competition. I hope it won't be, but it might. I don't want to look back in a few years and realise that I missed out on a once-in-a-lifetime experience.

I suppose I will find just enough to occupy me over the next three months. I've just thought – I can change my answerphone message at last! But life will be much poorer for the lack of football. Then again, it will be all the sweeter when it returns.

Roll on August.